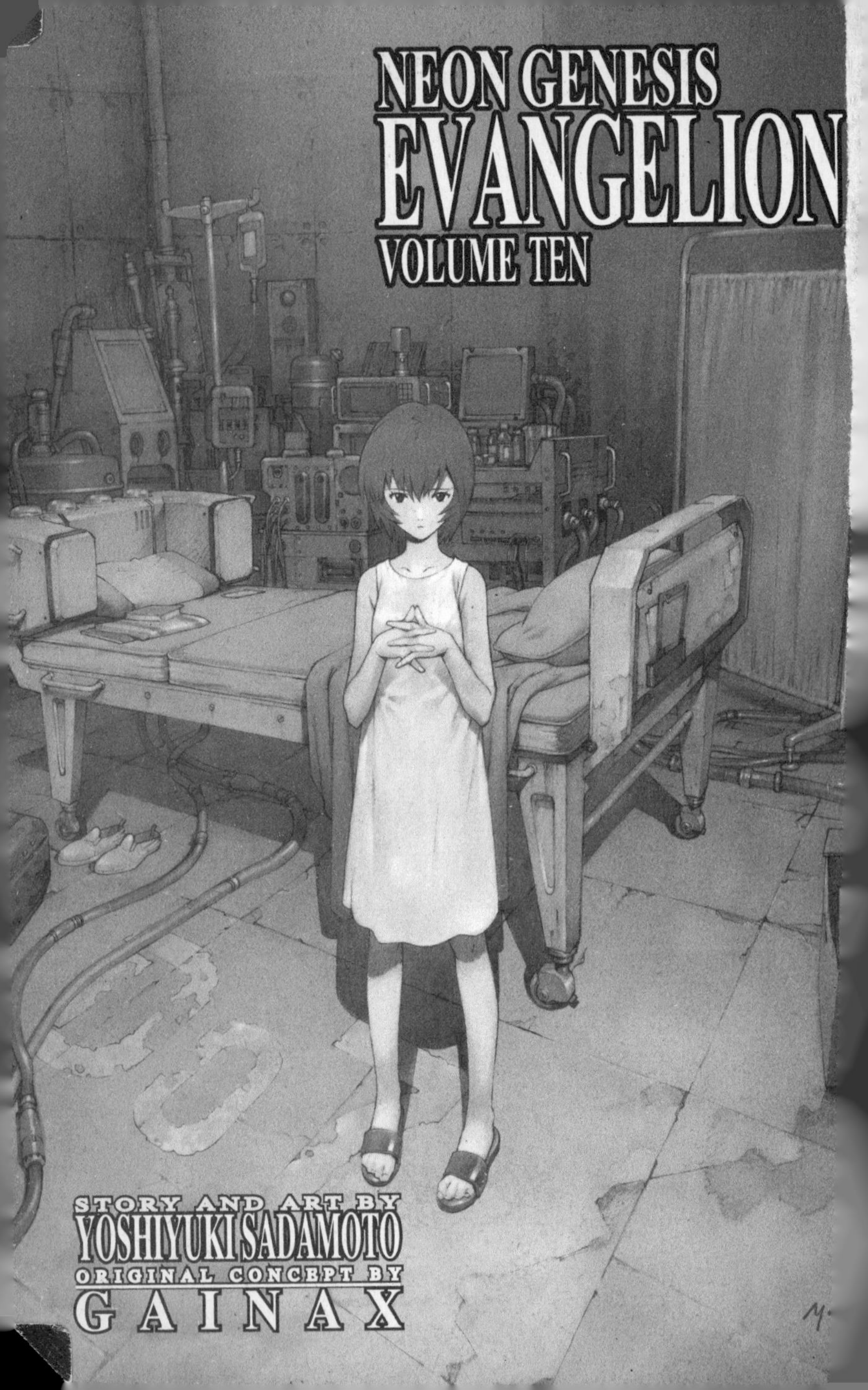

NEON GENESIS
EVANGELION
VOLUME TEN
STORY AND ART BY
YOSHIYUKI SADAMOTO
ORIGINAL CONCEPT BY
GAINAX

CONTENTS

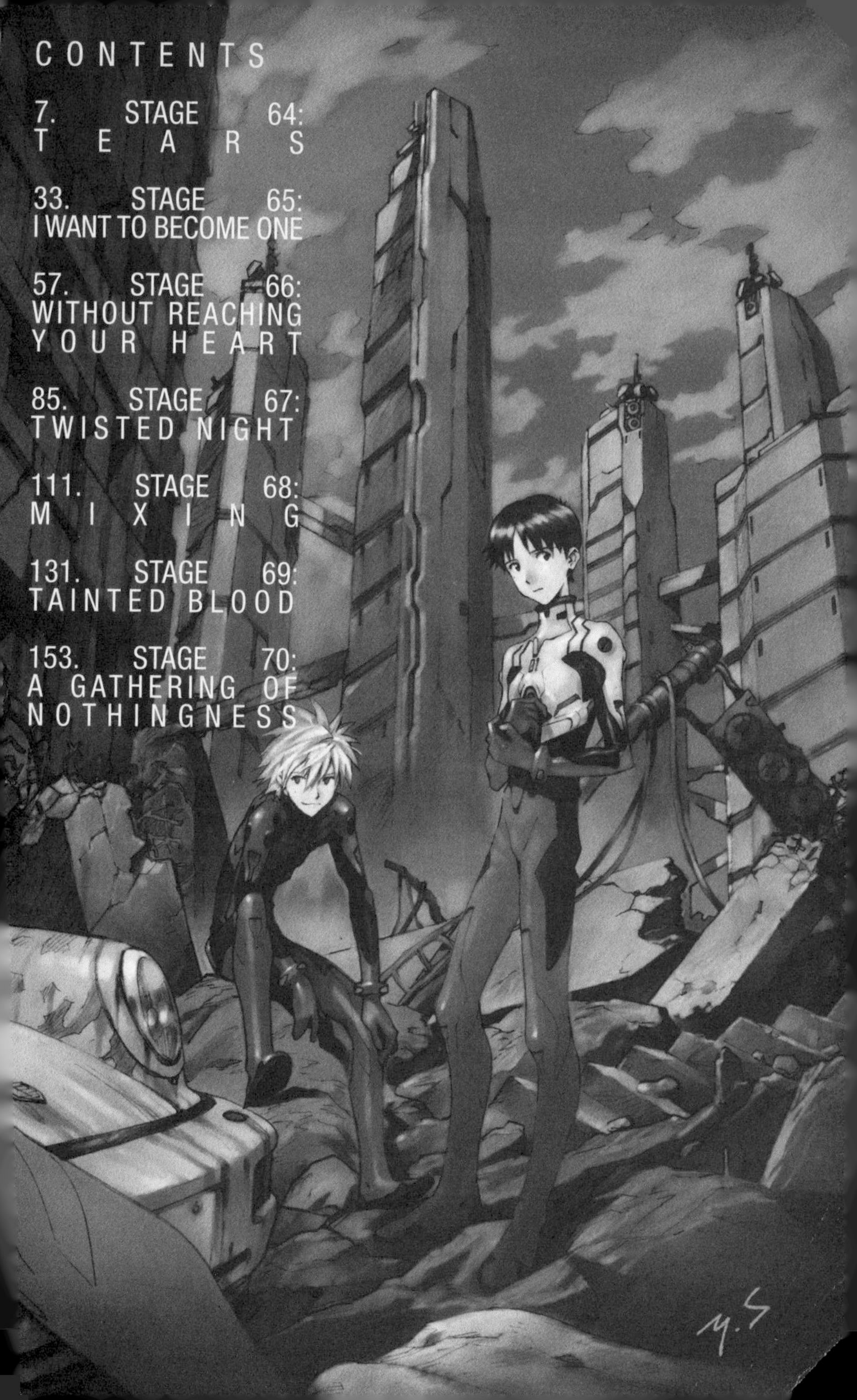

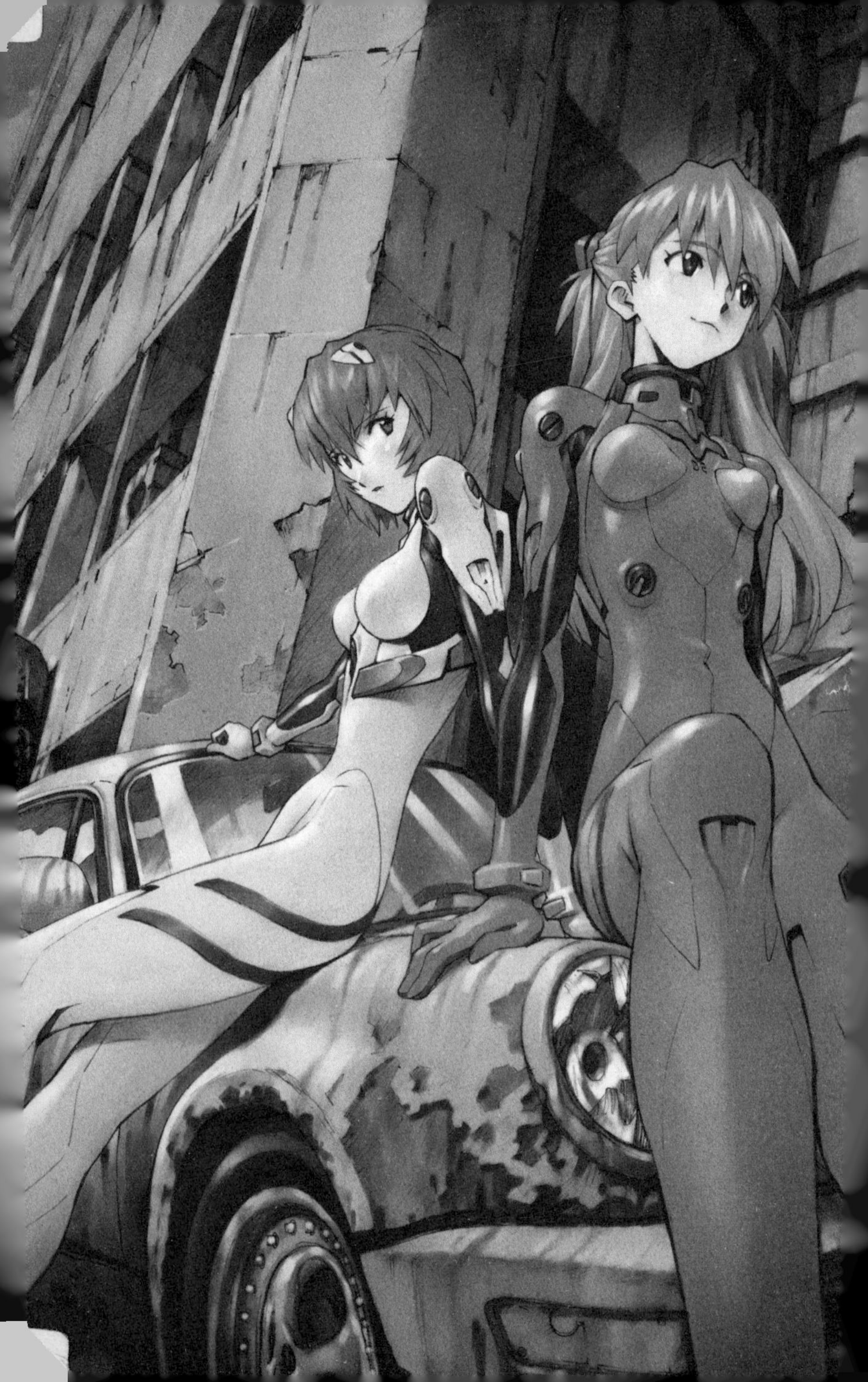

SHINJI IKARI

Identity: EVA UNIT-01 PILOT, NERV/MIDDLE SCHOOL STUDENT
Age: 14

Shinji is the pilot of "Unit 01" in NERV's series of monstrous, bioengineered giants code-named *Evangelion*. Despite his lack of training and alienation from his father, NERV's commander, Shinji has proven to be the best of the Eva pilots—owing to the unsettling discorporeal union his mother, scientist Yui Ikari, achieved with Unit-01 when Shinji was a small child; a union Shinji himself later experiences. His abilities have brought him no happiness, however, and have only drawn him deeper into the psychic and physical violence of NERV's war with the Angels.

REI AYANAMI

Identity: EVA UNIT-00 PILOT, NERV/MIDDLE SCHOOL STUDENT
Age: 14

The beautiful but sickly "First Child" assigned to pilot the prototype Eva Unit-00 has been closer to Gendo growing up than was Gendo's own son. Gendo's disturbing intimacy towards her has never bothered Rei until recently, as Shinji's presence has made her aware of the test subject-like nature of her life, an artificiality Rei compares to being made of straw. Shinji himself knows little about Rei's own secrets, including the fact she was used as the basis of the "dummy plug" system that overrode his command of Unit-01 and made the Eva kill his friend Toji.

ASUKA LANGLEY SORYU

Identity: EVA UNIT-02 PILOT, NERV/MIDDLE SCHOOL STUDENT
Age: 14

A United States citizen of mixed Japanese and German ancestry, Asuka—already a college graduate despite her assignment to Shinji's school—is a product of eugenic breeding. Asuka was selected to begin training as an Eva pilot from a very early age, but the "honor" was bound up inextricably with her attempts to please her mother, Kyoko, who had experienced an emotional breakdown from her husband leaving her; the delusional Kyoko apparently attempted to strangle Asuka, and then later hanged herself. Asuka's forced re-living of these memories by the Angel Arael has left her hospitalized in a catatonic state.

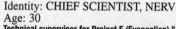

Dr. RITSUKO AKAGI

Identity: CHIEF SCIENTIST, NERV
Age: 30

Technical supervisor for Project E (Evangelion)," Dr. Akagi has developed the core technology of NERV first established by two other woman scientists—the Magi System built by her own mother, Naoko, and the Evangelion, engineered by Yui Ikari. A polymath genius whose fields include physics, genetics, and computer science, Dr. Akagi is also Rei's personal clinician but jealous and resentful of her, leading to a recent shocking assault. Although a friend of Misato and Kaji's since college, Ritsuko lacks their human warmth, and unlike them became increasingly detached from the profound moral consequences of her work.

MISATO KATSURAGI

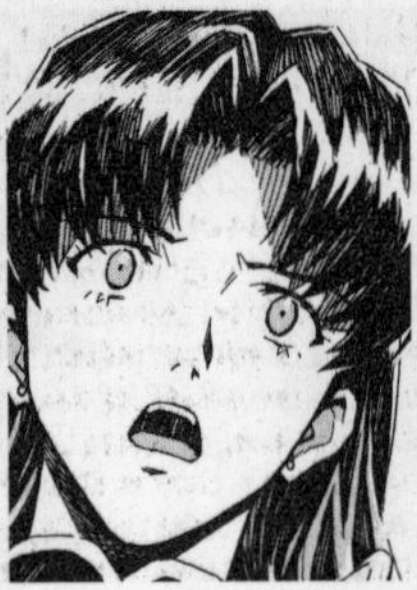

Identity: OPERATIONS CHIEF, NERV
Age: 29

Major Katsuragi is the only eyewitness to the manifestation of the Angel Adam in the "Second Impact" that devastated the Earth when she was 14. Saved at the cost of his own life by her father, Misato needed little motivation to join NERV and eventually become the tactical commander of the Eva pilots, but has tried to act as a family figure to those same children under her care. Her murdered lover, the spy Ryoji Kaji, made her aware that much of what she had been told about the war against the Angels was untrue; since his death, she has carried on his investigations.

KAWORU NAGISA

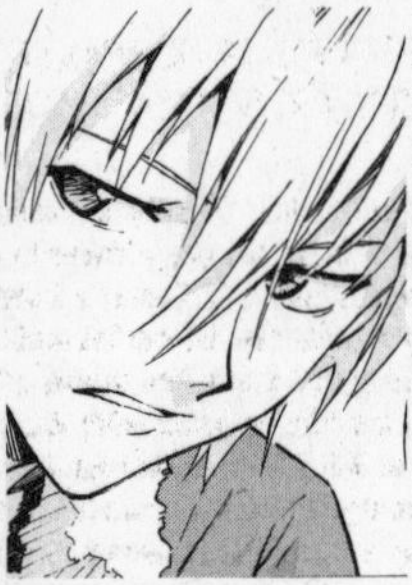

Identity: EVA PILOT, NERV/MIDDLE SCHOOL STUDENT
Age: 15 (?)

The "Fifth Child" designated to pilot the Eva Units; after Rei, Asuka, Shinji, and the deceased Toji Suzuhara. The previous Children were supposedly selected by Marduk, an elaborate front organization, but Kaworu was sent to NERV directly from SEELE. Kaworu is, in fact, Tabris, an Angel controlled by the Instrumentality Committee, and ordered to infiltrate Gendo's organization. He is oddly attracted to Shinji, but his blunt and even callous personality makes it hard for Shinji to even call him a friend—a remarkable contrast to the anime version of events.

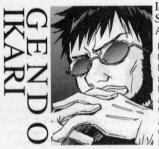

GENDO IKARI

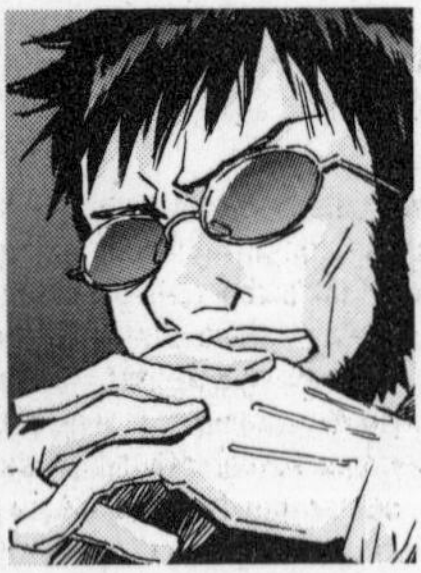

Identity: SUPREME COMMANDER, NERV
Age: 48

If Ritsuko Akagi is the mind behind the development of NERV's Evangelion system, this ruthless and enigmatic man, born Gendo Rokubungi, has served as the will. As an anti-social scholar at the University of Kyoto, he married the brilliant young scientist Yui Ikari and adopted her last name, although it was rumored his motive was to gain connections to SEELE, the mysterious organization backing her research. After Yui vanished during a preliminary test of the Eva Unit-01 in 2004, Gendo walked away from raising their son Shinji, leaving him in the care of his uncle and aunt.

LORENZ KIEL

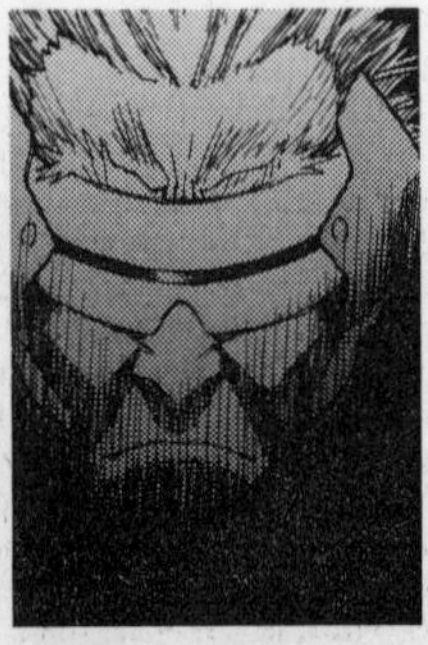

Identity: CHAIRMAN, INSTRUMENTALITY OF MAN COMMITTEE
Age: Unknown

Kiel, an elderly man seen only with dark glasses or a visor, is the evident leader of SEELE, German for the "Soul," a 13-member cabal—itself of possibly German origins. SEELE is believed to have existed for many years, and possessed of vast wealth, political influence, advanced scientific knowledge, and unique insight into the true origins of humankind and its destiny through access to certain Dead Sea Scrolls never made public. Kiel chairs SEELE's apparently five-man Instrumentality Committee, which trusted Gendo to carry out their plans but now views him as a renegade.

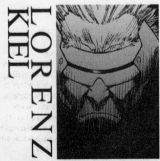

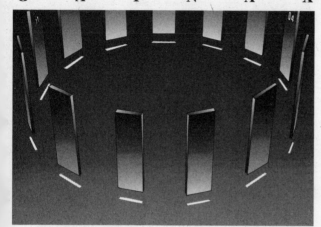

NEON GENESIS EVANGELION

VOLUME TEN

STORY AND ART BY
YOSHIYUKI SADAMOTO

ORIGINAL CONCEPT BY
GAINAX

ENGLISH ADAPTATION
CARL GUSTAV HORN

TRANSLATION
JUNE HONMA

LETTERING
JOHN CLARK

LAYOUT AND GRAPHIC DESIGN
SEAN LEE

SERIES COVER DESIGN AND EDITOR
CARL GUSTAV HORN

MANAGING EDITOR
ANNETTE ROMAN

EDITORIAL DIRECTOR
:LIZABETH KAWASAKI

EDITOR IN CHIEF, BOOKS
ALVIN LU

EDITOR IN CHIEF, MAGAZINES
MARC WEIDENBAUM

VP OF PUBLISHING LICENSING
RIKA INOUYE

VP OF SALES
GONZALO FERREYRA

SR. VP OF MARKETING
LIZA COPPOLA

PUBLISHER
HYOE NARITA

NTED IN THE U.S.A.

BLISHED BY VIZ MEDIA, LLC
. BOX 77064
N FRANCISCO, CA 94107

8 7 6 5 4 3 2
ST PRINTING, APRIL 2007
OND PRINTING, APRIL 2007

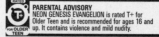

www.viz.com
store.viz.com

NEON GENESIS EVANGELION

STAGE 64: TEARS

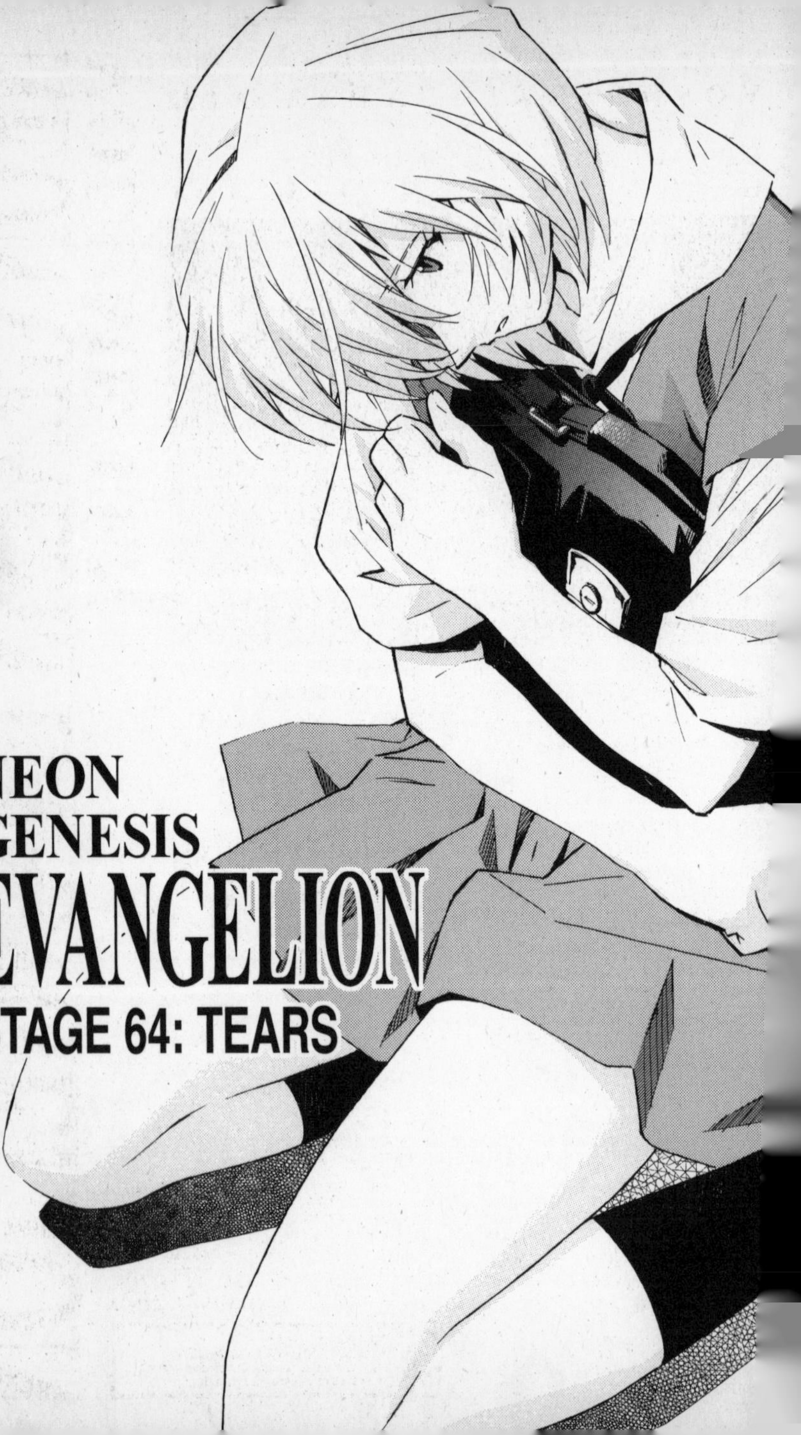

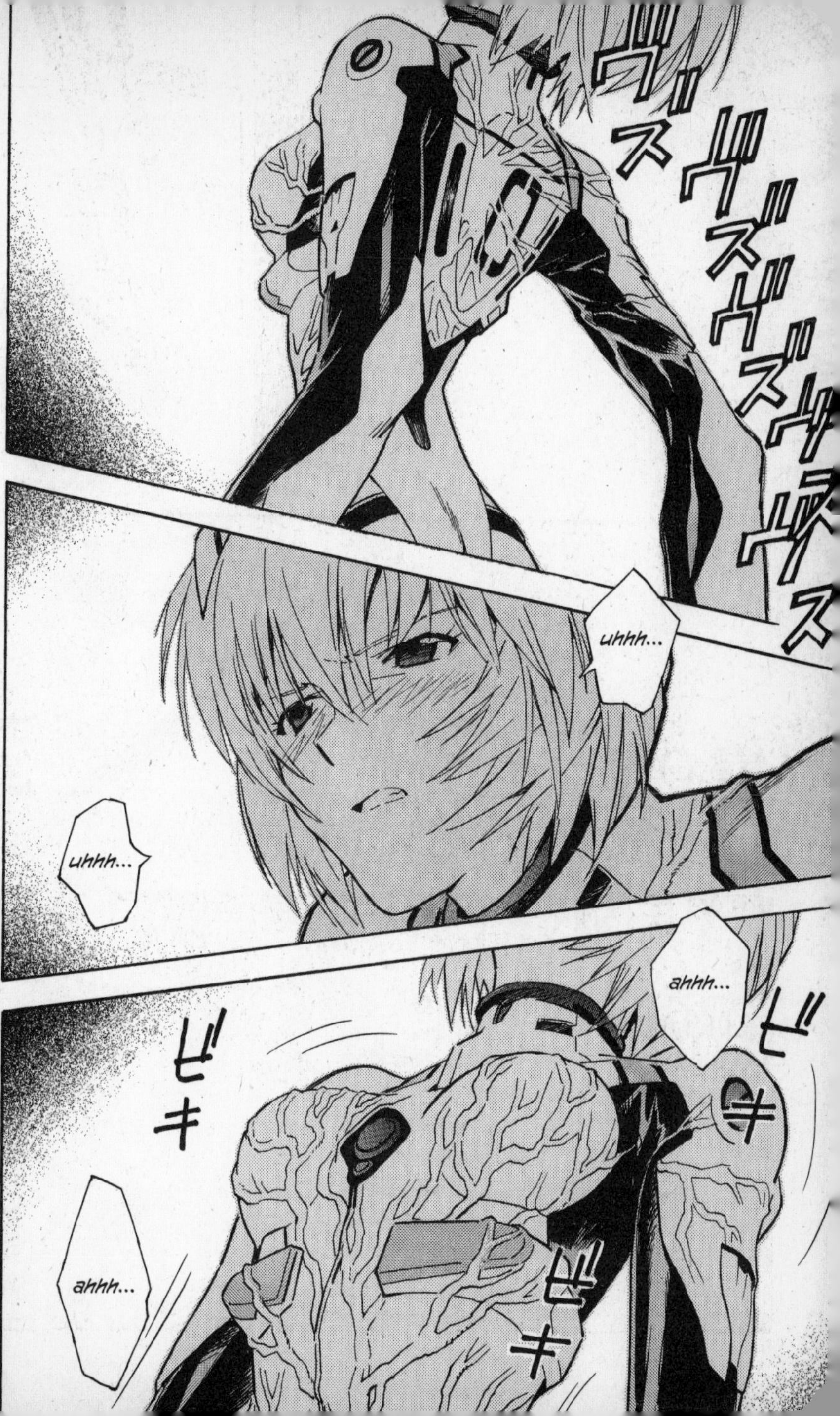
uhhh...
uhhh...
ahhh...
ビキ
ビキ
ビキ
ahhh...

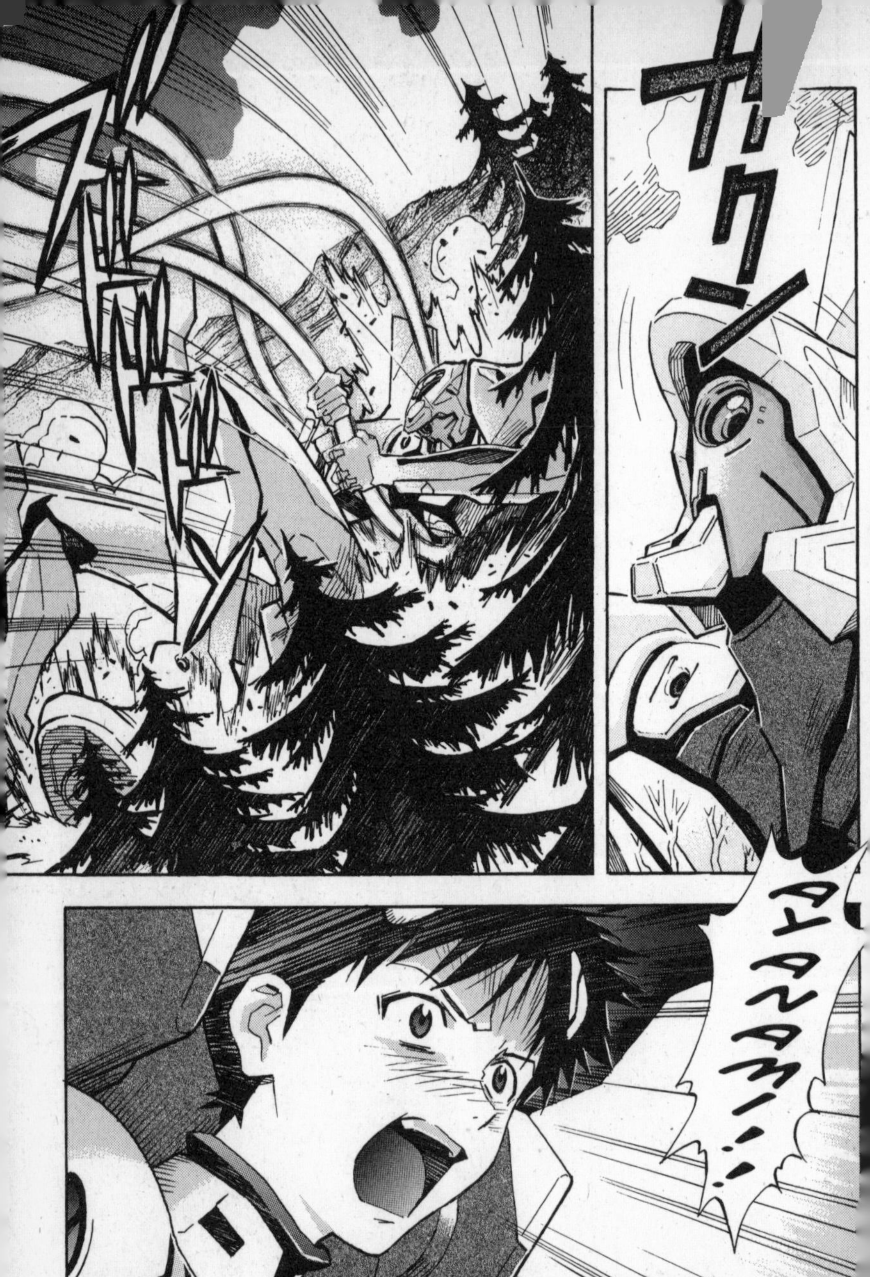
AYANAMI!!!

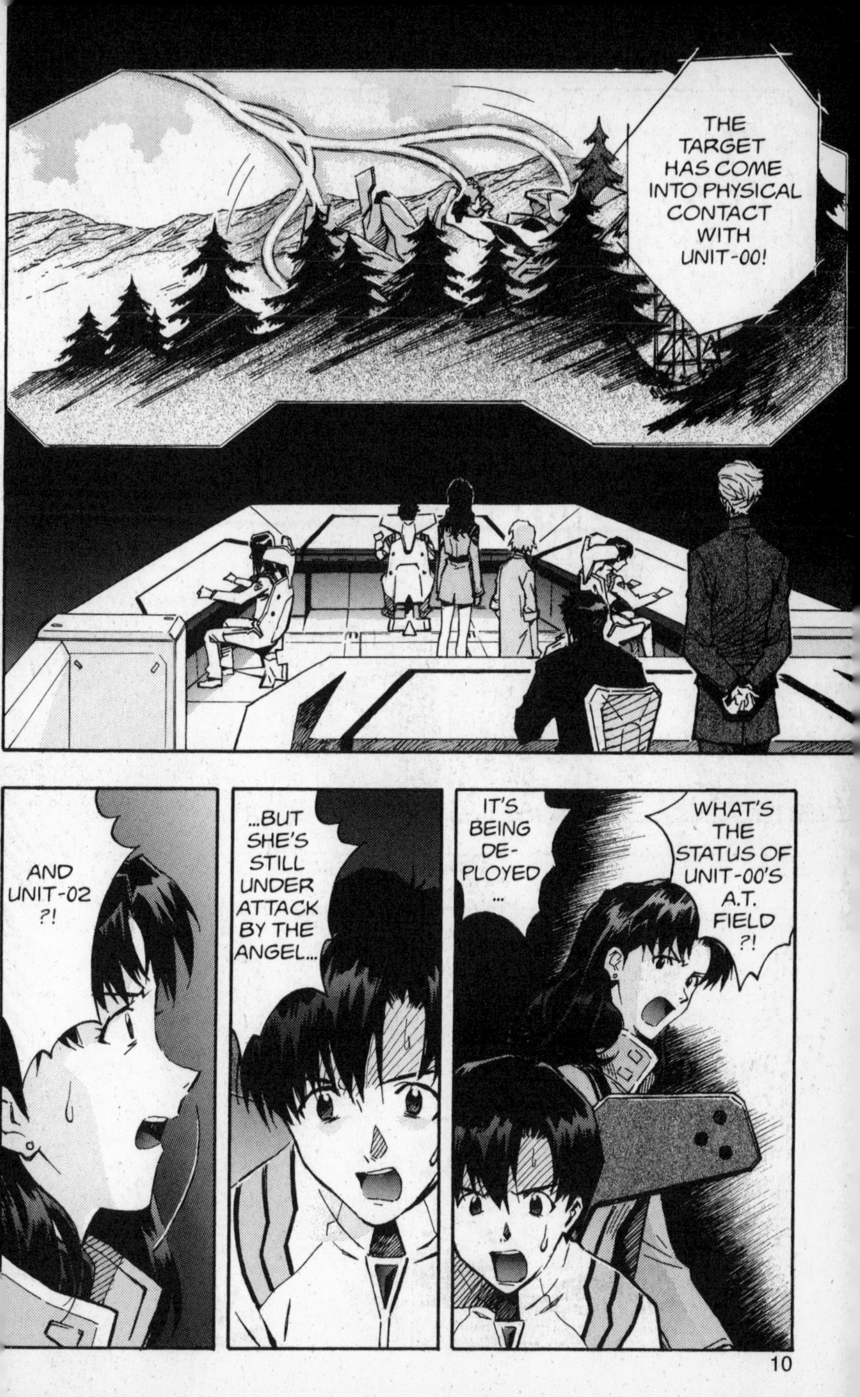
THE TARGET HAS COME INTO PHYSICAL CONTACT WITH UNIT-00!
WHAT'S THE STATUS OF UNIT-00'S A.T. FIELD ?!
IT'S BEING DE-PLOYED ...
...BUT SHE'S STILL UNDER ATTACK BY THE ANGEL...
AND UNIT-02 ?!

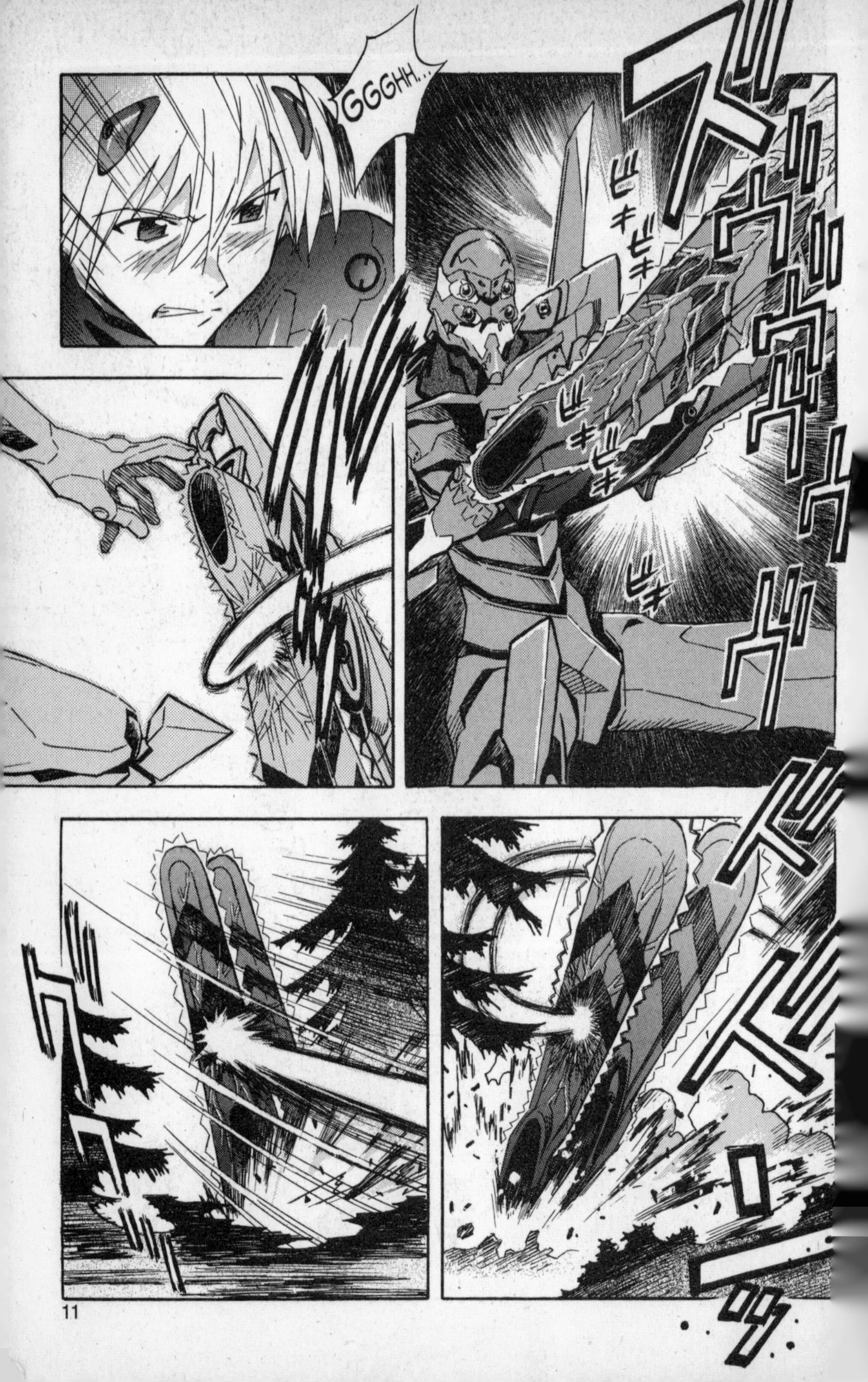
ビキビキ
ビキビキ
ビキ
GGGHH...

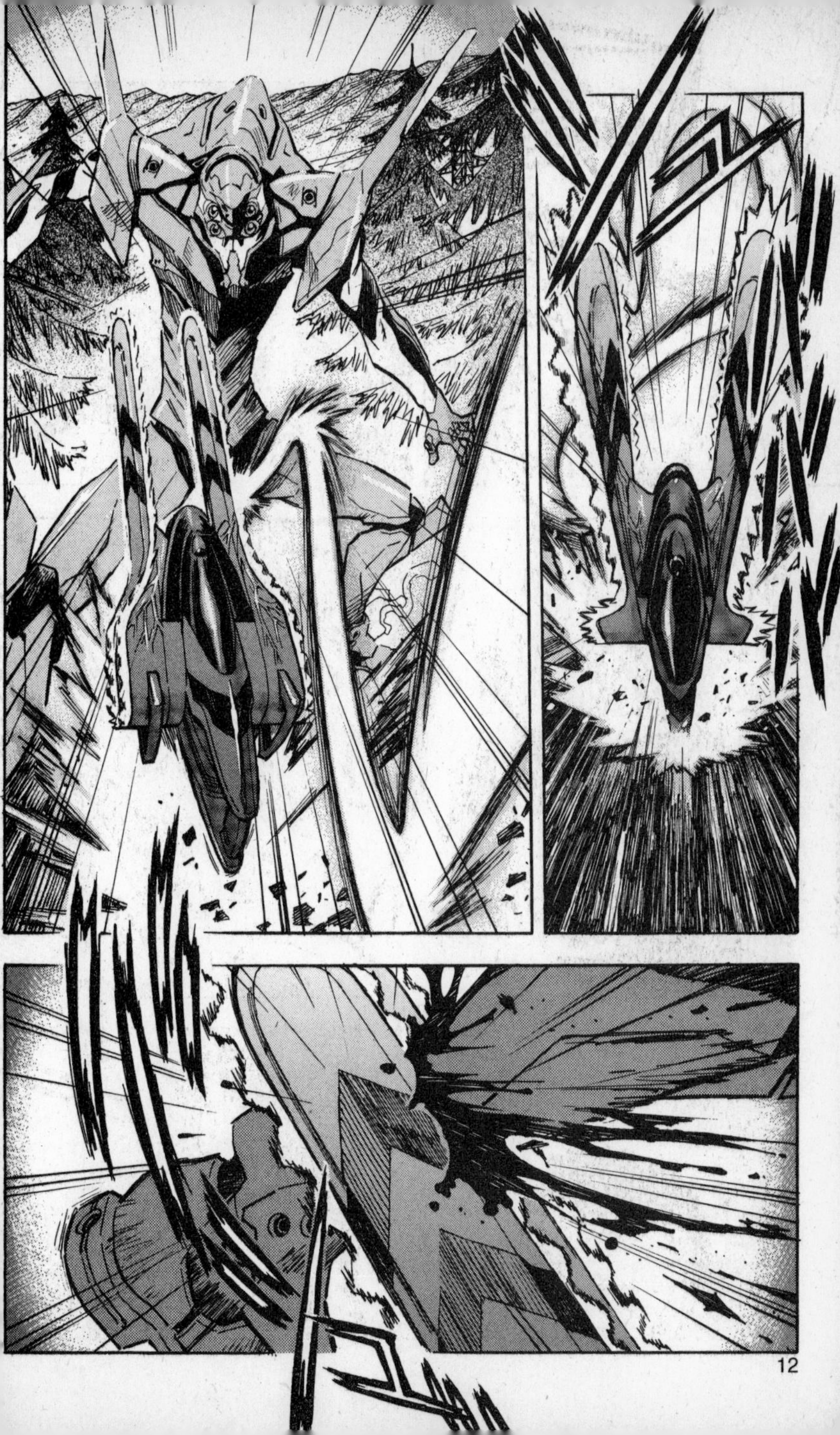

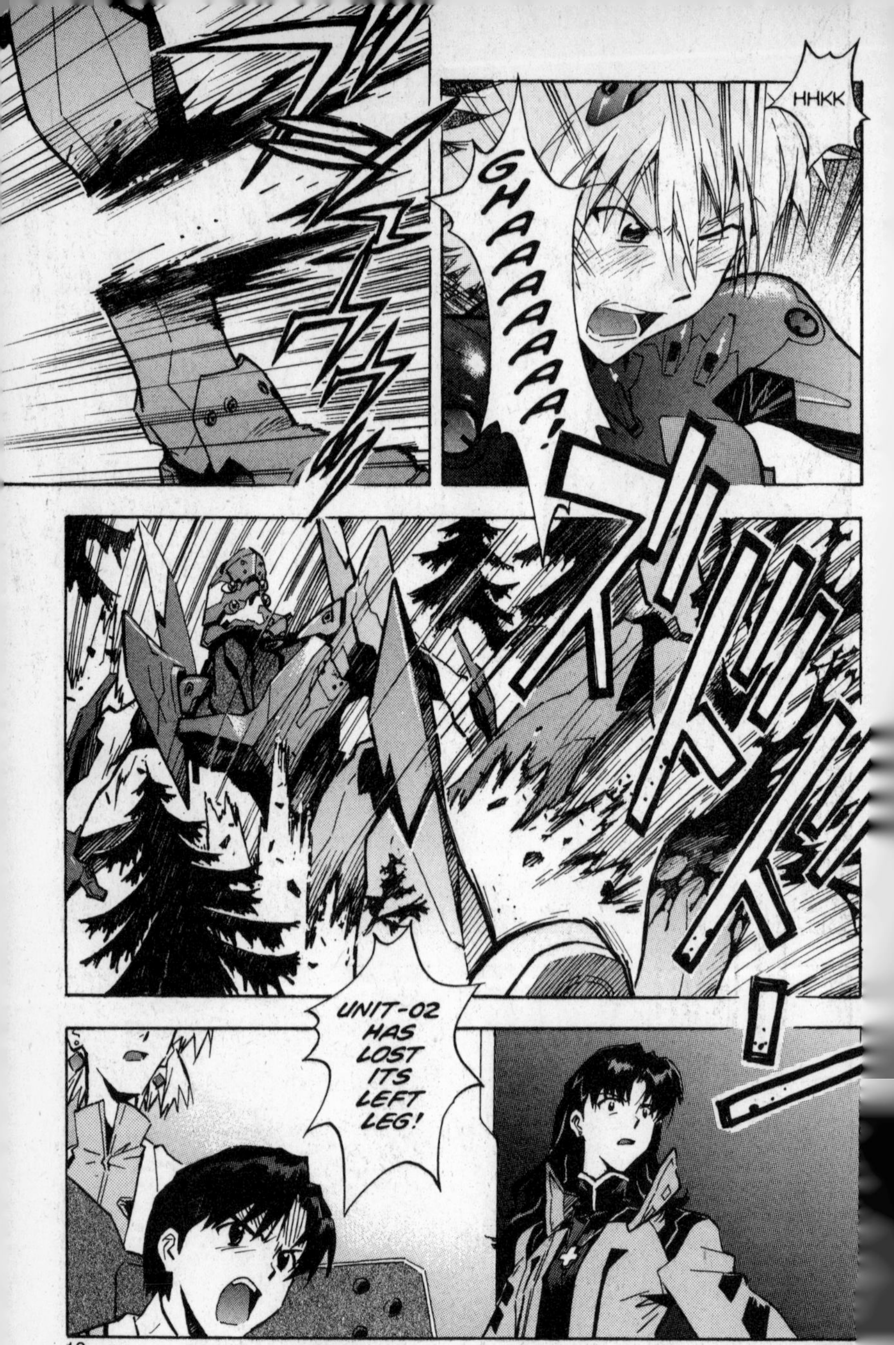
HHKK
GHAAAAAAAA!
UNIT-02 HAS LOST ITS LEFT LEG!

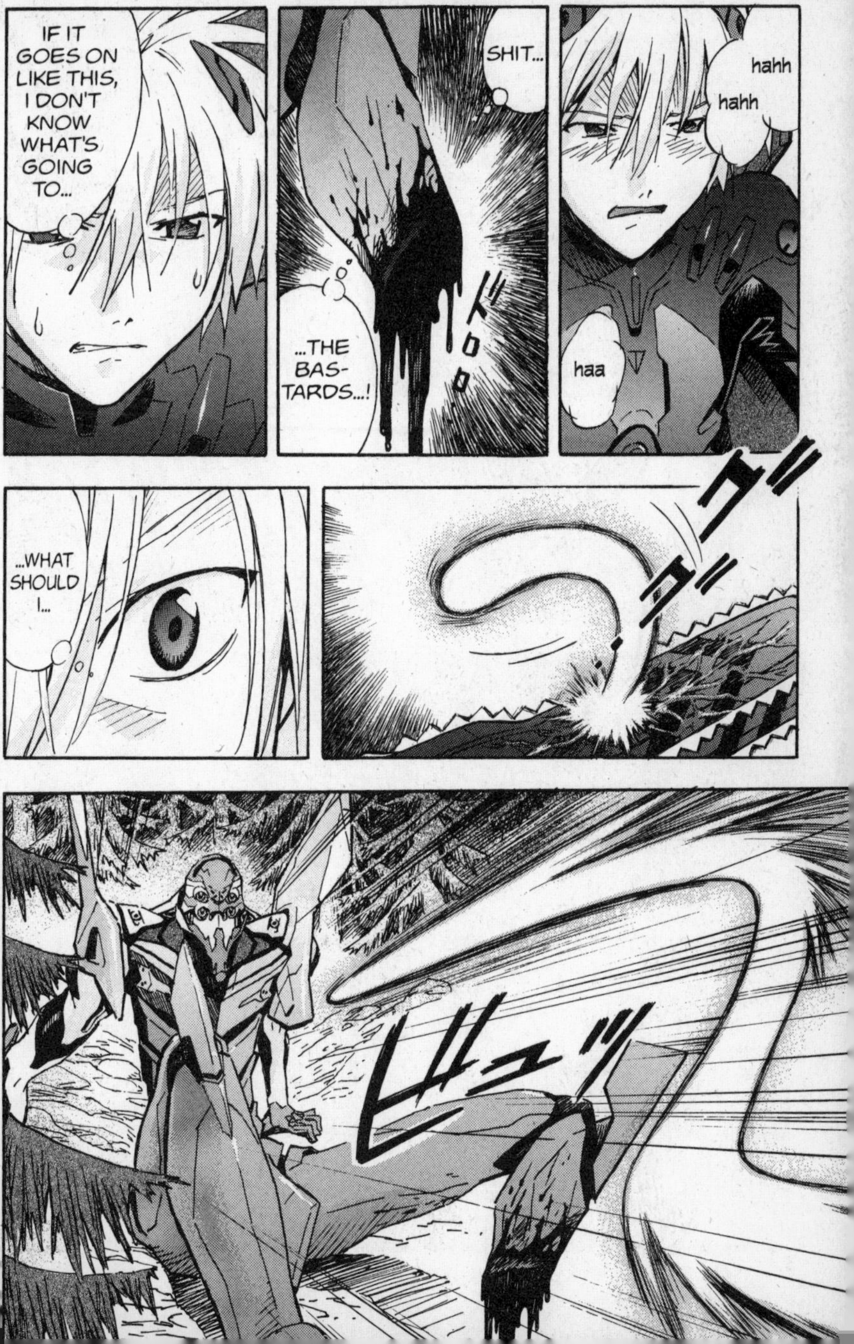
hahh
hahh
haa
SHIT...
...THE BAS-TARDS...!
ドロロ
IF IT GOES ON LIKE THIS, I DON'T KNOW WHAT'S GOING TO...
グ
グ
...WHAT SHOULD I...
ビュッ

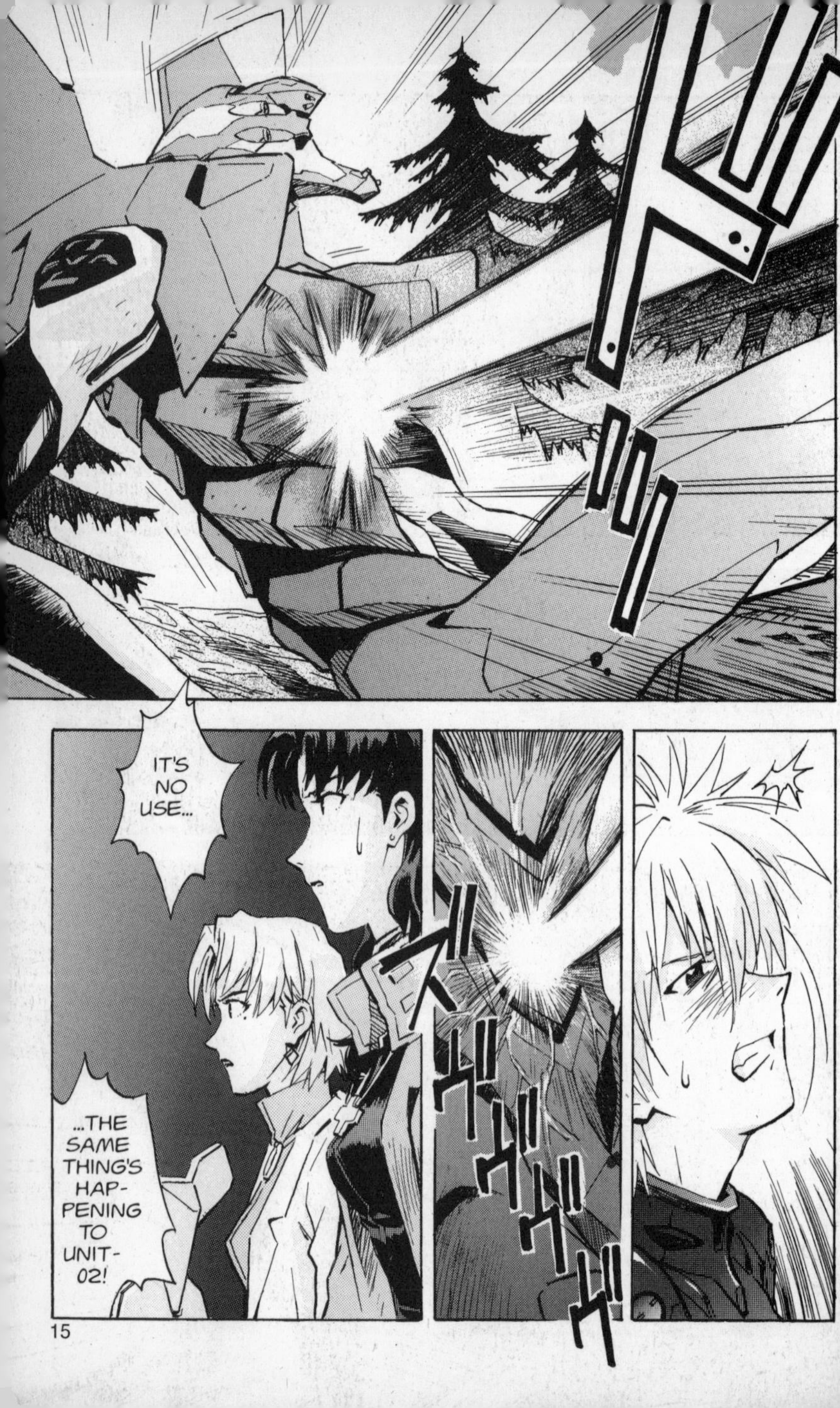
IT'S NO USE...
...THE SAME THING'S HAP-PENING TO UNIT-02!

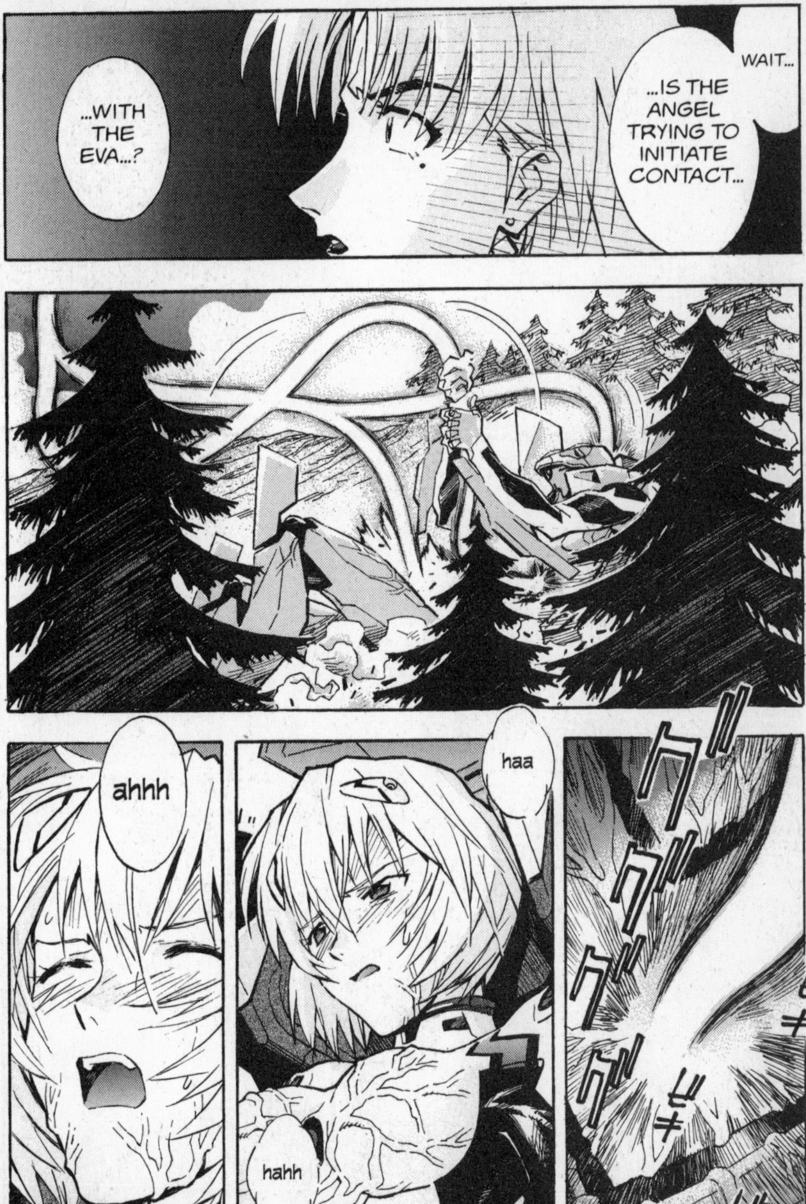
WAIT...
...IS THE ANGEL TRYING TO INITIATE CONTACT...
...WITH THE EVA...?
haa
hahh
ahhh

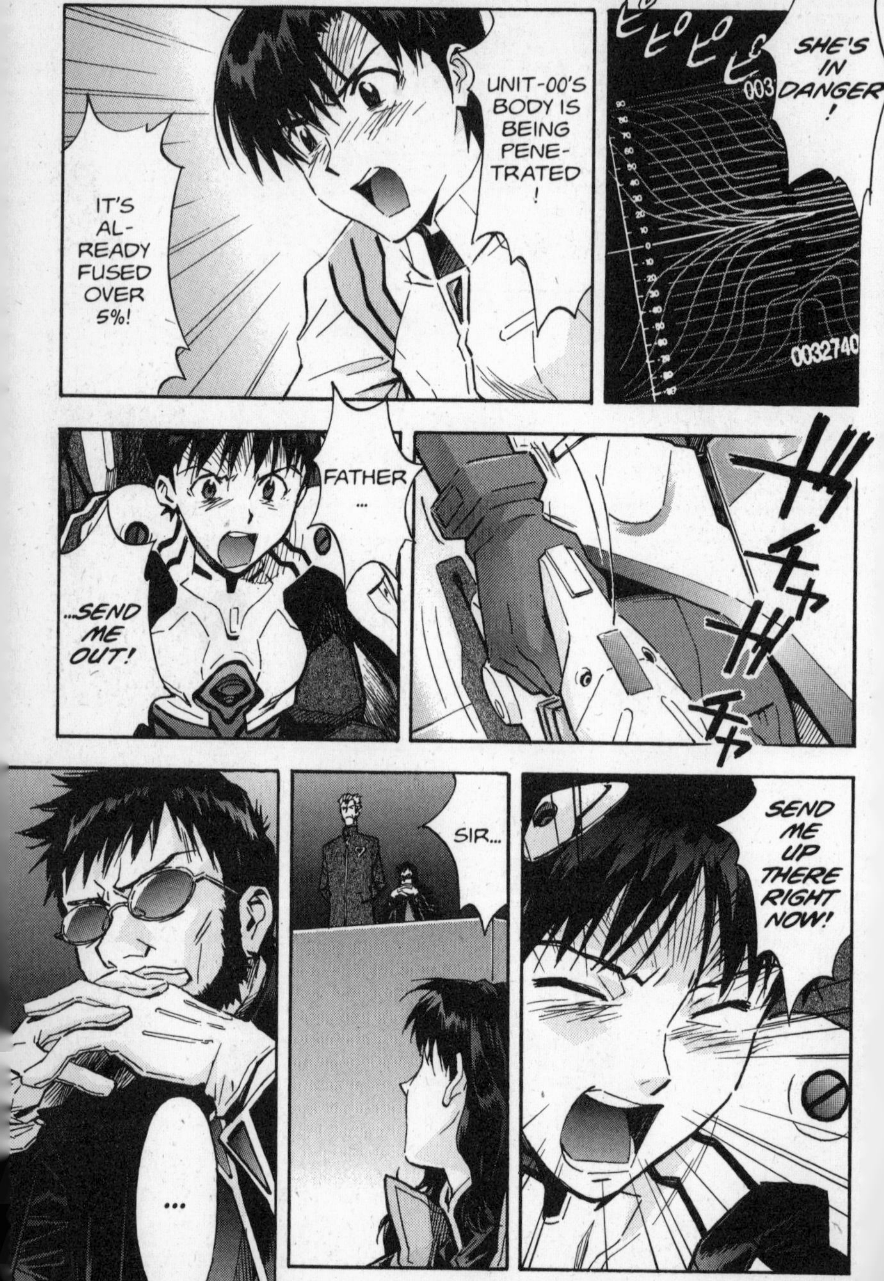
ピピピピ
003
SHE'S IN DANGER!
0032740
UNIT-00'S BODY IS BEING PENE-TRATED!
IT'S AL-READY FUSED OVER 5%!
ガチャガチャ
FATHER...
...SEND ME OUT!
SEND ME UP THERE RIGHT NOW!
SIR...
...

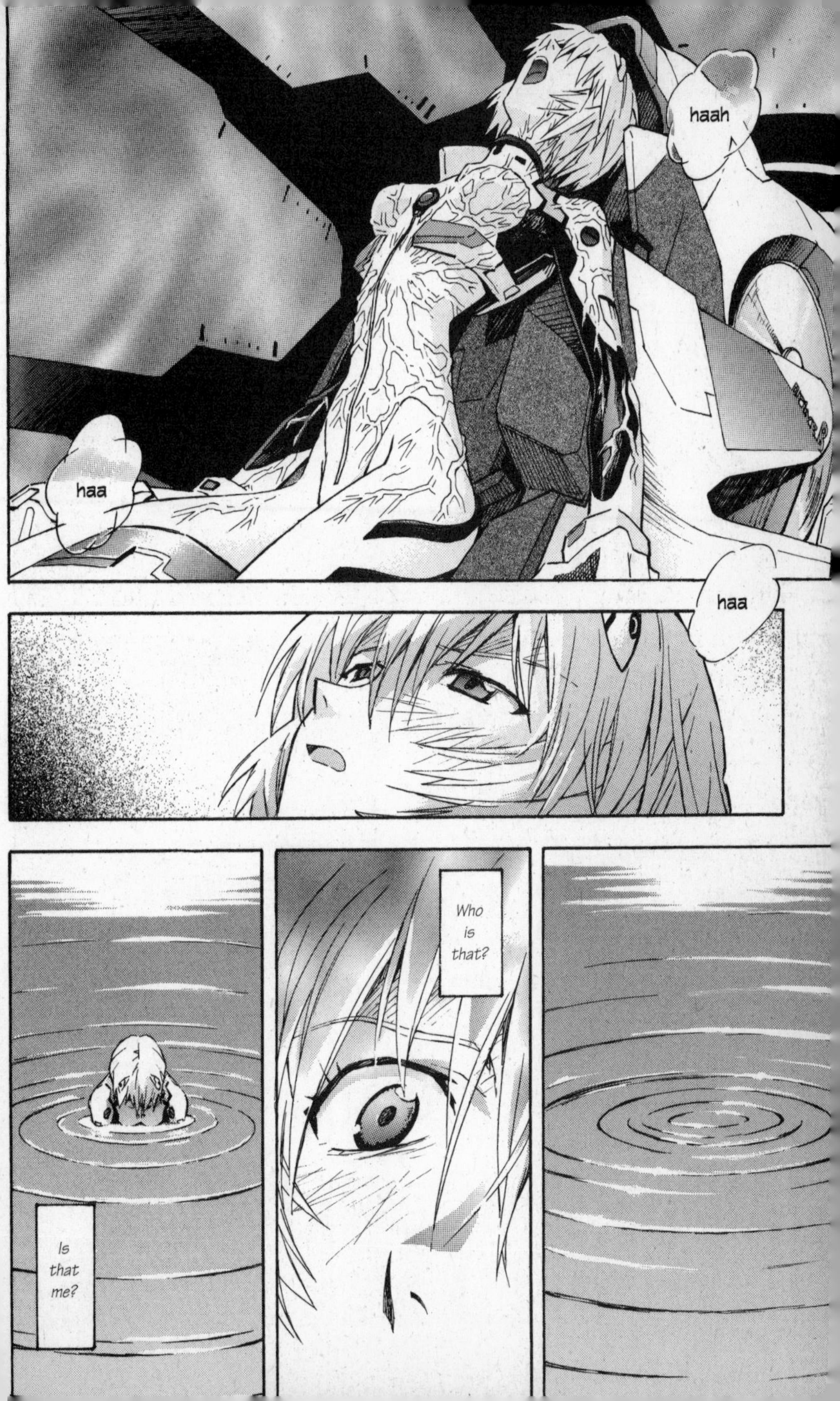
haah
haa
haa
Who is that?
Is that me?

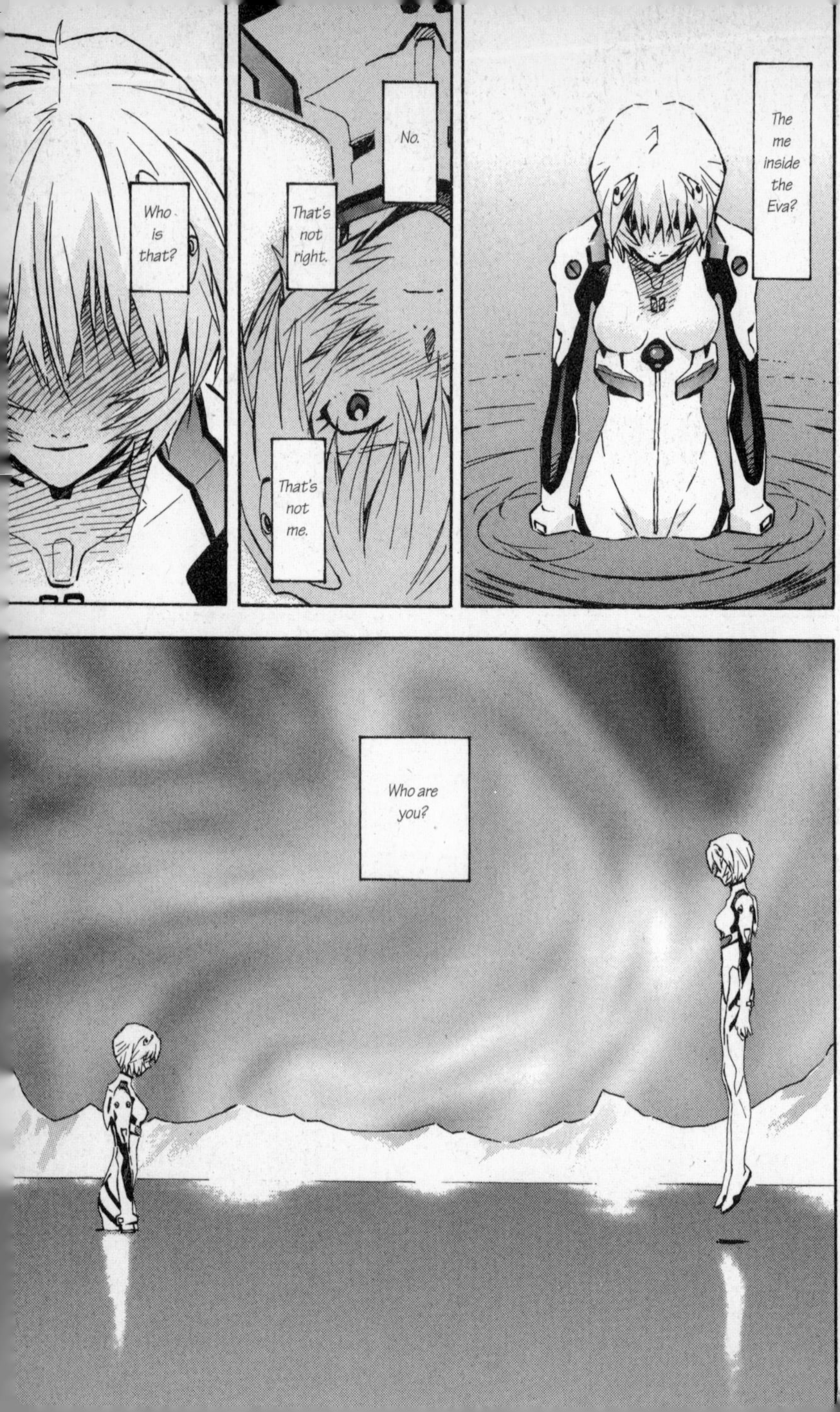

The me inside the Eva?
No.
That's not right.
That's not me.
Who is that?
Who are you?

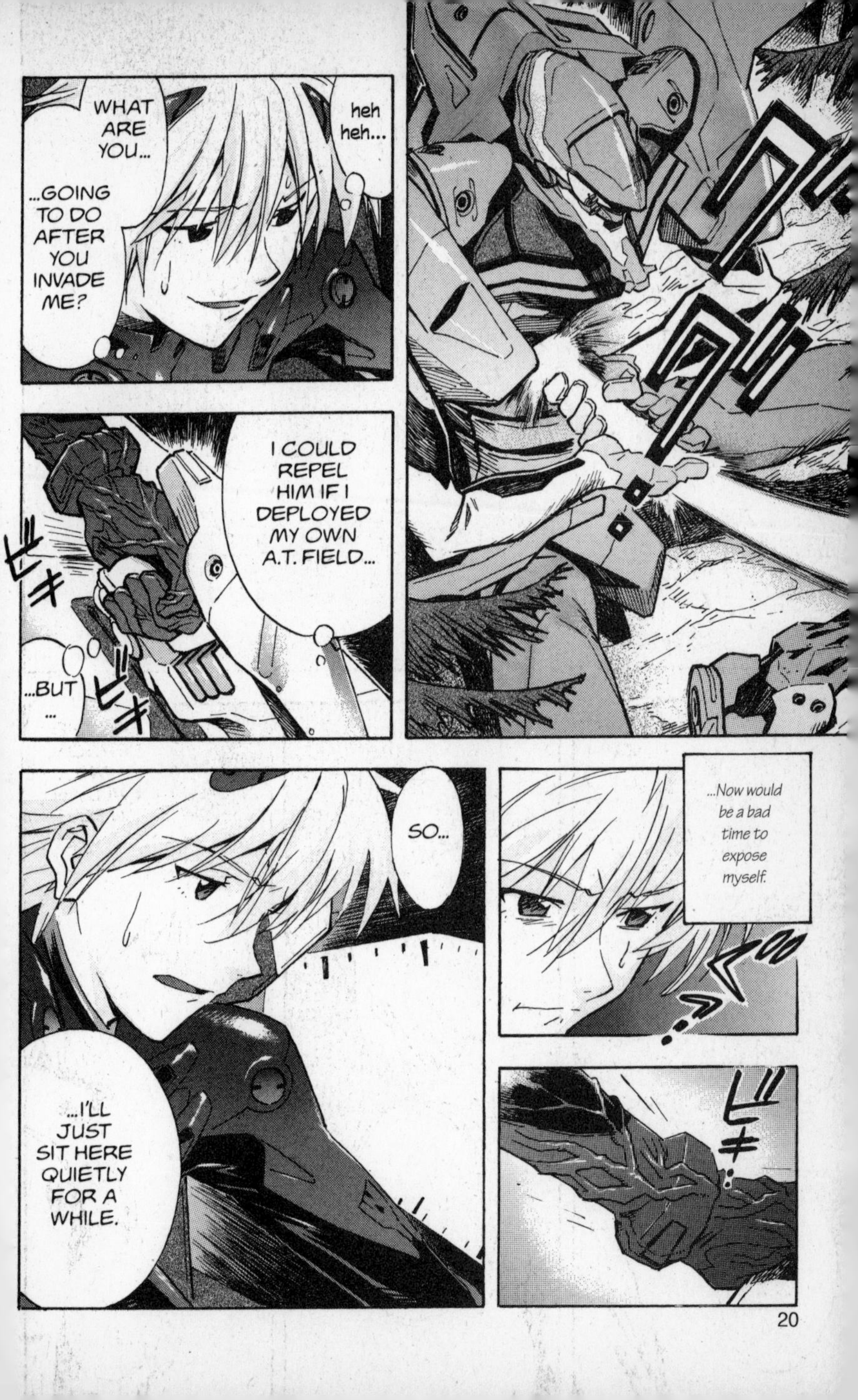
heh heh...
WHAT ARE YOU...
...GOING TO DO AFTER YOU INVADE ME?
I COULD REPEL HIM IF I DEPLOYED MY OWN A.T. FIELD...
ビキ
ビキ
...BUT ...
...Now would be a bad time to expose myself.
ビキ
SO...
...I'LL JUST SIT HERE QUIETLY FOR A WHILE.

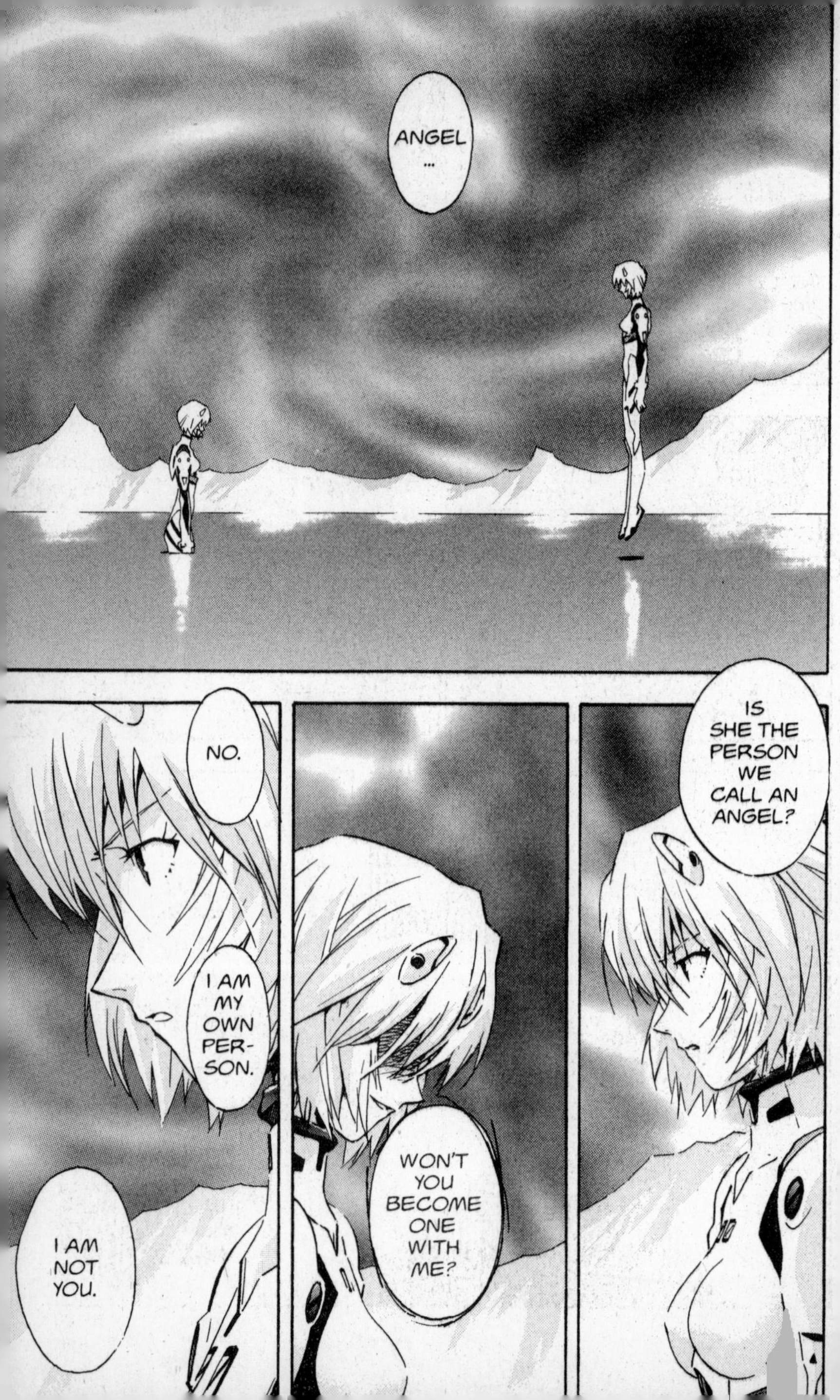
ANGEL ...
IS SHE THE PERSON WE CALL AN ANGEL?
WON'T YOU BECOME ONE WITH ME?
NO.
I AM MY OWN PERSON.
I AM NOT YOU.

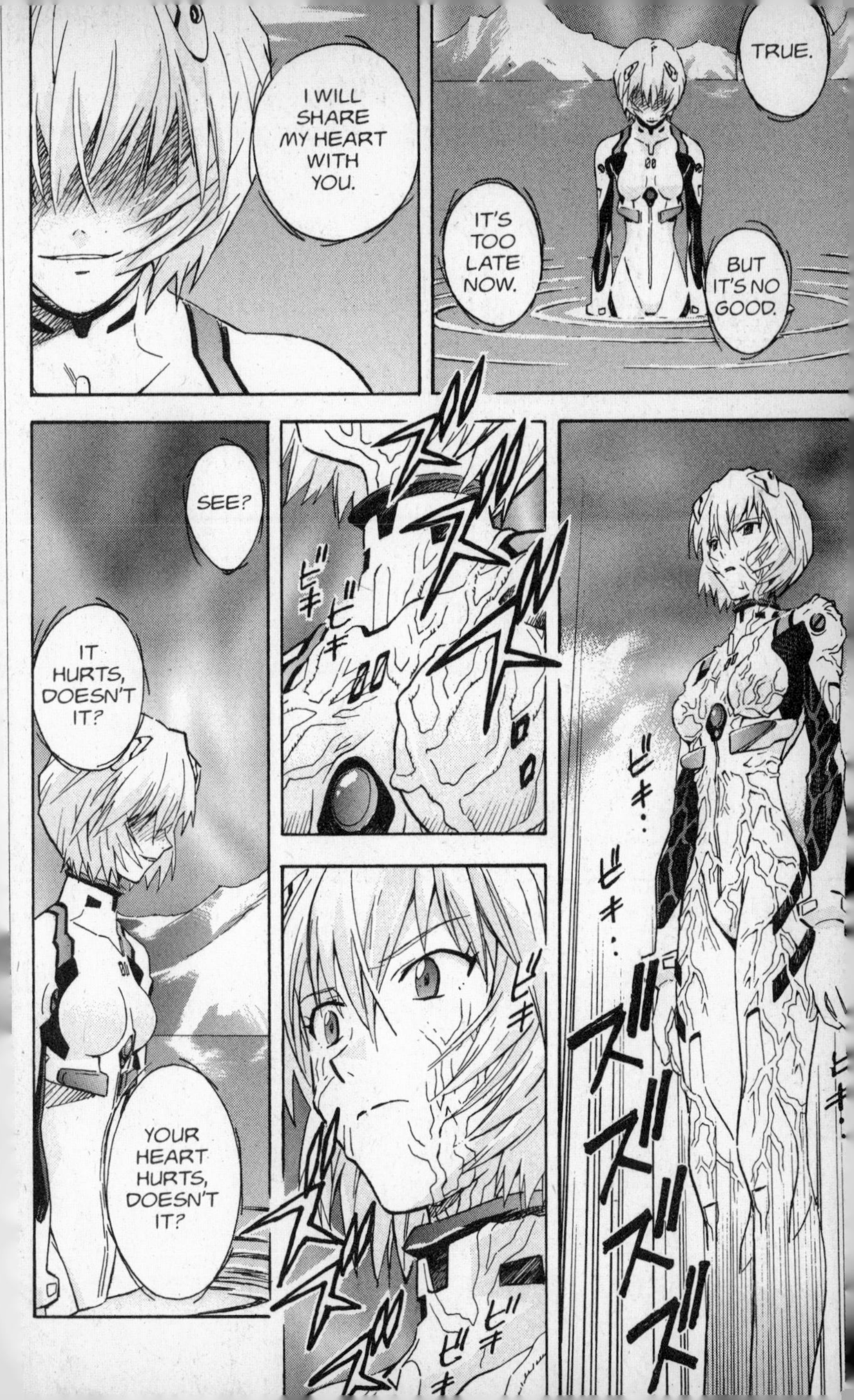
TRUE.
BUT IT'S NO GOOD.
IT'S TOO LATE NOW.
I WILL SHARE MY HEART WITH YOU.
ビキ…
ビキ…
ズズズズ
ビキ
ビキ
ビキ
SEE?
IT HURTS, DOESN'T IT?
YOUR HEART HURTS, DOESN'T IT?

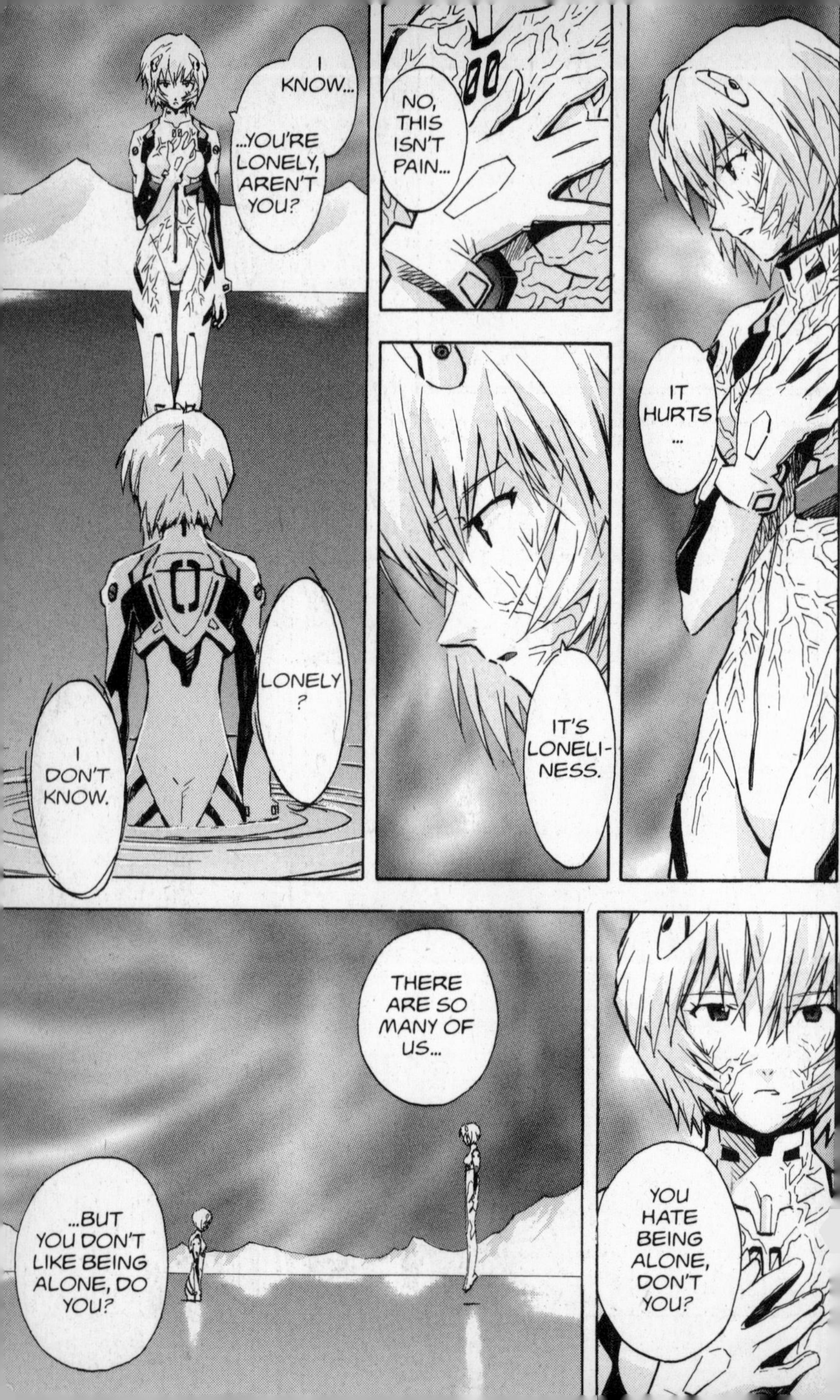
IT HURTS...
NO, THIS ISN'T PAIN...
IT'S LONELINESS.
I KNOW...
...YOU'RE LONELY, AREN'T YOU?
LONELY?
I DON'T KNOW.
YOU HATE BEING ALONE, DON'T YOU?
THERE ARE SO MANY OF US...
...BUT YOU DON'T LIKE BEING ALONE, DO YOU?

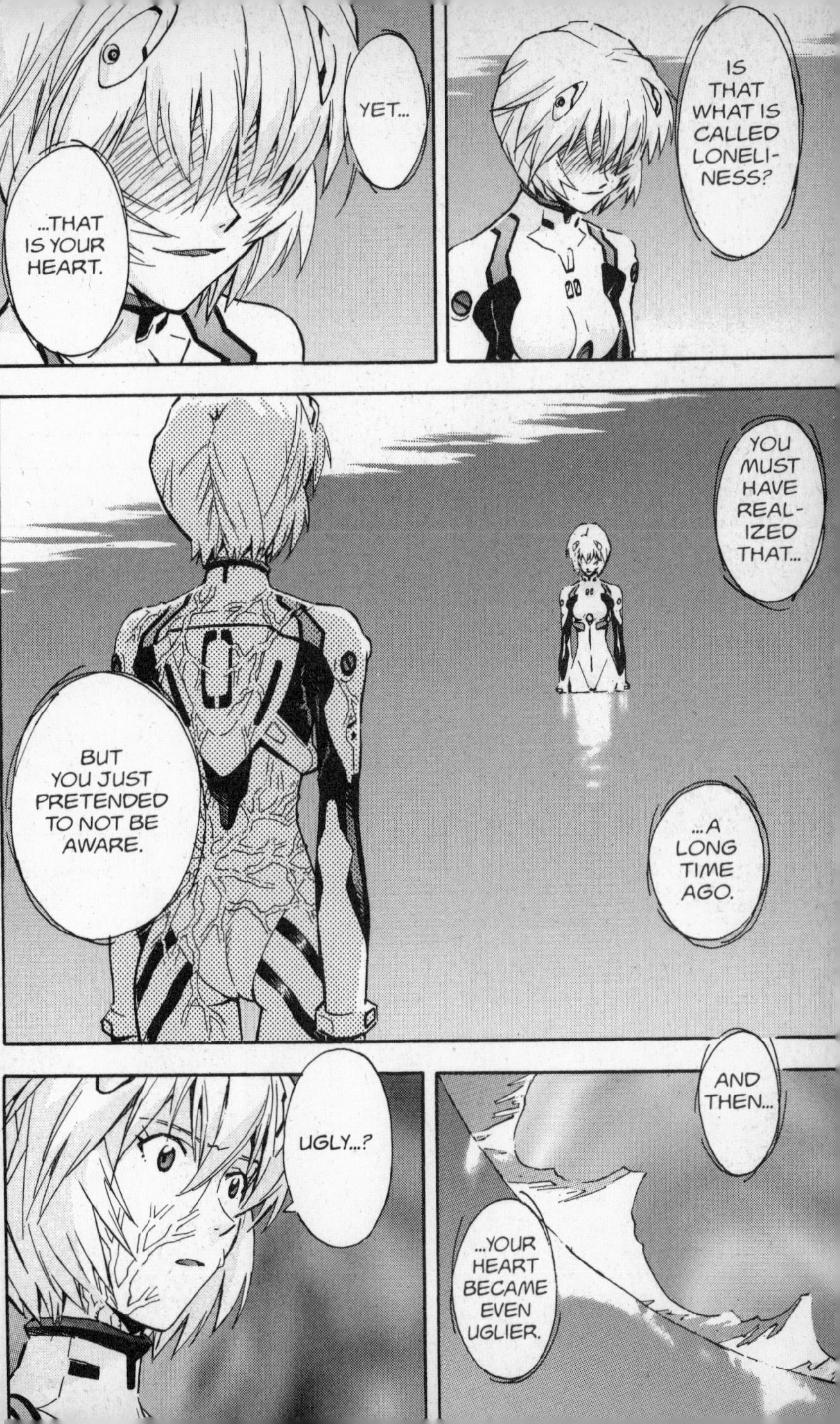
IS THAT WHAT IS CALLED LONELI-NESS?
YET...
...THAT IS YOUR HEART.
YOU MUST HAVE REAL-IZED THAT...
...A LONG TIME AGO.
BUT YOU JUST PRETENDED TO NOT BE AWARE.
AND THEN...
...YOUR HEART BECAME EVEN UGLIER.
UGLY...?

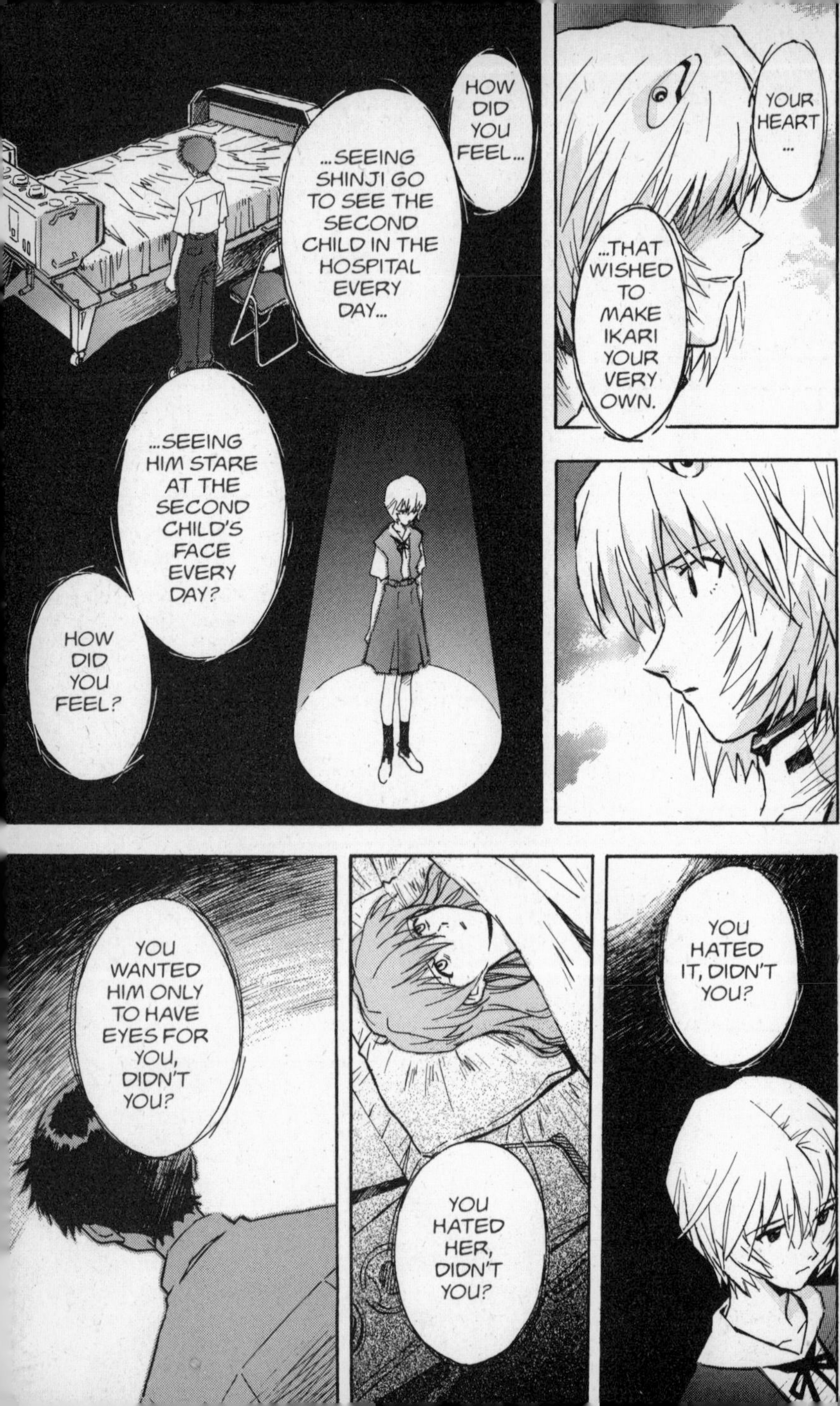
YOUR HEART ...
...THAT WISHED TO MAKE IKARI YOUR VERY OWN.
HOW DID YOU FEEL...
...SEEING SHINJI GO TO SEE THE SECOND CHILD IN THE HOSPITAL EVERY DAY...
...SEEING HIM STARE AT THE SECOND CHILD'S FACE EVERY DAY?
HOW DID YOU FEEL?
YOU HATED IT, DIDN'T YOU?
YOU HATED HER, DIDN'T YOU?
YOU WANTED HIM ONLY TO HAVE EYES FOR YOU, DIDN'T YOU?

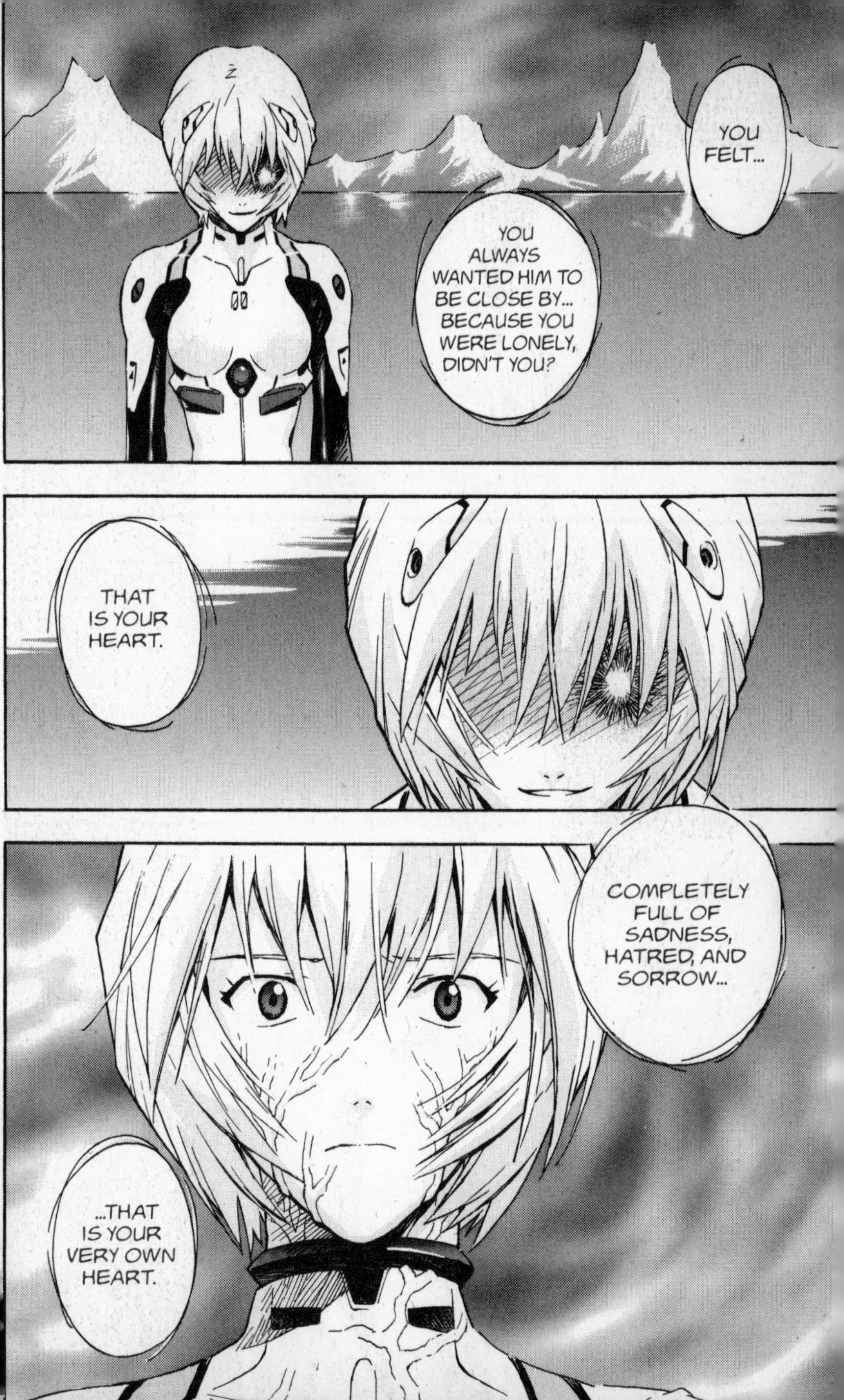
YOU FELT...
YOU ALWAYS WANTED HIM TO BE CLOSE BY... BECAUSE YOU WERE LONELY, DIDN'T YOU?
THAT IS YOUR HEART.
COMPLETELY FULL OF SADNESS, HATRED, AND SORROW...
...THAT IS YOUR VERY OWN HEART.

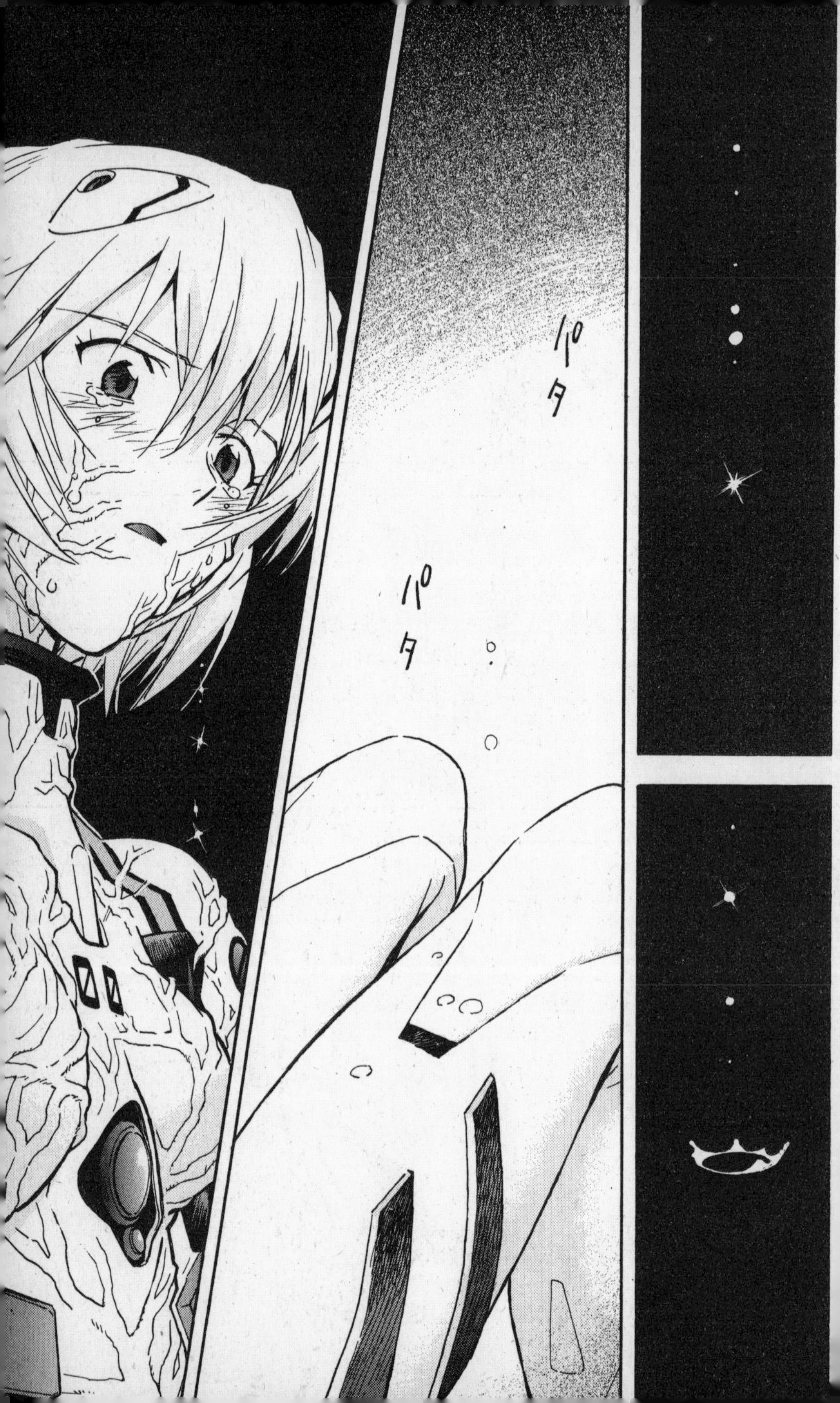

パタ
パタ

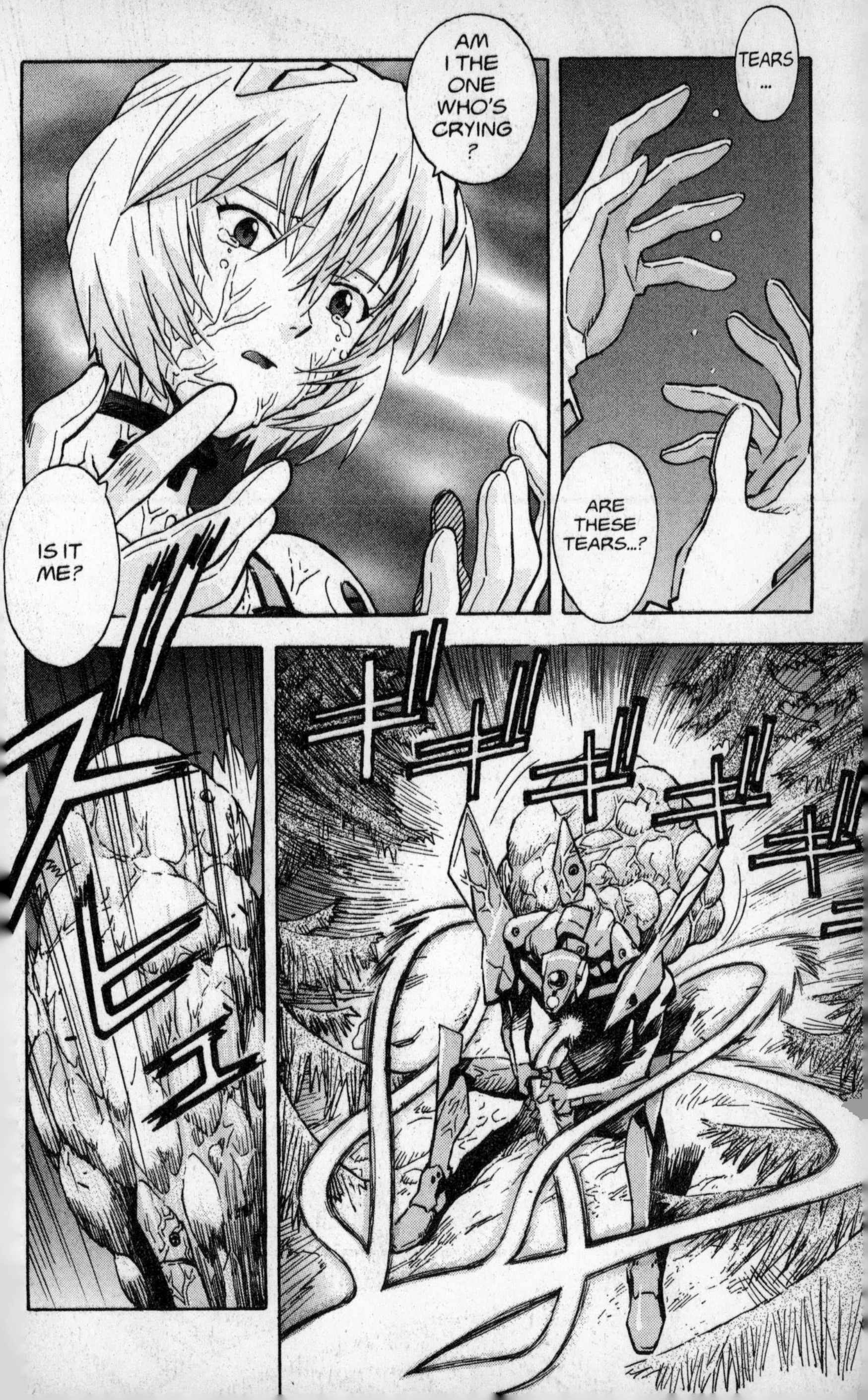
TEARS...
ARE THESE TEARS...?
AM I THE ONE WHO'S CRYING?
IS IT ME?

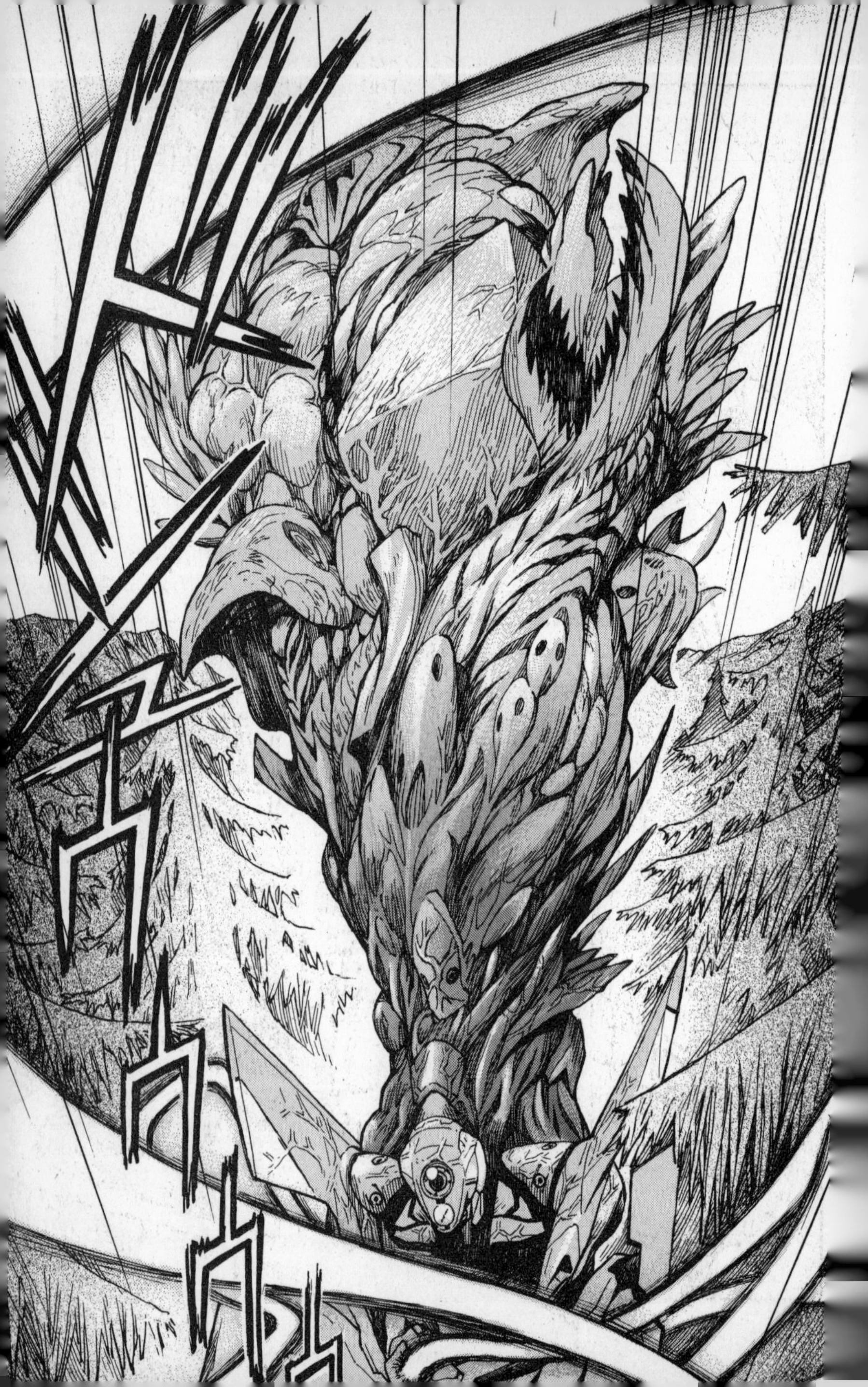

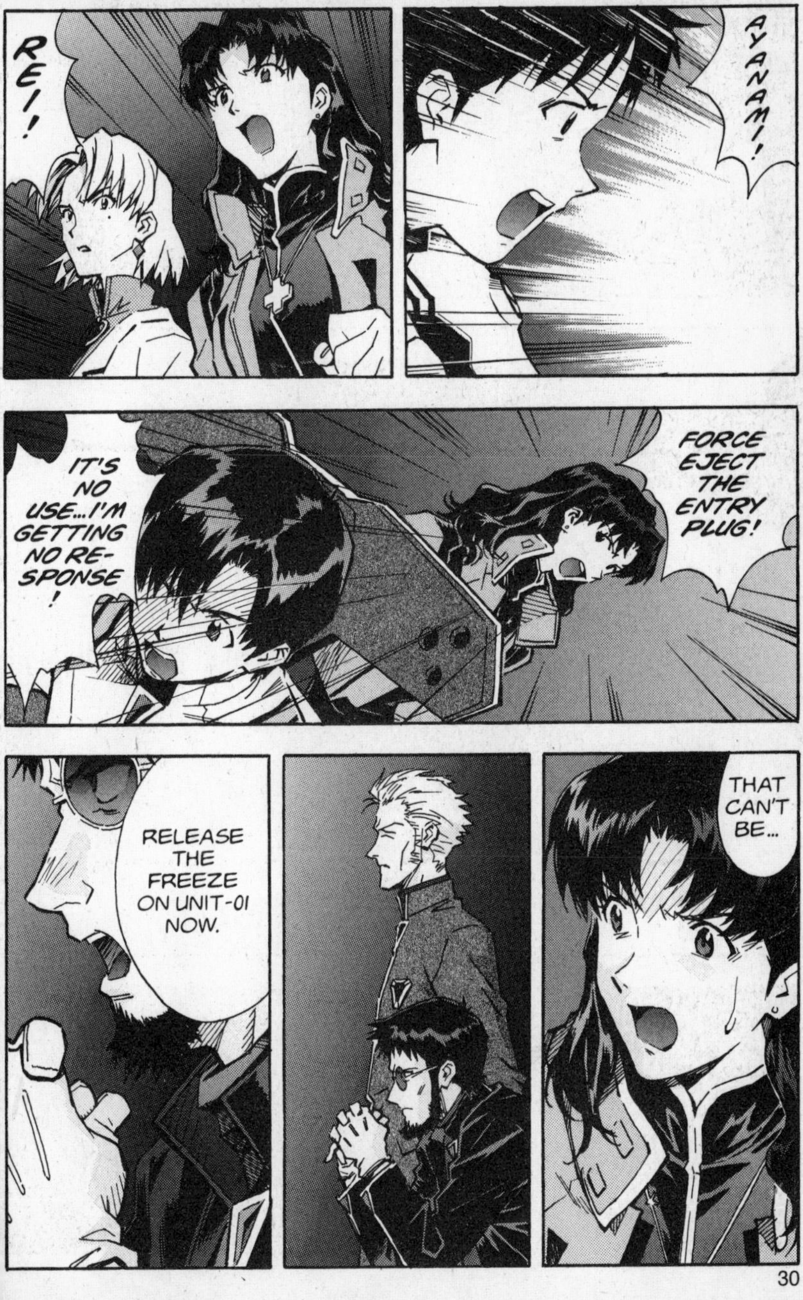
AYANAMI!
REI!
FORCE EJECT THE ENTRY PLUG!
IT'S NO USE...I'M GETTING NO RE-SPONSE!
THAT CAN'T BE...
RELEASE THE FREEZE ON UNIT-01 NOW.

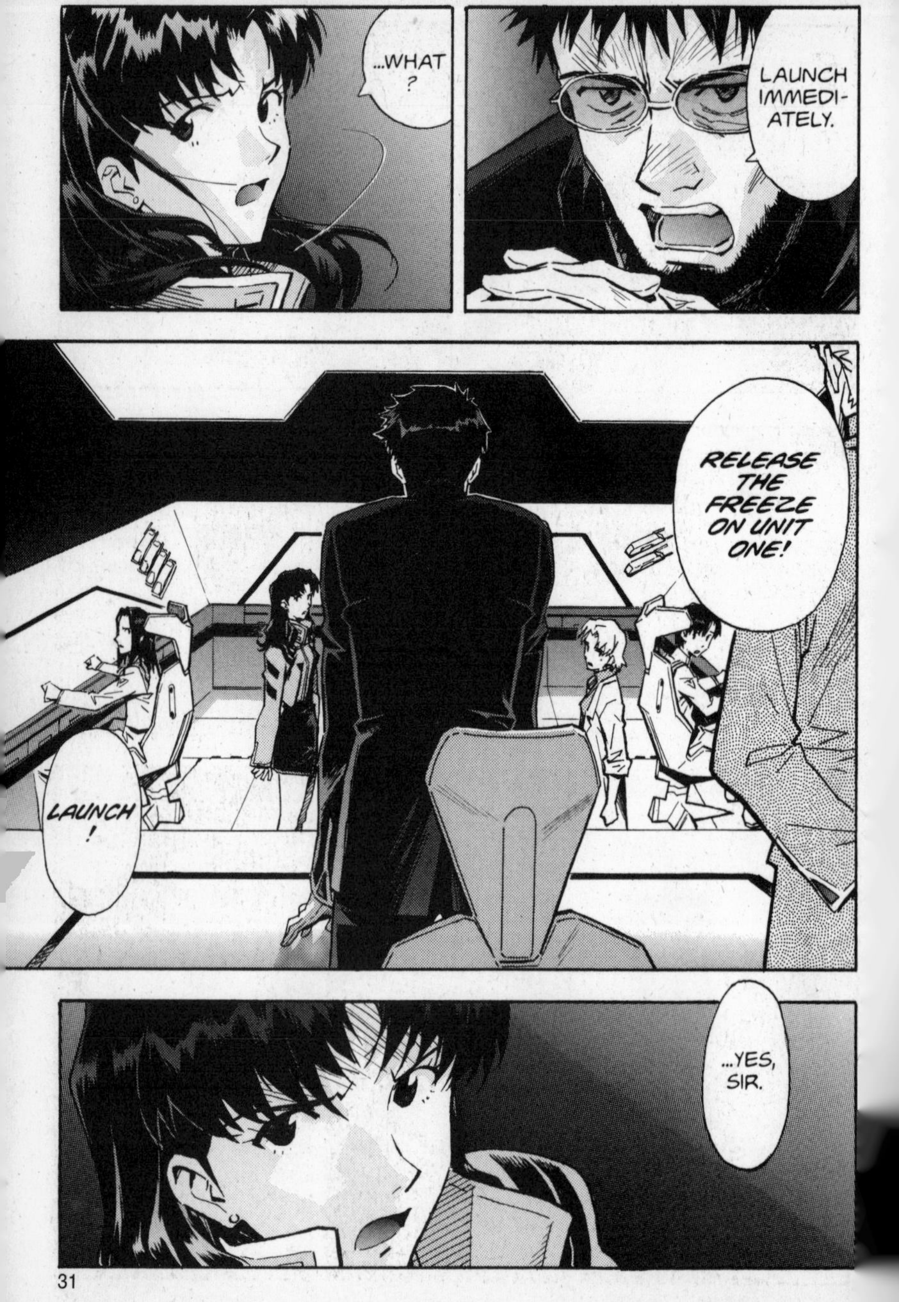
LAUNCH IMMEDIATELY.
...WHAT?
RELEASE THE FREEZE ON UNIT ONE!
LAUNCH!
...YES, SIR.

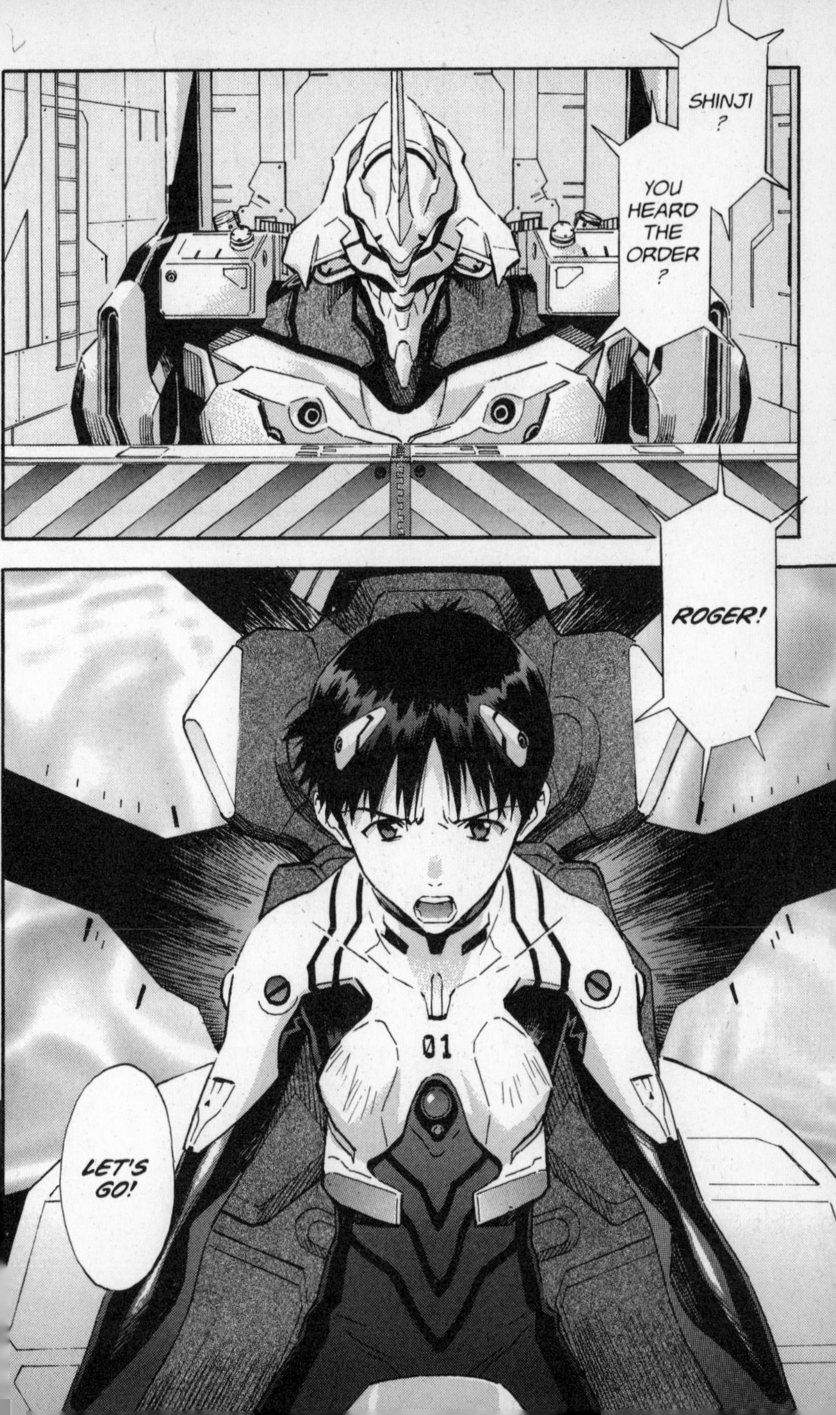
SHINJI?
YOU HEARD THE ORDER?
ROGER!
LET'S GO!

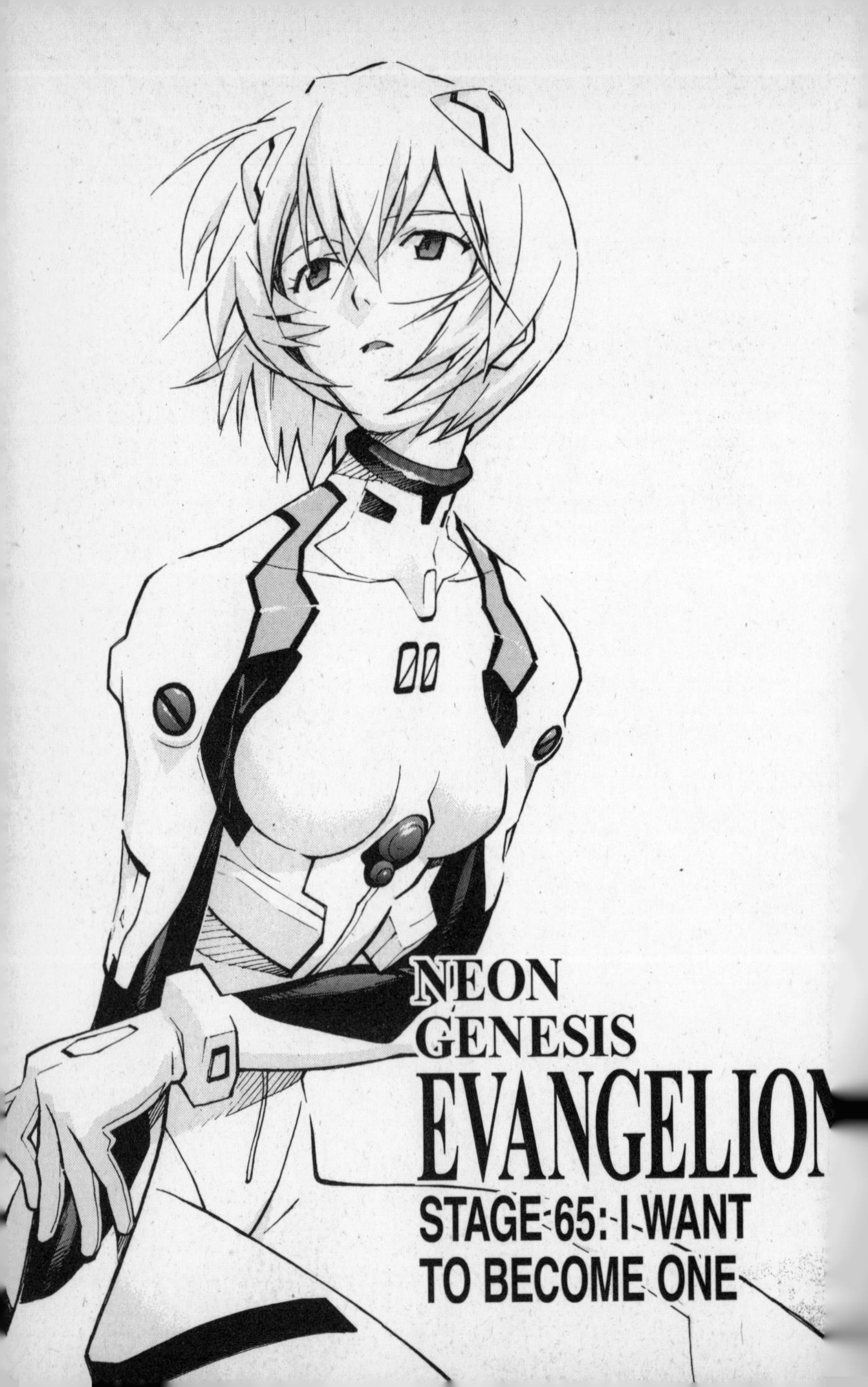
NEON GENESIS
EVANGELION
STAGE 65: I WANT TO BECOME ONE

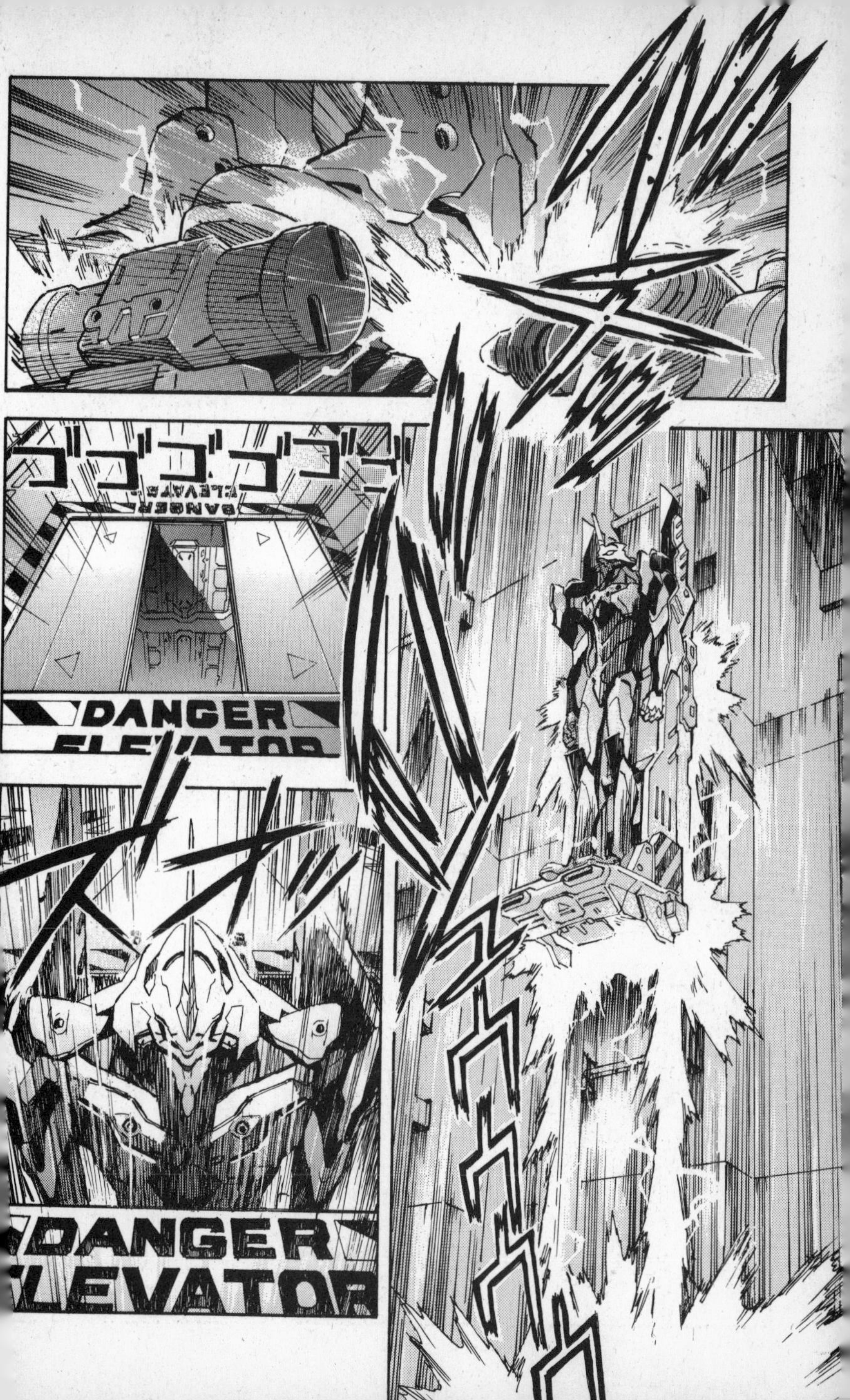
ゴゴゴゴゴ
DANGER
DANGER
ELEVATOR

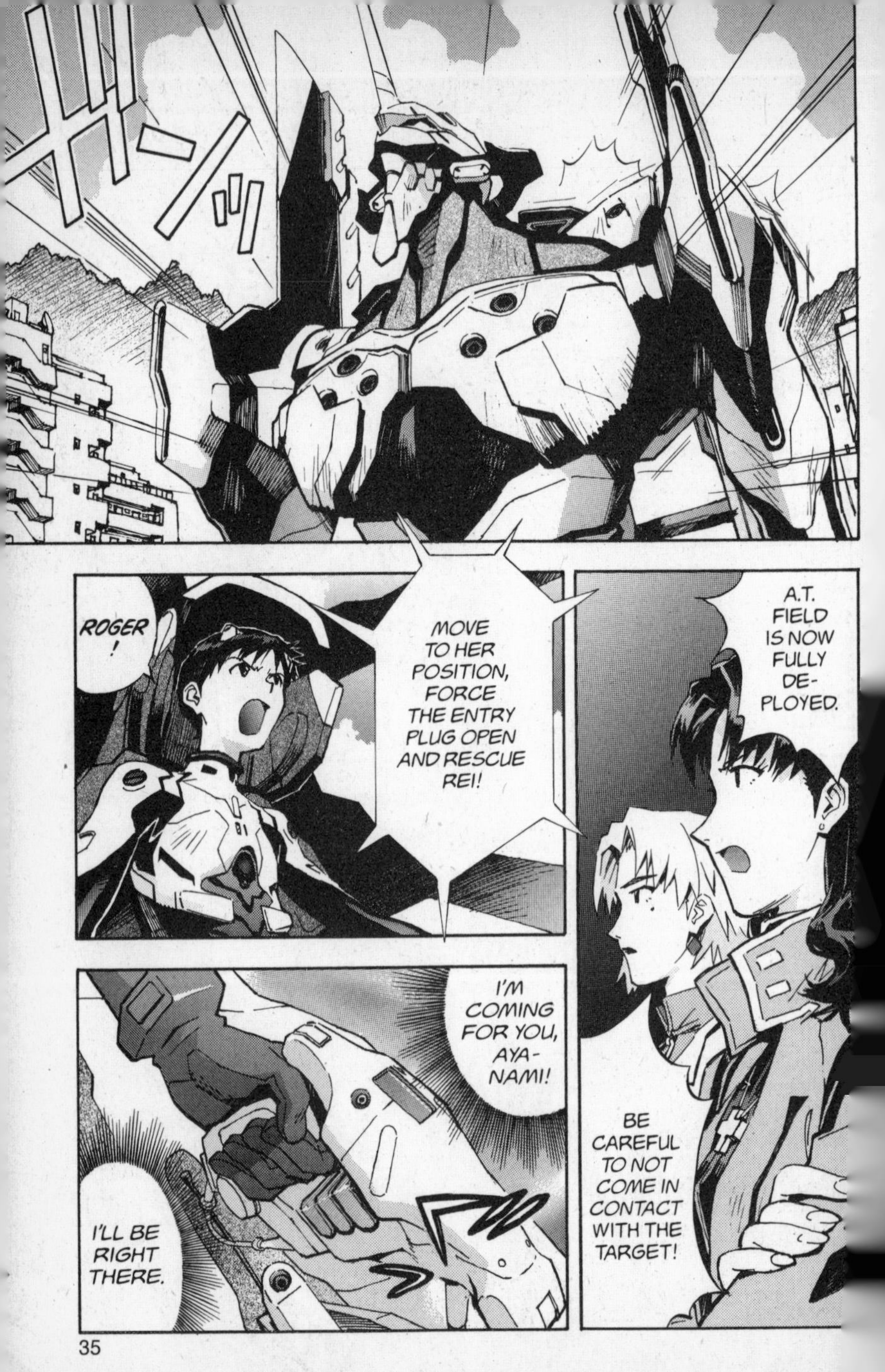
A.T. FIELD IS NOW FULLY DE-PLOYED.
BE CAREFUL TO NOT COME IN CONTACT WITH THE TARGET!
MOVE TO HER POSITION, FORCE THE ENTRY PLUG OPEN AND RESCUE REI!
ROGER!
I'M COMING FOR YOU, AYA-NAMI!
I'LL BE RIGHT THERE.

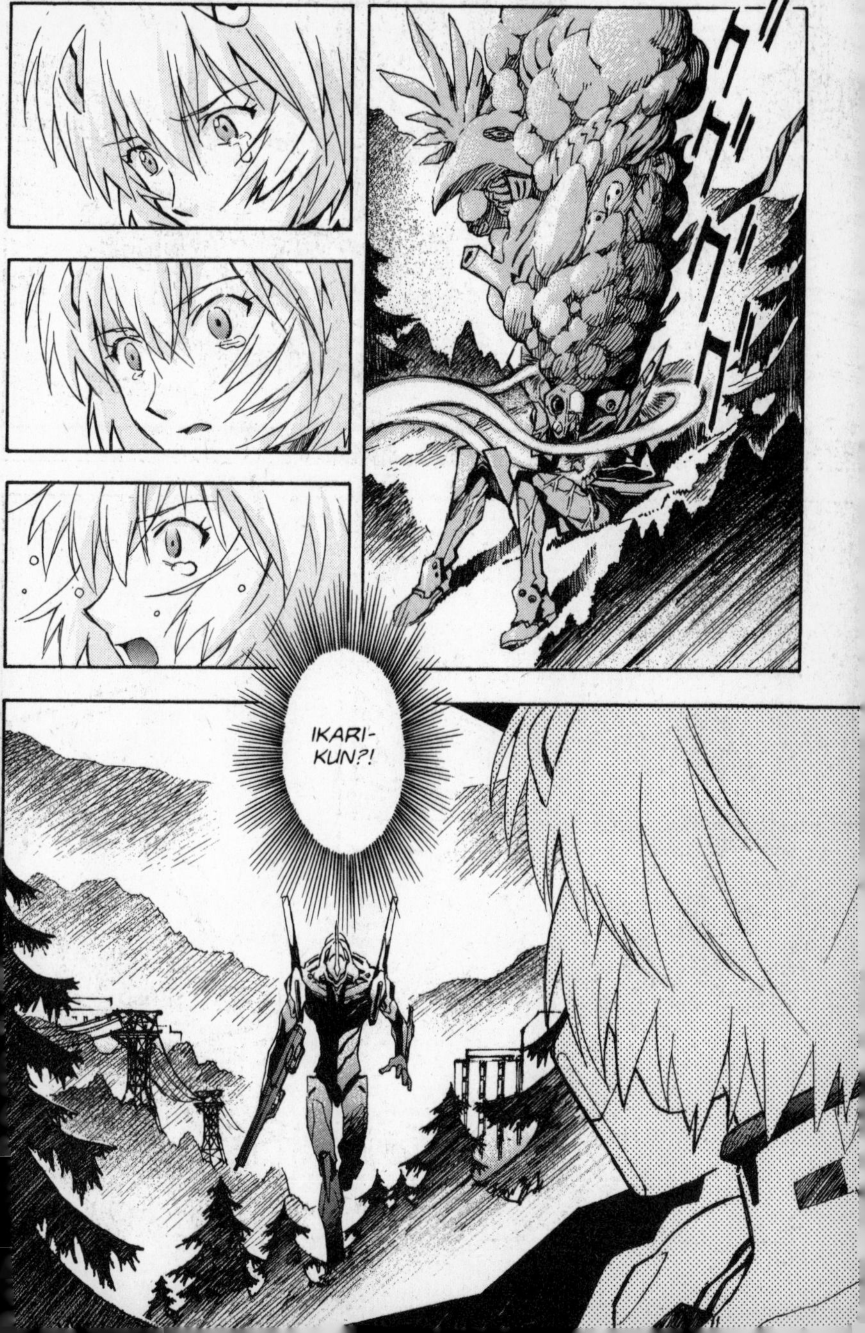
IKARI-
KUN?!

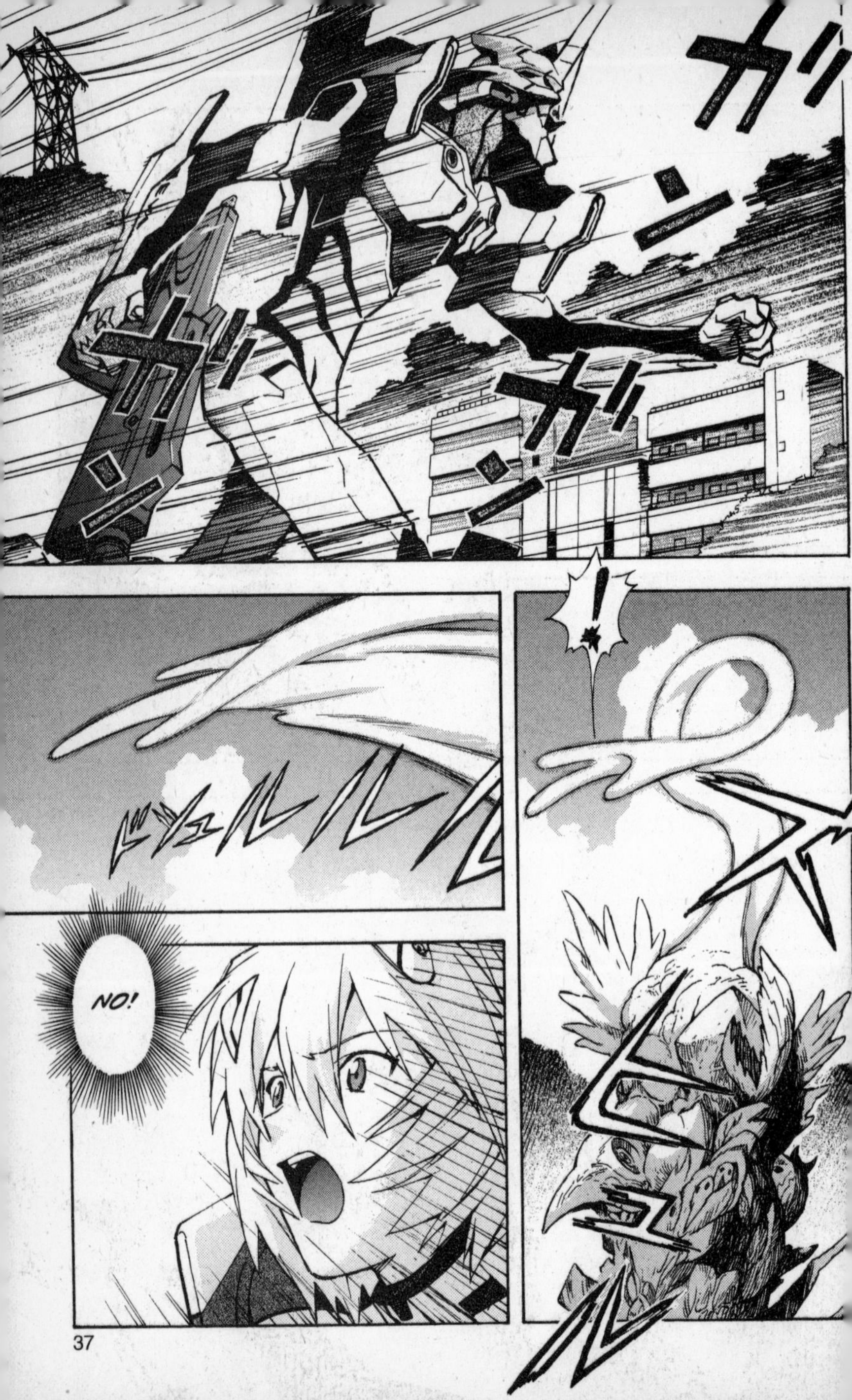
ガッ
ドシュルルル
!
NO!

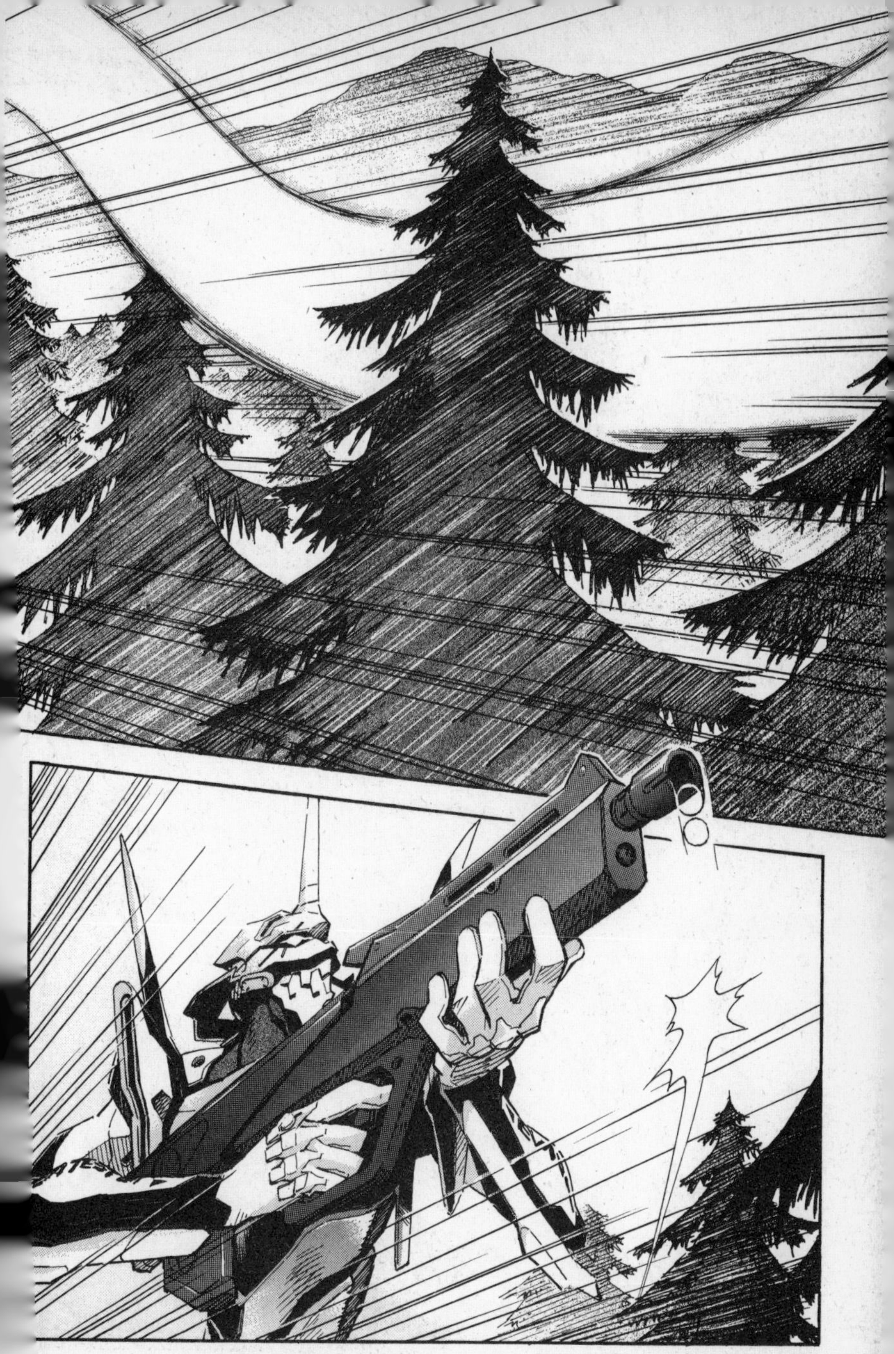

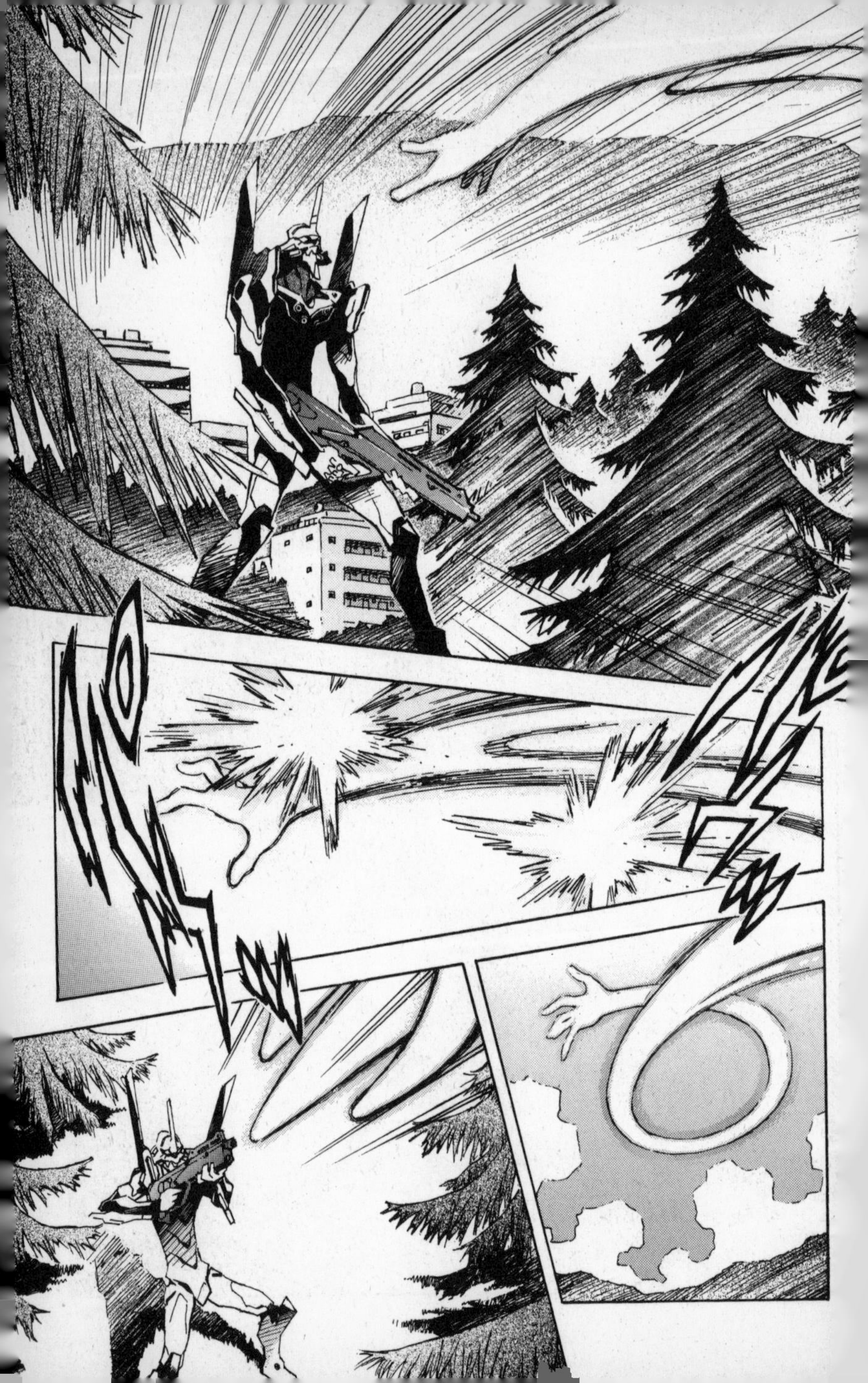

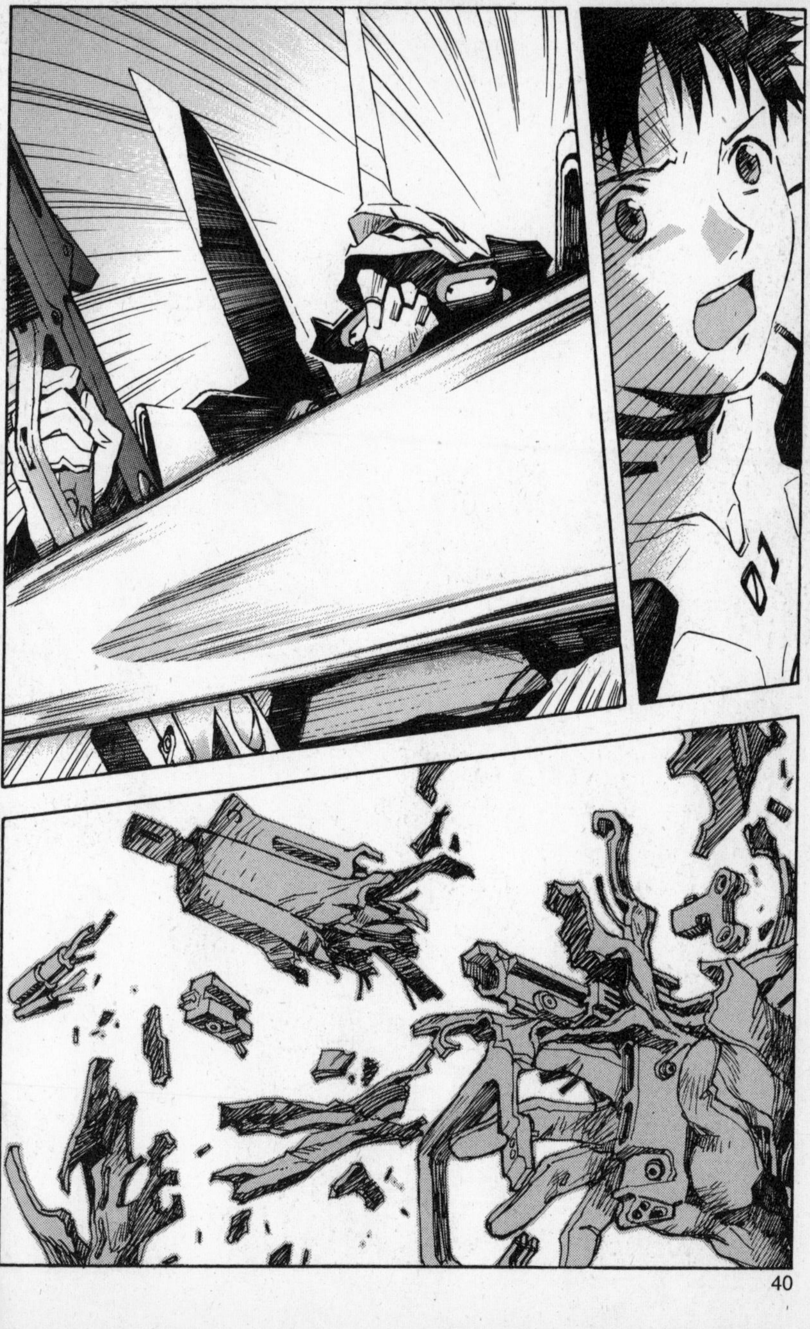

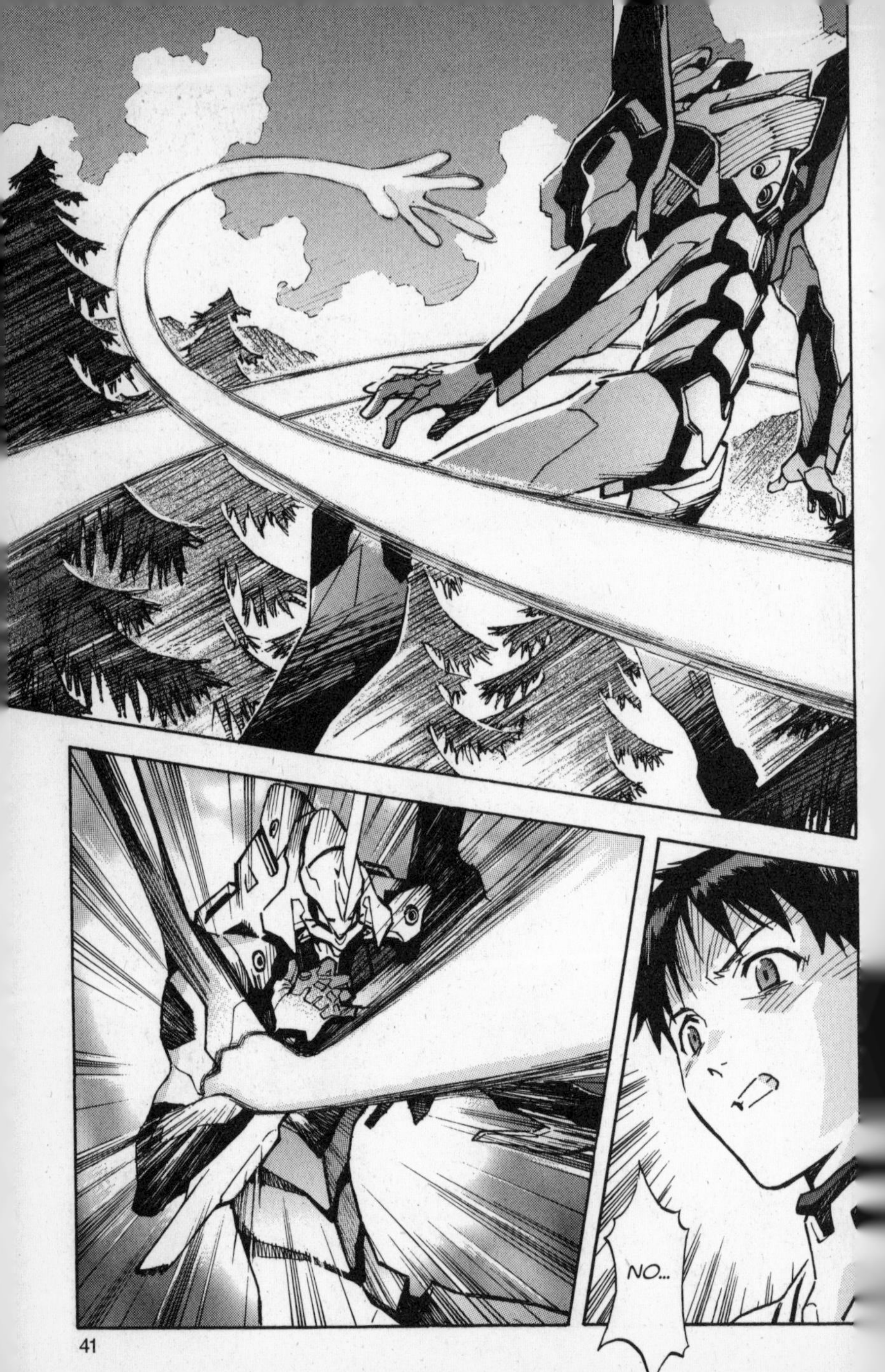
NO...

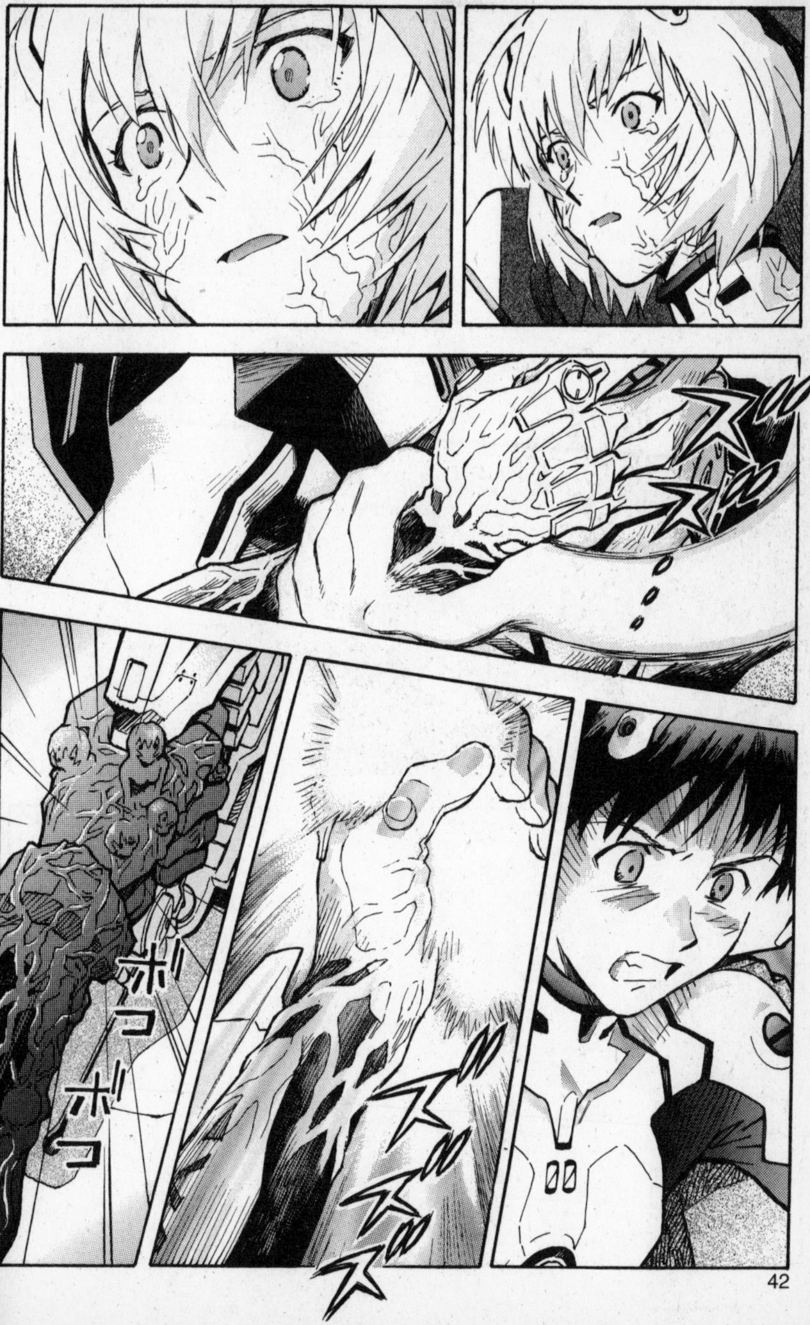
ボコ
ボコ

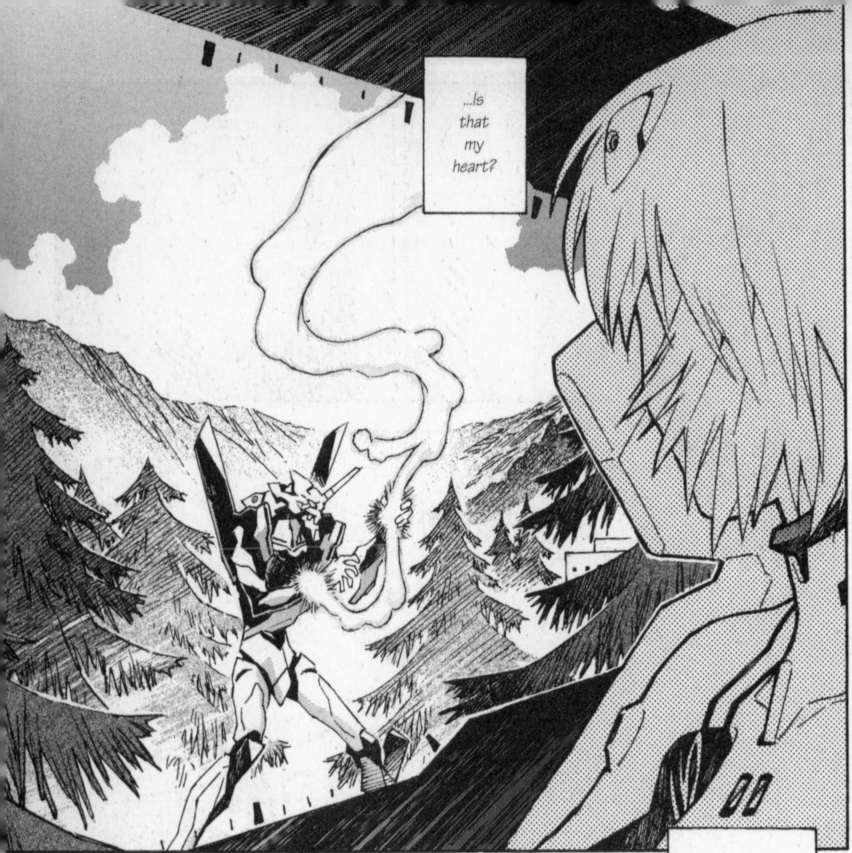
...Is that my heart?
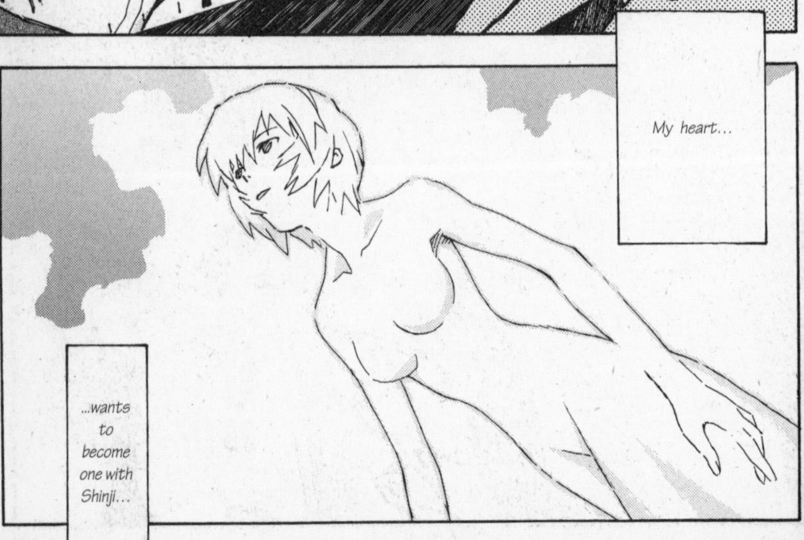
My heart...
...wants to become one with Shinji...

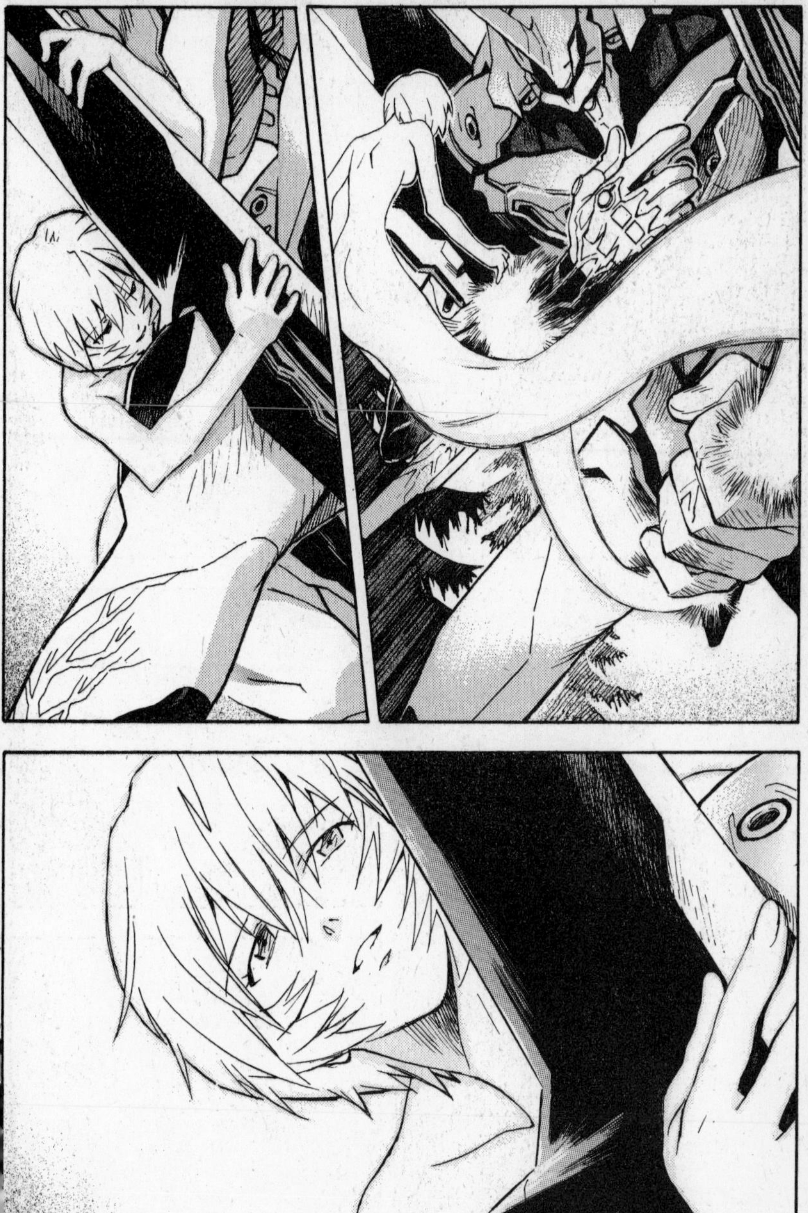

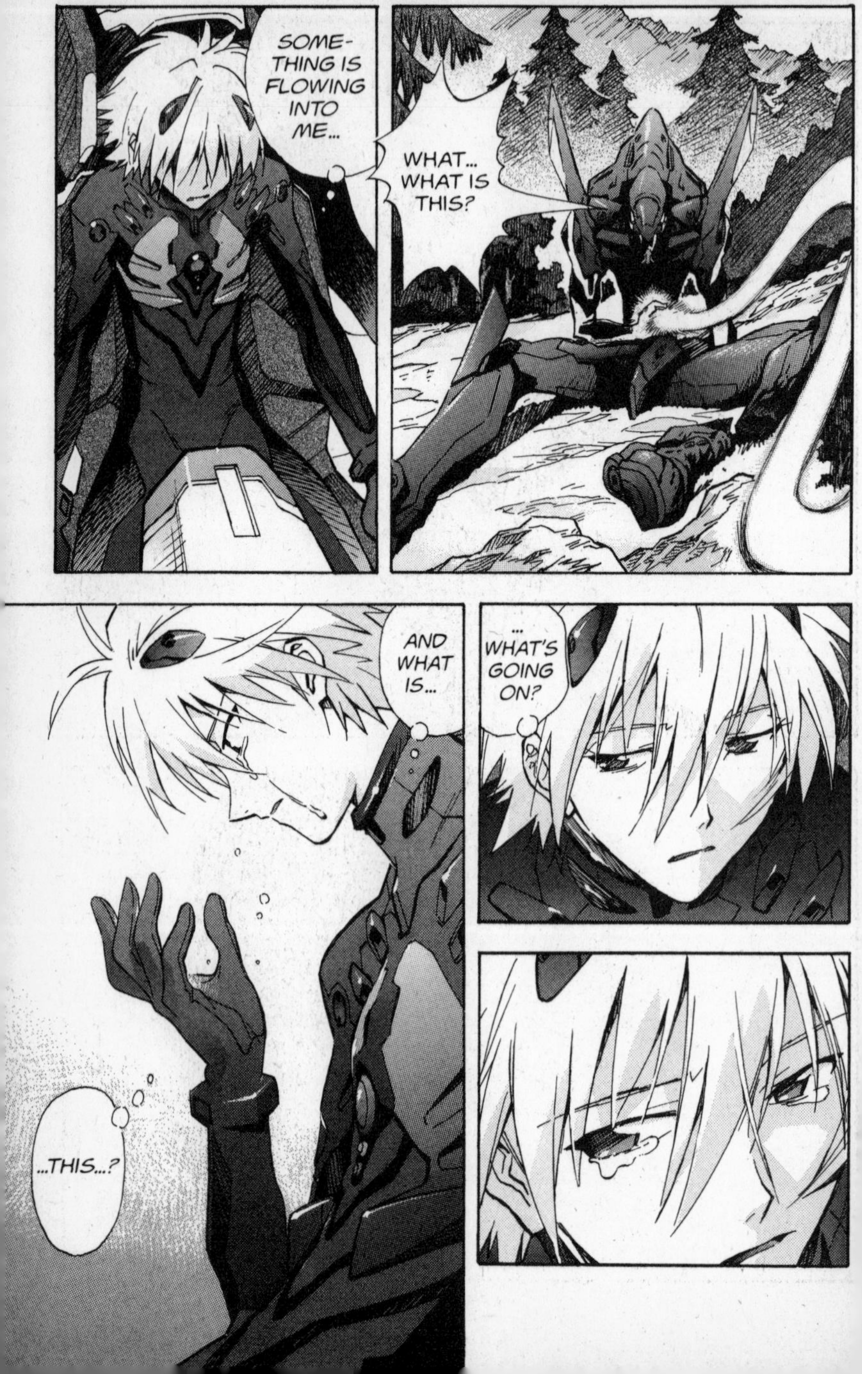
WHAT... WHAT IS THIS?
SOME-THING IS FLOWING INTO ME...
...WHAT'S GOING ON?
AND WHAT IS...
...THIS...?

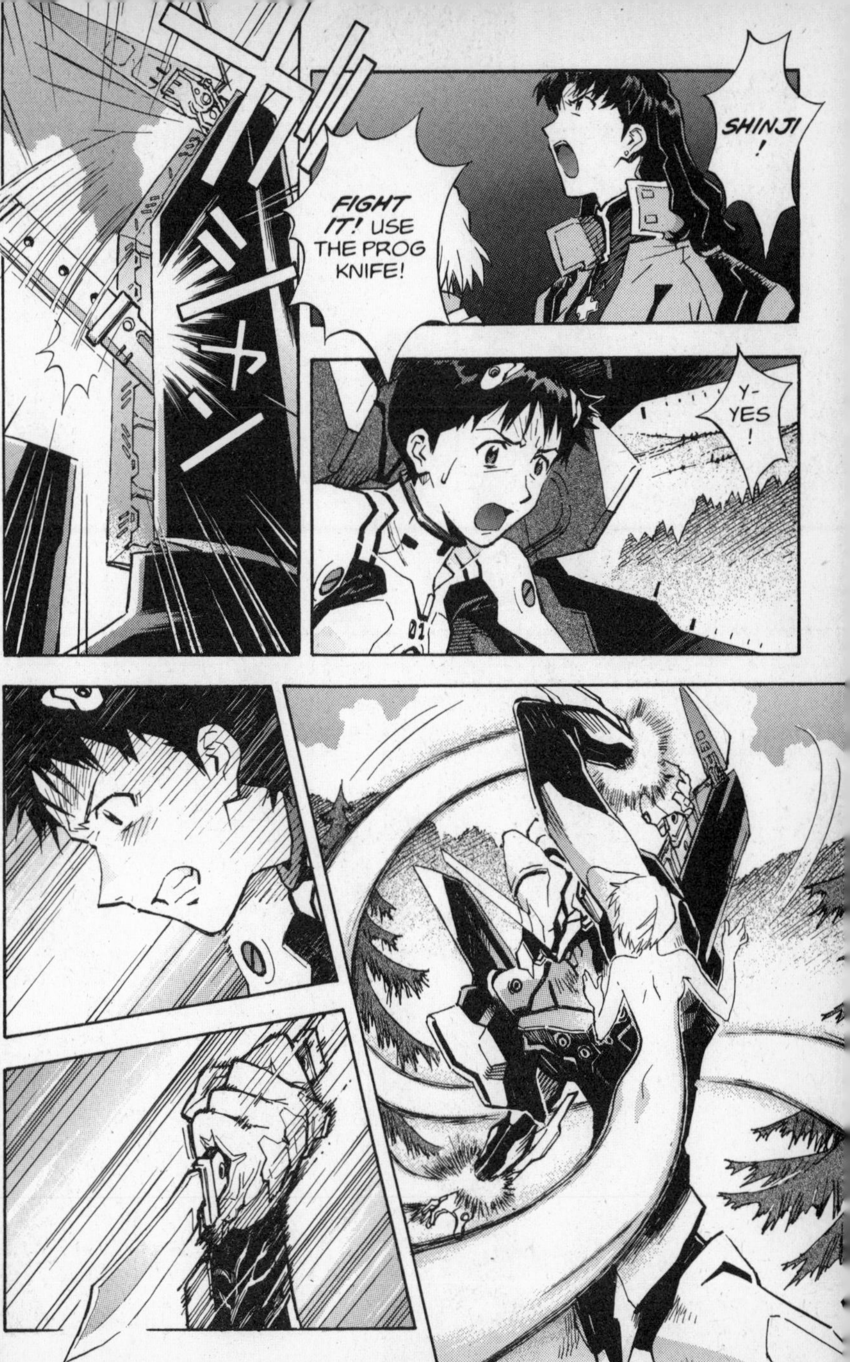
SHINJI!
FIGHT IT! USE THE PROG KNIFE!
Y-YES!

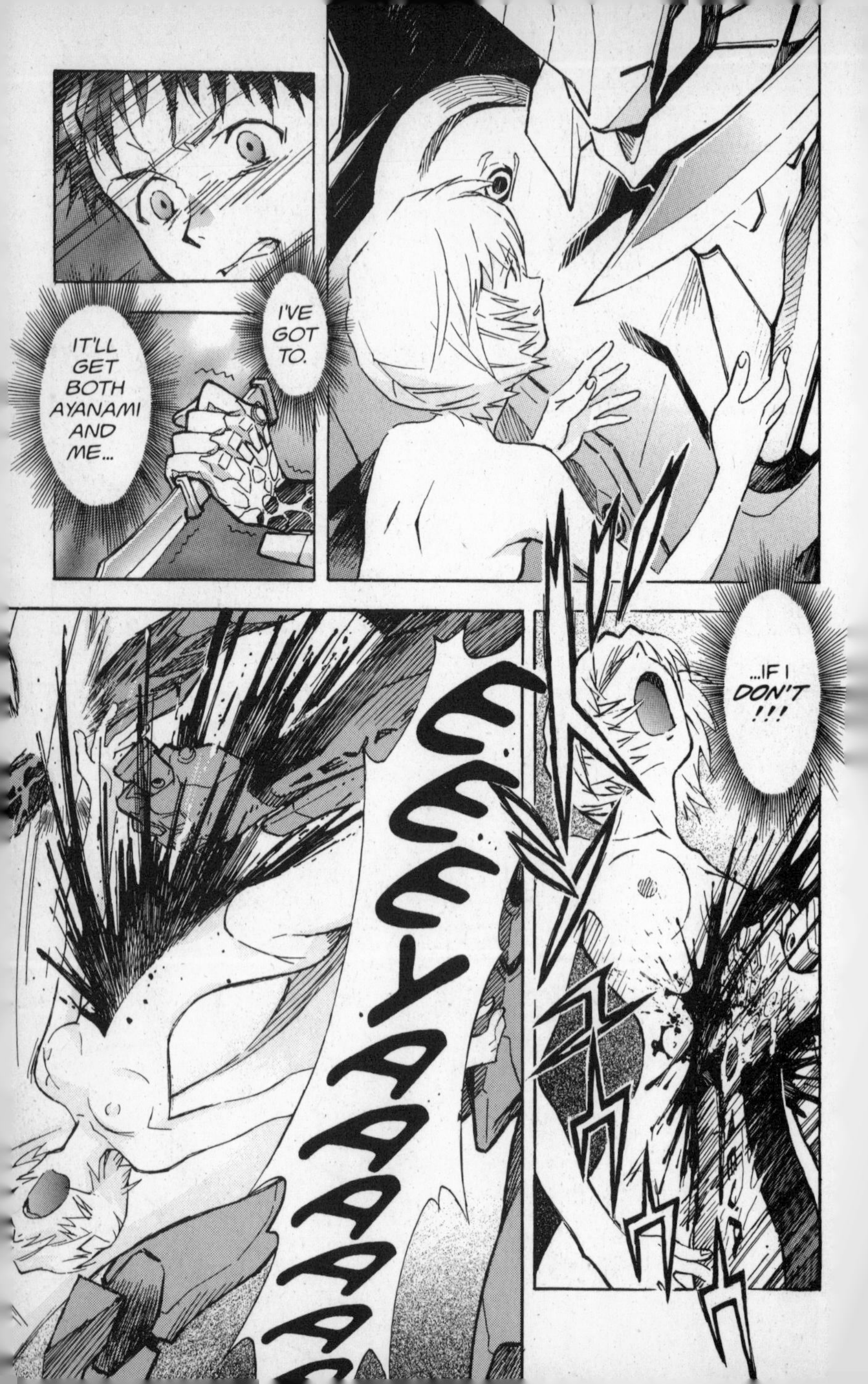
I'VE GOT TO.
IT'LL GET BOTH AYANAMI AND ME...
...IF I DON'T!!!
EEEEYAAAAAAAAA

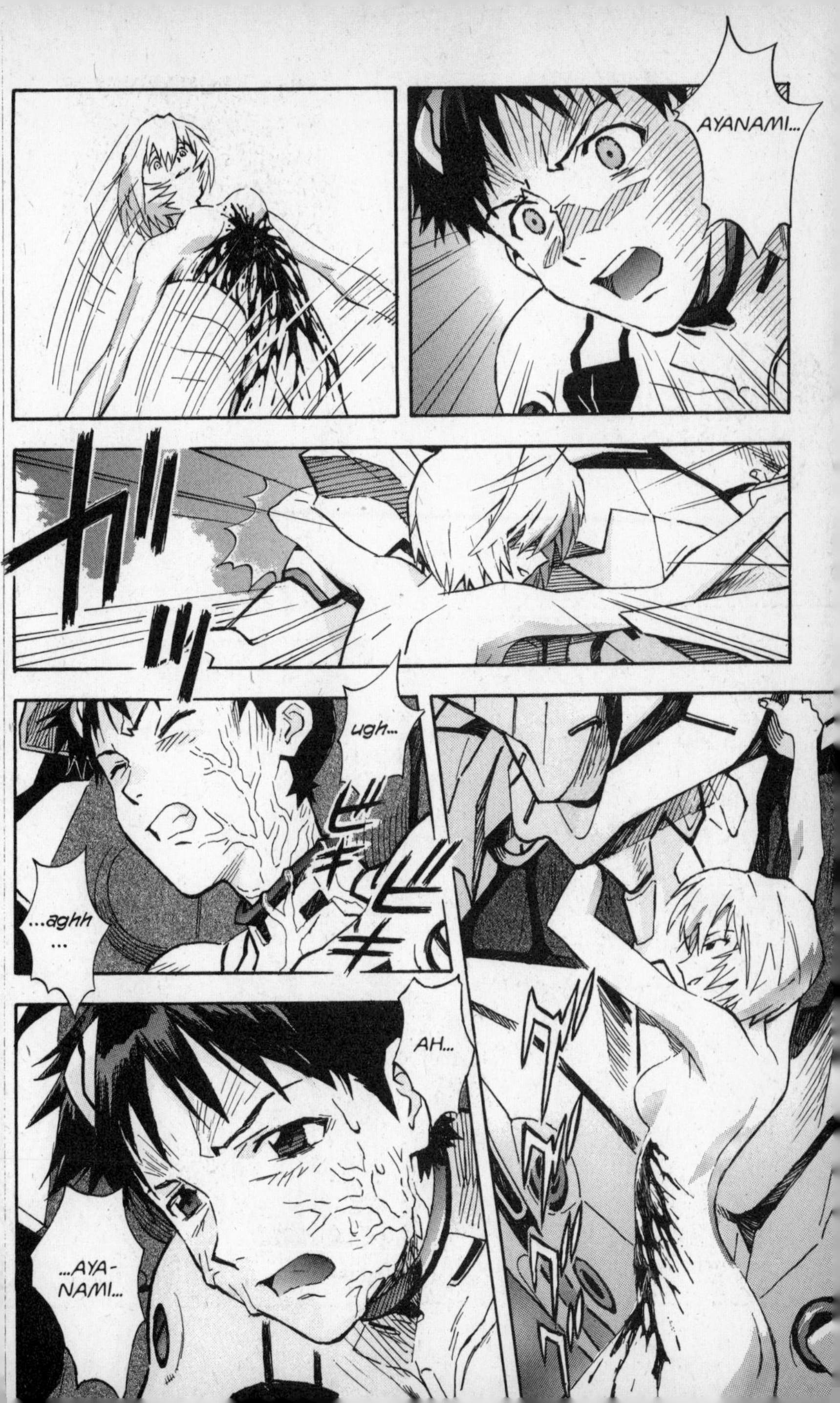
AYANAMI...
ugh...
...aghh ...
AH...
...AYA-
NAMI...

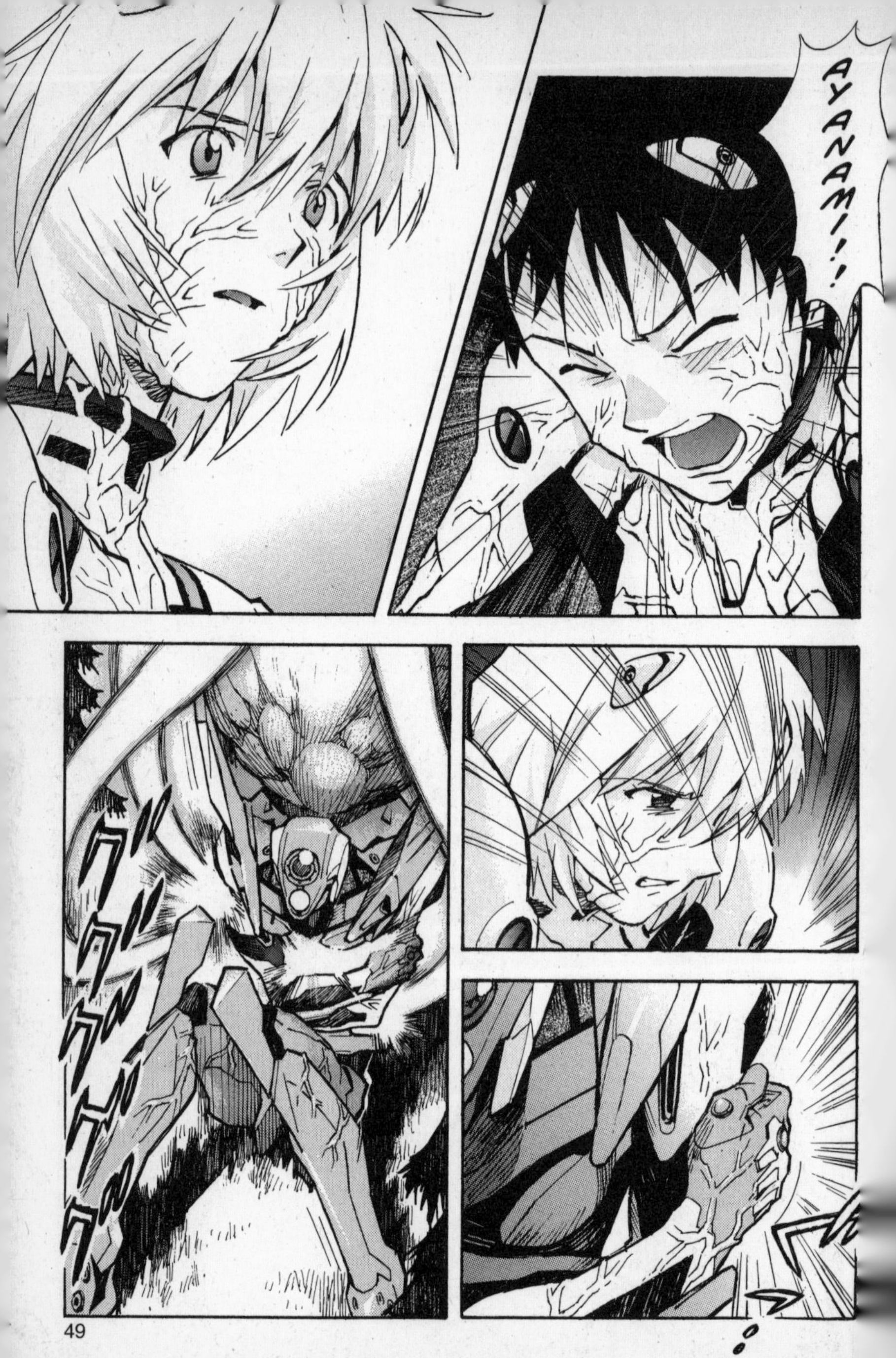
AYANAMI!!

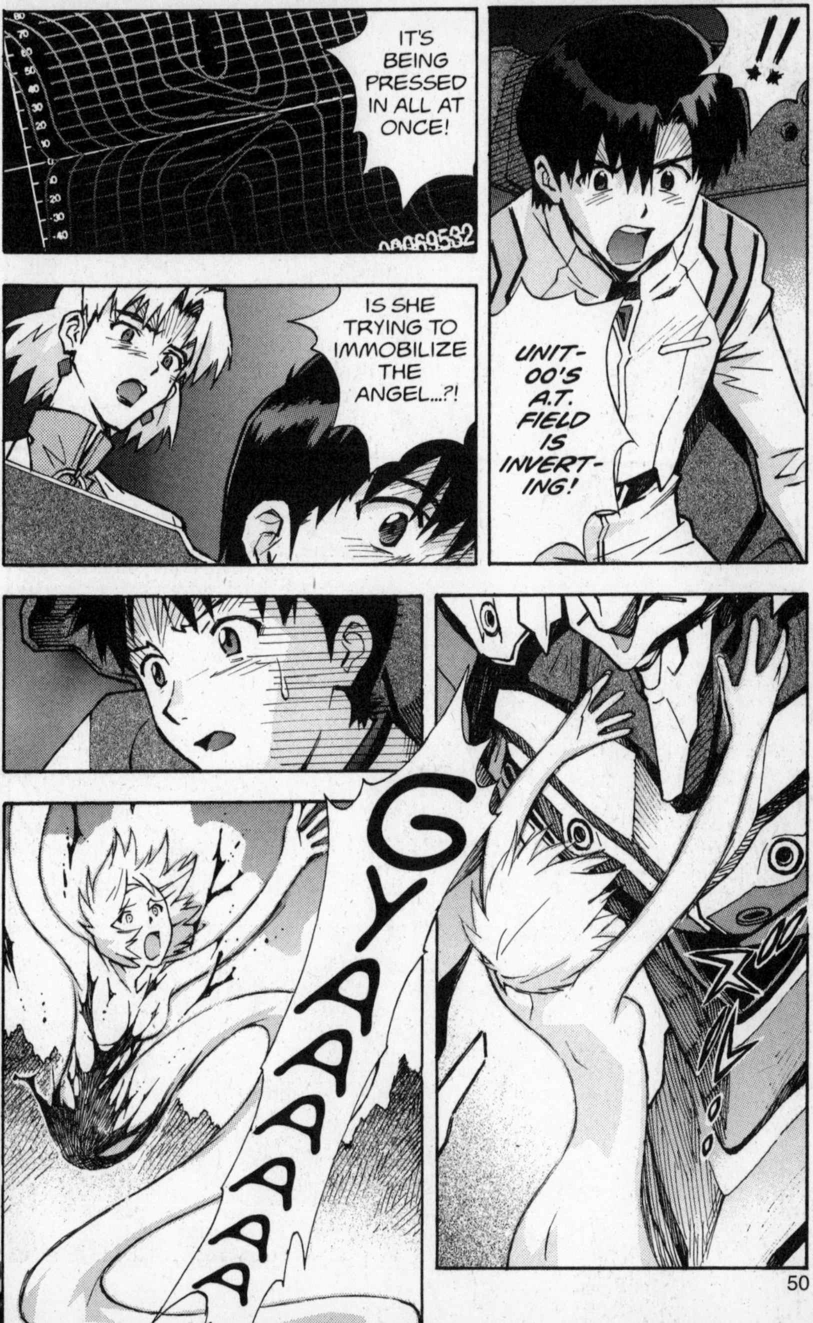
!!
UNIT-00'S A.T. FIELD IS INVERTING!
IT'S BEING PRESSED IN ALL AT ONCE!
IS SHE TRYING TO IMMOBILIZE THE ANGEL...?!
GYAAAAAAA

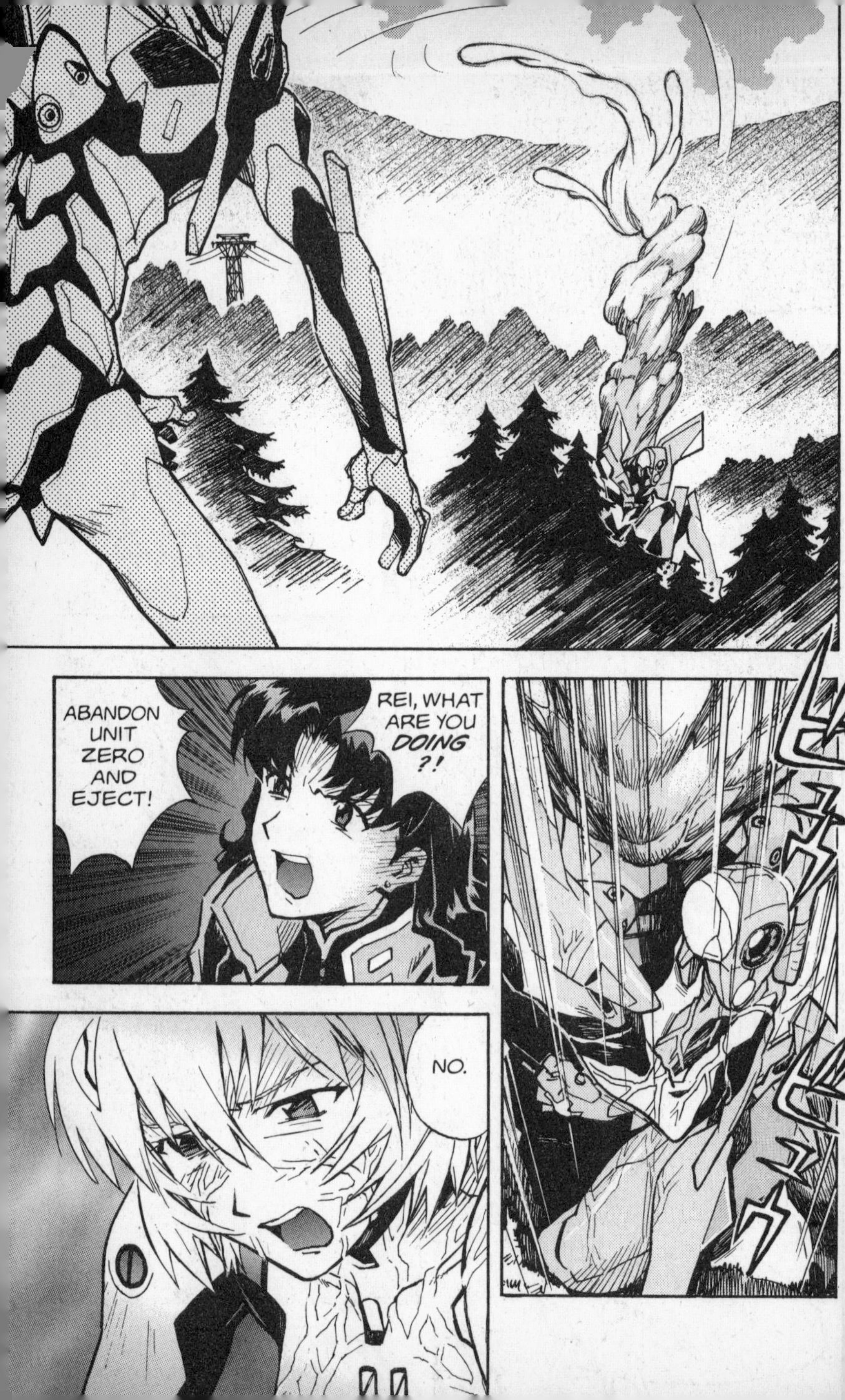
REI, WHAT ARE YOU DOING?!
ABANDON UNIT ZERO AND EJECT!
NO.

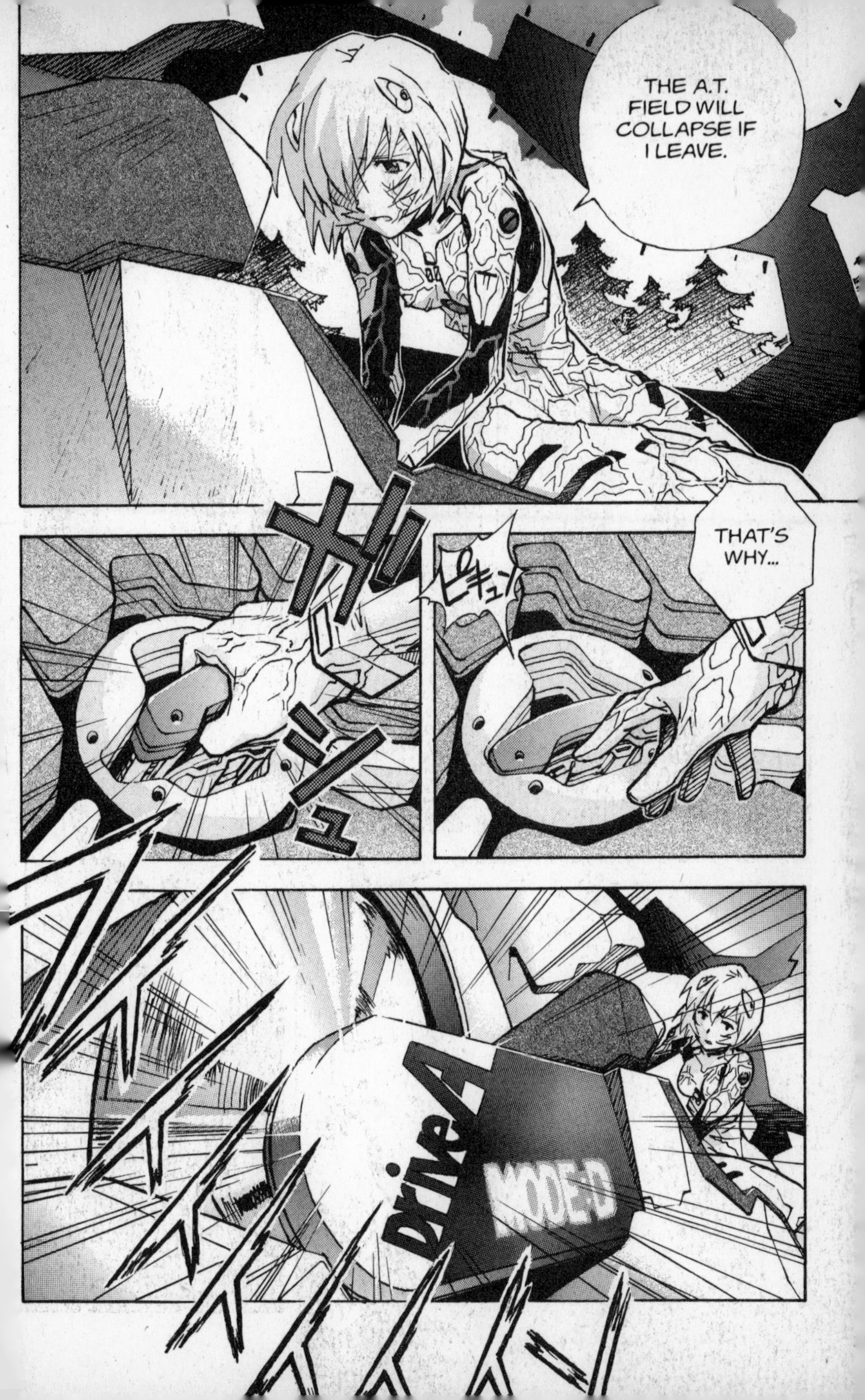
THE A.T. FIELD WILL COLLAPSE IF I LEAVE.
THAT'S WHY...
Drive A
MODE:D

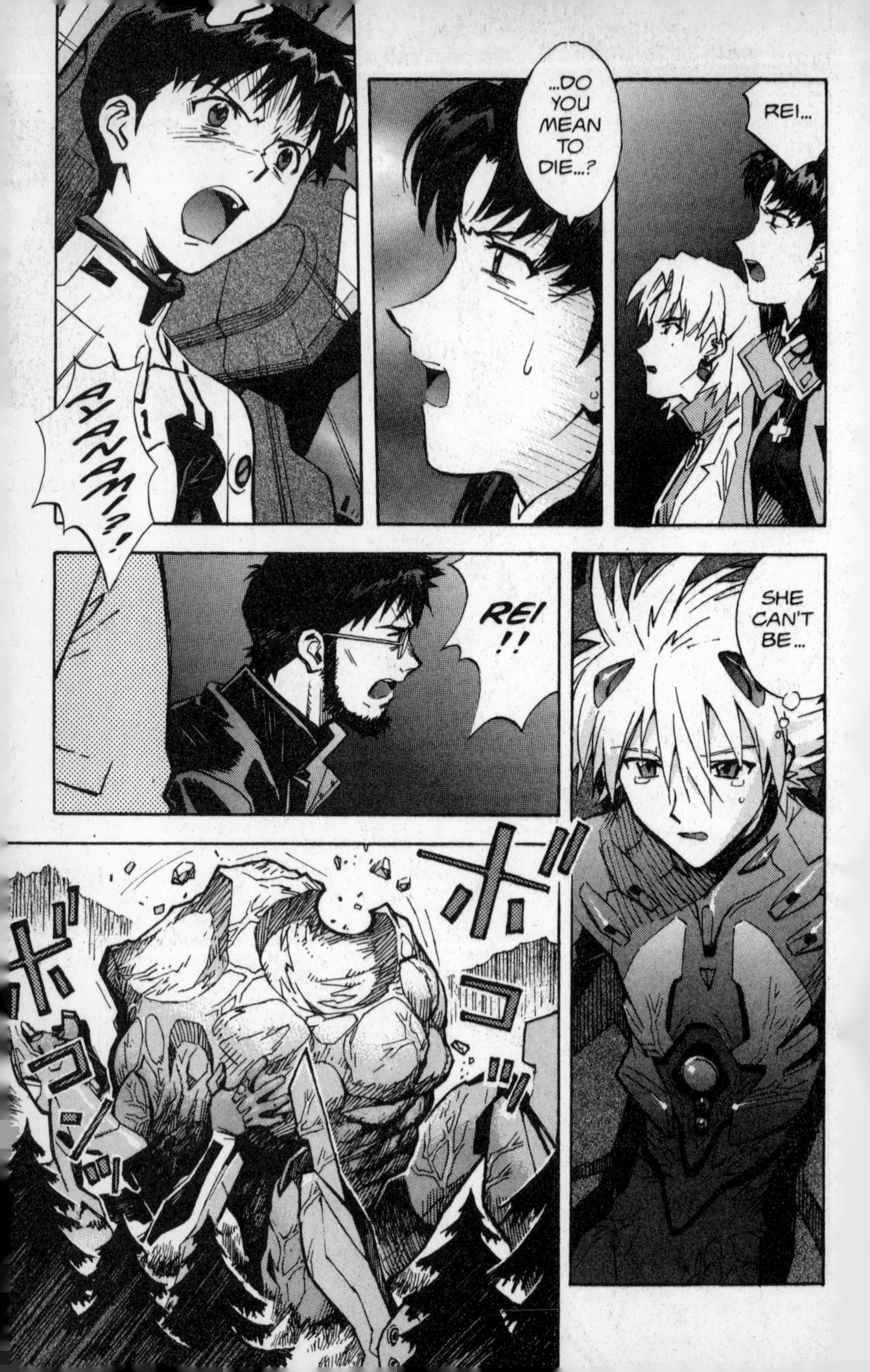
REI...
...DO YOU MEAN TO DIE...?
AYANAMI?!
SHE CAN'T BE...
REI!!

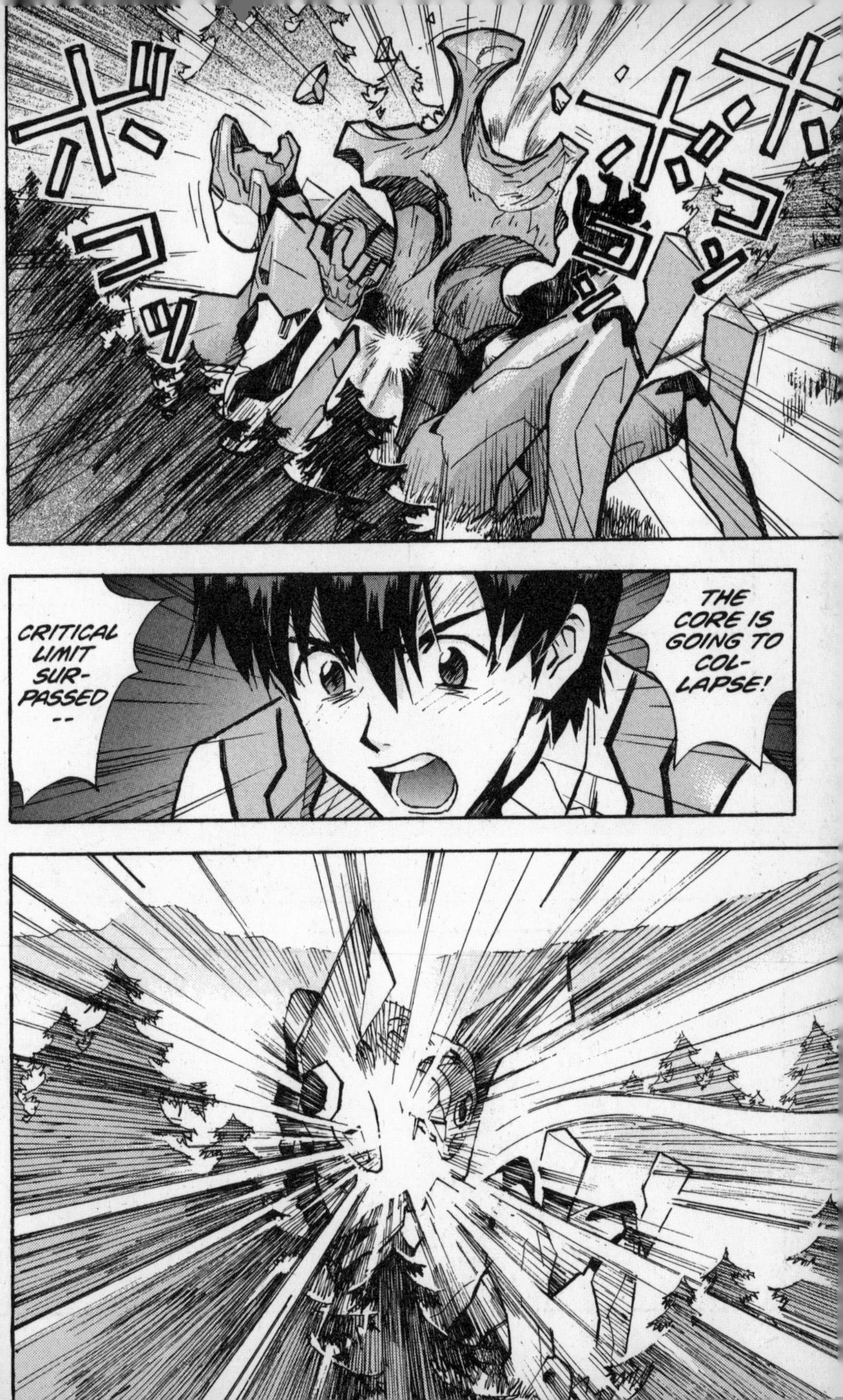
THE CORE IS GOING TO COL-LAPSE!
CRITICAL LIMIT SUR-PASSED --

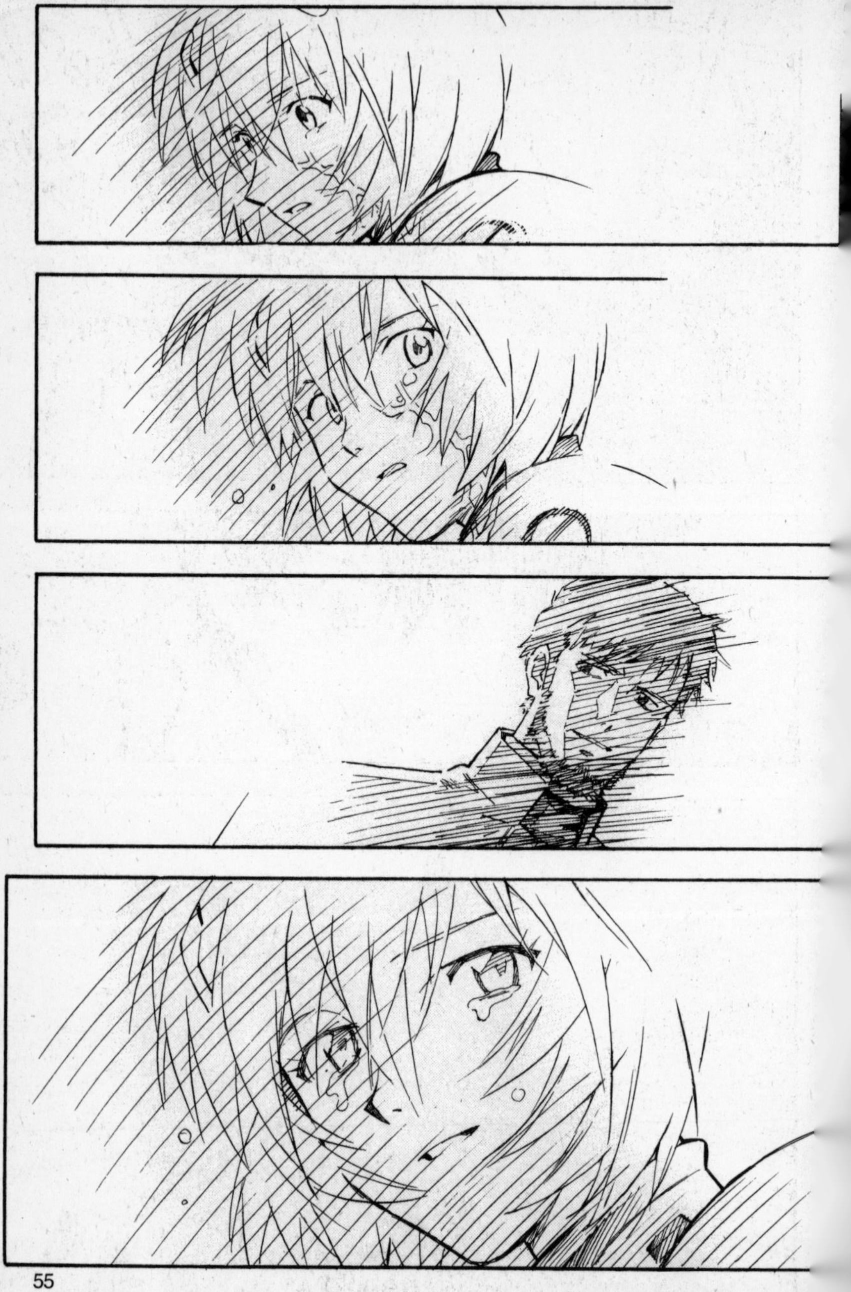

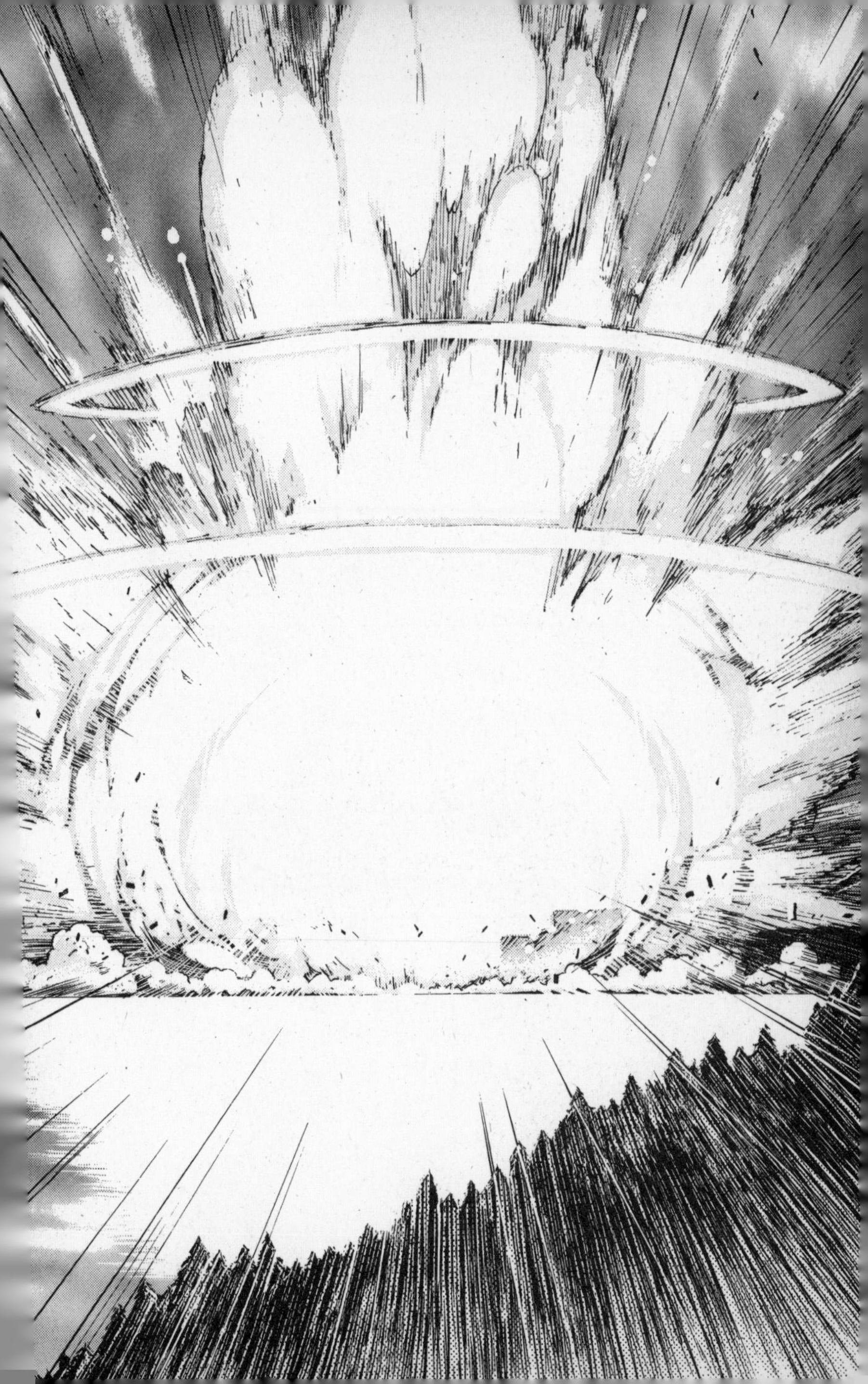

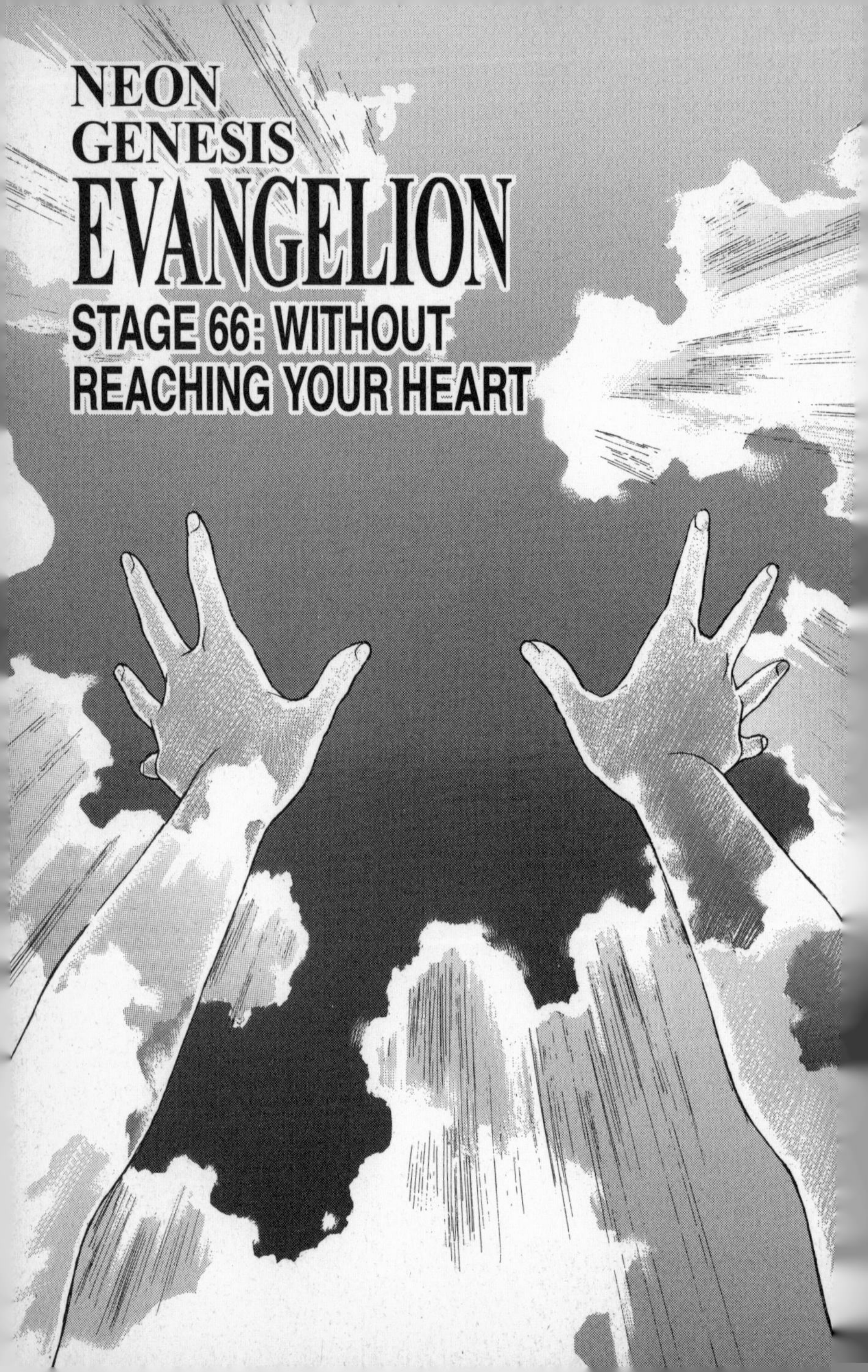
NEON
GENESIS
EVANGELION
STAGE 66: WITHOUT
REACHING YOUR HEART

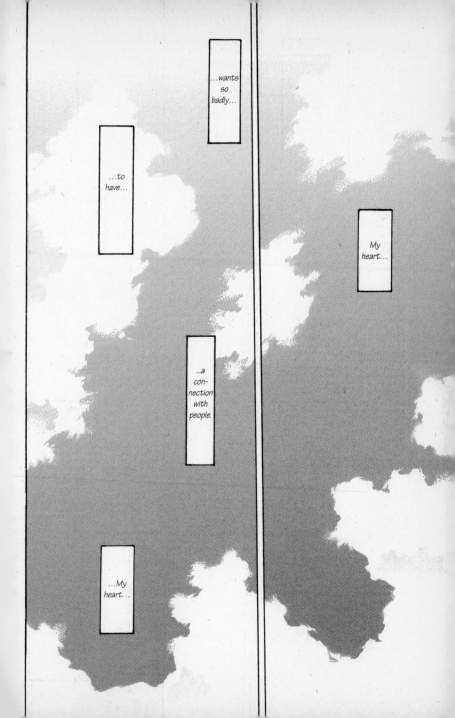

...wants
so
badly...

...to
have...

My
heart...

...a
con-
nection
with
people.

...My
heart...

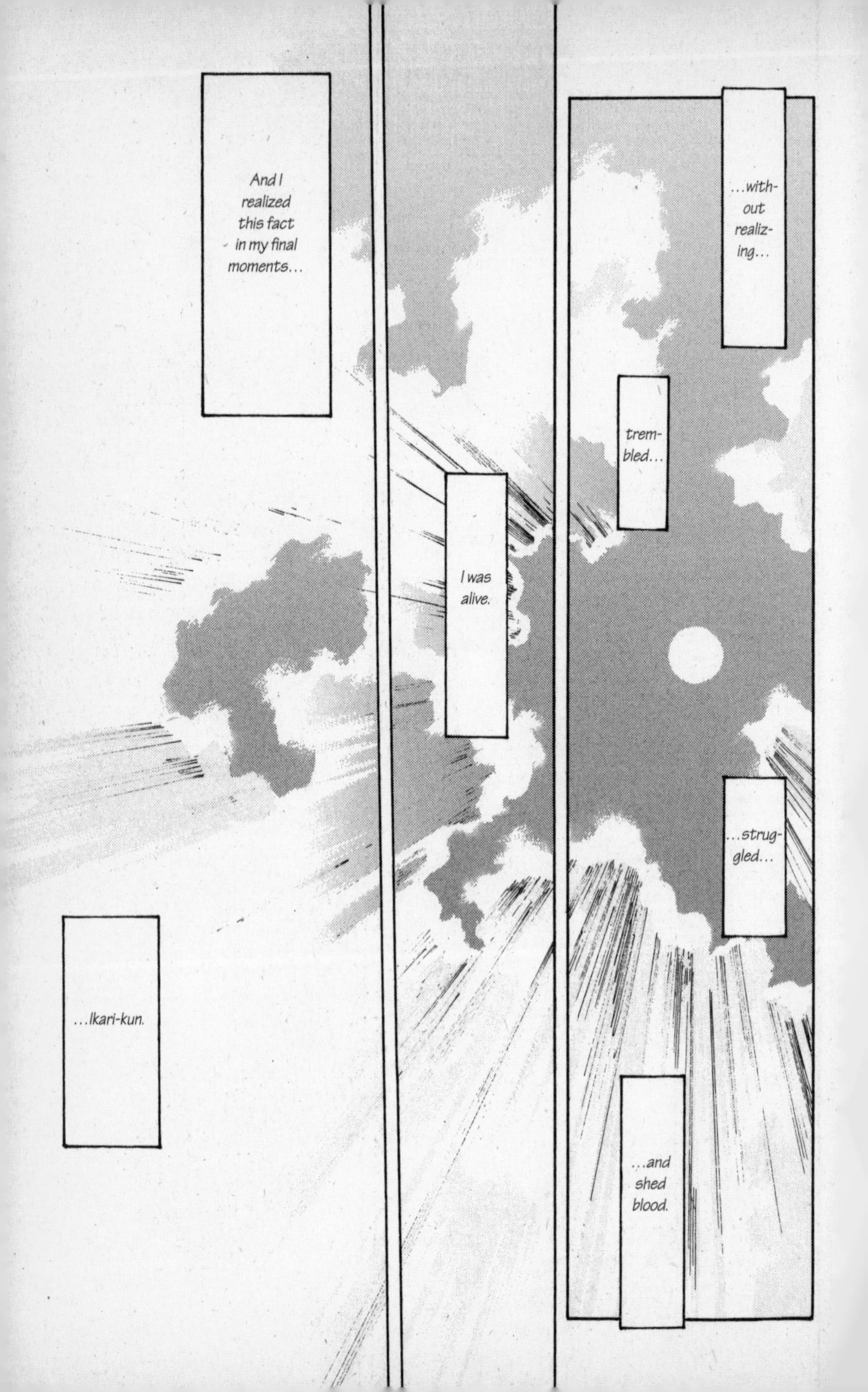
...with-out realiz-ing...
trem-bled...
...strug-gled...
...and shed blood.
I was alive.
And I realized this fact in my final moments...
...Ikari-kun.

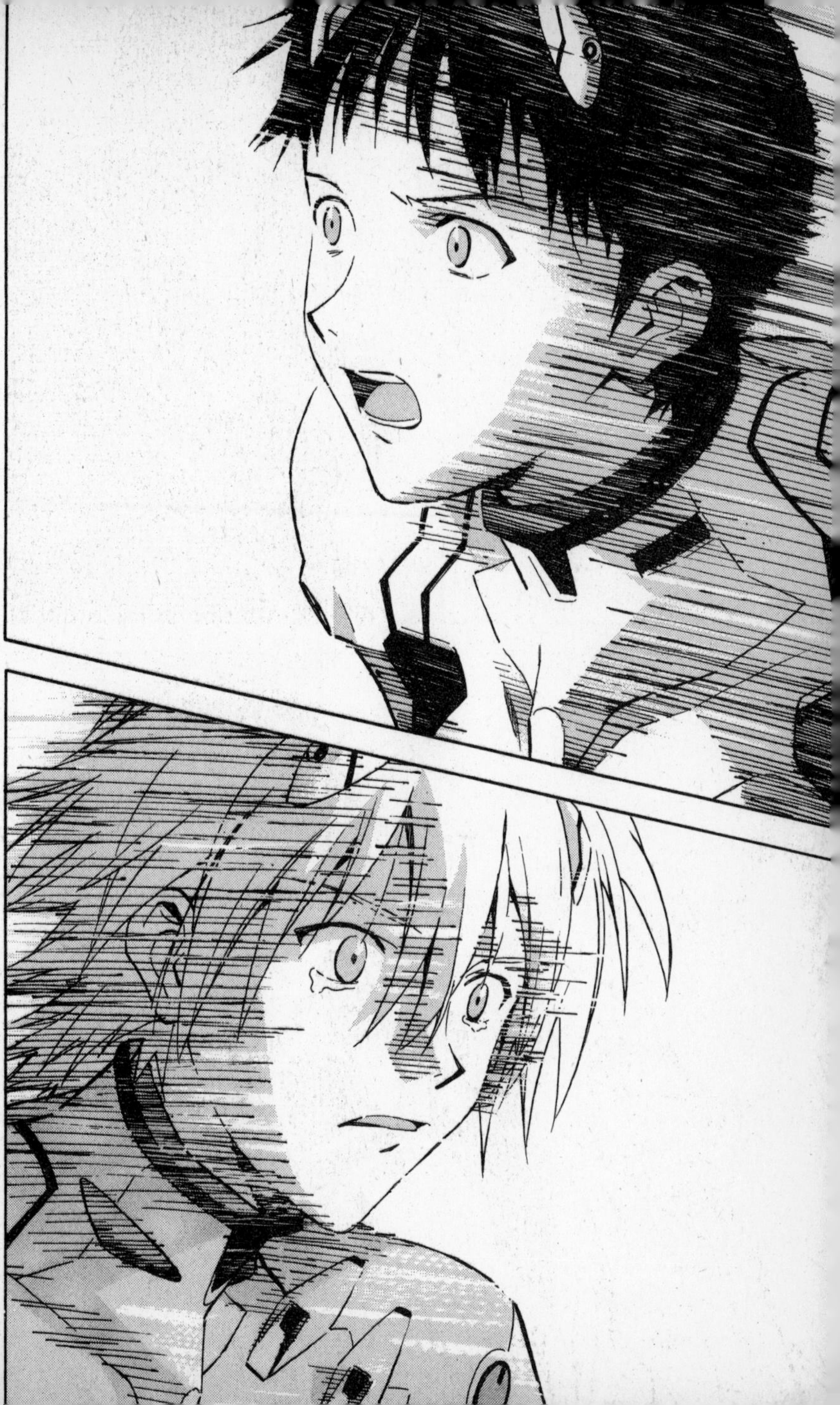

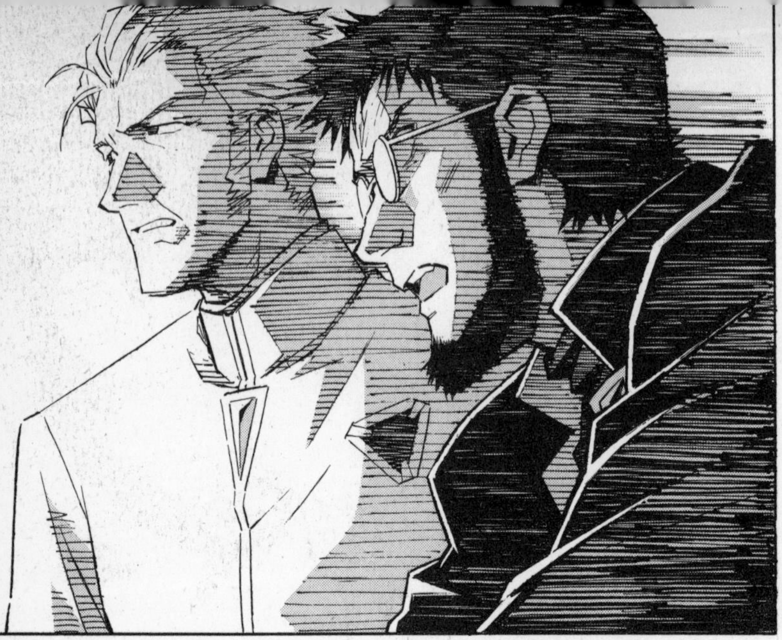
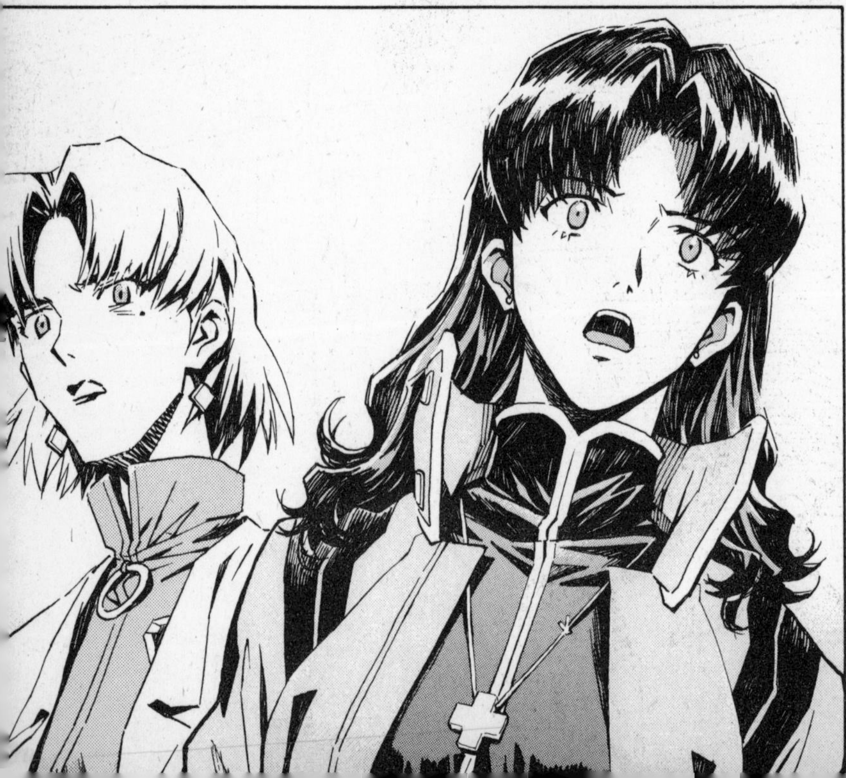

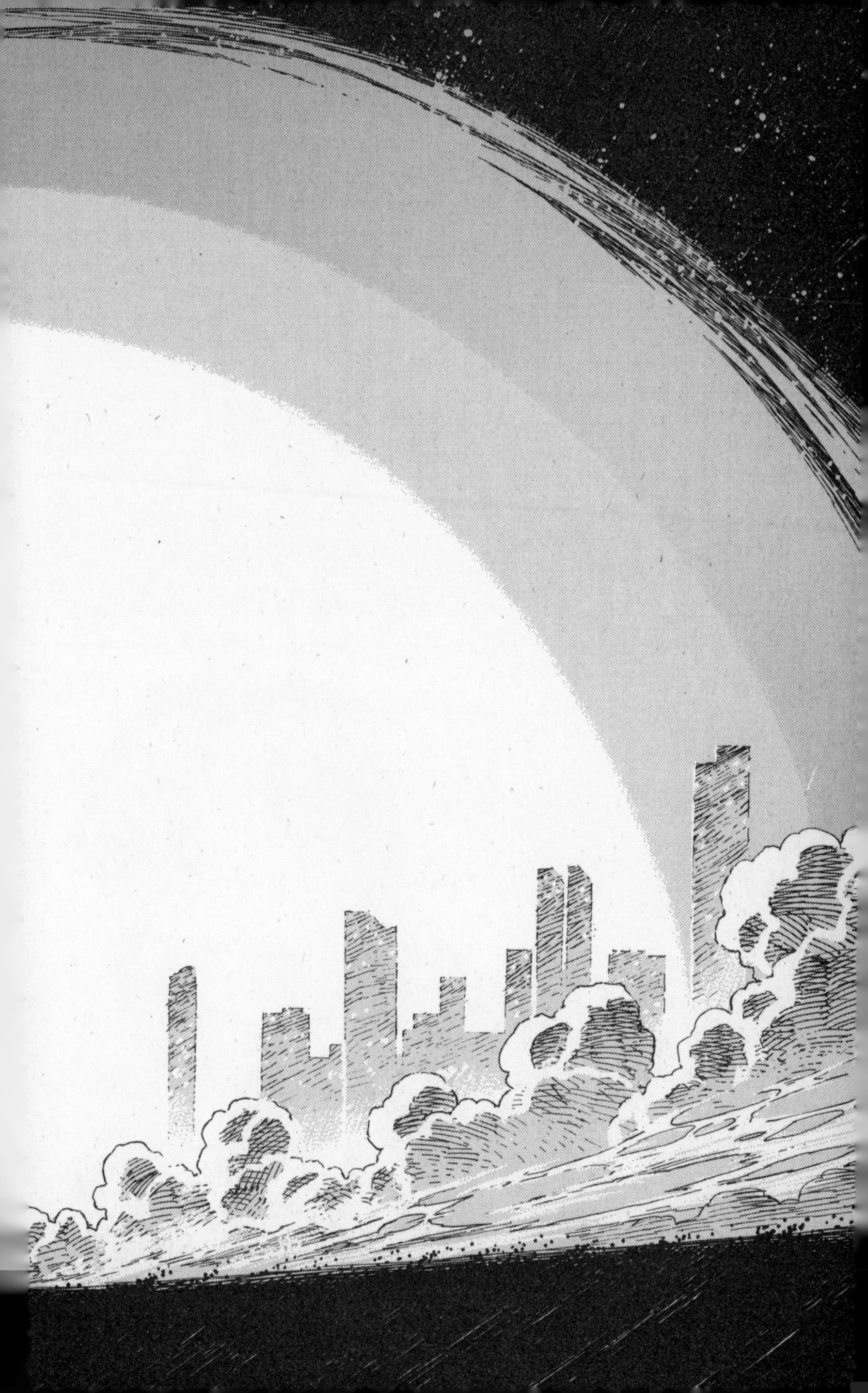

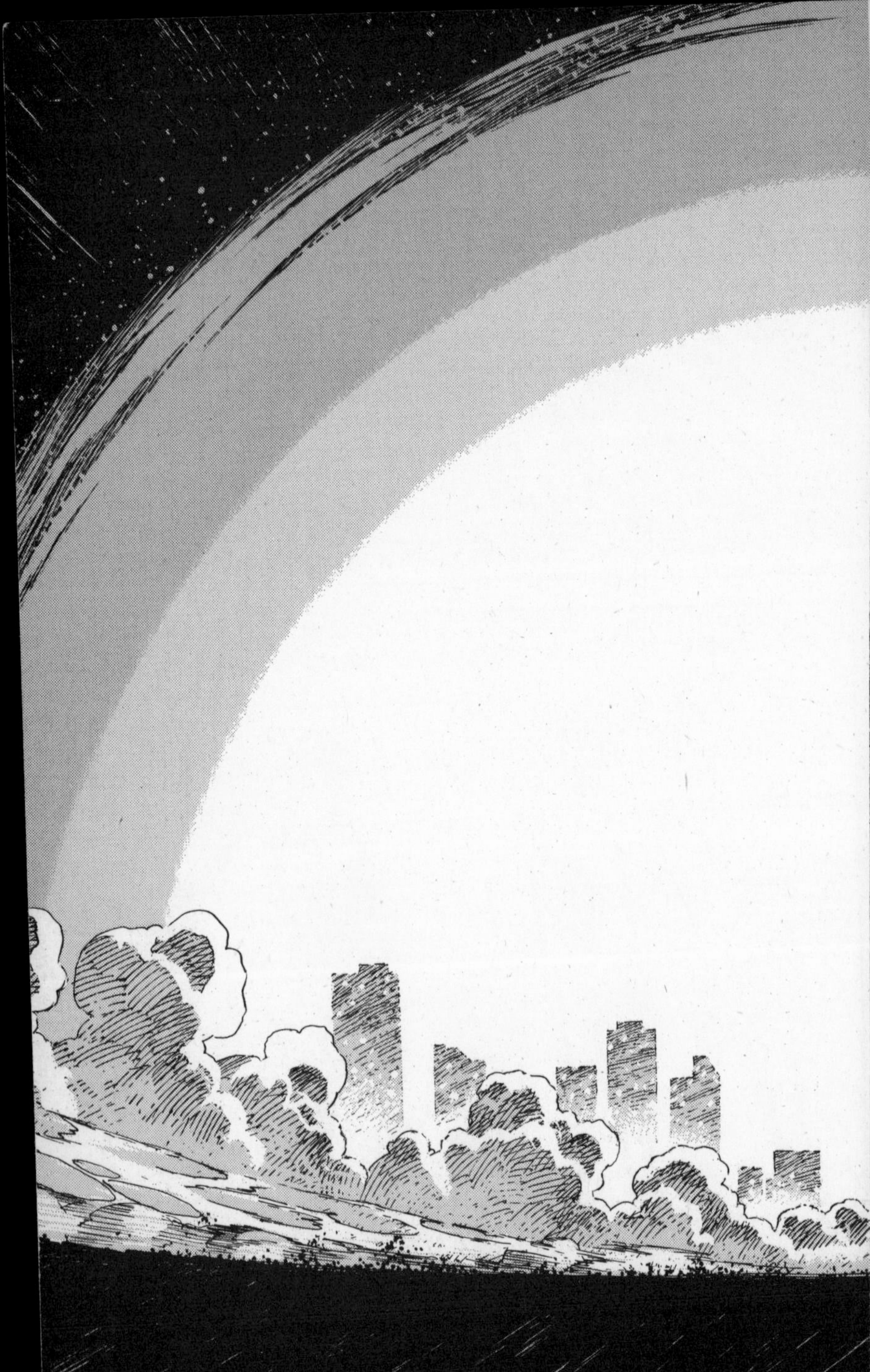

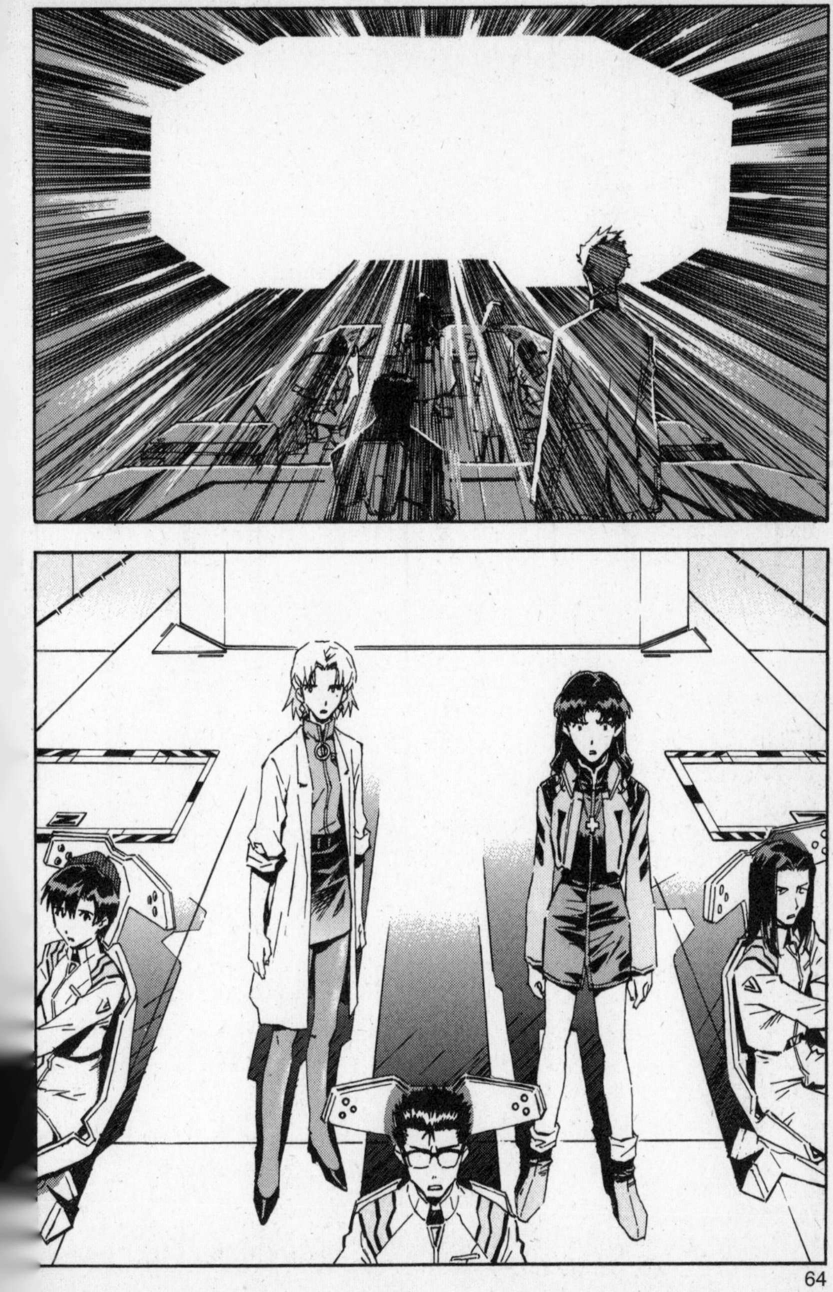

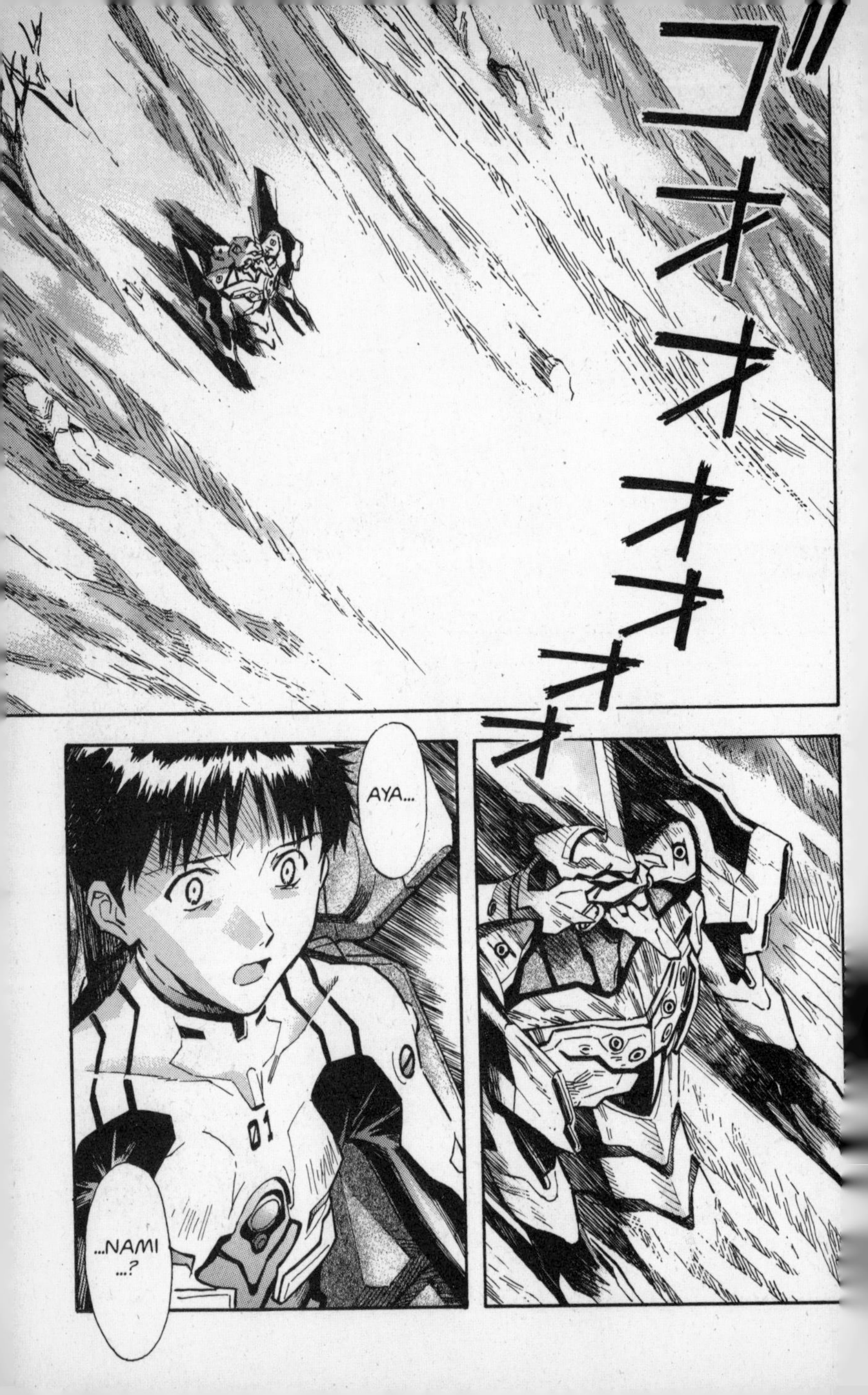
ゴオオオオオオ
AYA...
...NAMI
...?

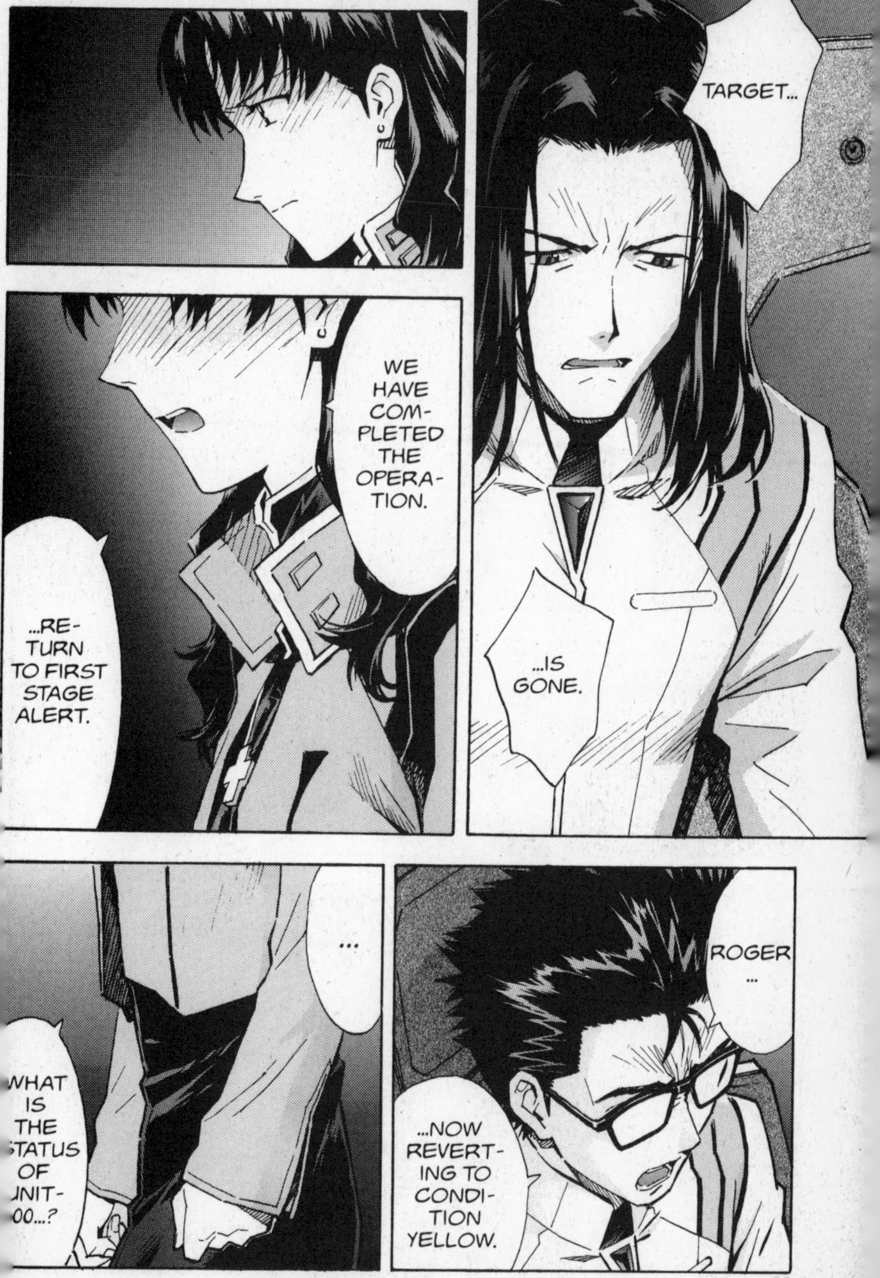
TARGET...
...IS GONE.
WE HAVE COMPLETED THE OPERATION.
...RETURN TO FIRST STAGE ALERT.
ROGER...
...NOW REVERTING TO CONDITION YELLOW.
...
WHAT IS THE STATUS OF UNIT-00...?

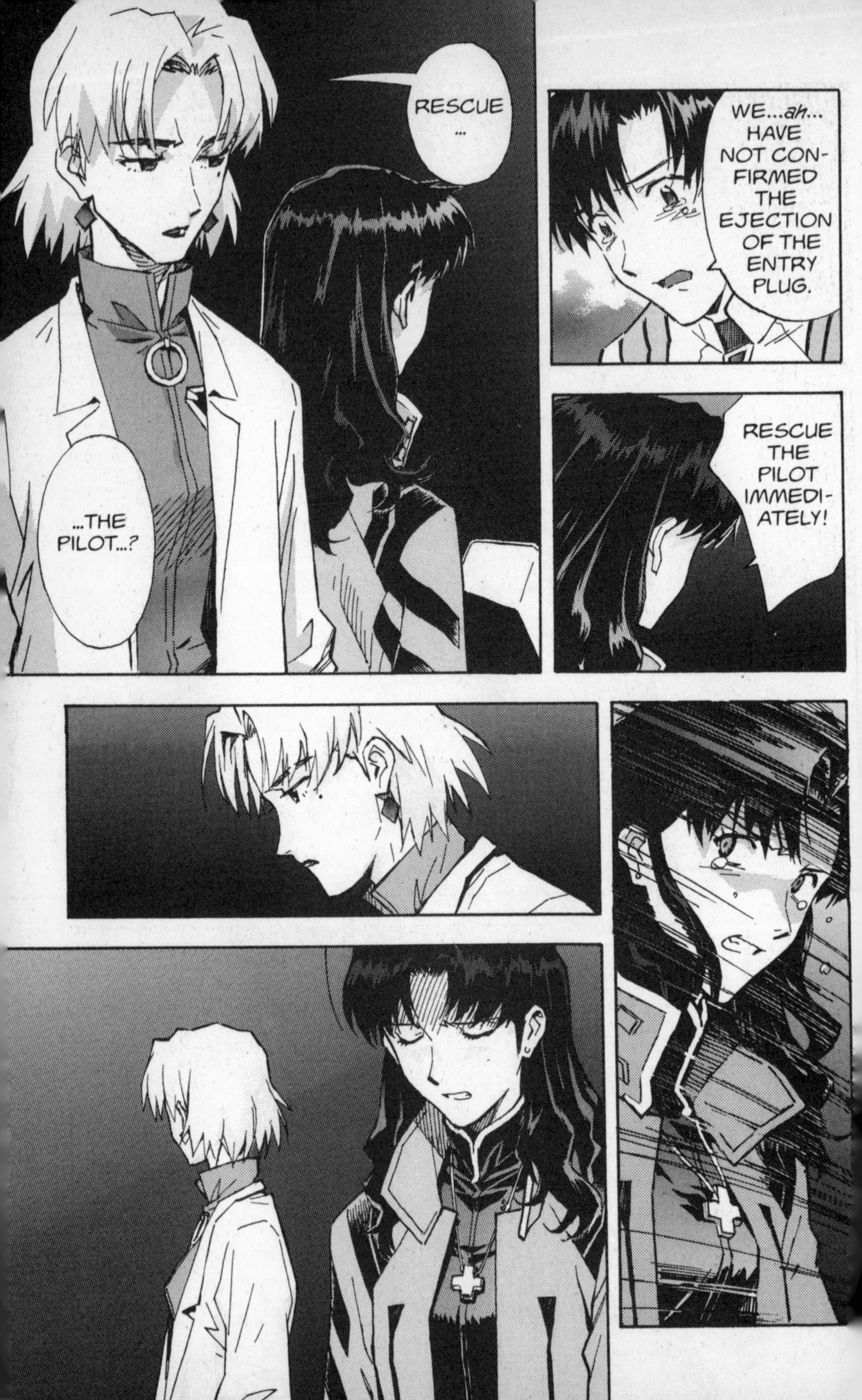
WE...ah... HAVE NOT CON-FIRMED THE EJECTION OF THE ENTRY PLUG.
RESCUE THE PILOT IMMEDI-ATELY!
RESCUE ...
...THE PILOT...?

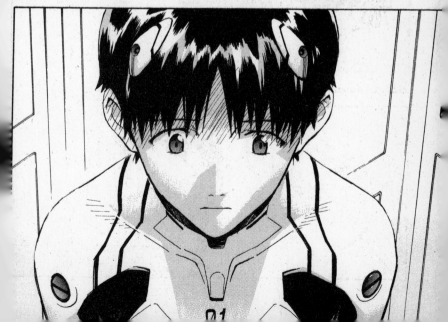

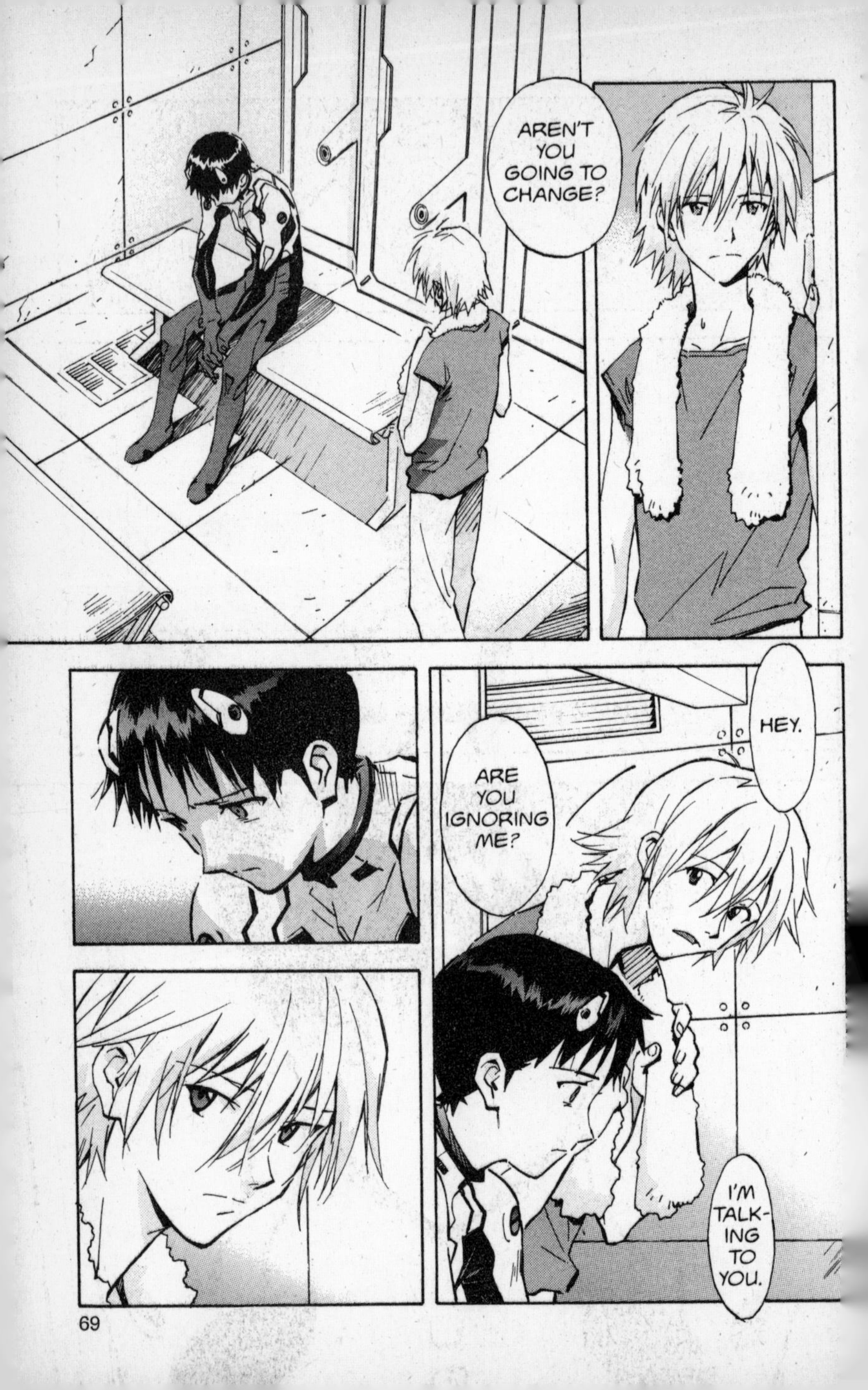
AREN'T YOU GOING TO CHANGE?
HEY.
ARE YOU IGNORING ME?
I'M TALK-ING TO YOU.

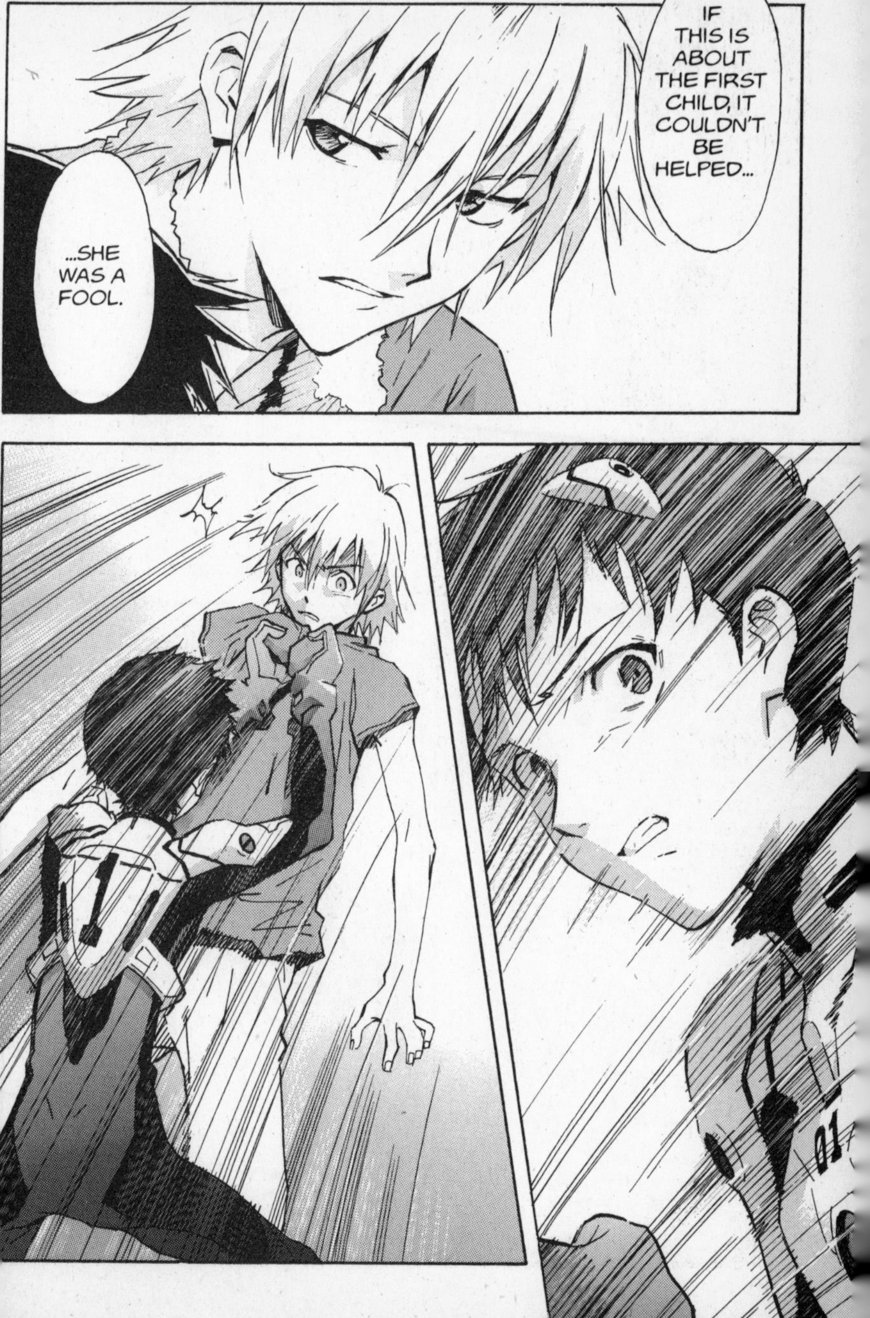
IF THIS IS ABOUT THE FIRST CHILD, IT COULDN'T BE HELPED...
...SHE WAS A FOOL.

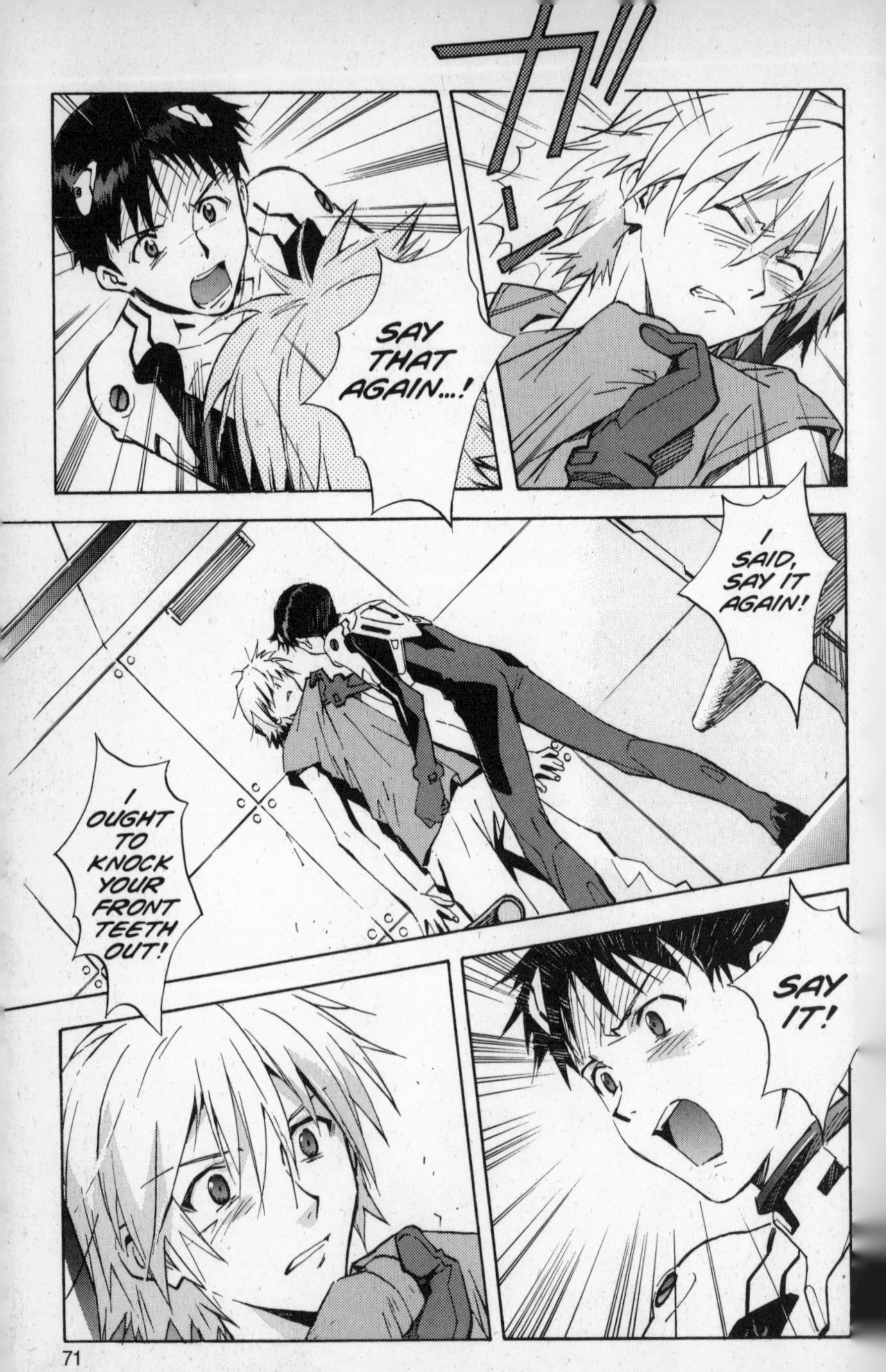
SAY THAT AGAIN...!
I SAID, SAY IT AGAIN!
I OUGHT TO KNOCK YOUR FRONT TEETH OUT!
SAY IT!

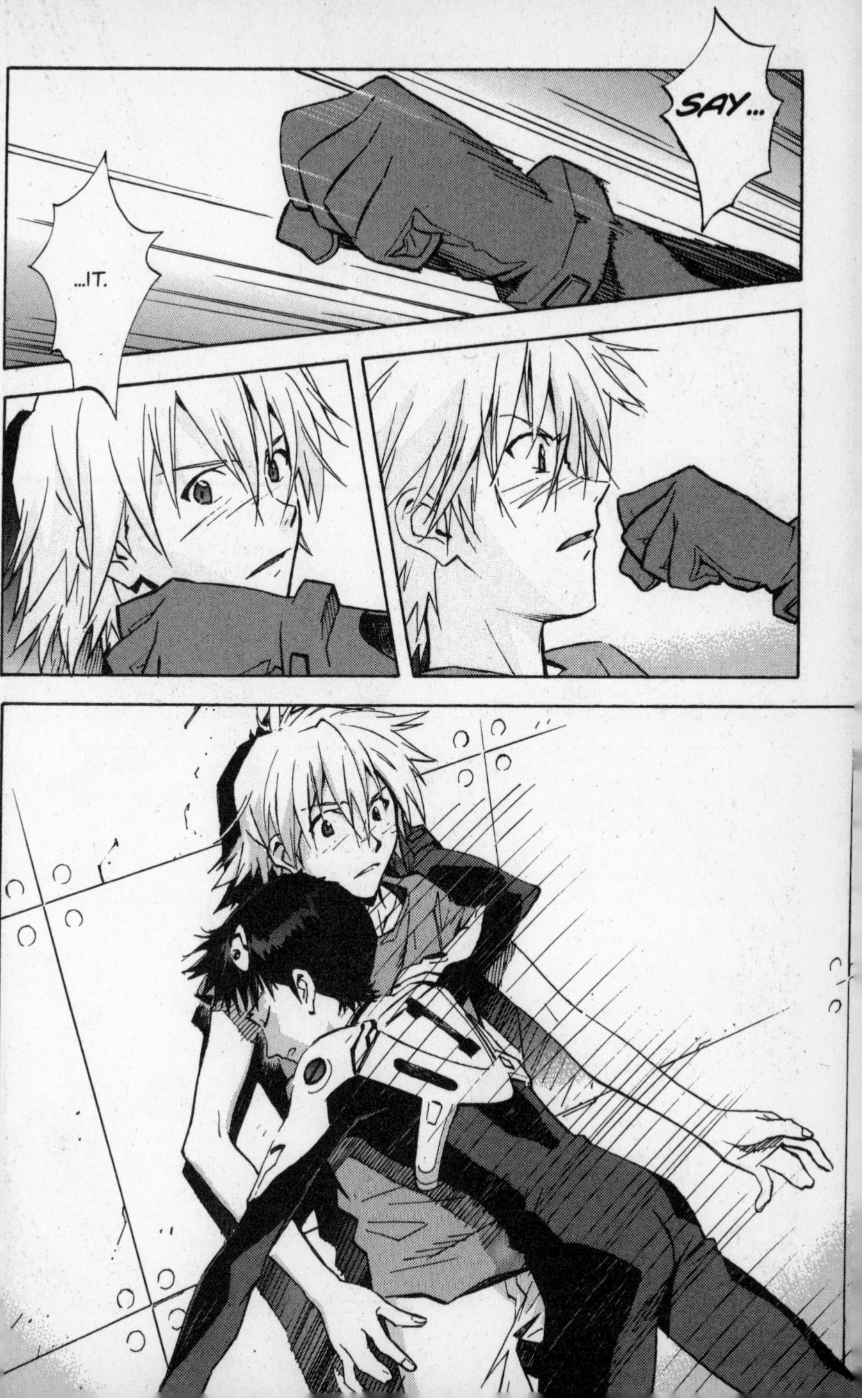
SAY...
...IT.

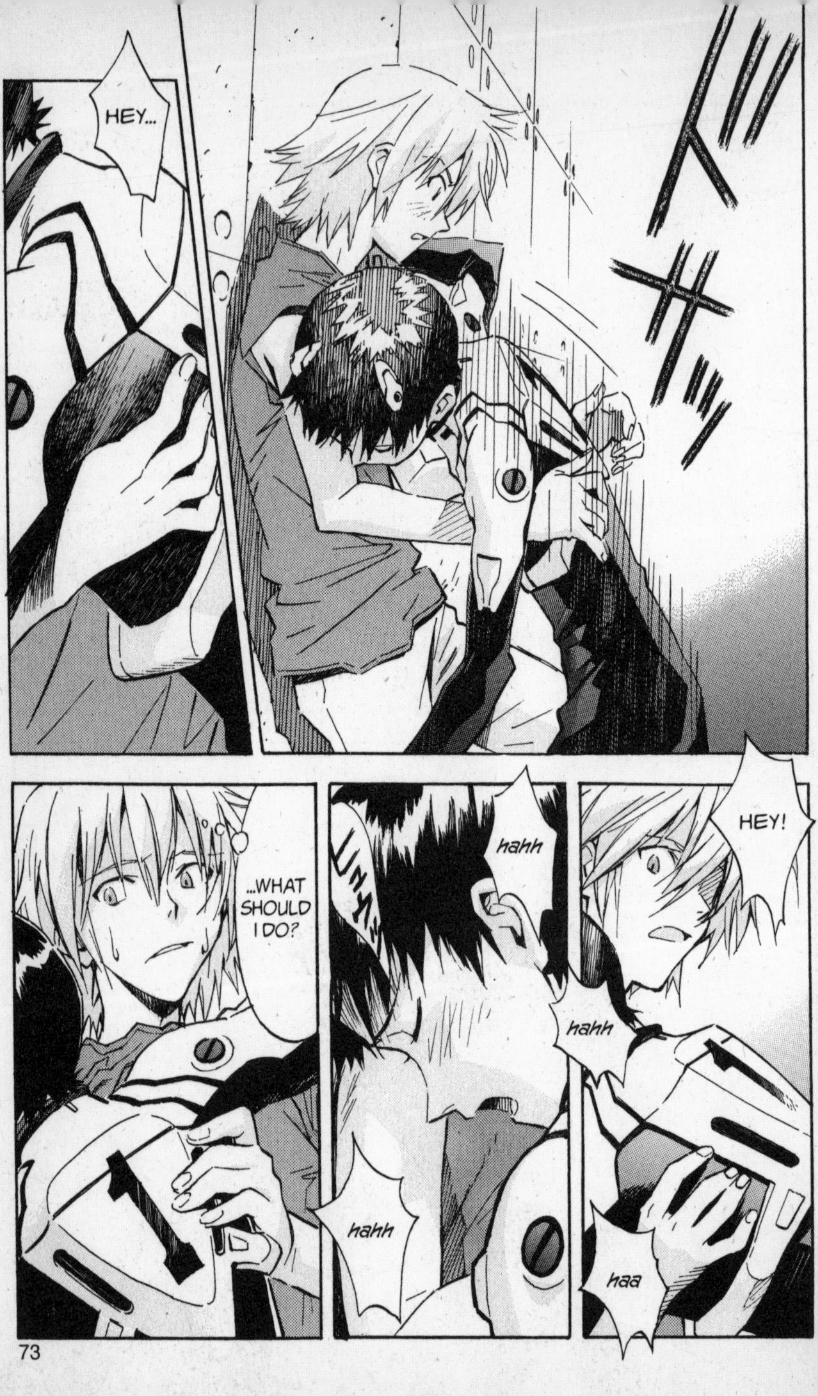
HEY...
HEY!
hahh
haa
hahh
hahh
...WHAT SHOULD I DO?

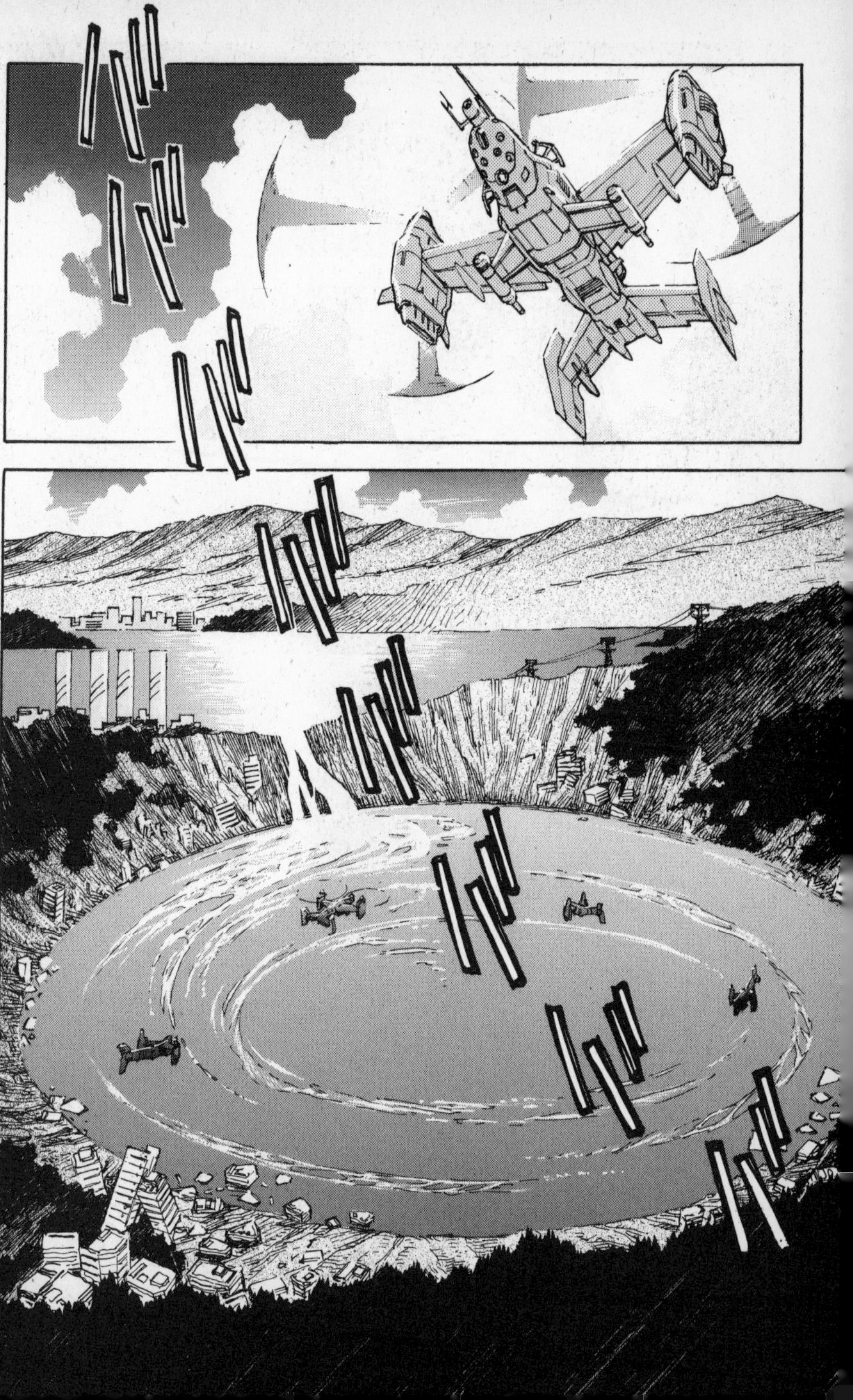

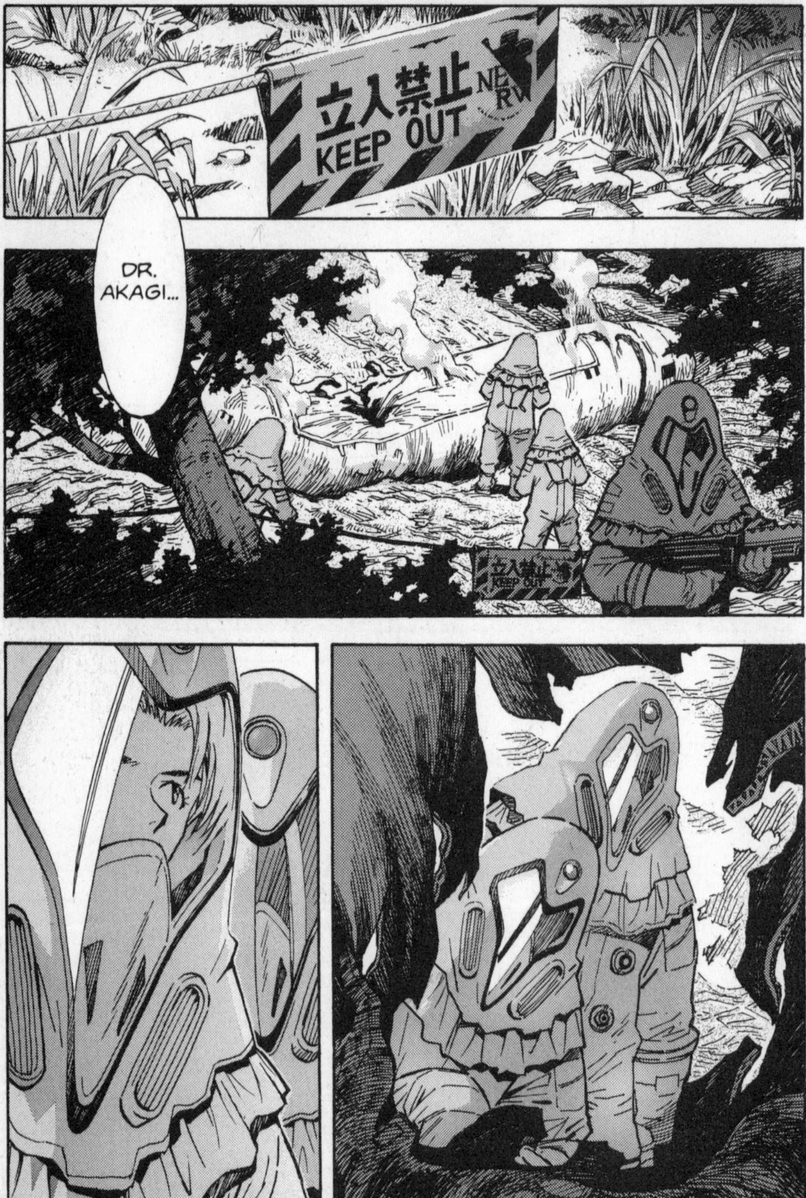
立入禁止
KEEP OUT
DR. AKAGI...
立入禁止
KEEP OUT

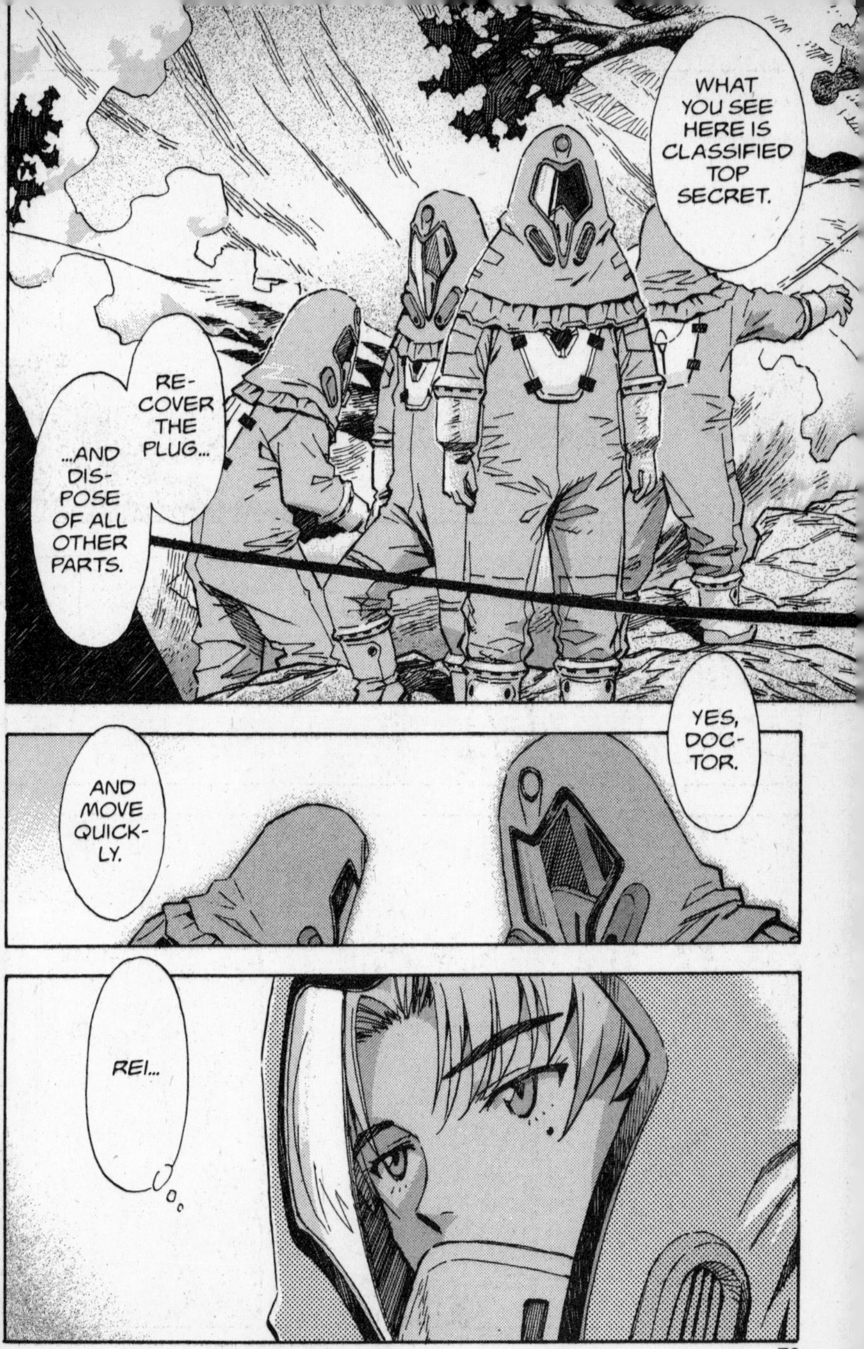
WHAT YOU SEE HERE IS CLASSIFIED TOP SECRET.
RE-COVER THE PLUG...
...AND DIS-POSE OF ALL OTHER PARTS.
YES, DOC-TOR.
AND MOVE QUICK-LY.
REI...

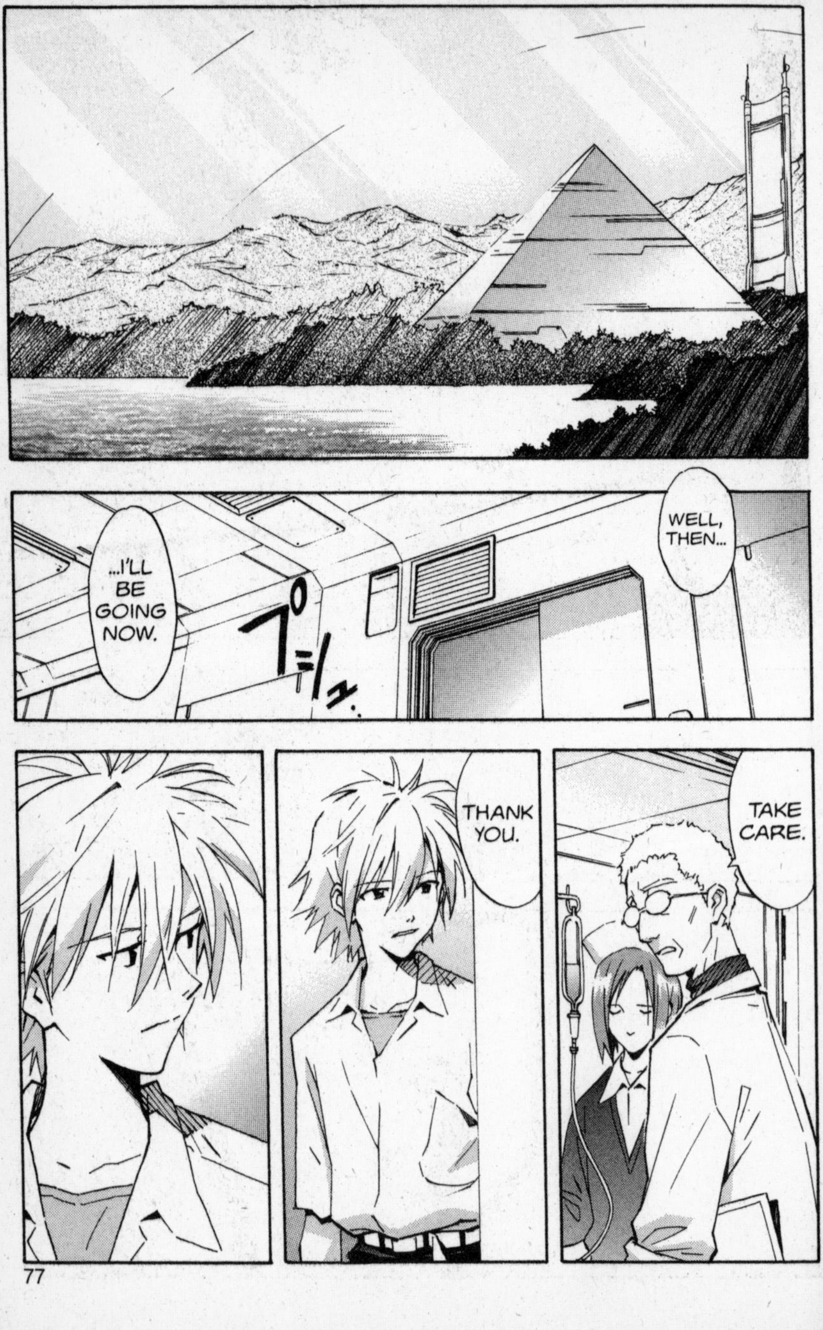
WELL, THEN...
...I'LL BE GOING NOW.
プシュ..
TAKE CARE.
THANK YOU.

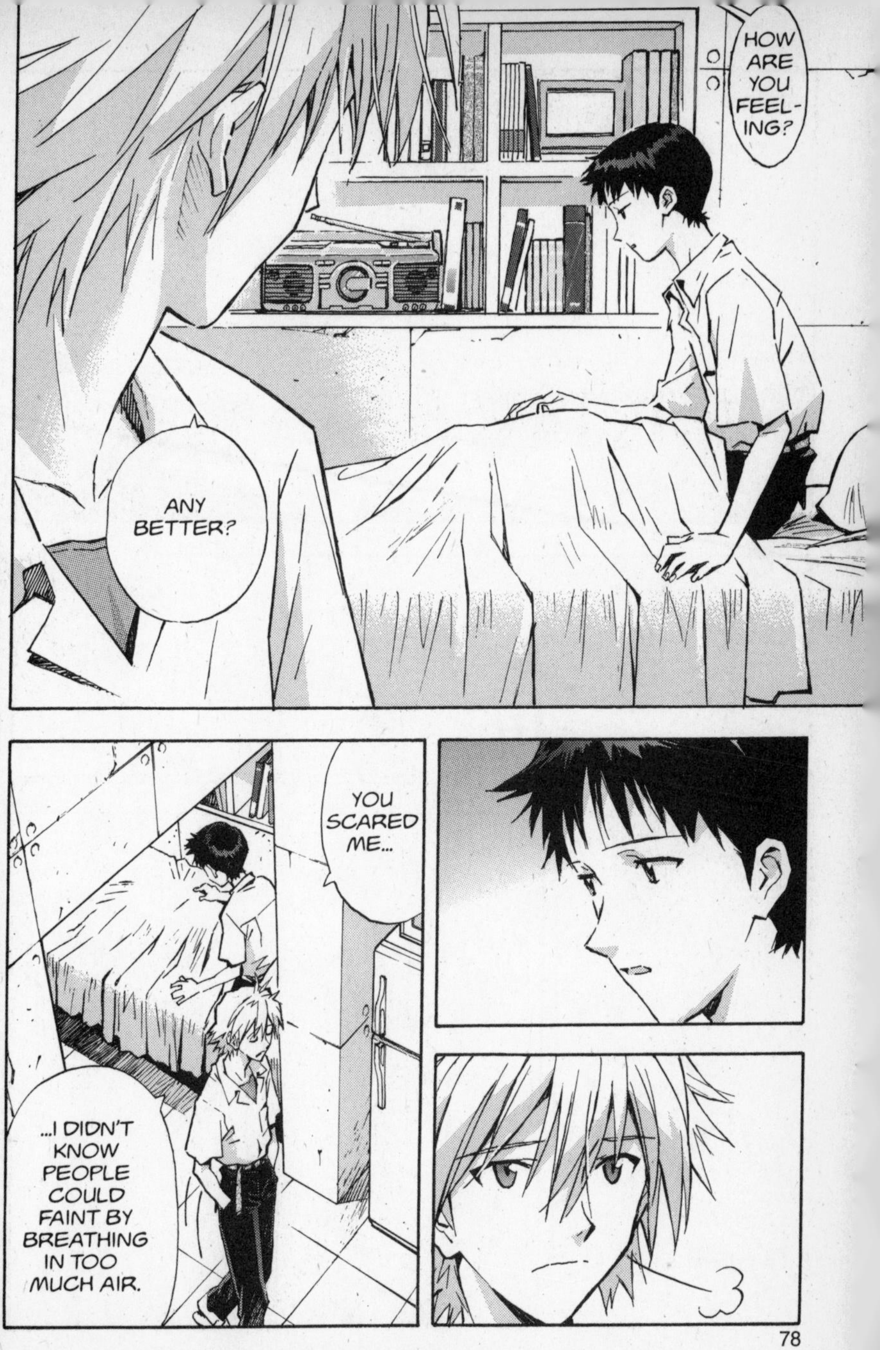
HOW ARE YOU FEEL-ING?
ANY BETTER?
YOU SCARED ME...
...I DIDN'T KNOW PEOPLE COULD FAINT BY BREATHING IN TOO MUCH AIR.

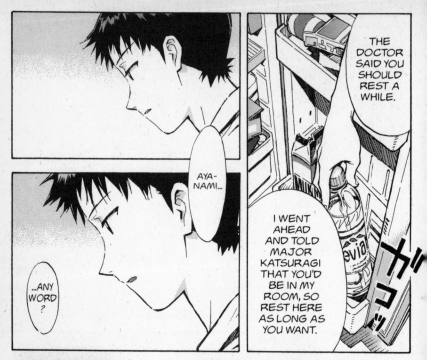

THE DOCTOR SAID YOU SHOULD REST A WHILE.

AYA-NAMI...

...ANY WORD?

I WENT AHEAD AND TOLD MAJOR KATSURAGI THAT YOU'D BE IN MY ROOM, SO REST HERE AS LONG AS YOU WANT.

I'VE HEARD NO NEWS...

...THIS WAS DIFFERENT FROM BEFORE.

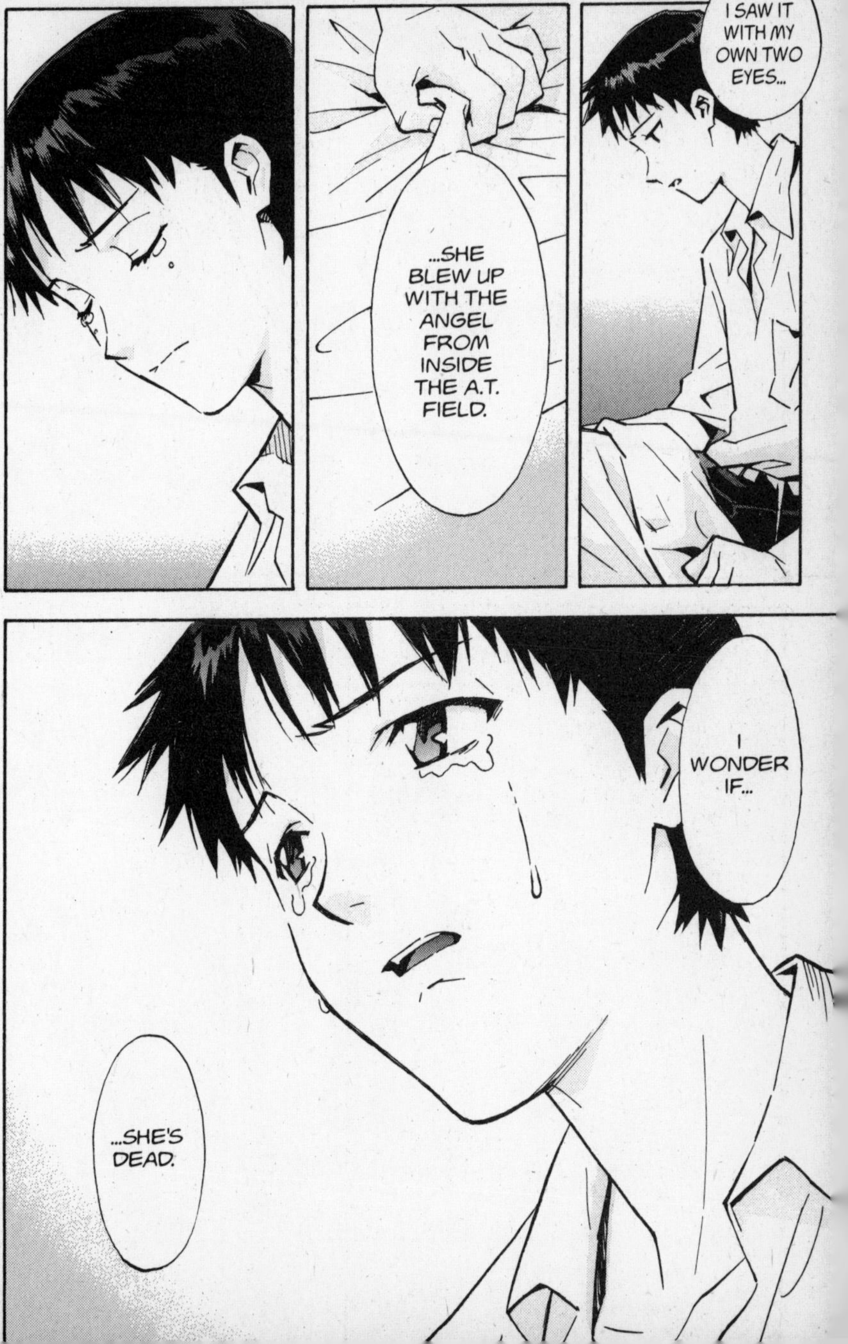
I SAW IT WITH MY OWN TWO EYES...
...SHE BLEW UP WITH THE ANGEL FROM INSIDE THE A.T. FIELD.
I WONDER IF...
...SHE'S DEAD.

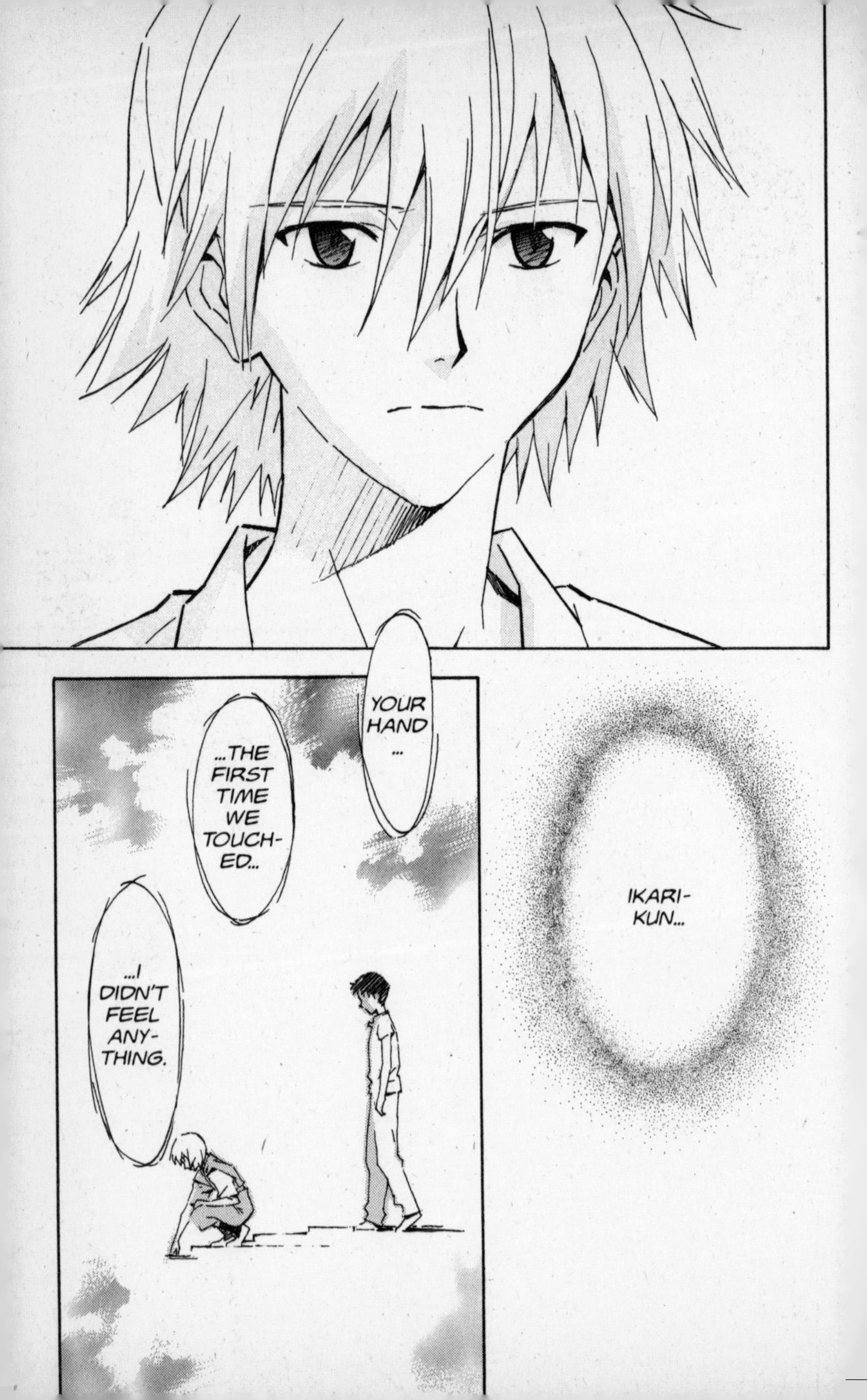
IKARI-KUN...
YOUR HAND...
...THE FIRST TIME WE TOUCHED...
...I DIDN'T FEEL ANYTHING.

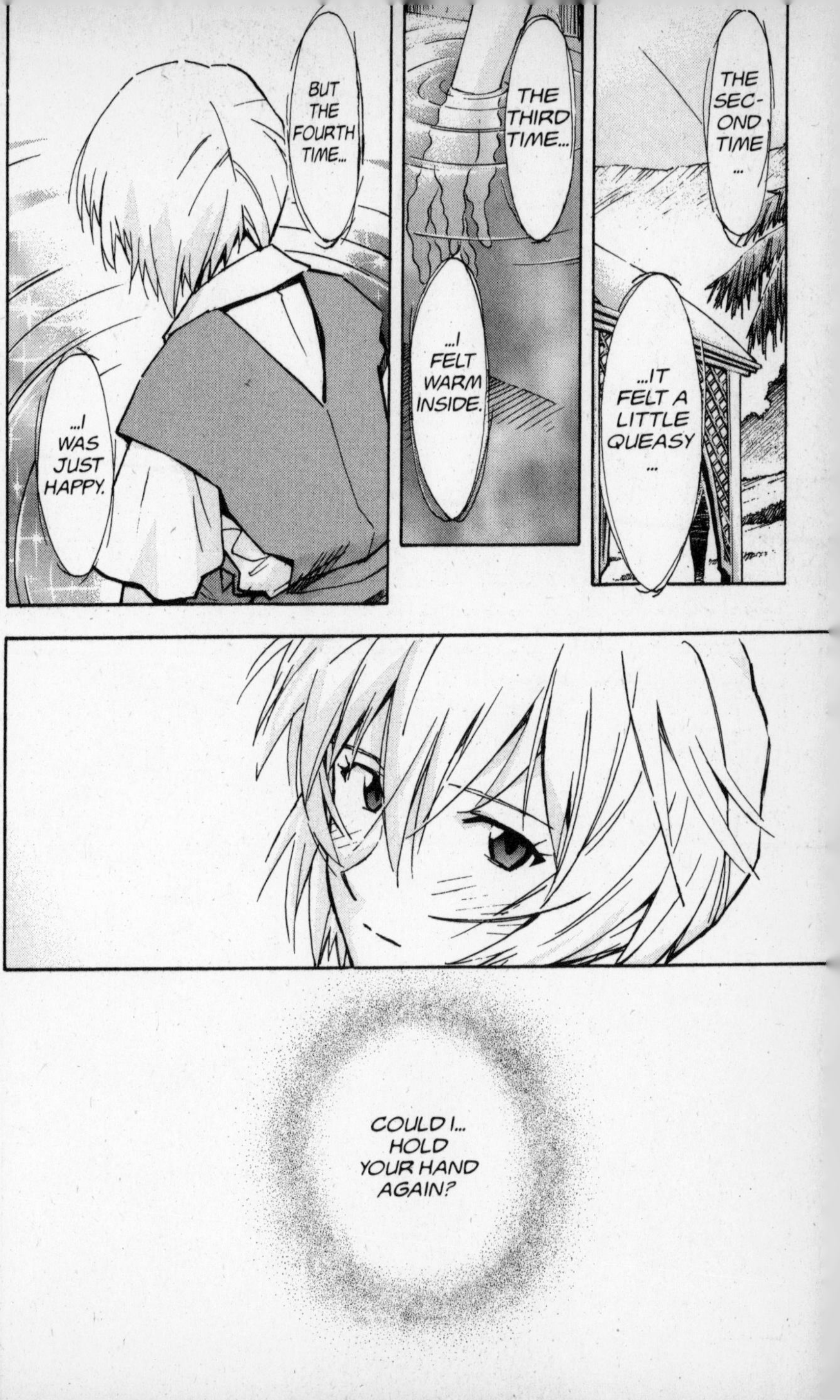
THE SECOND TIME...
...IT FELT A LITTLE QUEASY...
THE THIRD TIME...
...I FELT WARM INSIDE.
BUT THE FOURTH TIME...
...I WAS JUST HAPPY.
COULD I... HOLD YOUR HAND AGAIN?

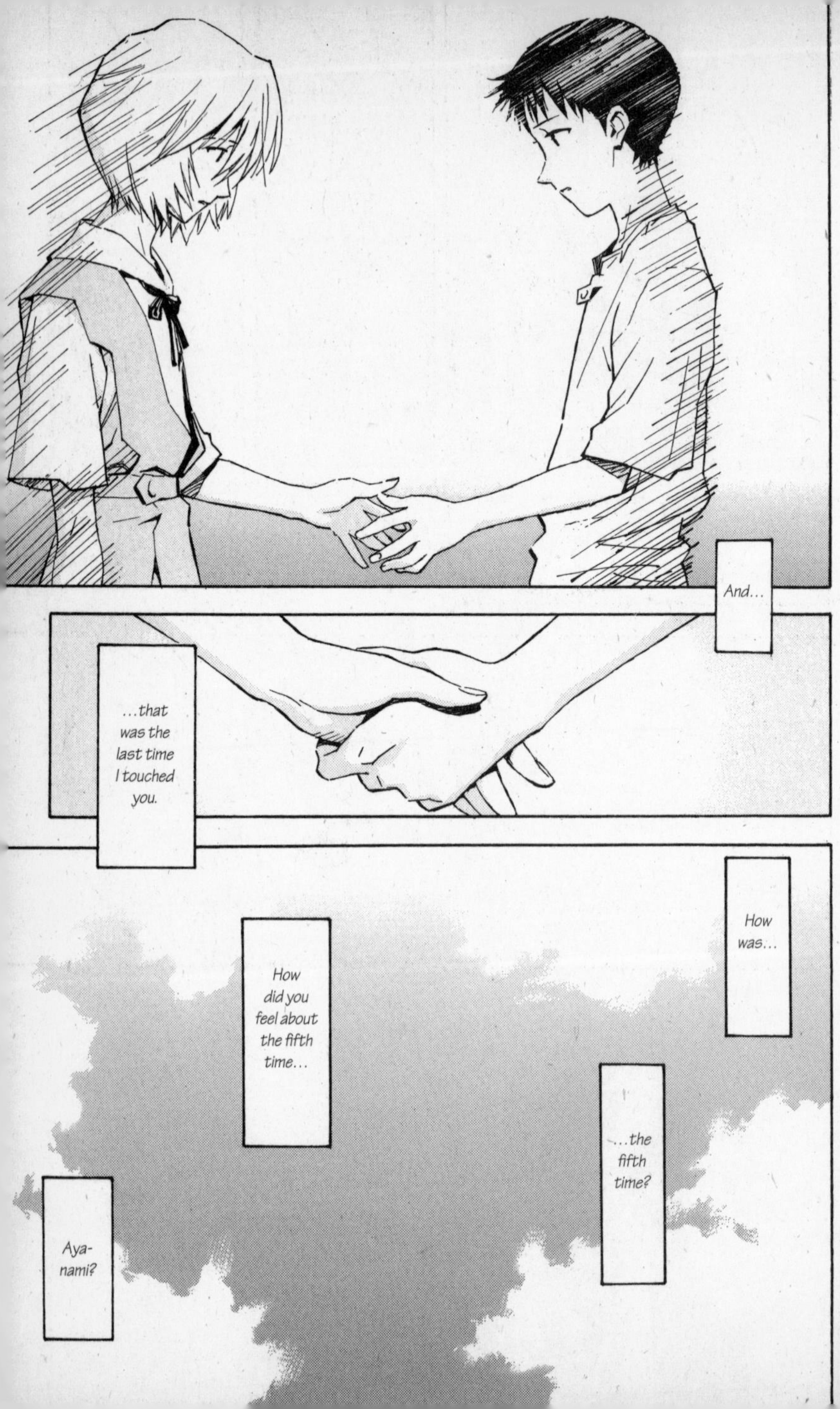
And...
...that was the last time I touched you.
How was...
How did you feel about the fifth time...
...the fifth time?
Aya-nami?

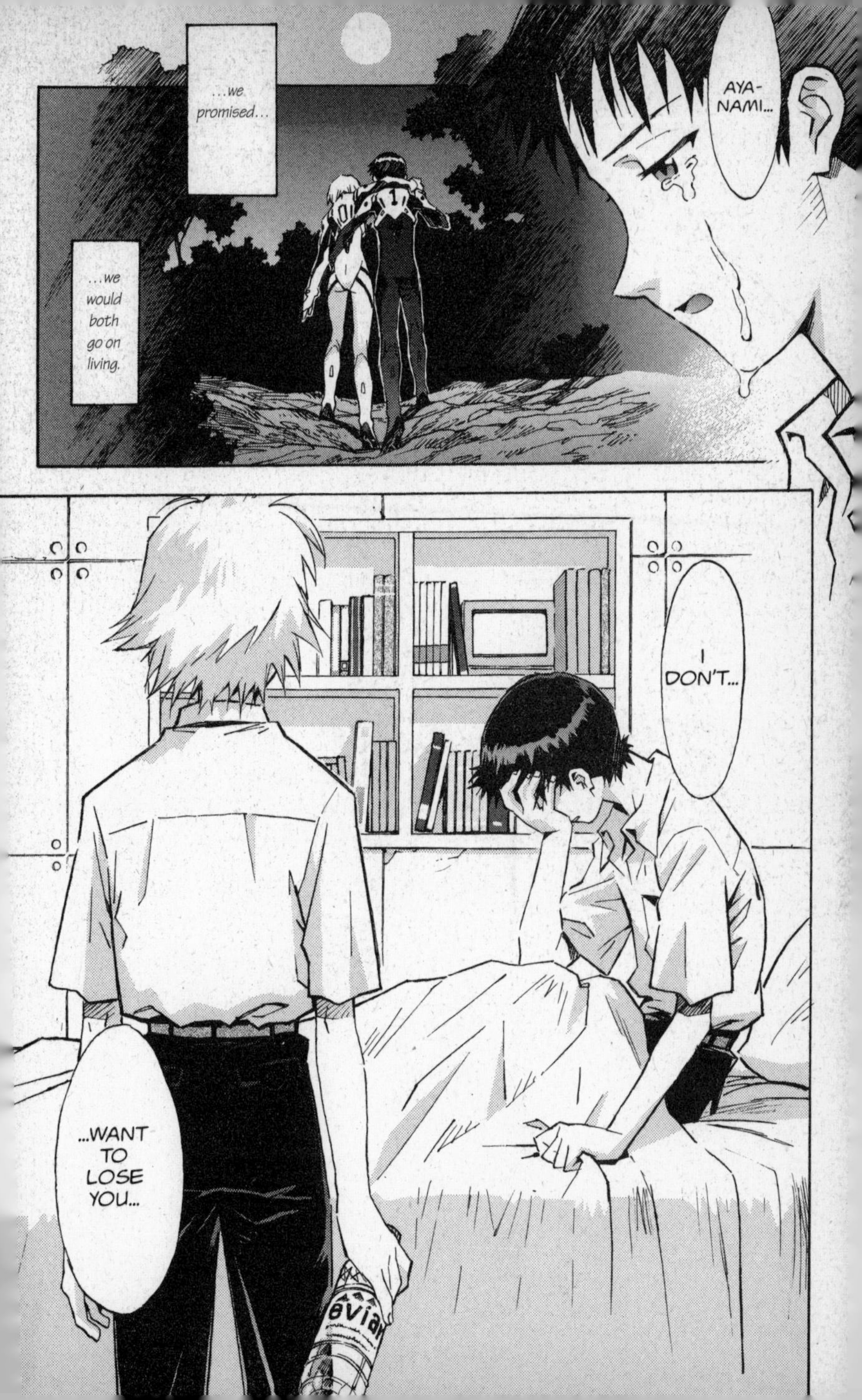
AYA-NAMI...
...we promised...
...we would both go on living.
I DON'T...
...WANT TO LOSE YOU...
evian

NEON GENESIS EVANGELION

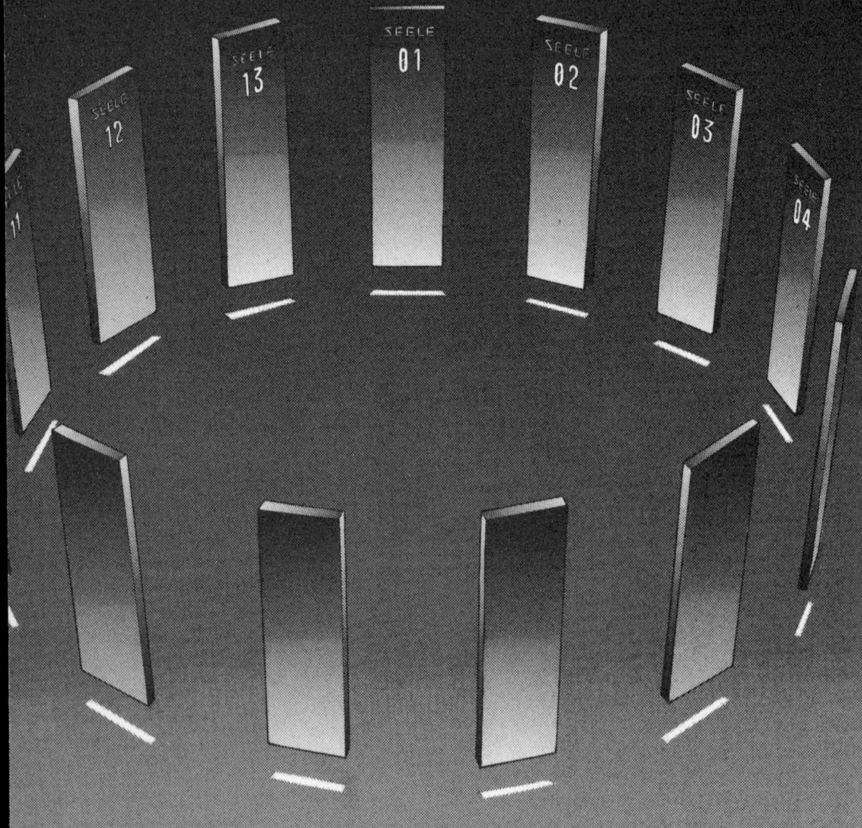
SEELE 01
SEELE 02
SEELE 03
SEELE 04
SEELE 12
SEELE 13

STAGE 67: TWISTED NIGHT

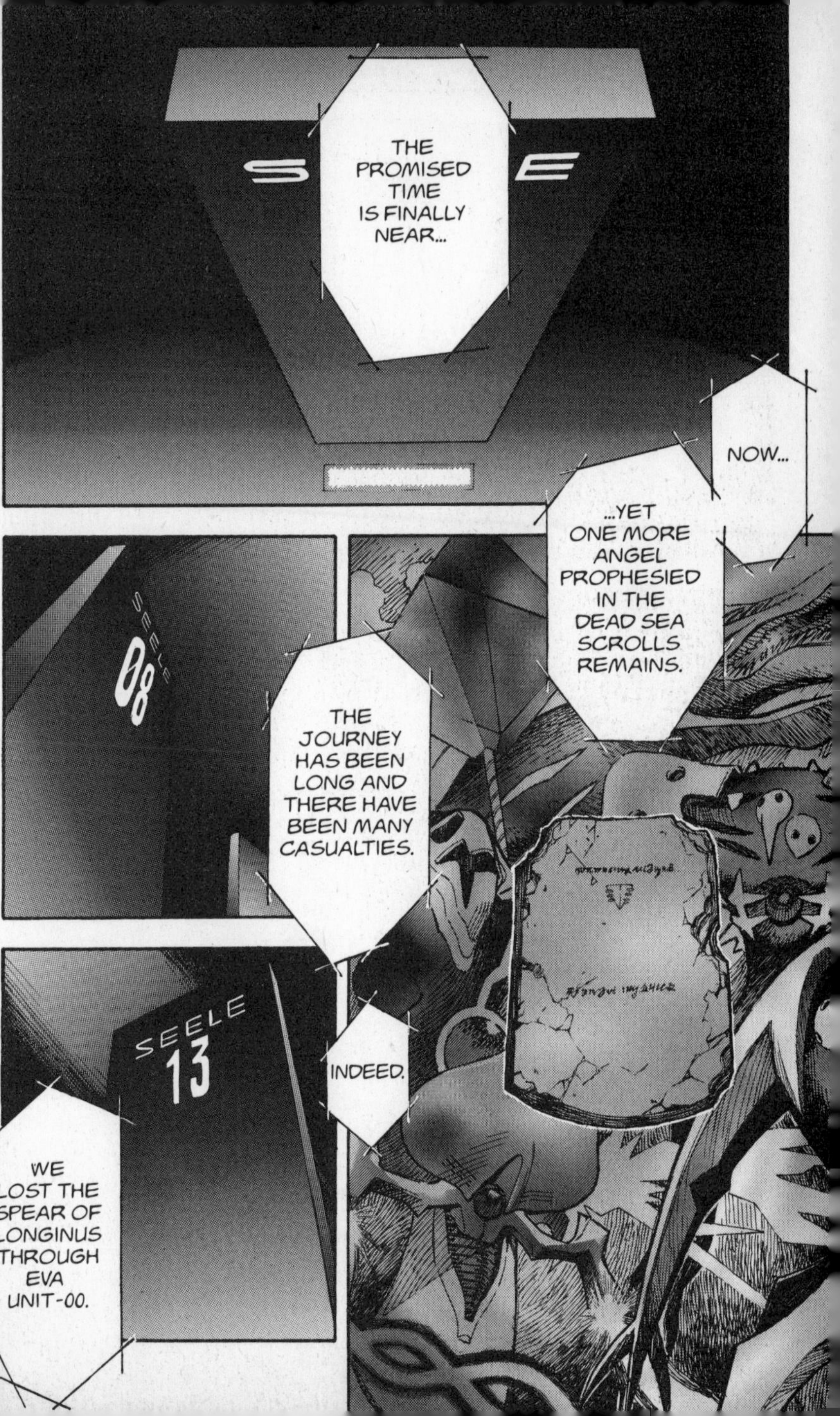
S
E
THE PROMISED TIME IS FINALLY NEAR...
NOW...
...YET ONE MORE ANGEL PROPHESIED IN THE DEAD SEA SCROLLS REMAINS.
SEELE
08
THE JOURNEY HAS BEEN LONG AND THERE HAVE BEEN MANY CASUALTIES.
SEELE
13
INDEED.
WE LOST THE SPEAR OF LONGINUS THROUGH EVA UNIT-00.

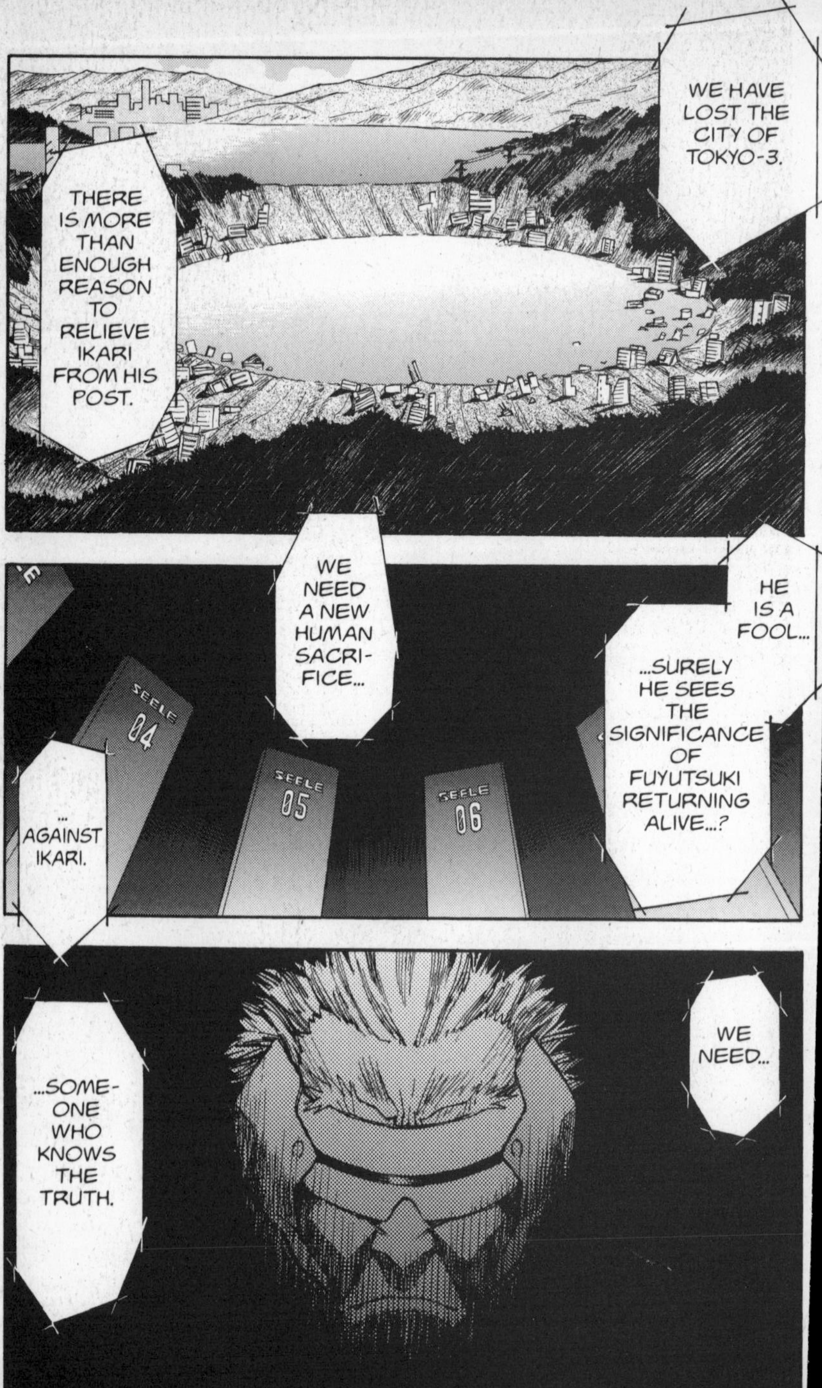
WE HAVE LOST THE CITY OF TOKYO-3.
THERE IS MORE THAN ENOUGH REASON TO RELIEVE IKARI FROM HIS POST.
HE IS A FOOL...
...SURELY HE SEES THE SIGNIFICANCE OF FUYUTSUKI RETURNING ALIVE...?
WE NEED A NEW HUMAN SACRI-FICE...
SEELE 04
SEELE 05
SEELE 06
... AGAINST IKARI.
WE NEED...
...SOME-ONE WHO KNOWS THE TRUTH.

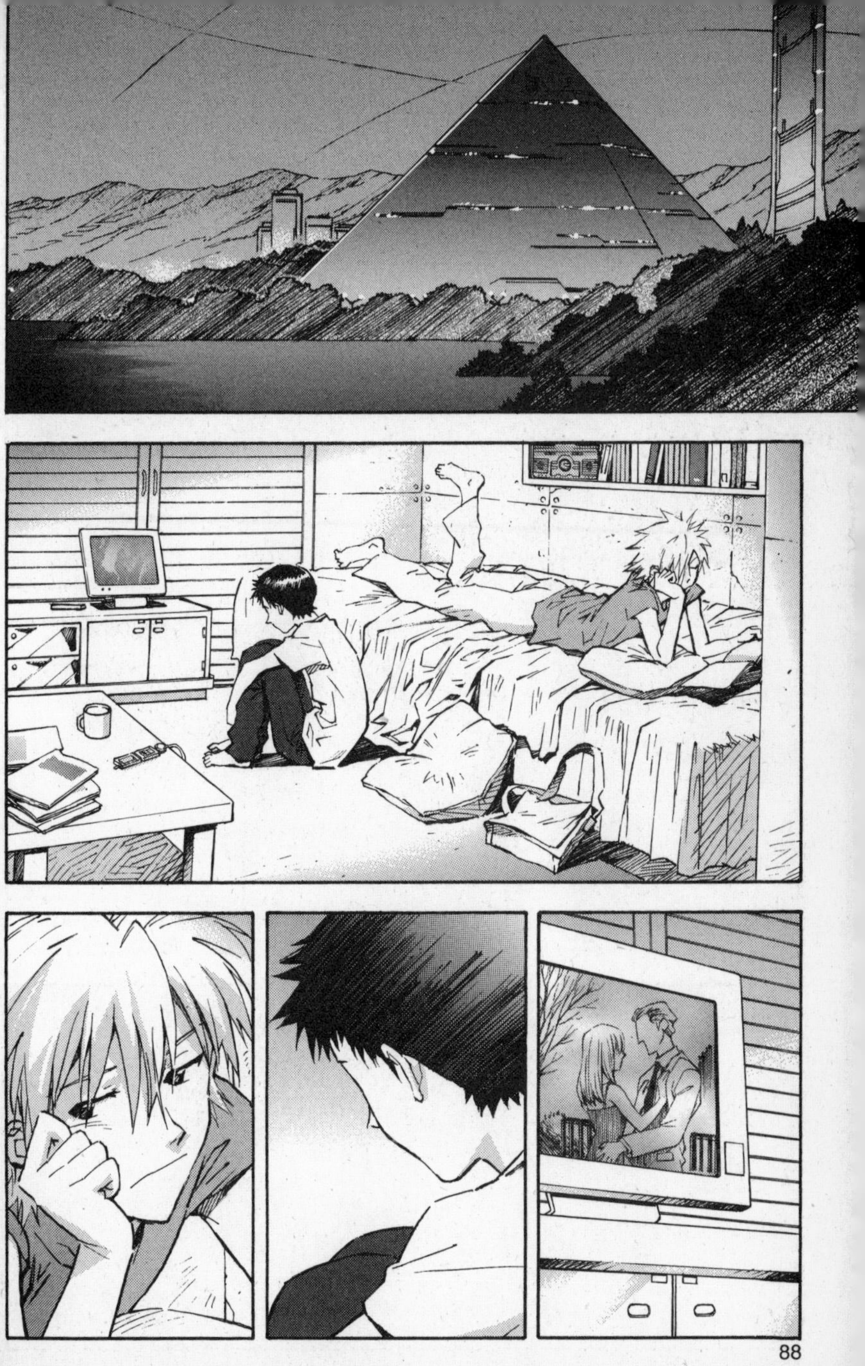

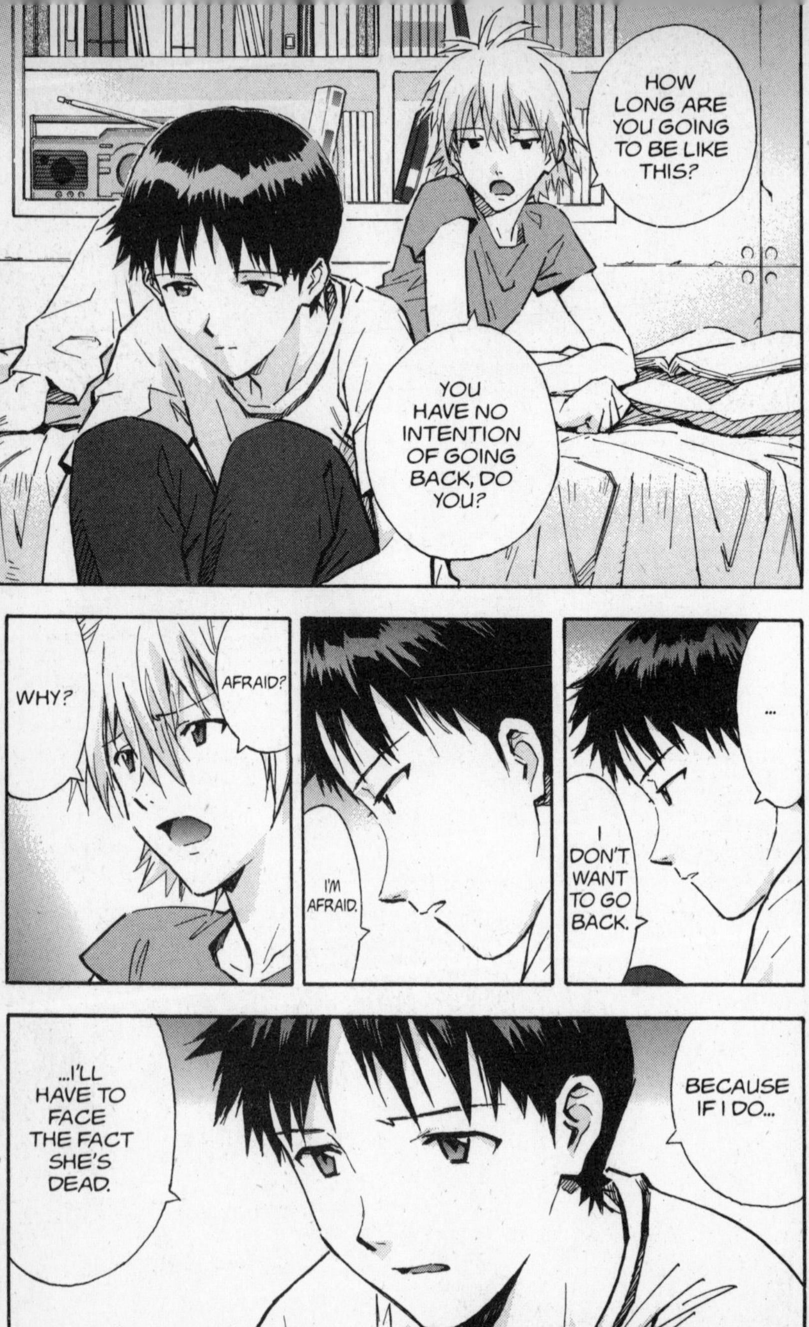
HOW LONG ARE YOU GOING TO BE LIKE THIS?
YOU HAVE NO INTENTION OF GOING BACK, DO YOU?
...
I DON'T WANT TO GO BACK.
I'M AFRAID.
AFRAID?
WHY?
BECAUSE IF I DO...
...I'LL HAVE TO FACE THE FACT SHE'S DEAD.

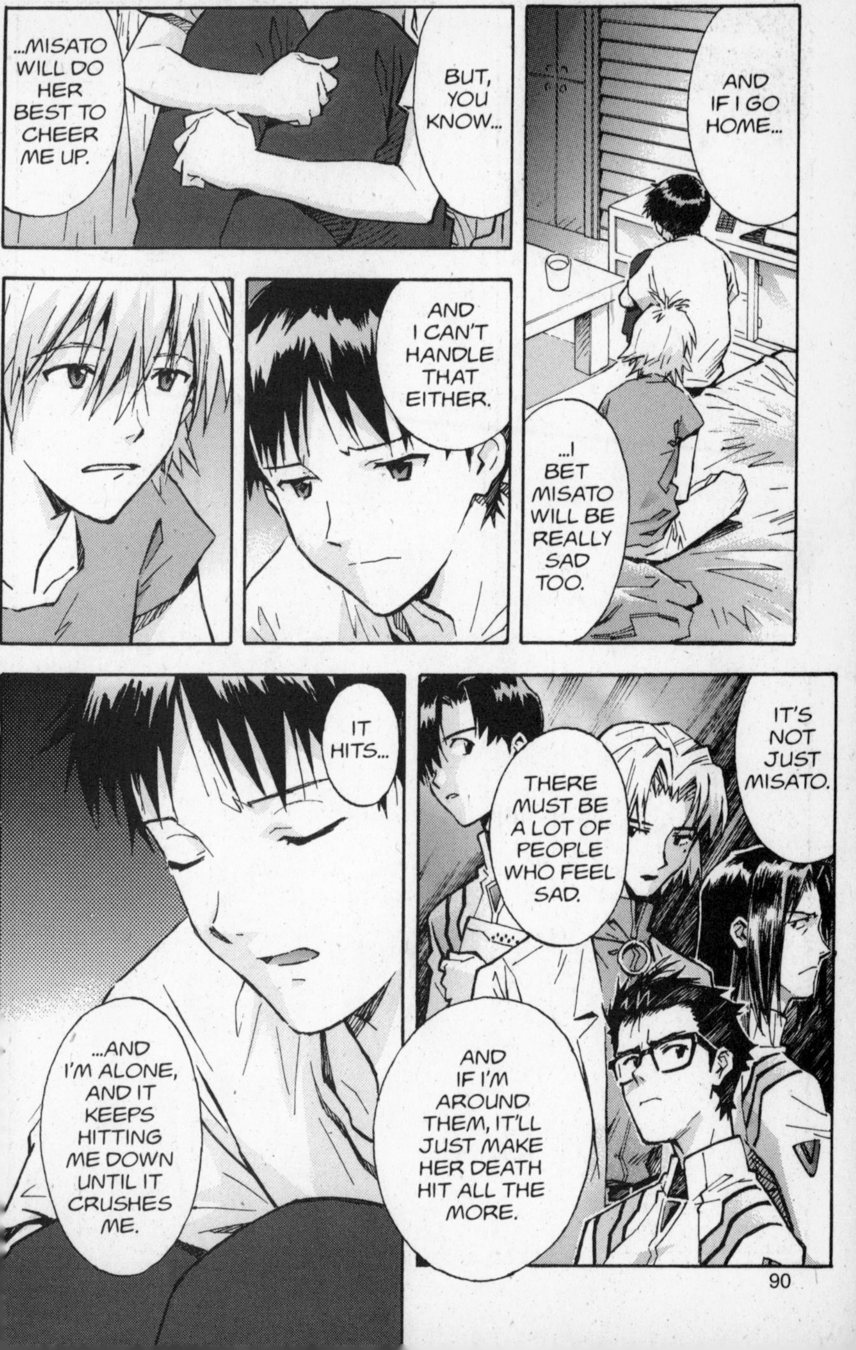
AND IF I GO HOME...
...I BET MISATO WILL BE REALLY SAD TOO.
BUT, YOU KNOW...
...MISATO WILL DO HER BEST TO CHEER ME UP.
AND I CAN'T HANDLE THAT EITHER.
IT'S NOT JUST MISATO.
THERE MUST BE A LOT OF PEOPLE WHO FEEL SAD.
AND IF I'M AROUND THEM, IT'LL JUST MAKE HER DEATH HIT ALL THE MORE.
IT HITS...
...AND I'M ALONE, AND IT KEEPS HITTING ME DOWN UNTIL IT CRUSHES ME.

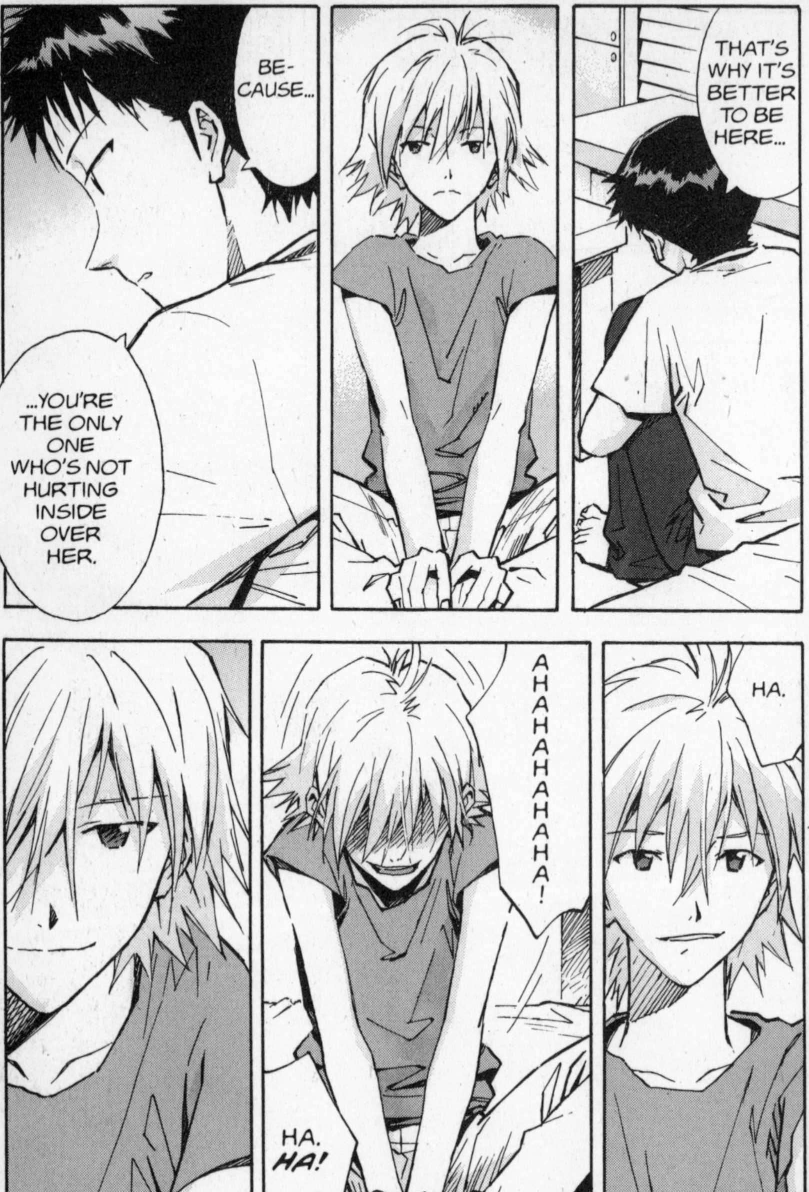
THAT'S WHY IT'S BETTER TO BE HERE...
BE-CAUSE...
...YOU'RE THE ONLY ONE WHO'S NOT HURTING INSIDE OVER HER.
HA.
AHAHAHAHAHA!
HA. *HA!*

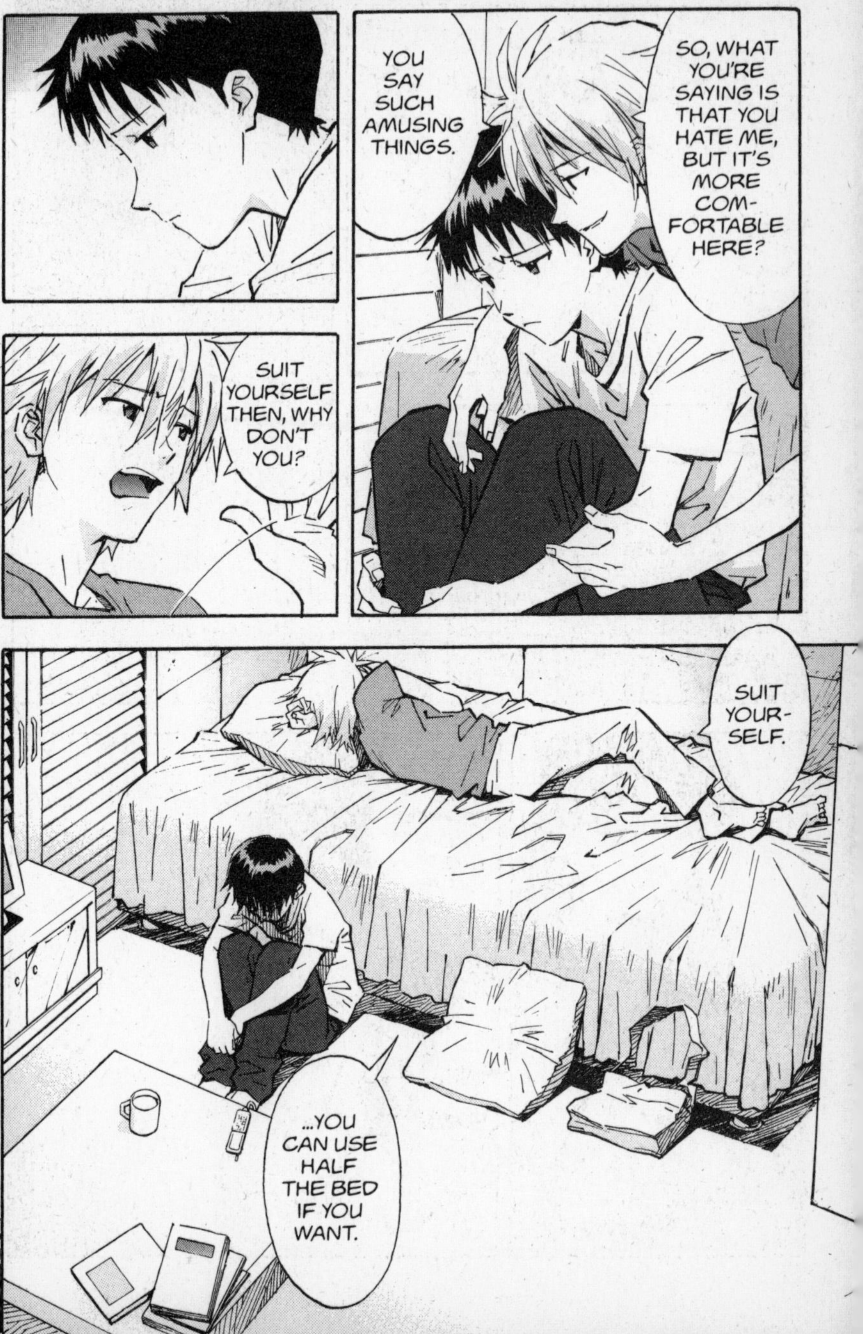
SO, WHAT YOU'RE SAYING IS THAT YOU HATE ME, BUT IT'S MORE COM-FORTABLE HERE?
YOU SAY SUCH AMUSING THINGS.
SUIT YOURSELF THEN, WHY DON'T YOU?
SUIT YOUR-SELF.
...YOU CAN USE HALF THE BED IF YOU WANT.

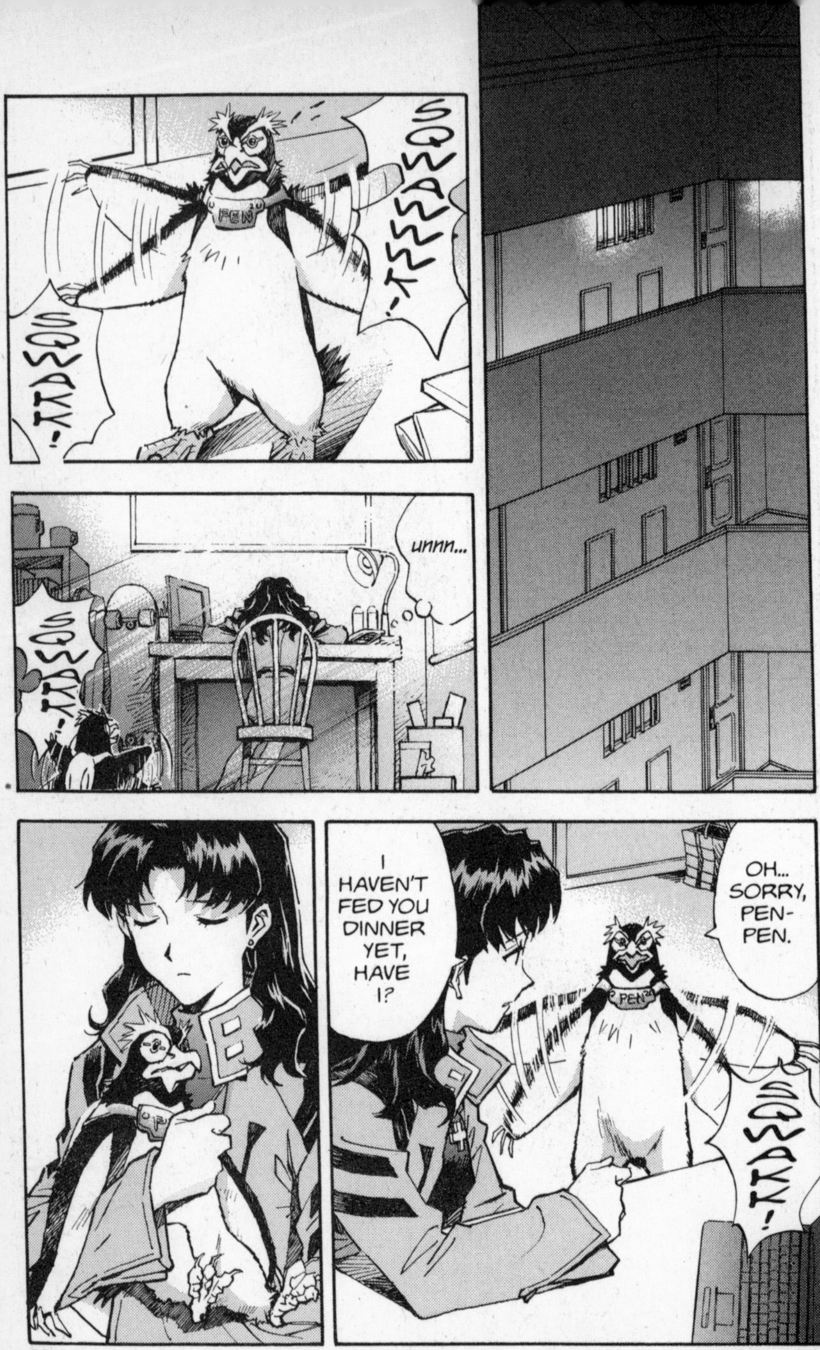
SQWAWWWK!
SQWAKK!
unnn...
SQWAKK!
OH... SORRY, PEN-PEN.
I HAVEN'T FED YOU DINNER YET, HAVE I?
SQWAKK!

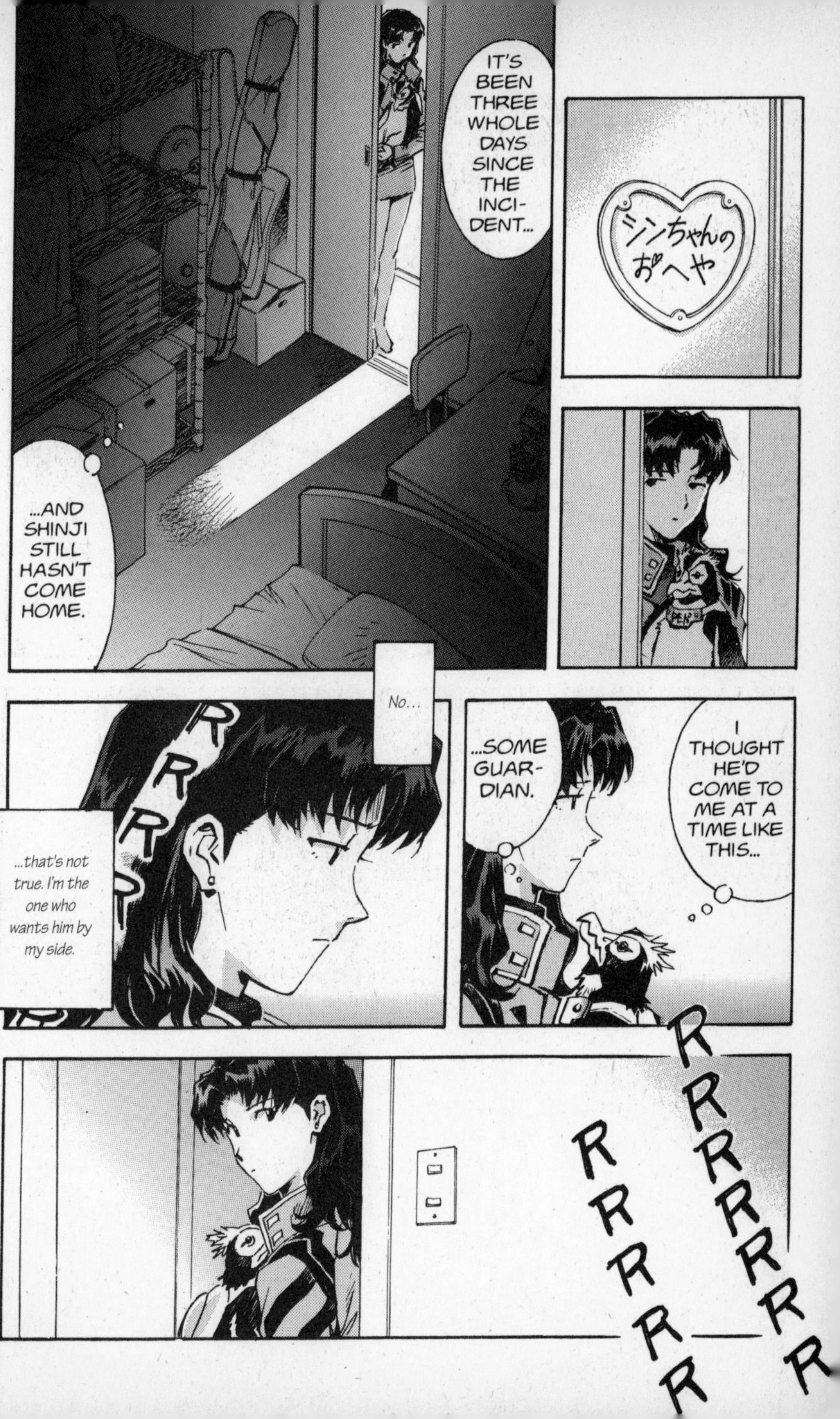
シンちゃんの
お♡へや
IT'S BEEN THREE WHOLE DAYS SINCE THE INCI-DENT...
...AND SHINJI STILL HASN'T COME HOME.
I THOUGHT HE'D COME TO ME AT A TIME LIKE THIS...
...SOME GUARDIAN.
No...
...that's not true. I'm the one who wants him by my side.
RRRR
RRRRRRRRRR

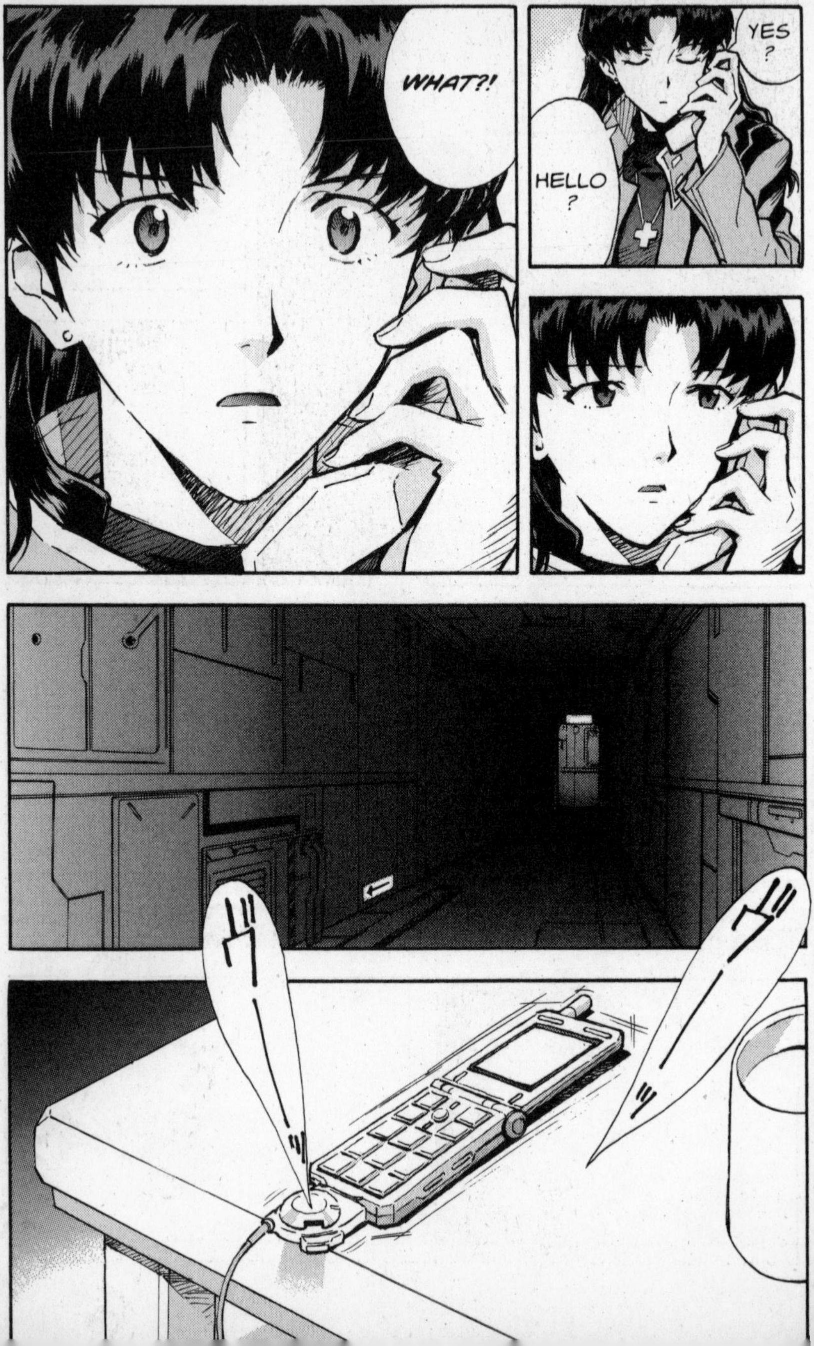
YES ?
HELLO ?
WHAT?!

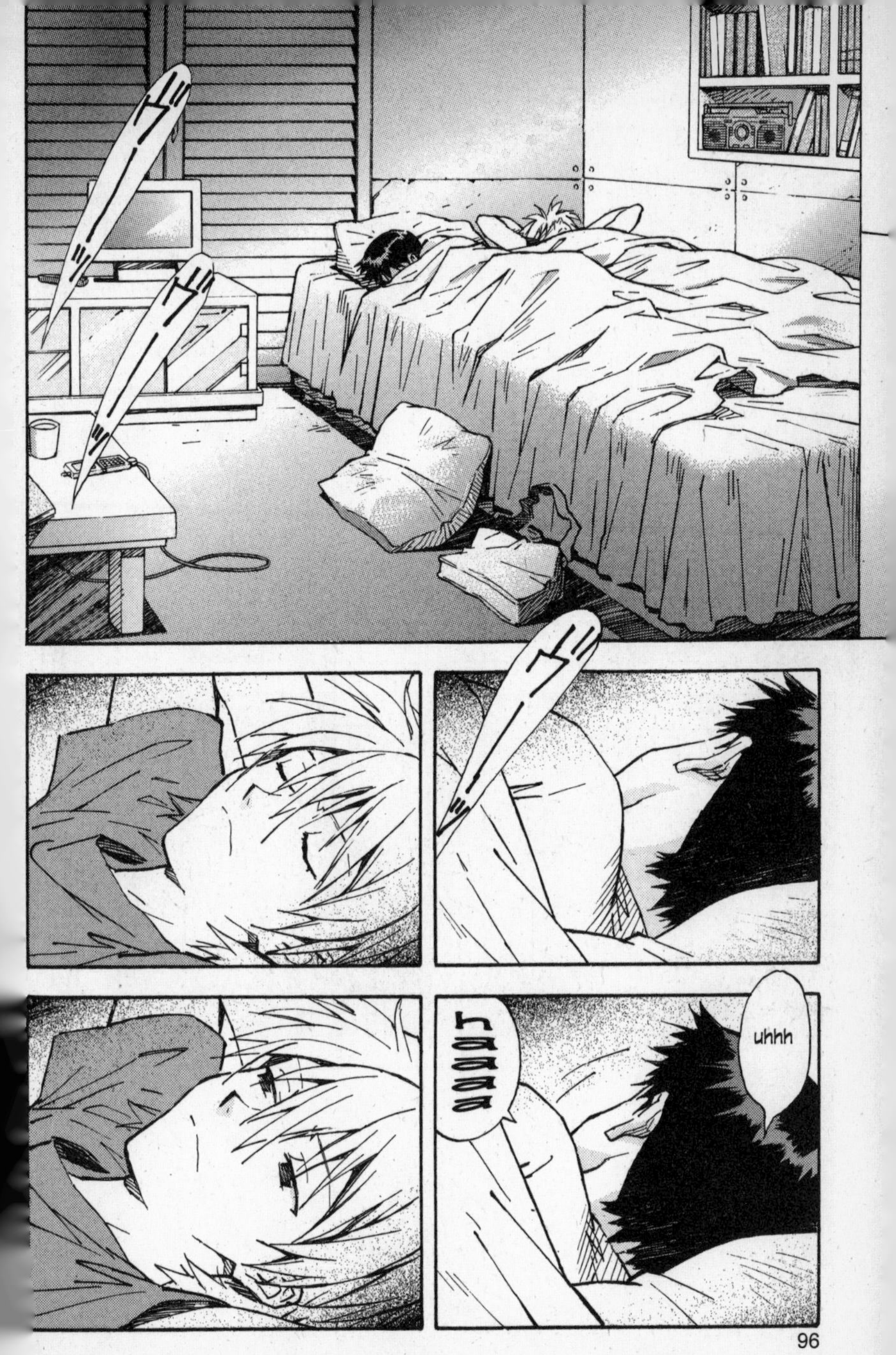
uhhh
haaaa

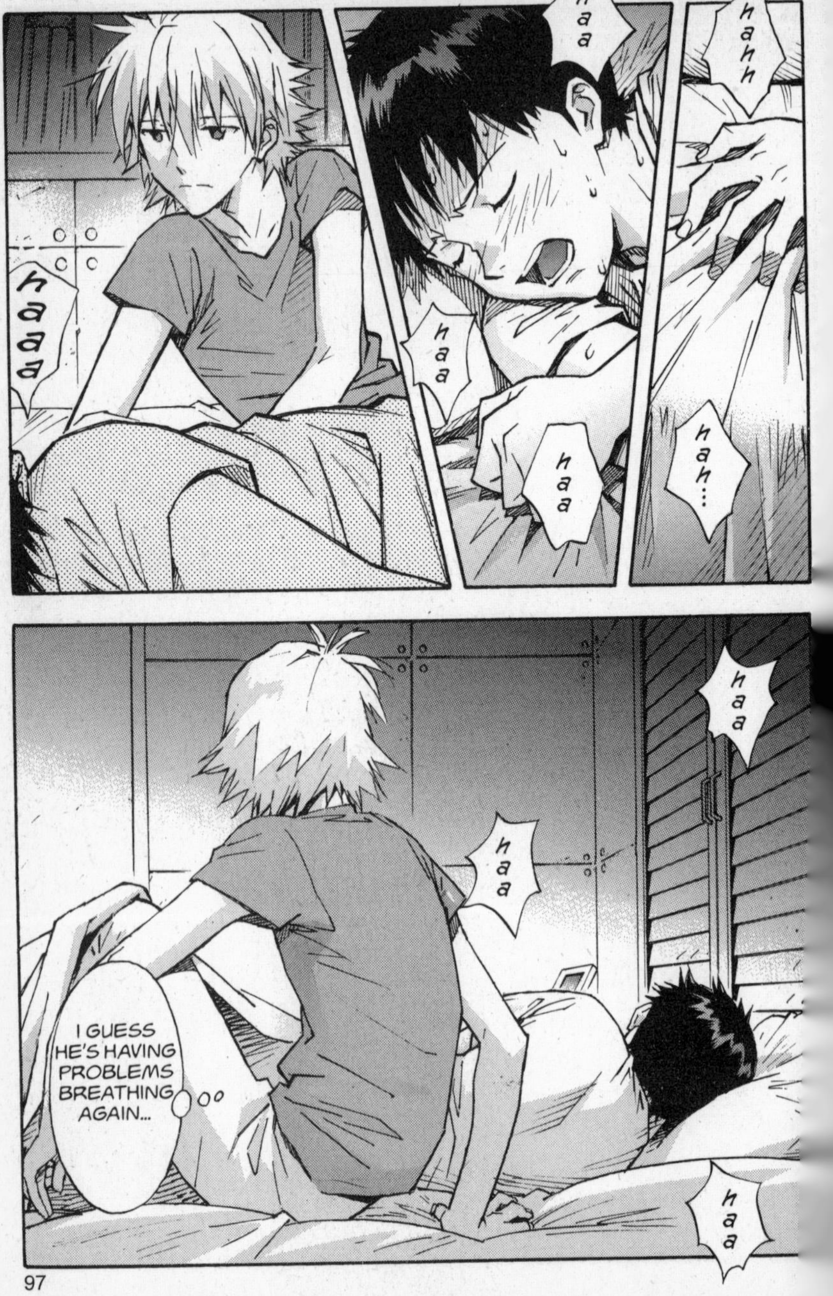
hahh
hah...
haa
haa
haa
haaa
haa
haa
I GUESS HE'S HAVING PROBLEMS BREATHING AGAIN...
haa

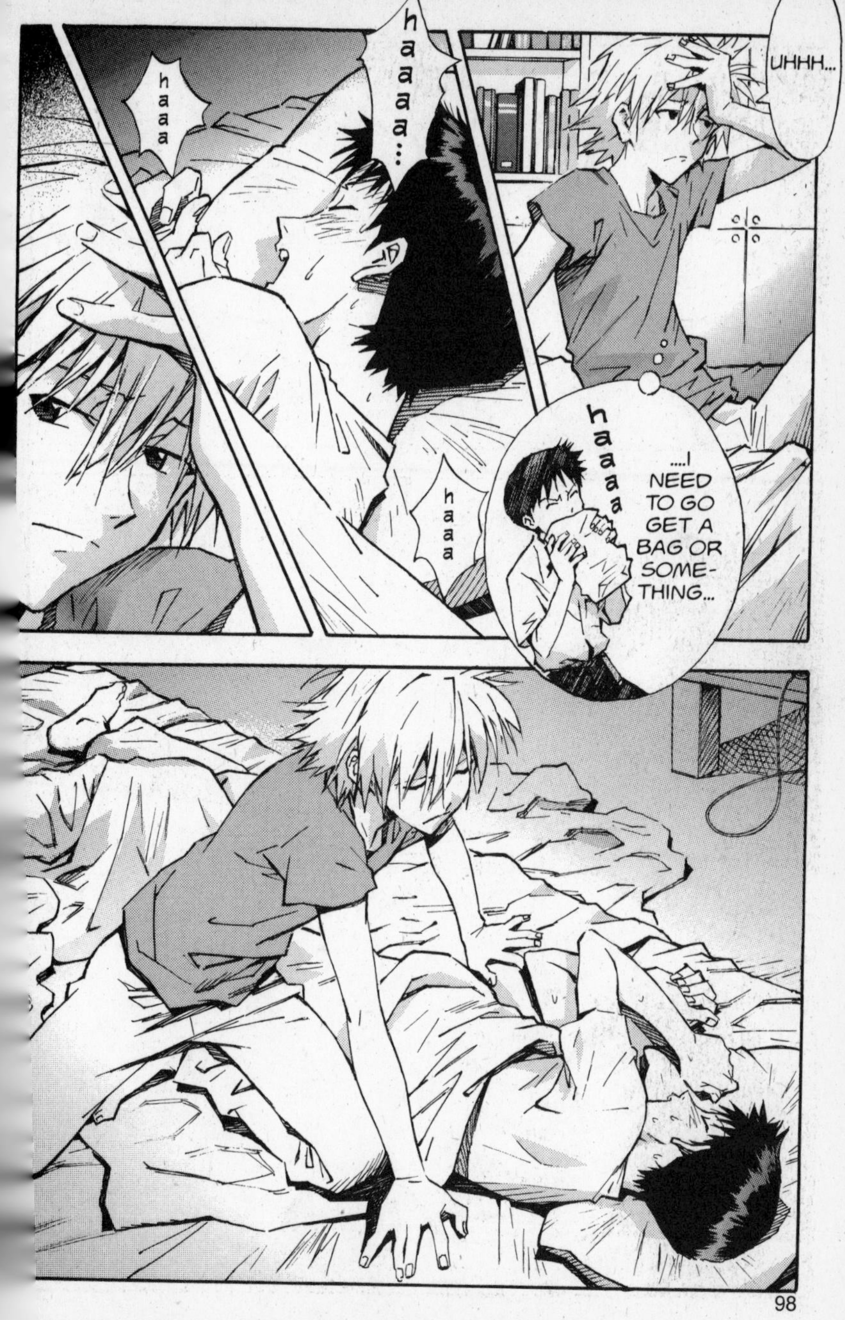
UHHH...
haaaa
....I NEED TO GO GET A BAG OR SOME-THING...
haaaa...
haaa
haaa

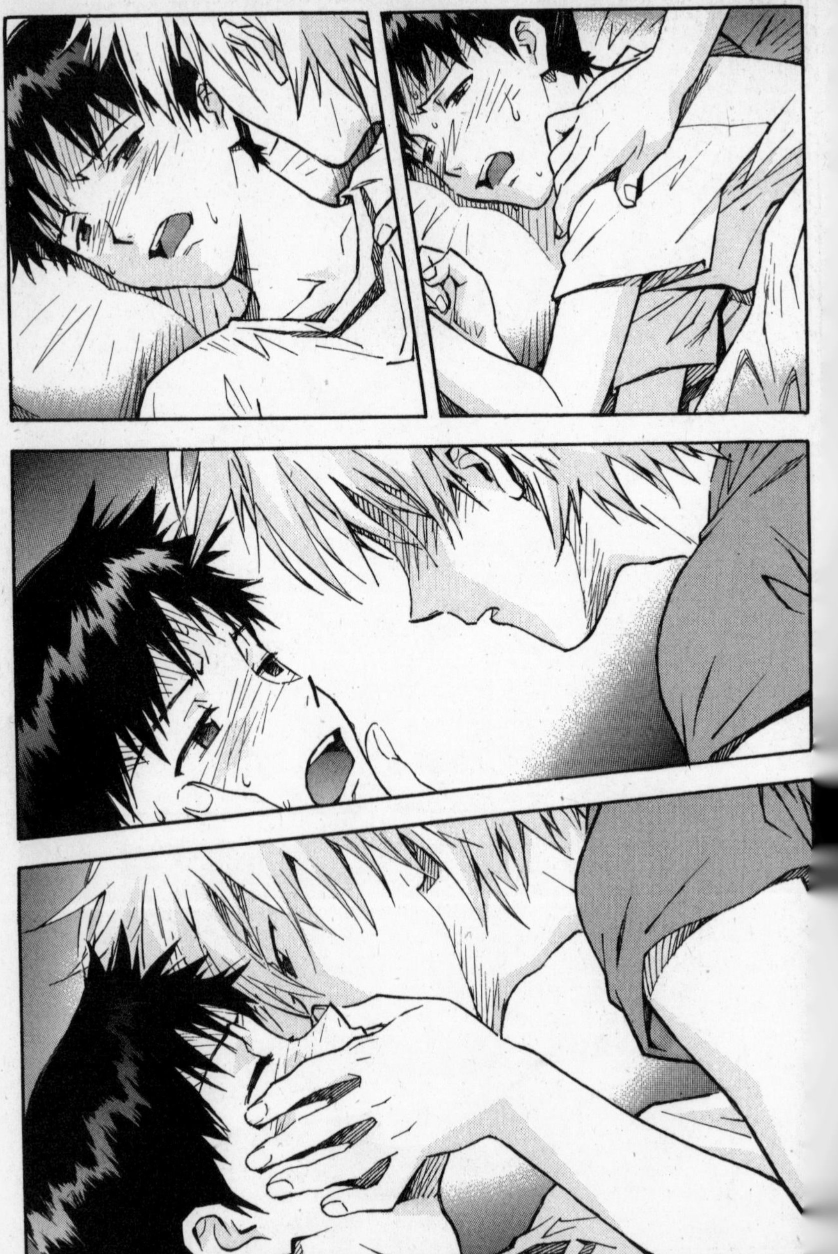

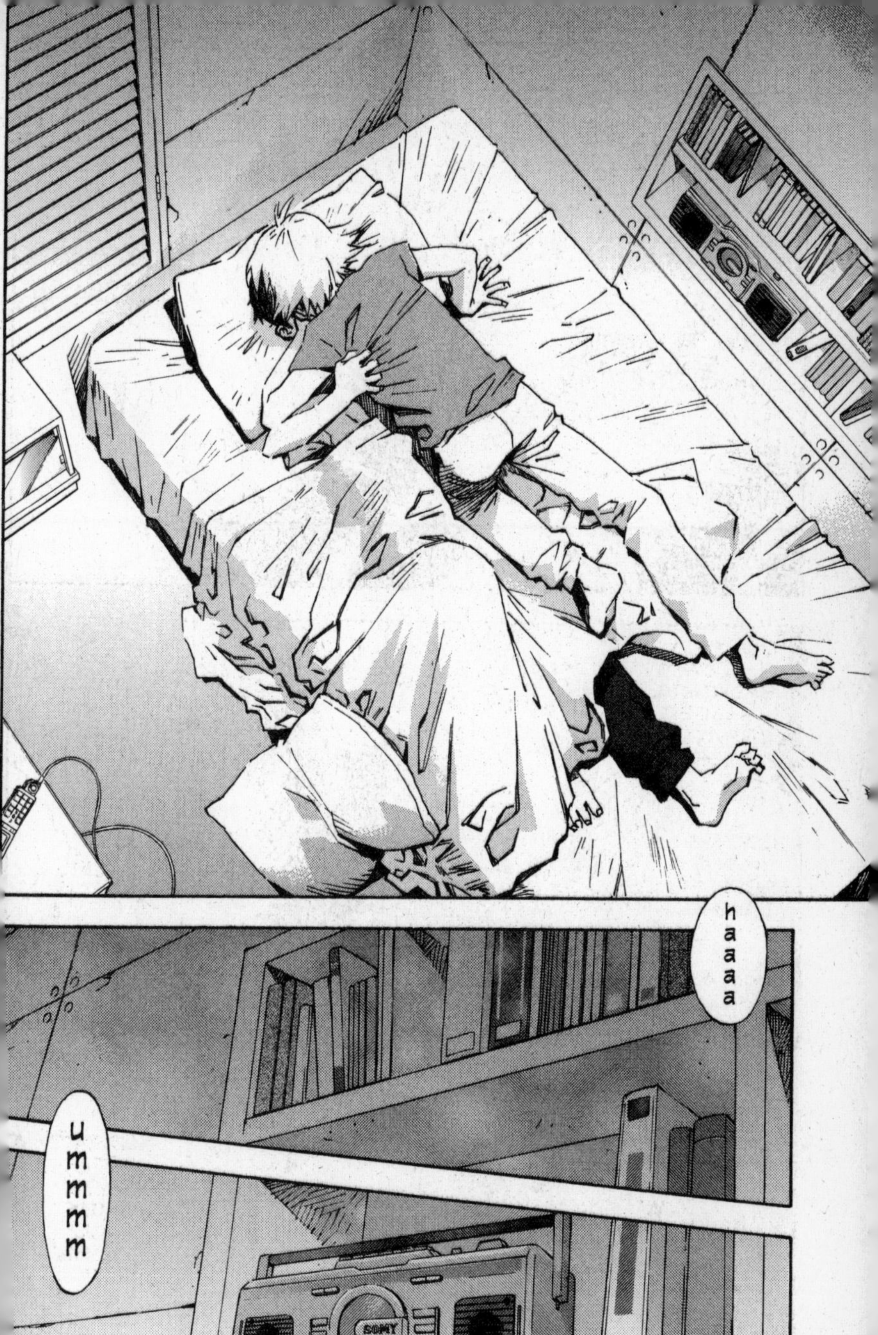
haaaa
ummmm

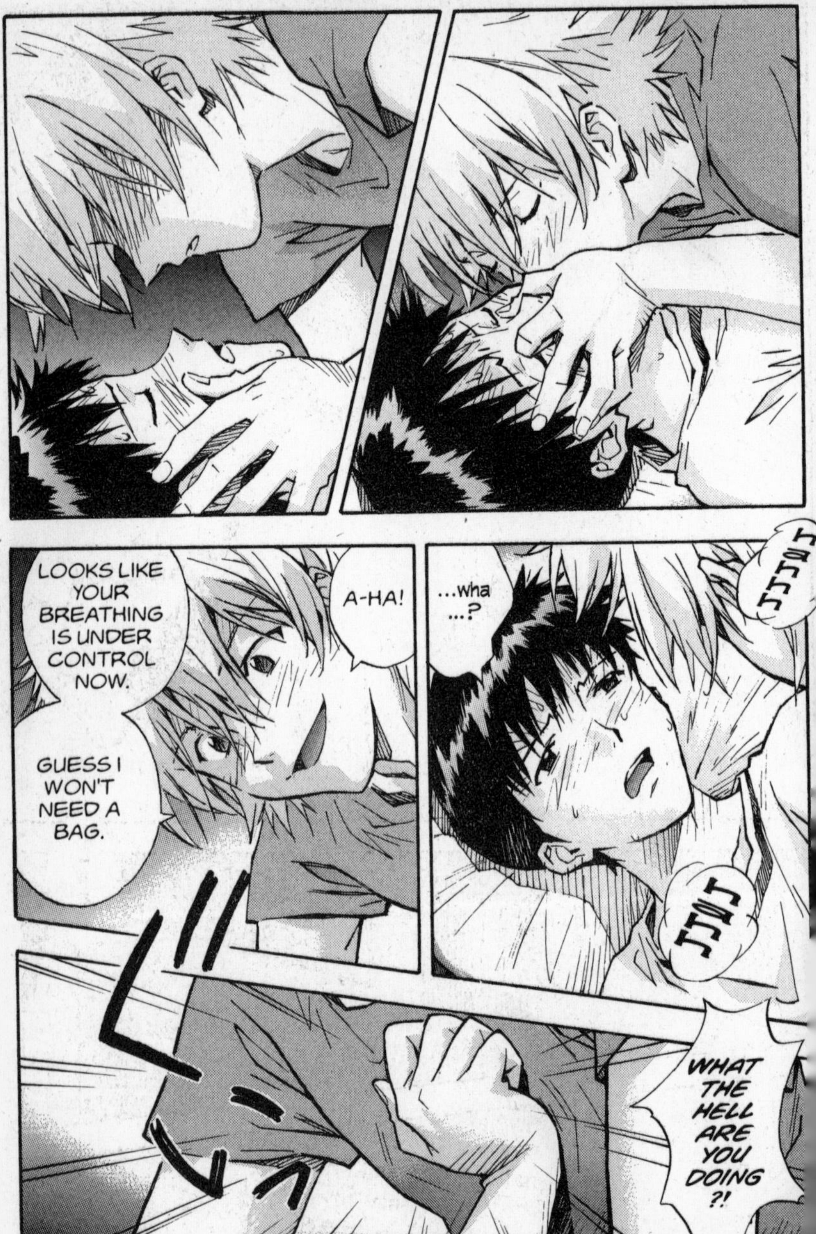
...wha ...?
A-HA!
LOOKS LIKE YOUR BREATHING IS UNDER CONTROL NOW.
GUESS I WON'T NEED A BAG.
WHAT THE HELL ARE YOU DOING?!

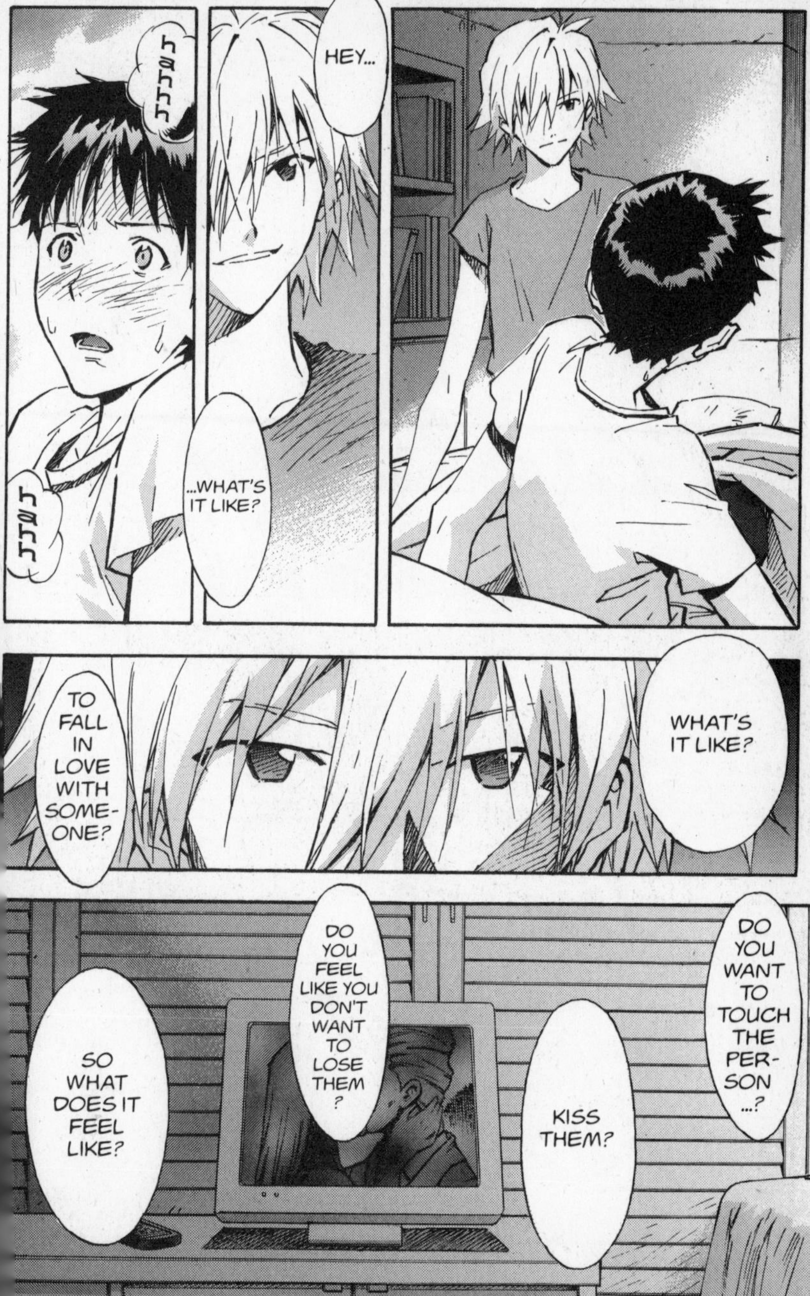
HEY...
...WHAT'S IT LIKE?
hahhh
hahh
WHAT'S IT LIKE?
TO FALL IN LOVE WITH SOME-ONE?
DO YOU WANT TO TOUCH THE PER-SON ...?
KISS THEM?
DO YOU FEEL LIKE YOU DON'T WANT TO LOSE THEM ?
SO WHAT DOES IT FEEL LIKE?

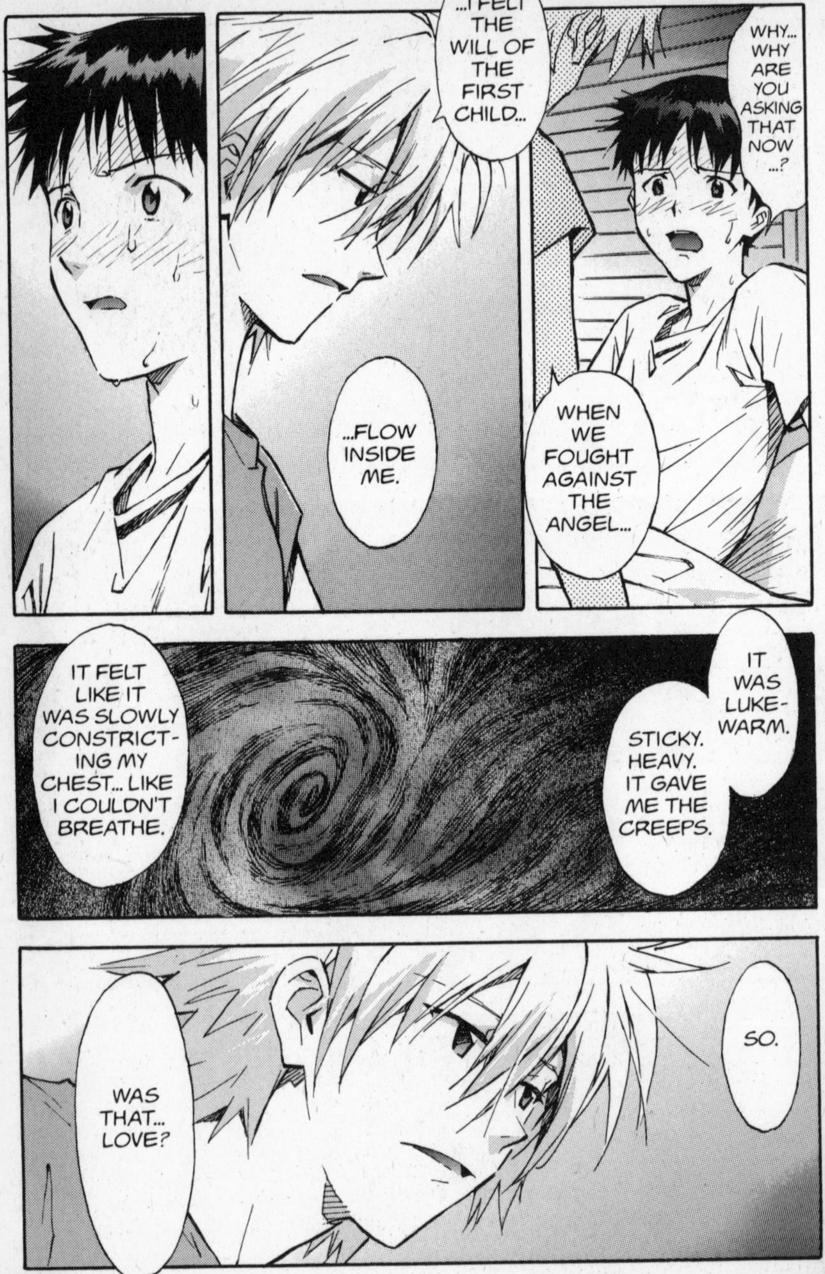
WHY... WHY ARE YOU ASKING THAT NOW ...?
WHEN WE FOUGHT AGAINST THE ANGEL...
...I FELT THE WILL OF THE FIRST CHILD...
...FLOW INSIDE ME.
IT WAS LUKE-WARM.
STICKY. HEAVY. IT GAVE ME THE CREEPS.
IT FELT LIKE IT WAS SLOWLY CONSTRICT-ING MY CHEST... LIKE I COULDN'T BREATHE.
SO.
WAS THAT... LOVE?

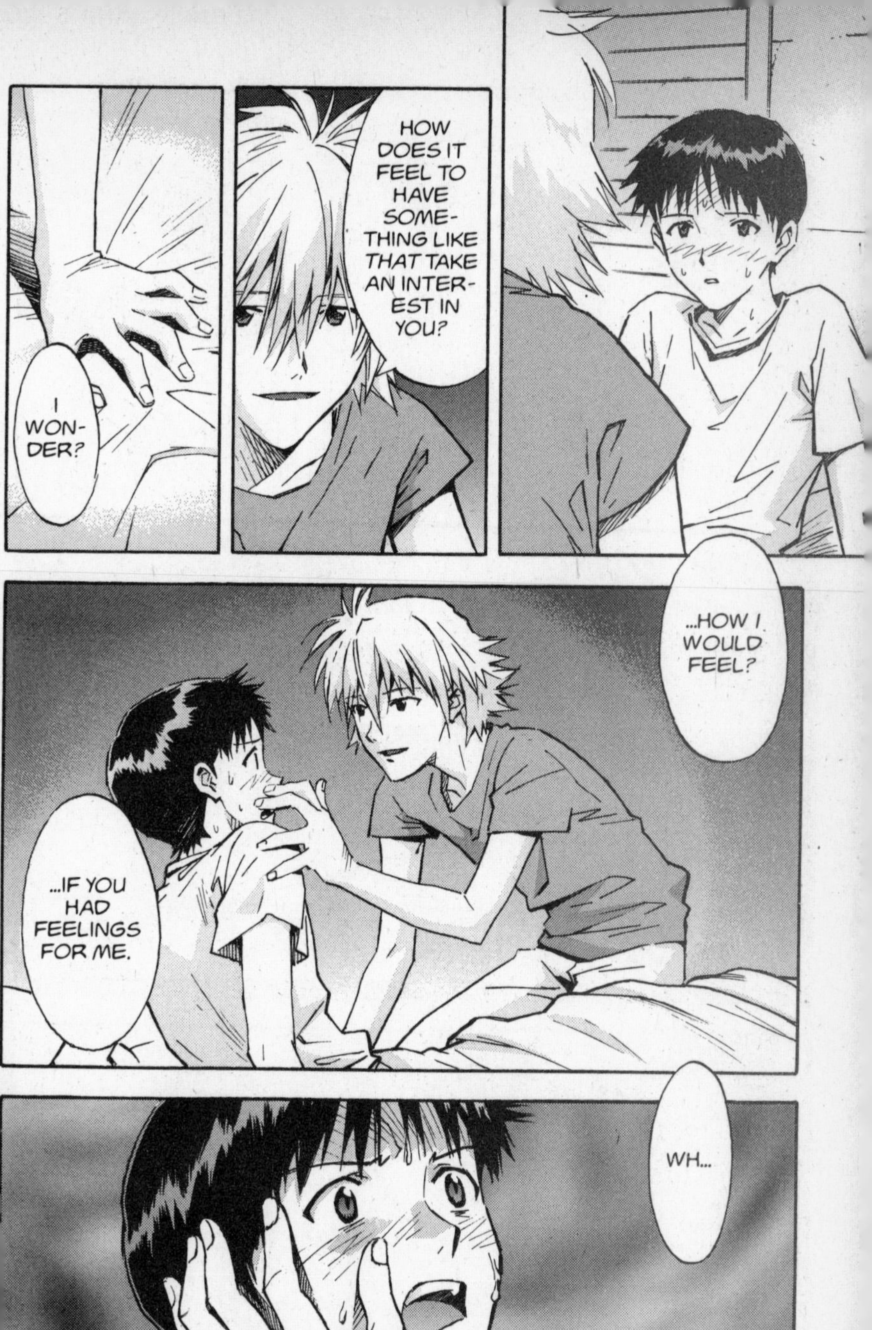
HOW DOES IT FEEL TO HAVE SOME-THING LIKE THAT TAKE AN INTER-EST IN YOU?
I WON-DER?
...HOW I WOULD FEEL?
...IF YOU HAD FEELINGS FOR ME.
WH...

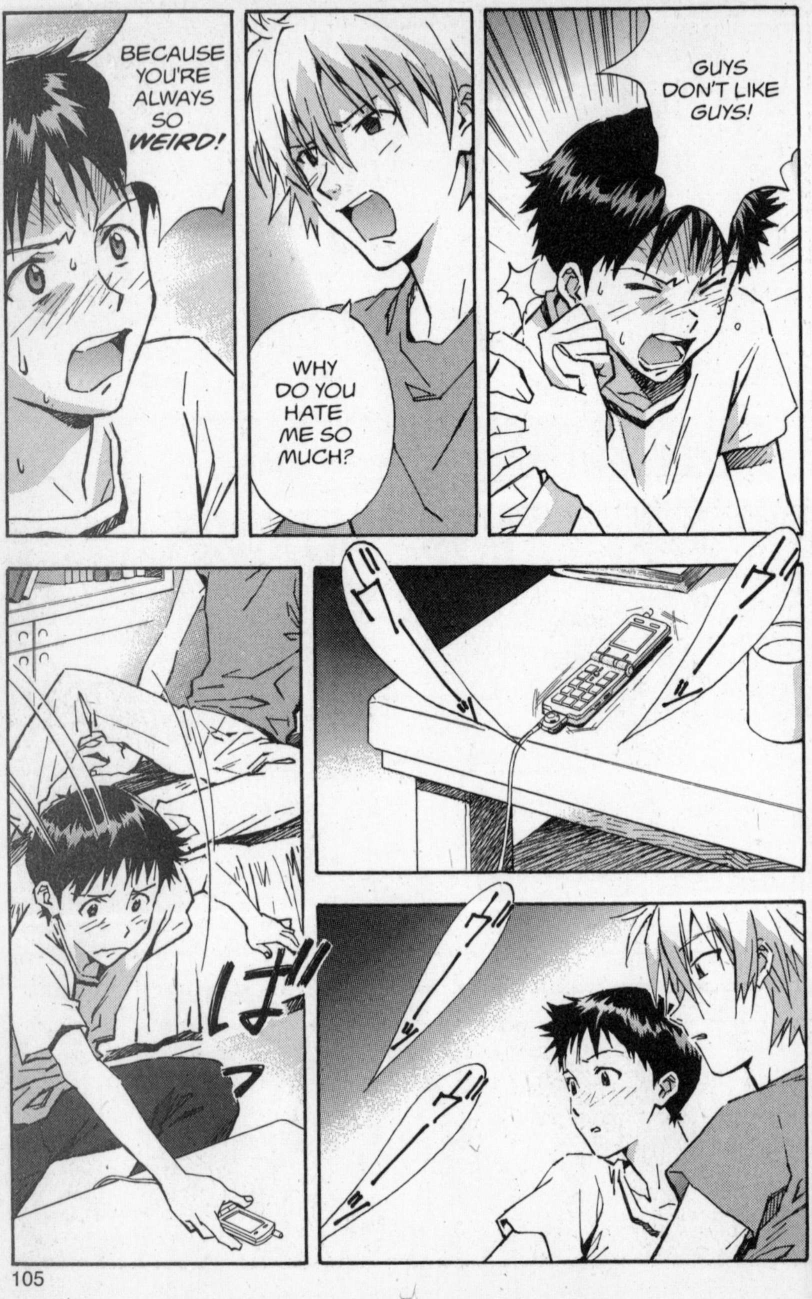
GUYS DON'T LIKE GUYS!
WHY DO YOU HATE ME SO MUCH?
BECAUSE YOU'RE ALWAYS SO *WEIRD!*

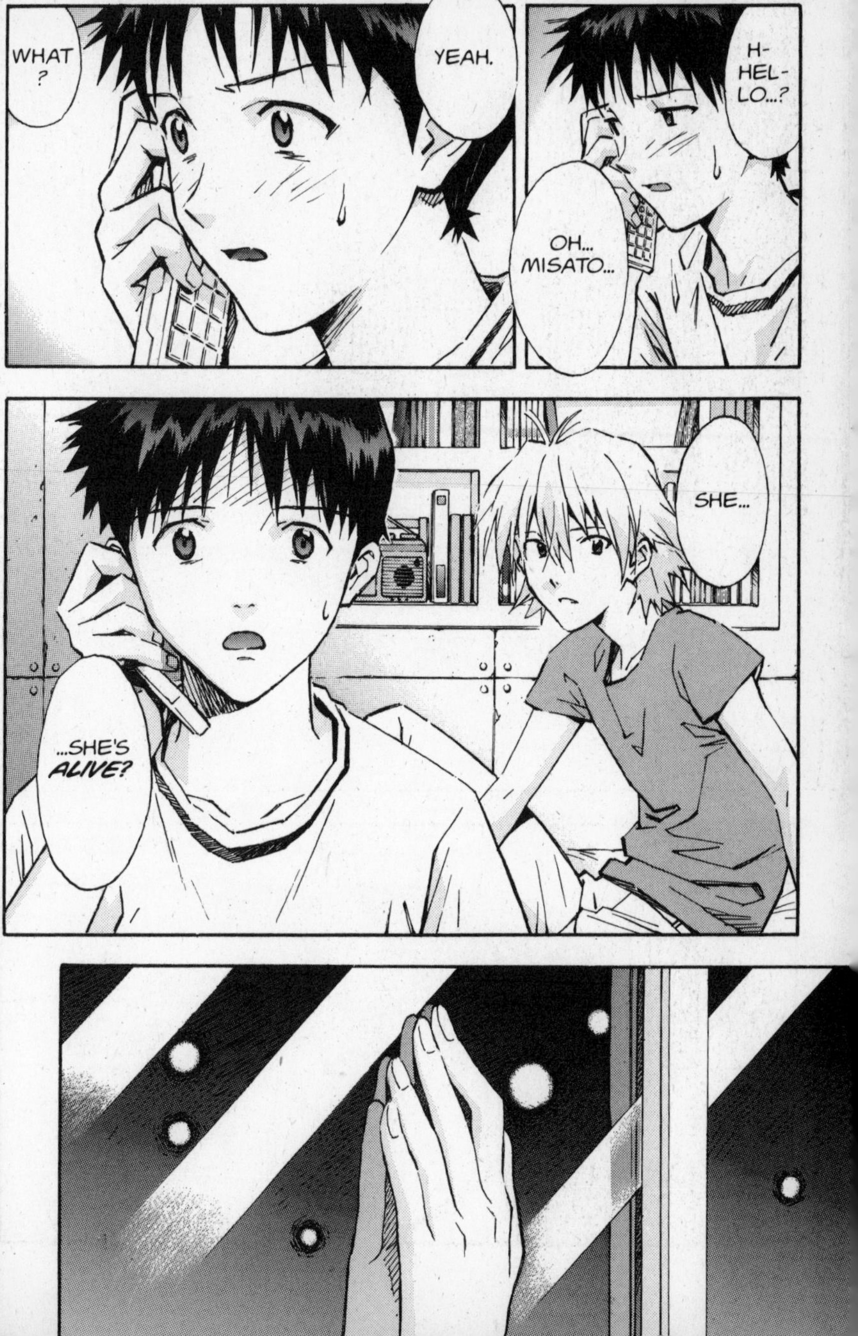
H-HEL-LO...?
OH... MISATO...
YEAH.
WHAT?
SHE...
...SHE'S ALIVE?

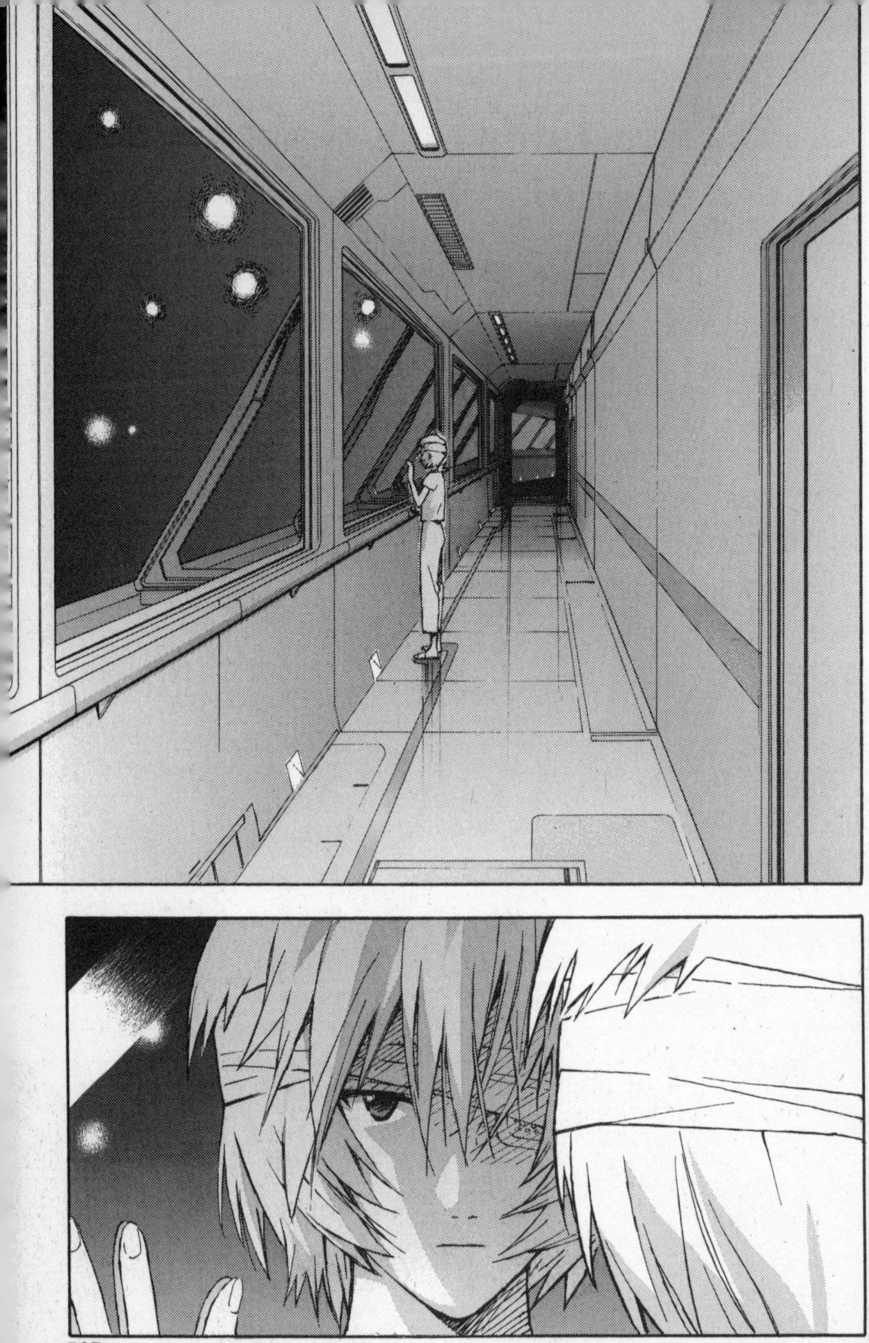

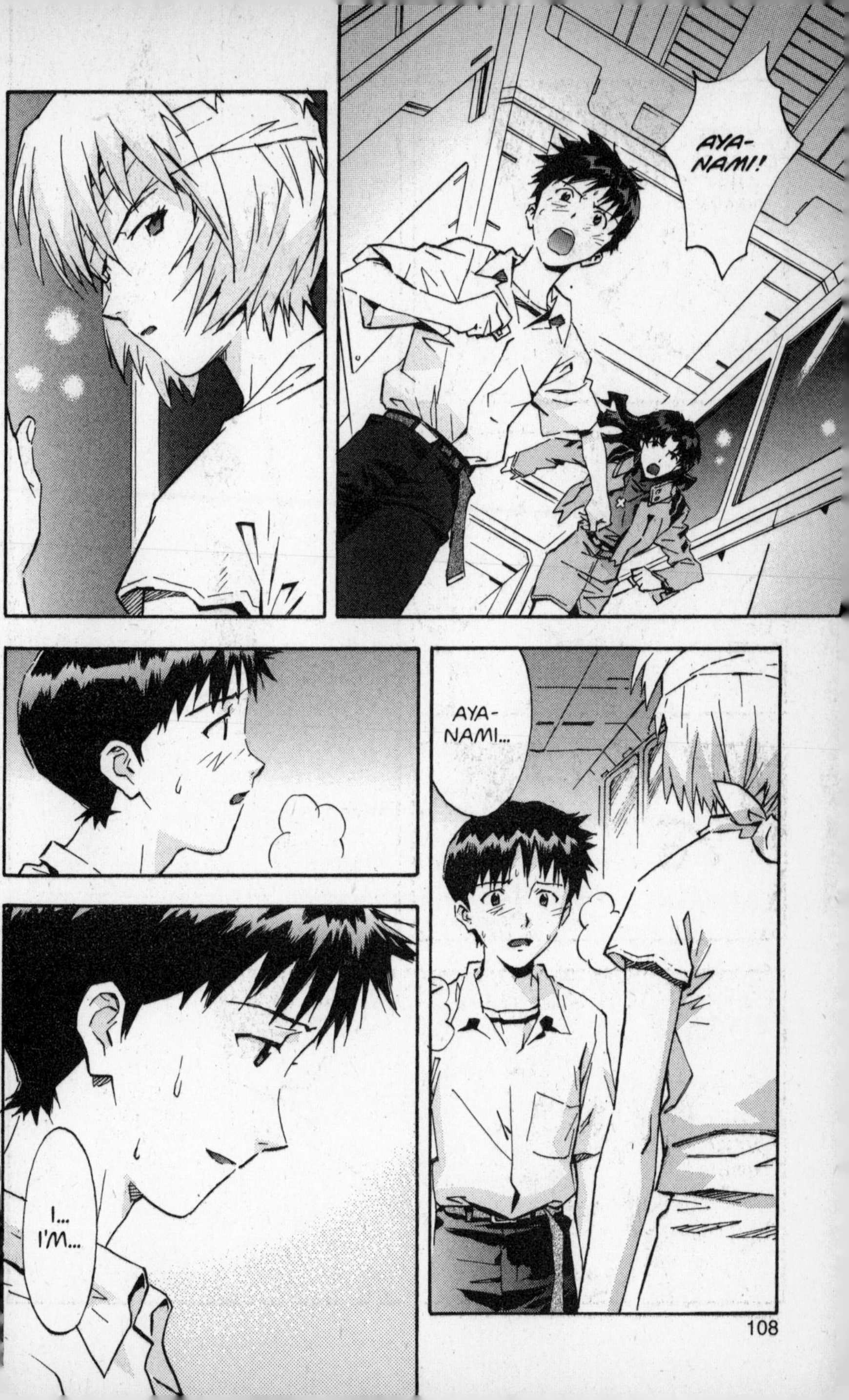
AYA-
NAMI!
AYA-
NAMI...
I...
I'M...

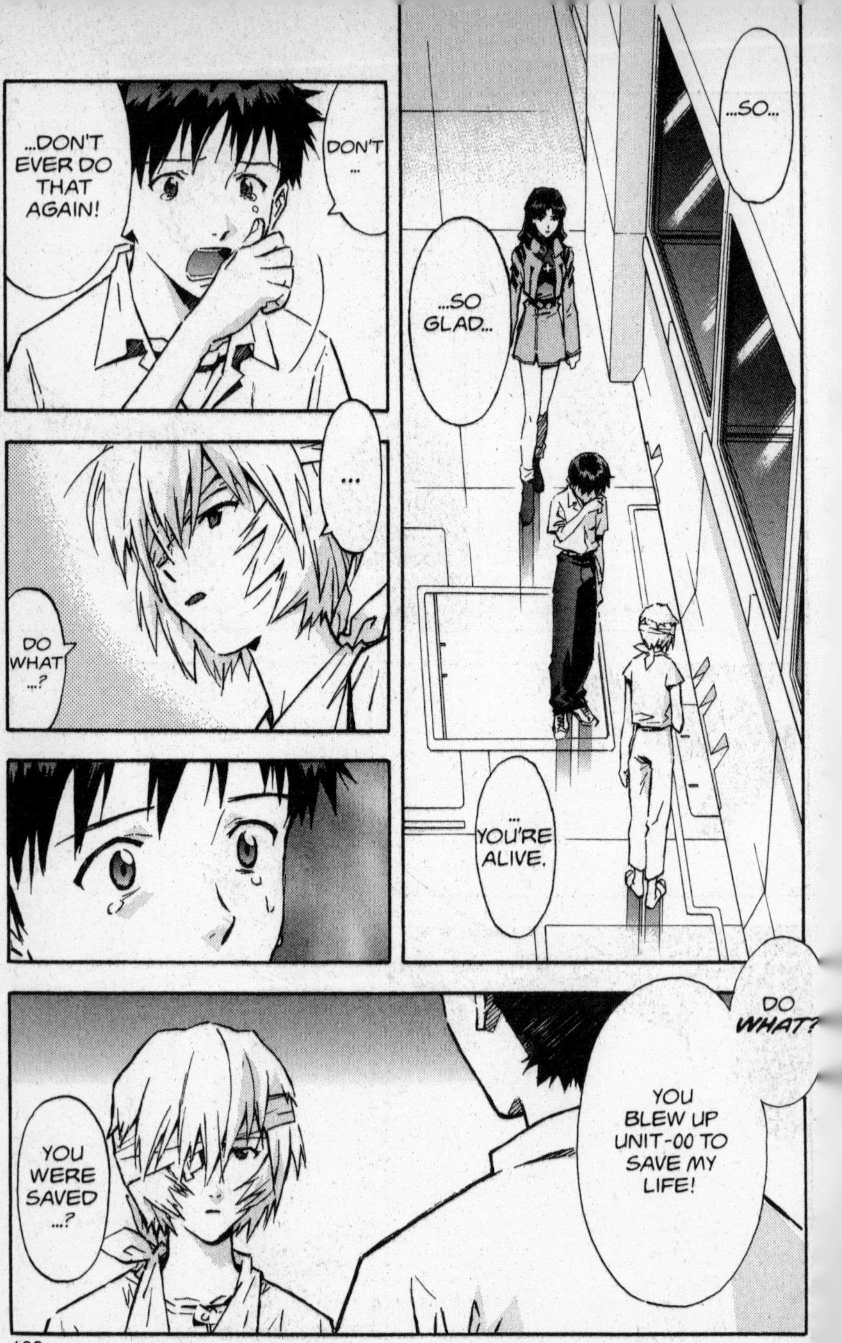
...SO...
...SO GLAD...
... YOU'RE ALIVE.
DON'T ...
...DON'T EVER DO THAT AGAIN!
...
DO WHAT ...?
DO WHAT?
YOU BLEW UP UNIT-00 TO SAVE MY LIFE!
YOU WERE SAVED ...?

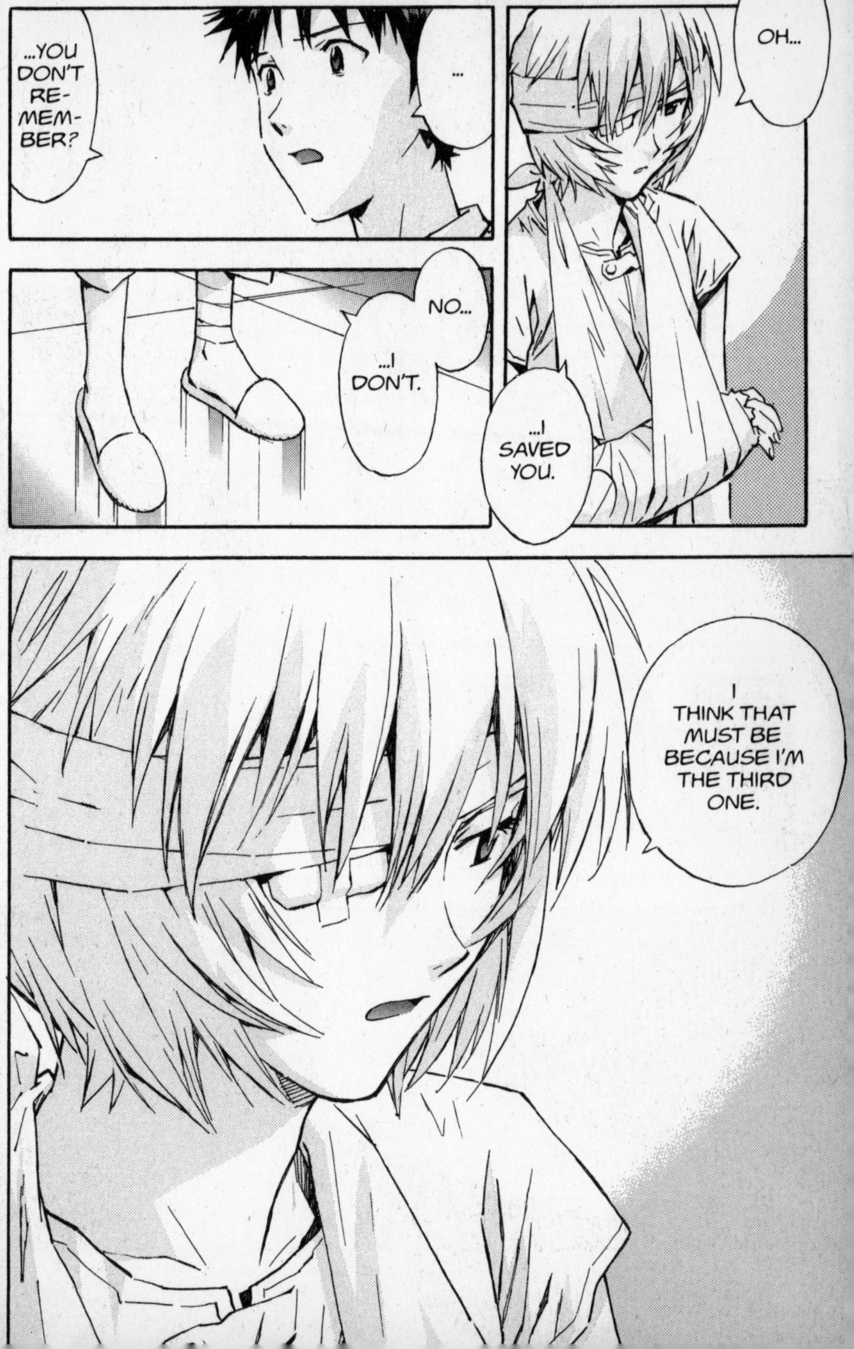
OH...
...I SAVED YOU.
...
...YOU DON'T RE-MEM-BER?
NO...
...I DON'T.
I THINK THAT MUST BE BECAUSE I'M THE THIRD ONE.

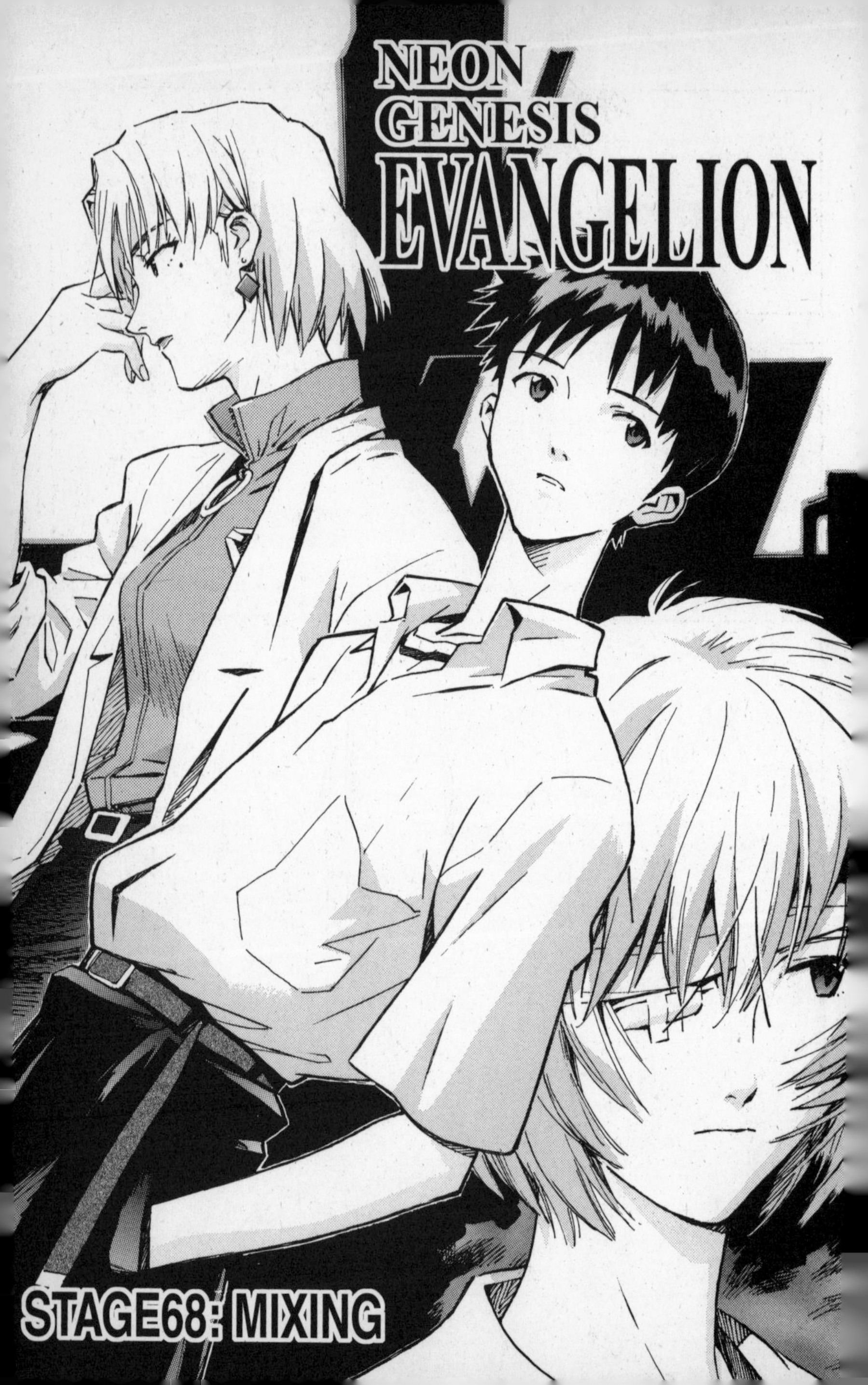
NEON GENESIS EVANGELION
STAGE 68: MIXING

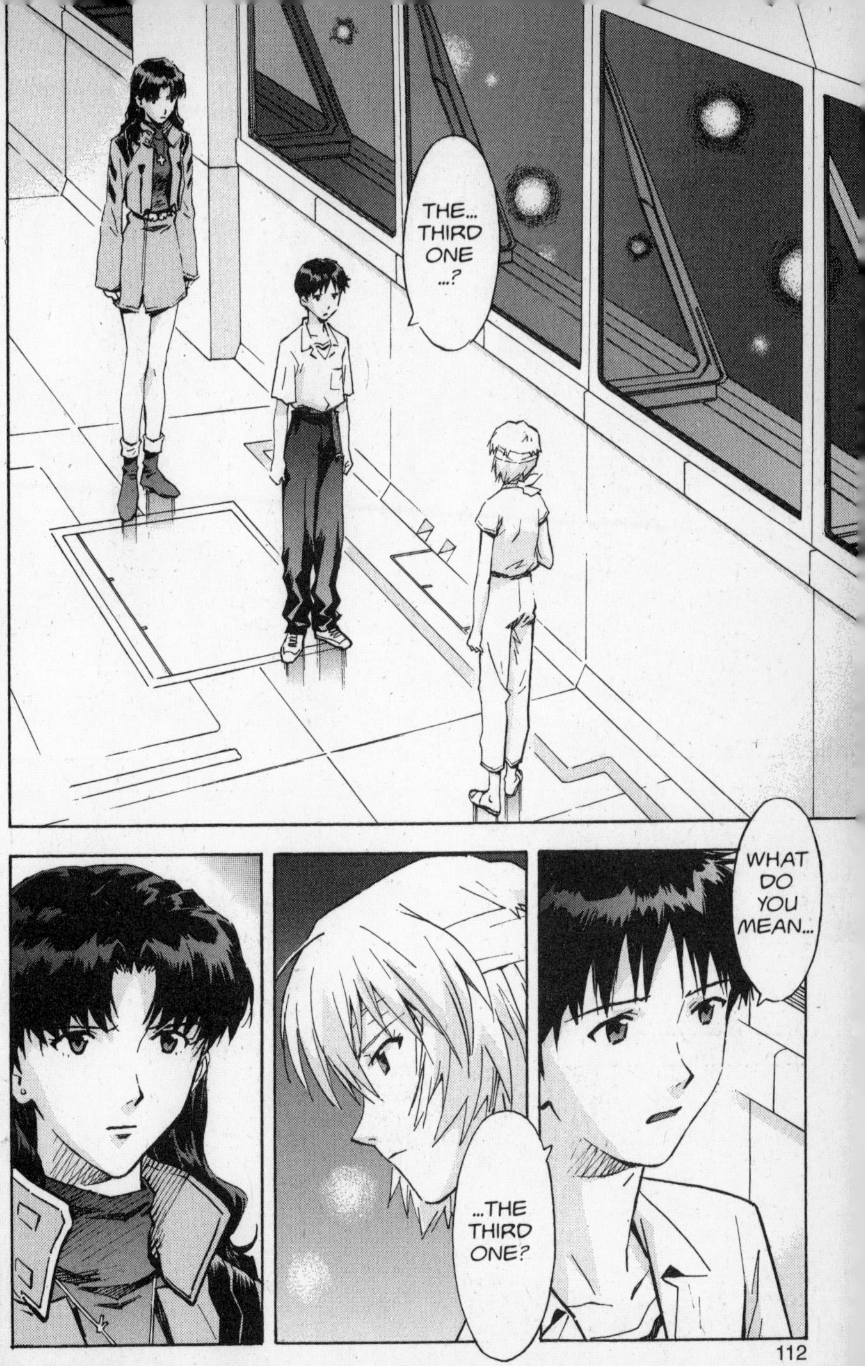
THE... THIRD ONE ...?
WHAT DO YOU MEAN...
...THE THIRD ONE?

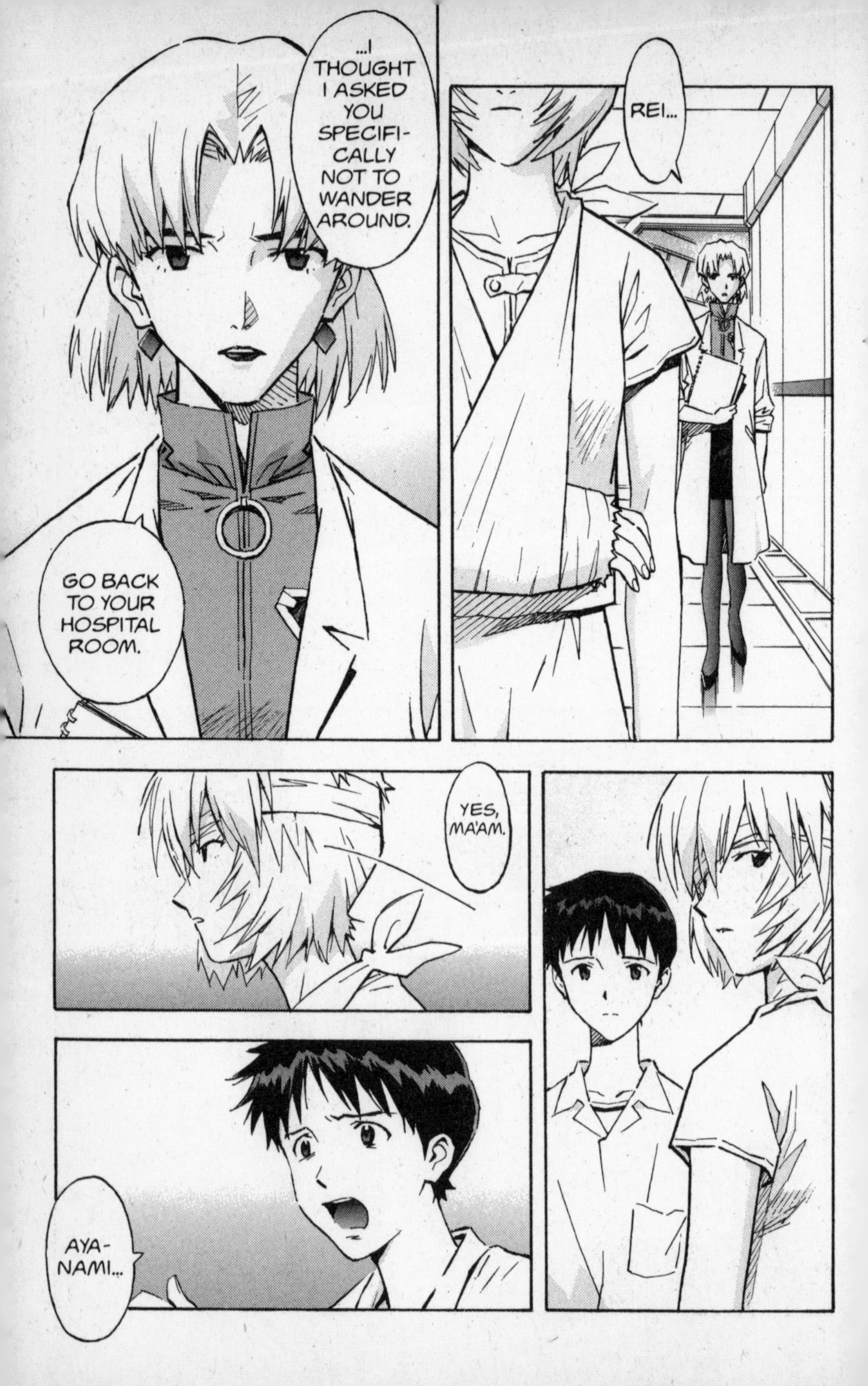
REI...
...I THOUGHT I ASKED YOU SPECIFICALLY NOT TO WANDER AROUND.
GO BACK TO YOUR HOSPITAL ROOM.
YES, MA'AM.
AYA-NAMI...

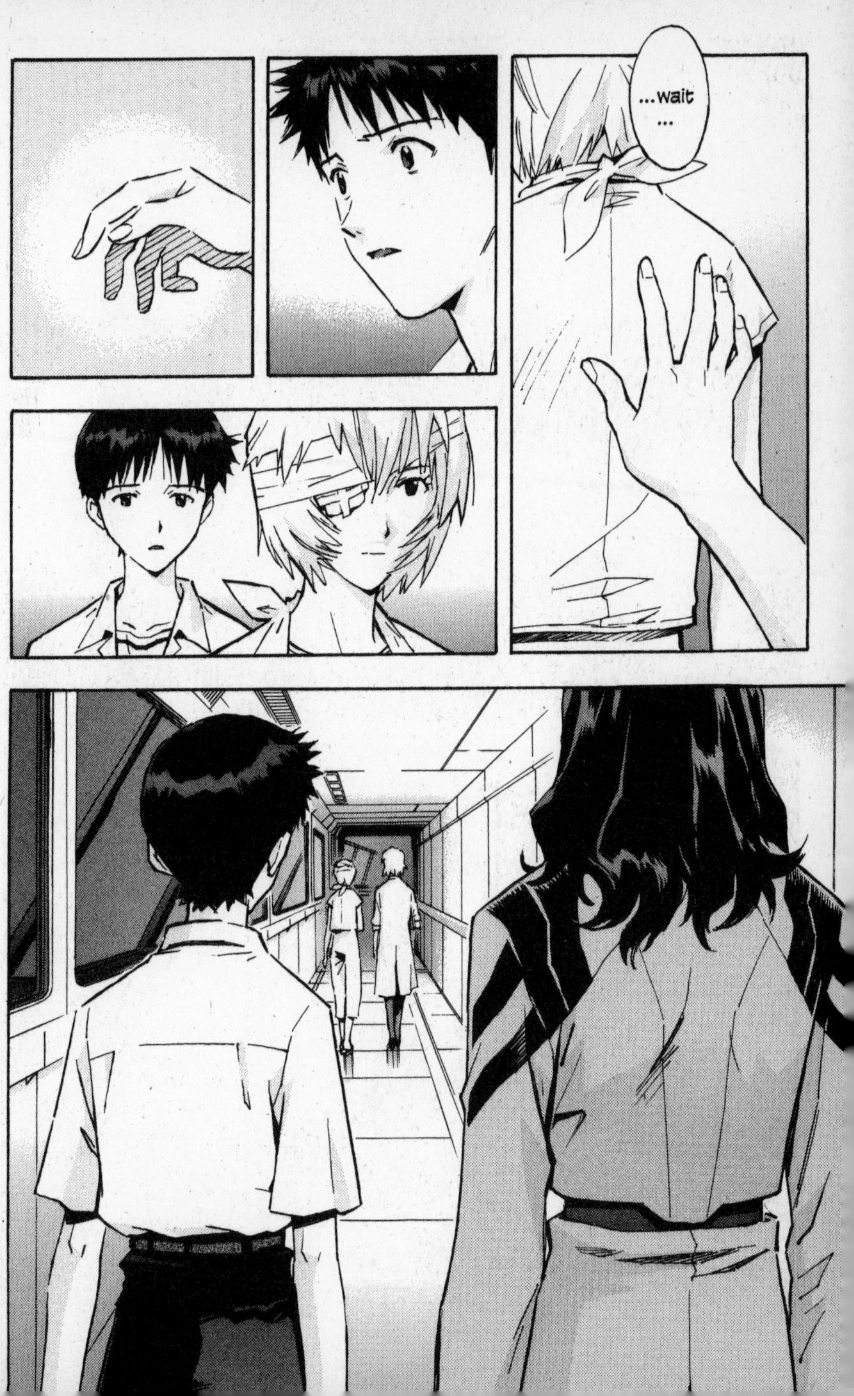
...wait
...

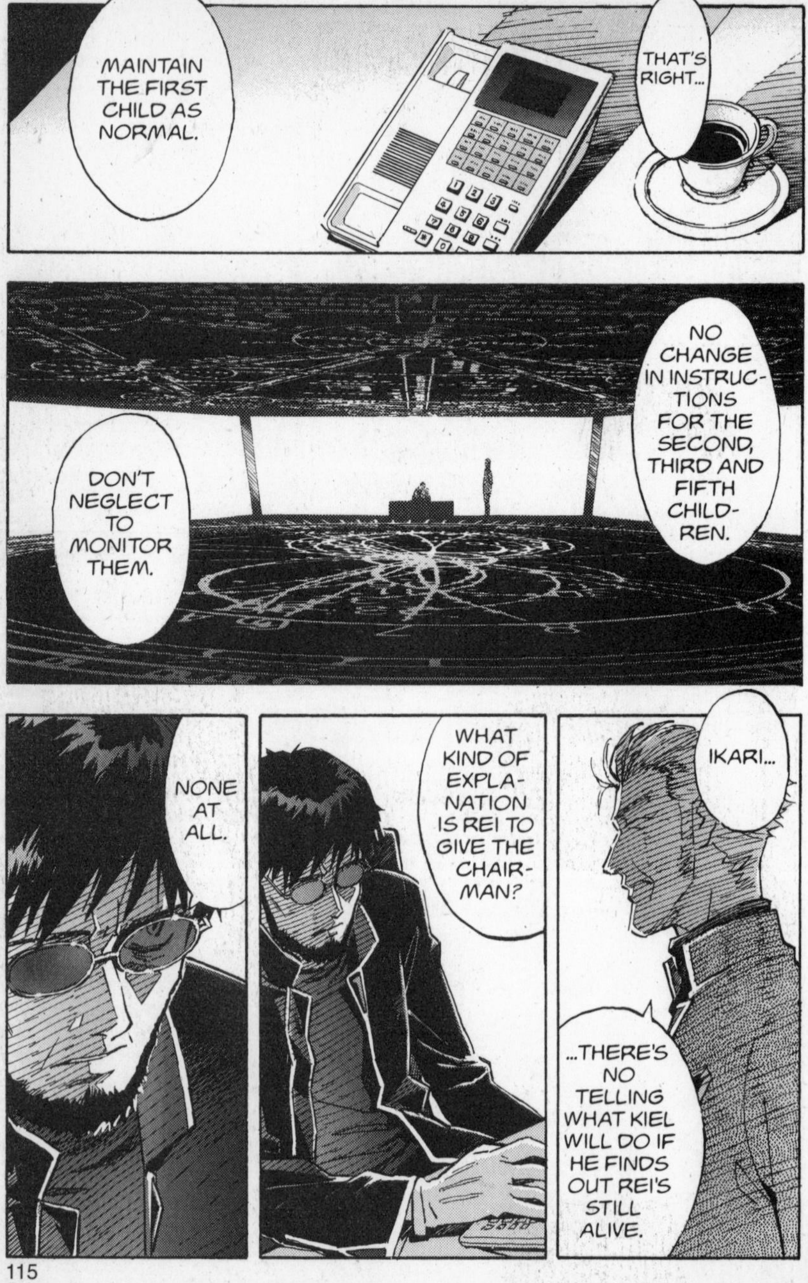
THAT'S RIGHT...
MAINTAIN THE FIRST CHILD AS NORMAL.
NO CHANGE IN INSTRUCTIONS FOR THE SECOND, THIRD AND FIFTH CHILDREN.
DON'T NEGLECT TO MONITOR THEM.
IKARI...
...THERE'S NO TELLING WHAT KIEL WILL DO IF HE FINDS OUT REI'S STILL ALIVE.
WHAT KIND OF EXPLANATION IS REI TO GIVE THE CHAIRMAN?
NONE AT ALL.

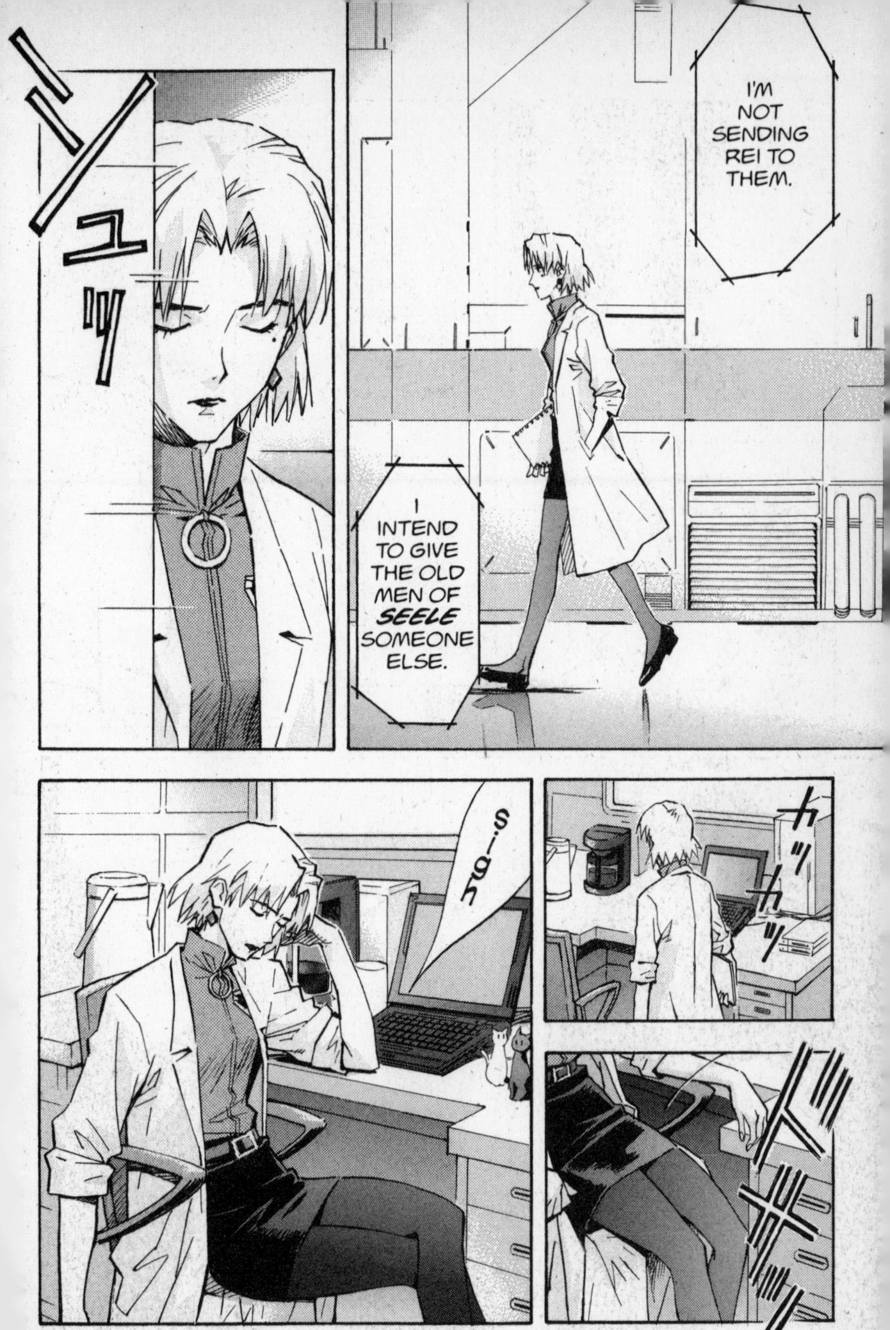
I'M NOT SENDING REI TO THEM.
I INTEND TO GIVE THE OLD MEN OF ***SEELE*** SOMEONE ELSE.
シュッ
カッカッ
sigh

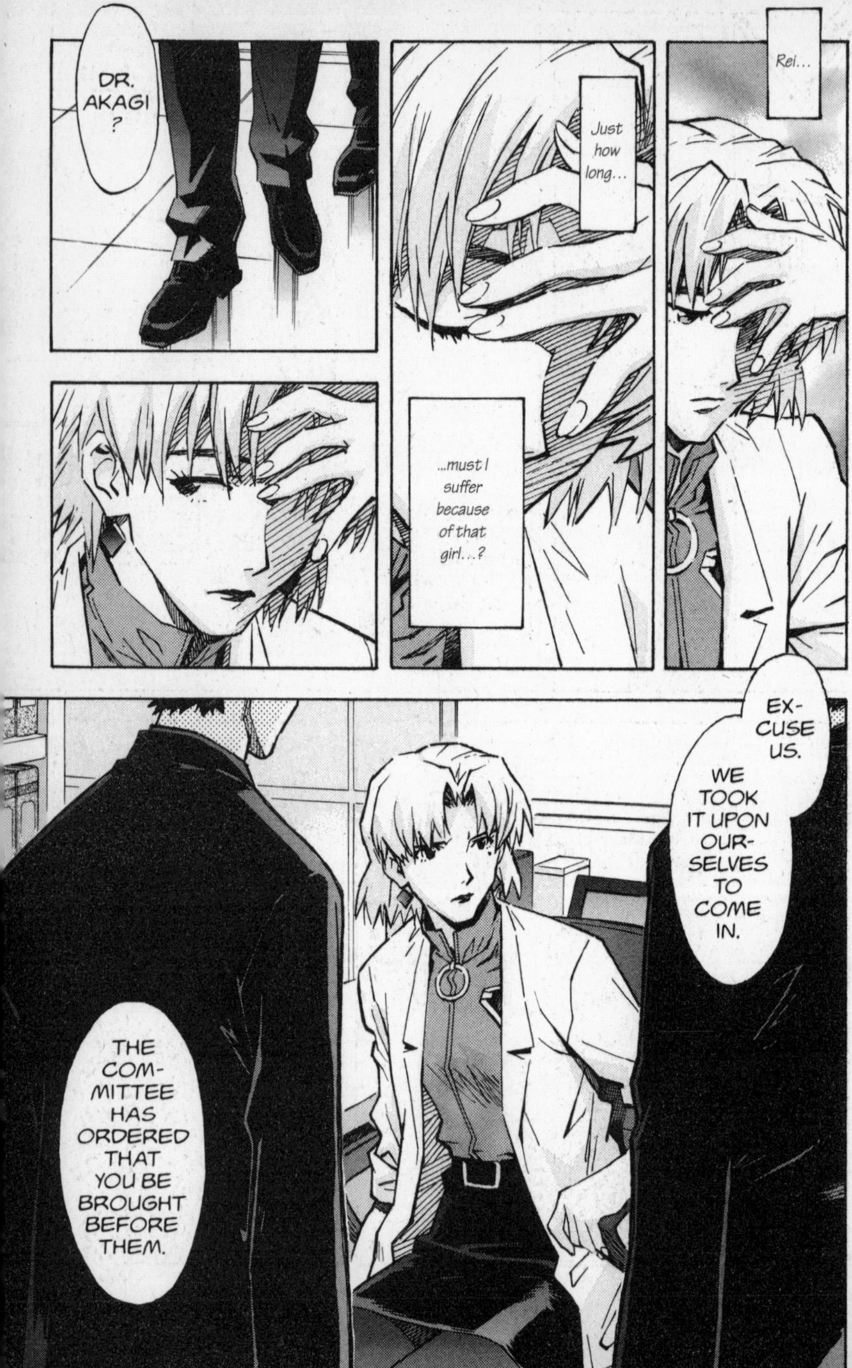
Rei...
Just how long...
...must I suffer because of that girl...?
DR. AKAGI?
EX-CUSE US. WE TOOK IT UPON OUR-SELVES TO COME IN.
THE COM-MITTEE HAS ORDERED THAT YOU BE BROUGHT BEFORE THEM.

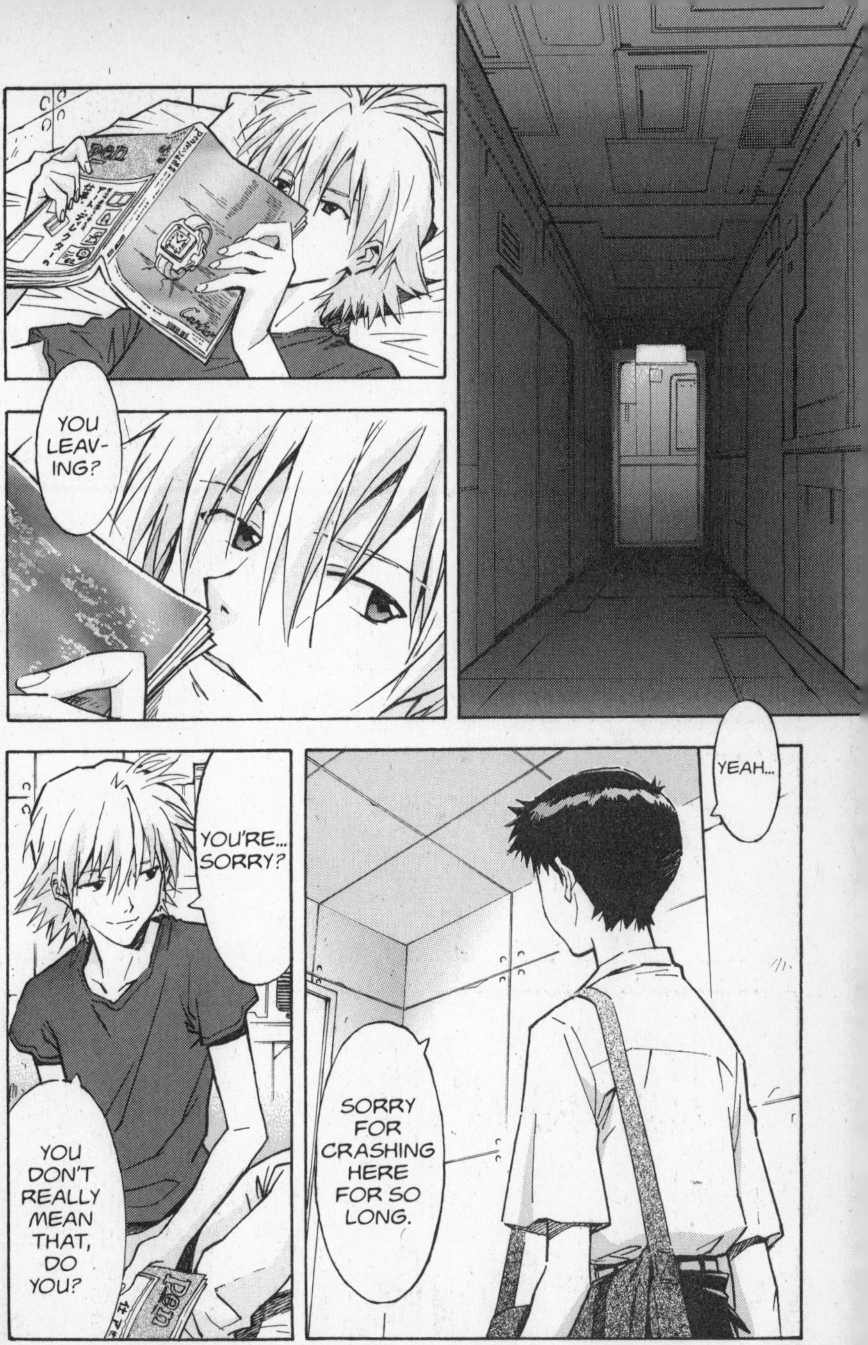
YOU LEAV-ING?
YEAH...
SORRY FOR CRASHING HERE FOR SO LONG.
YOU'RE... SORRY?
YOU DON'T REALLY MEAN THAT, DO YOU?

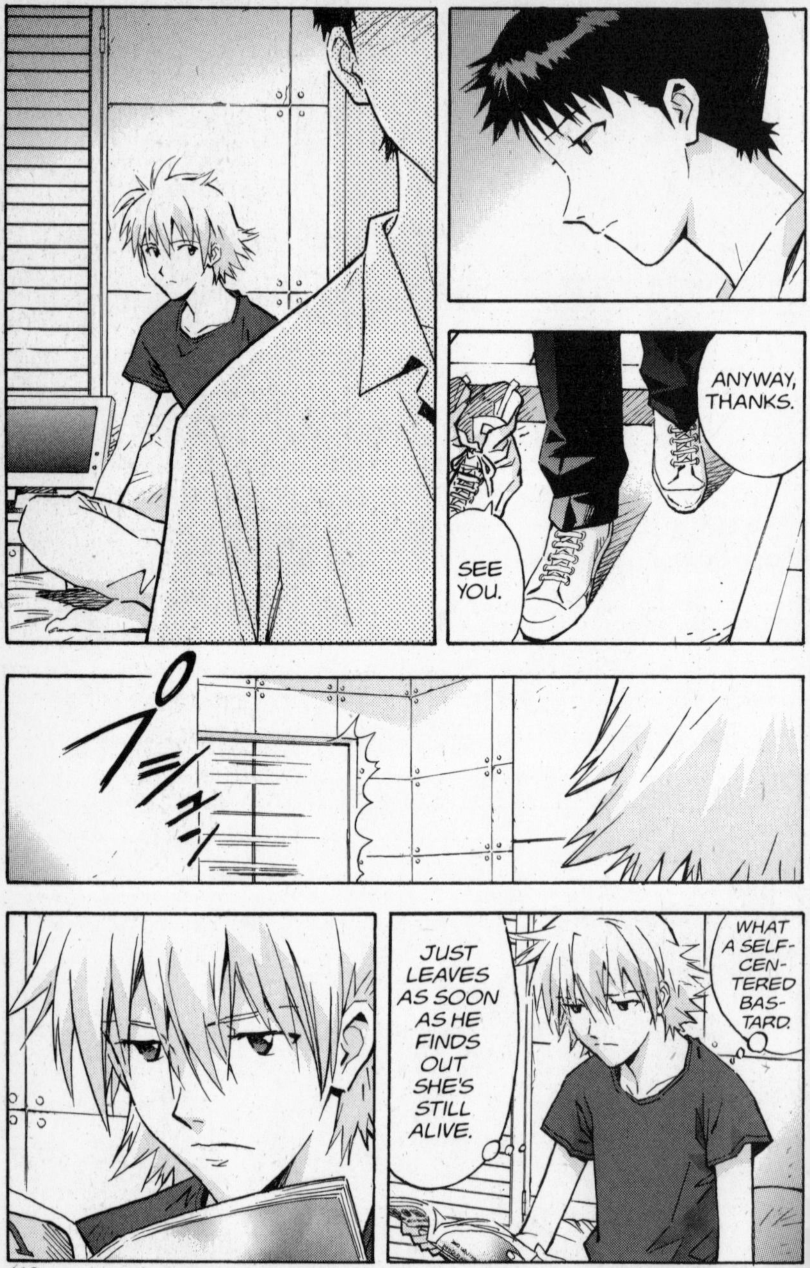
ANYWAY, THANKS.
SEE YOU.
プシュッ
WHAT A SELF-CENTERED BASTARD.
JUST LEAVES AS SOON AS HE FINDS OUT SHE'S STILL ALIVE.

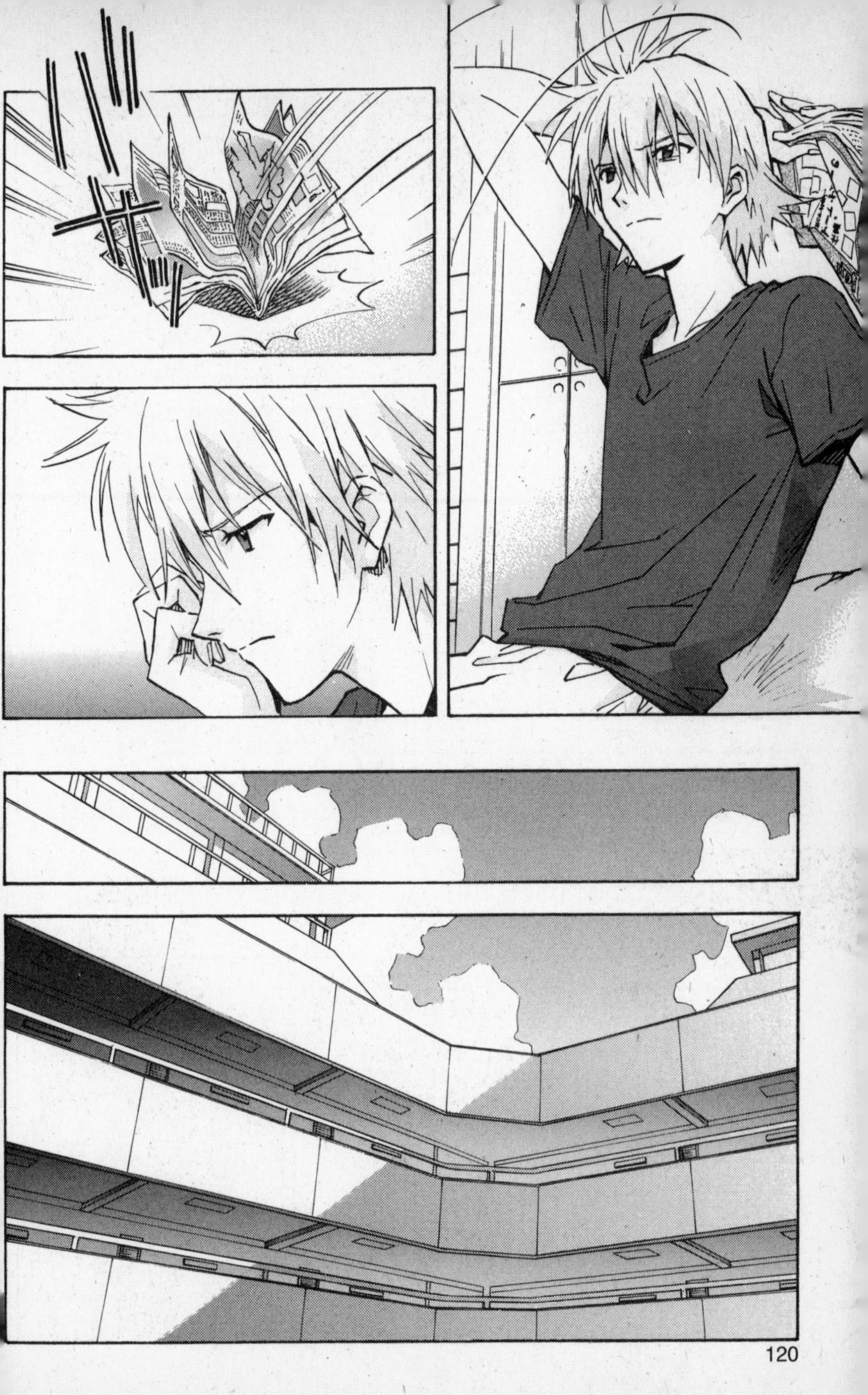

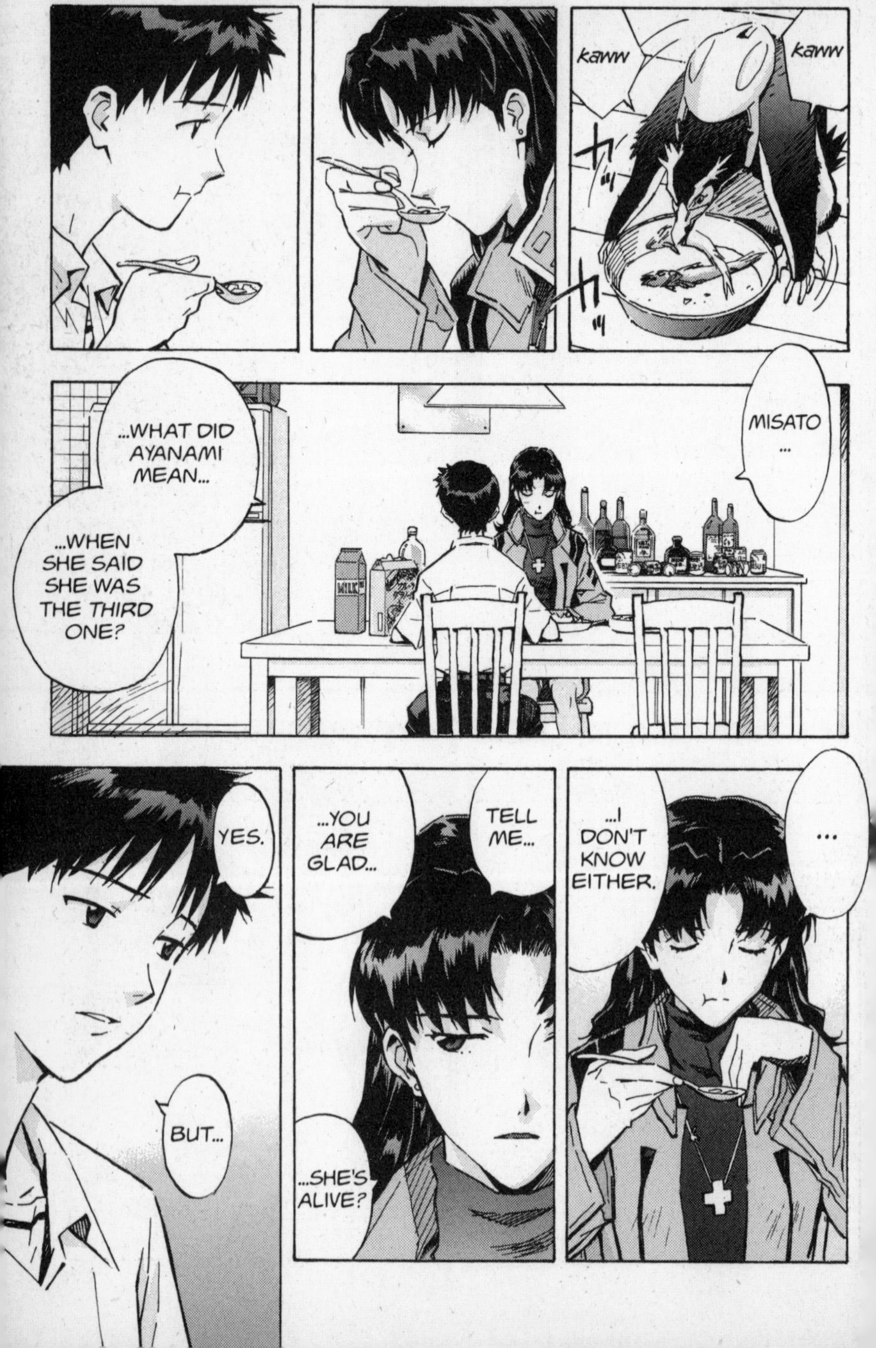
kaww
kaww
MISATO ...
...WHAT DID AYANAMI MEAN...
...WHEN SHE SAID SHE WAS THE THIRD ONE?
...
...I DON'T KNOW EITHER.
TELL ME...
...YOU ARE GLAD...
...SHE'S ALIVE?
YES.
BUT...

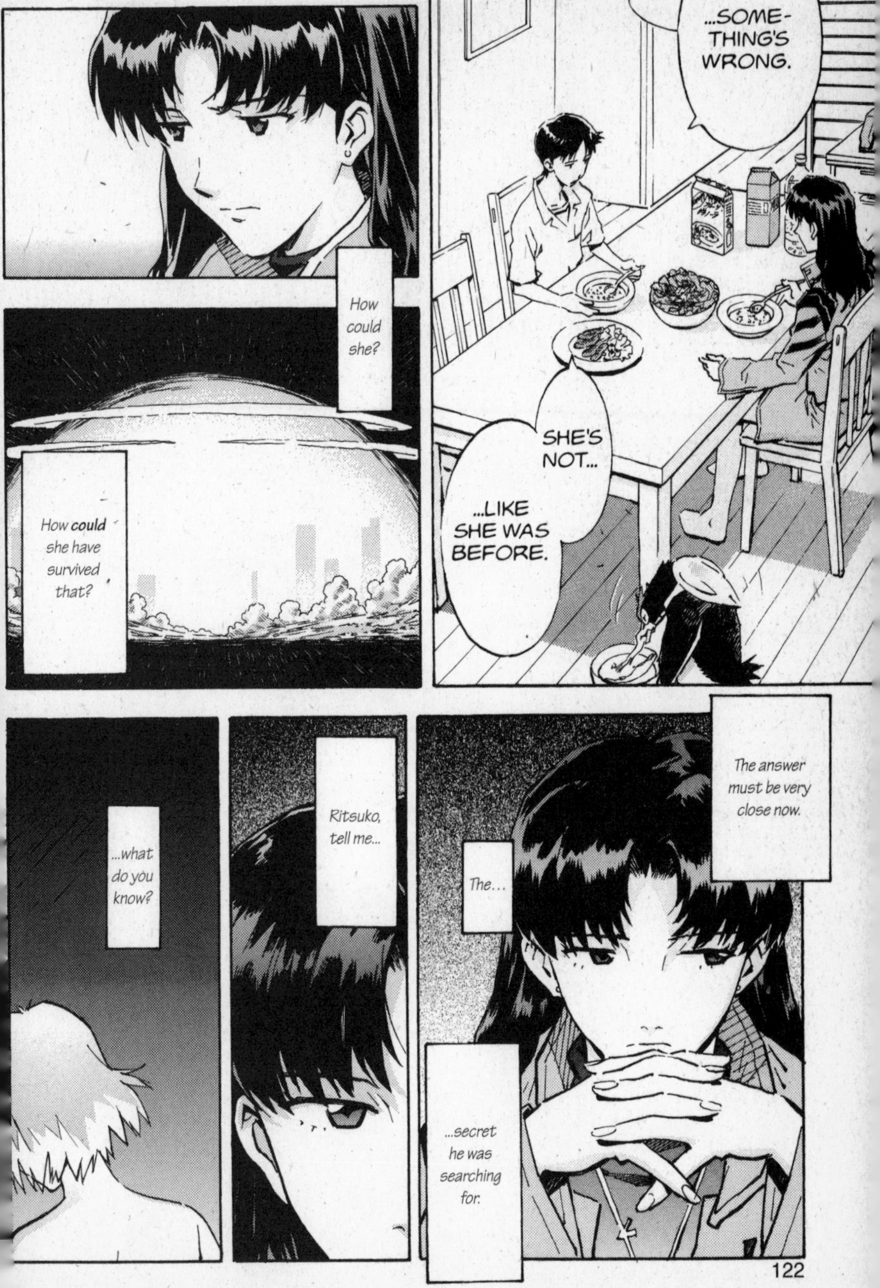
...SOME-THING'S WRONG.
SHE'S NOT...
...LIKE SHE WAS BEFORE.
How could she?
How **could** she have survived that?
The answer must be very close now.
The...
...secret he was searching for.
Ritsuko, tell me...
...what do you know?

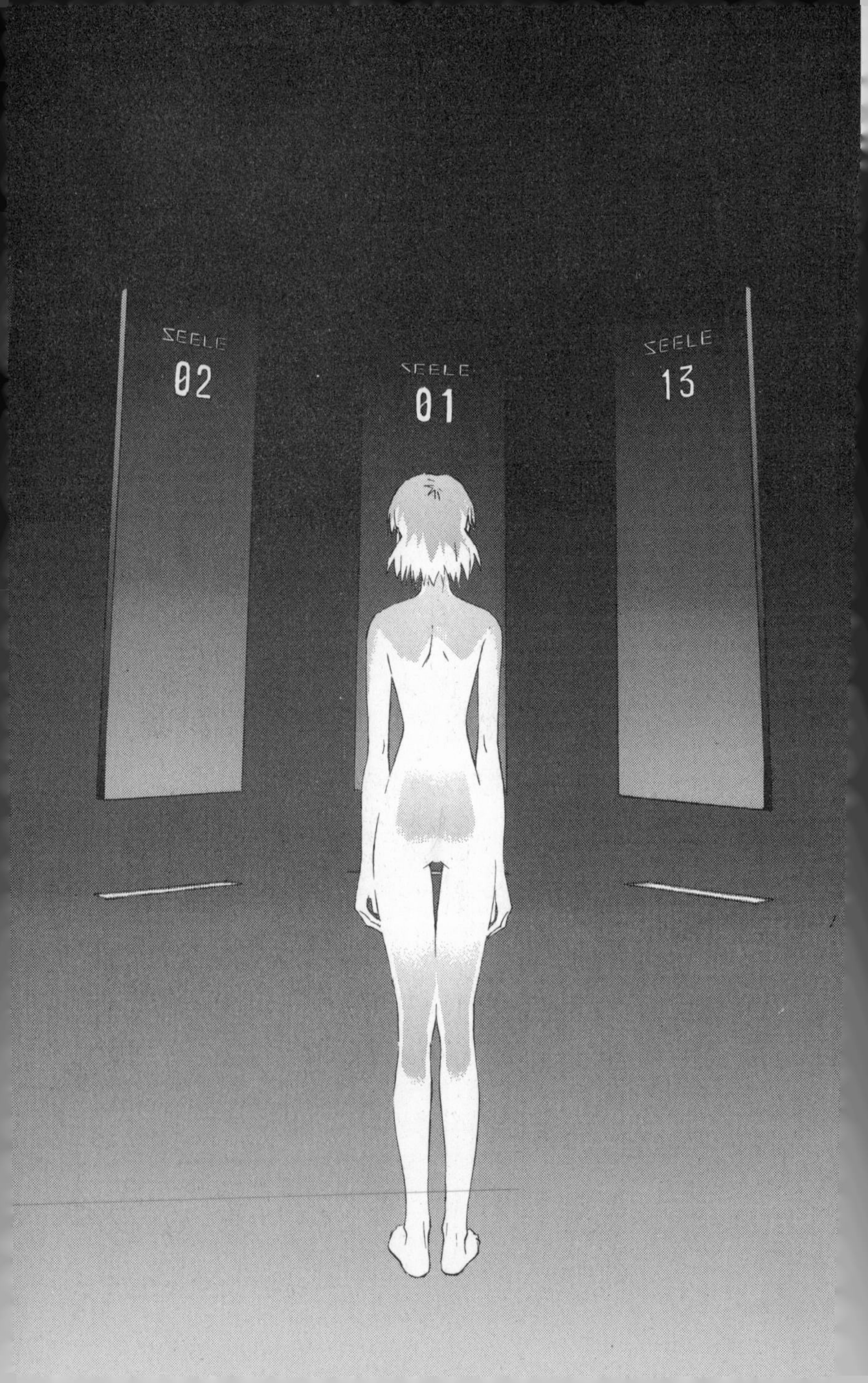
SEELE 01
SEELE 02
SEELE 13

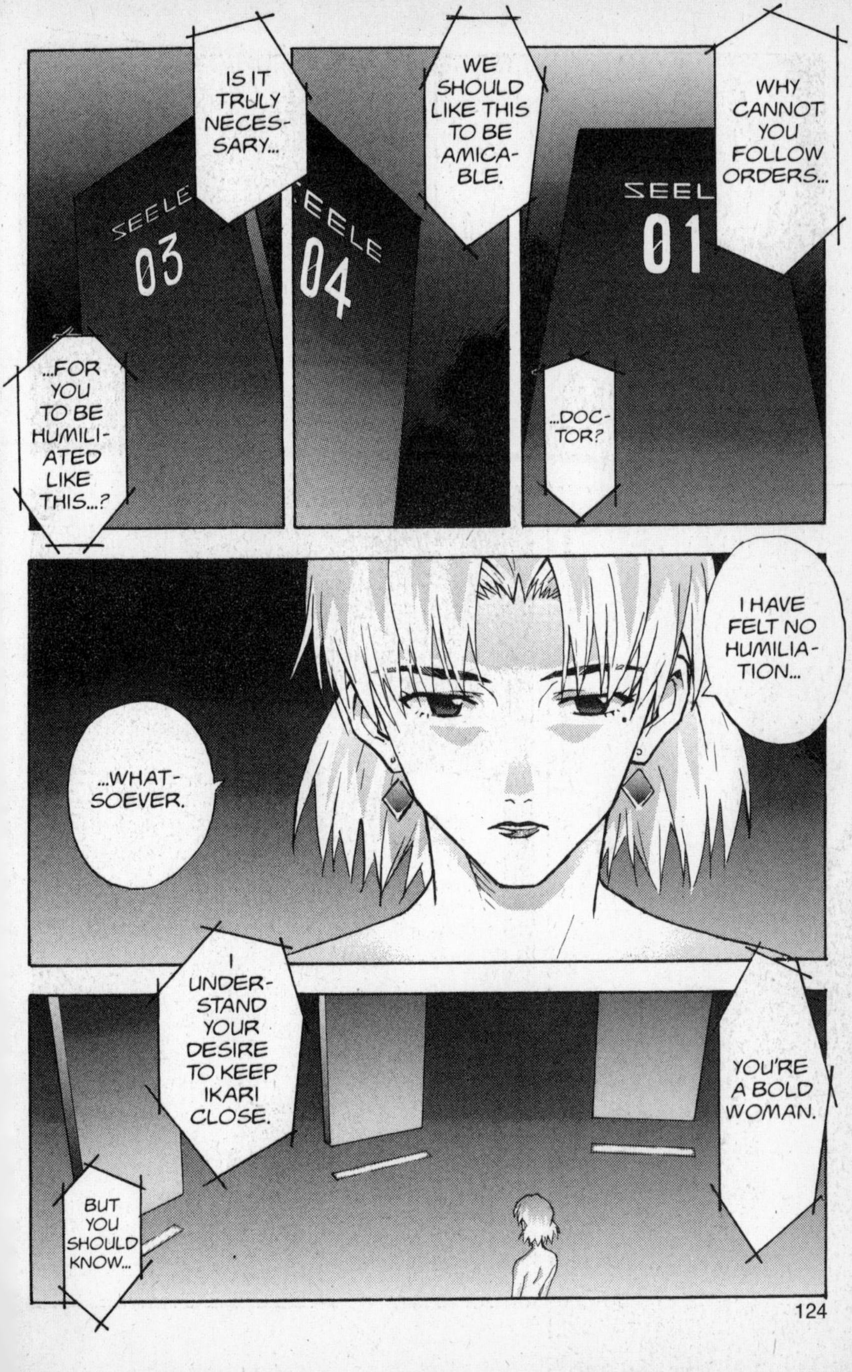
WHY CANNOT YOU FOLLOW ORDERS...
01
...DOCTOR?
WE SHOULD LIKE THIS TO BE AMICABLE.
04
IS IT TRULY NECESSARY...
SEELE 03
...FOR YOU TO BE HUMILIATED LIKE THIS...?
I HAVE FELT NO HUMILIATION...
...WHATSOEVER.
YOU'RE A BOLD WOMAN.
I UNDERSTAND YOUR DESIRE TO KEEP IKARI CLOSE.
BUT YOU SHOULD KNOW...

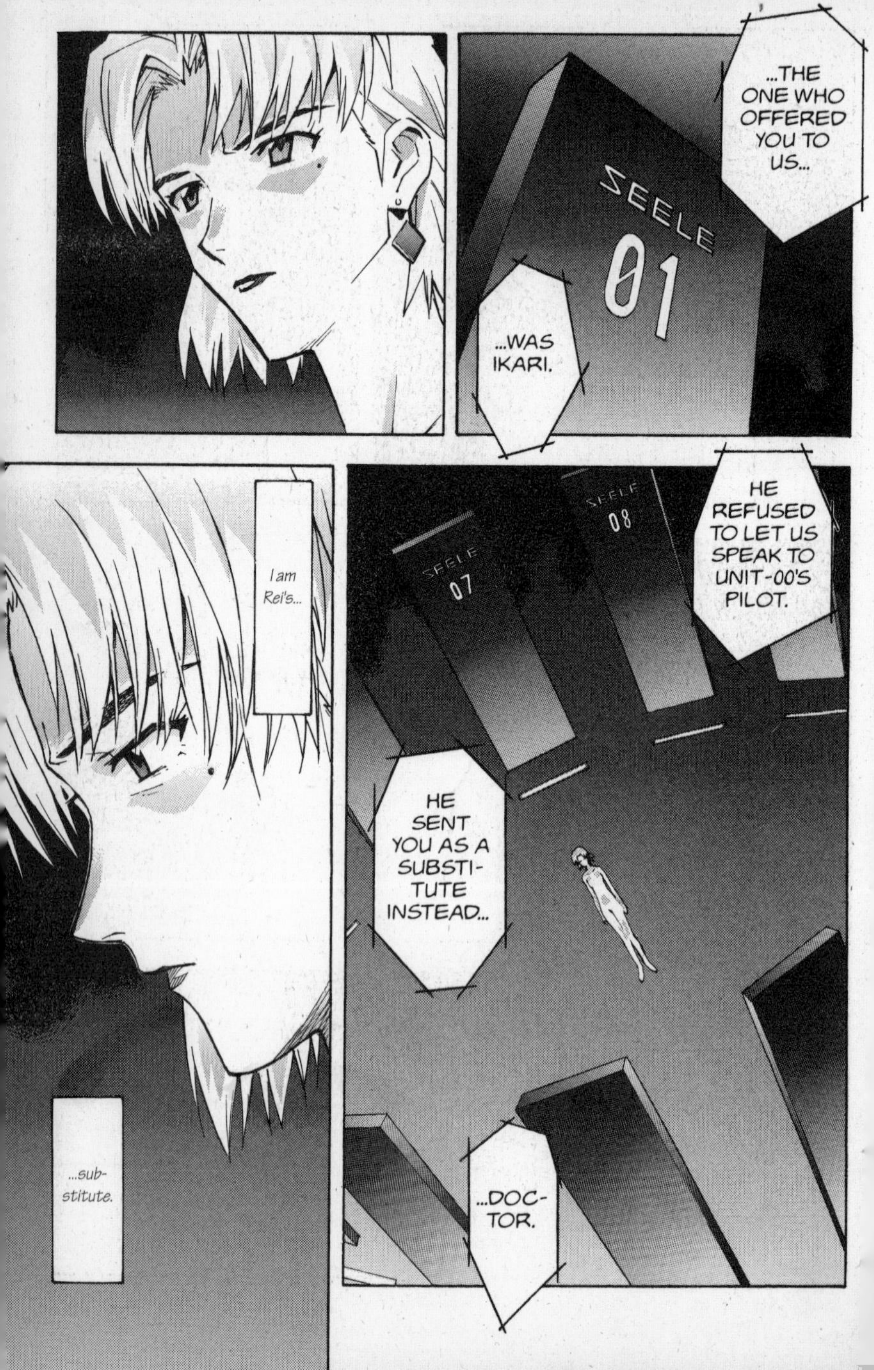
...THE ONE WHO OFFERED YOU TO US...
SEELE 01
...WAS IKARI.
HE REFUSED TO LET US SPEAK TO UNIT-00'S PILOT.
SEELE 08
SEELE 07
HE SENT YOU AS A SUBSTITUTE INSTEAD...
...DOCTOR.
I am Rei's...
...substitute.

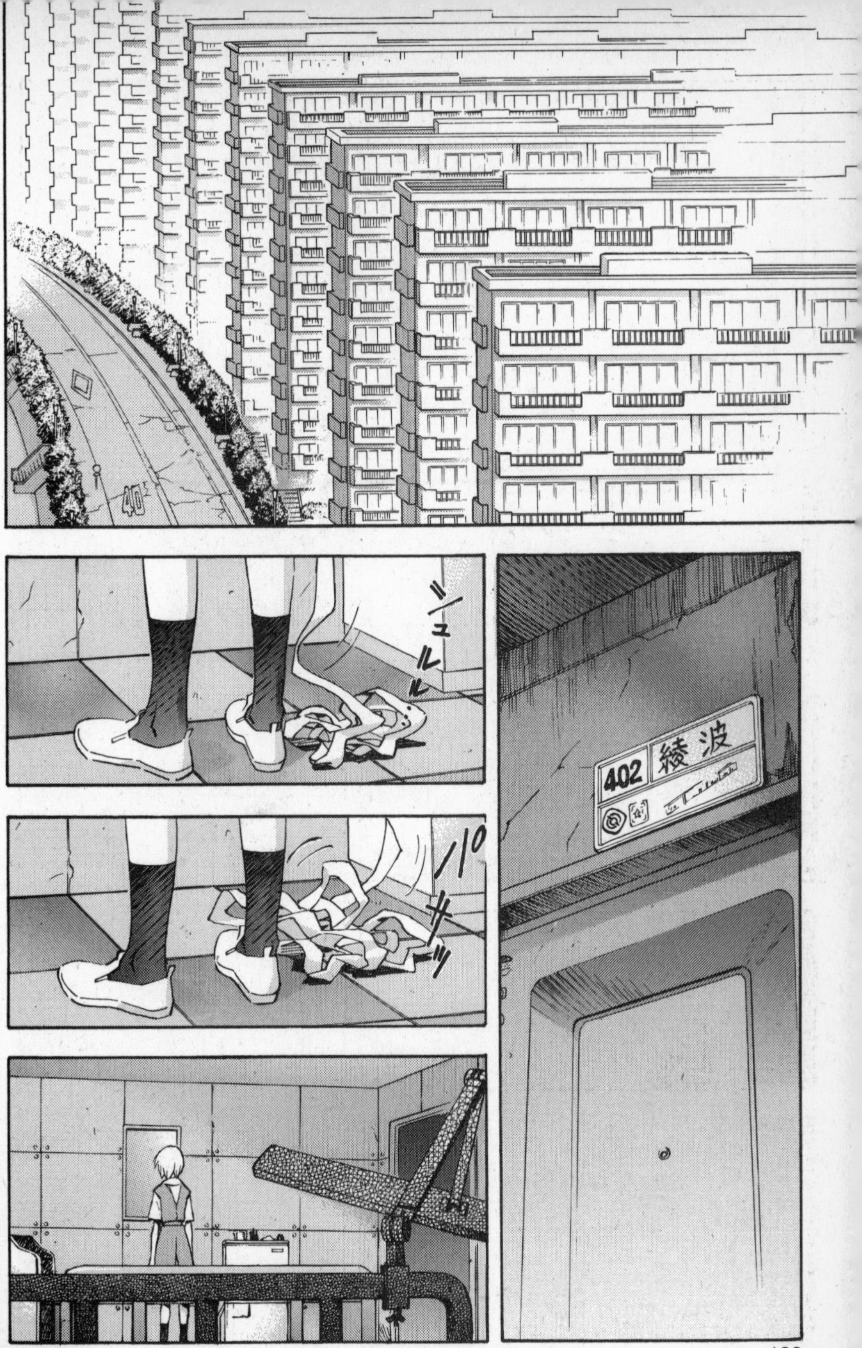
40
402
綾波
シュルル
パサッ

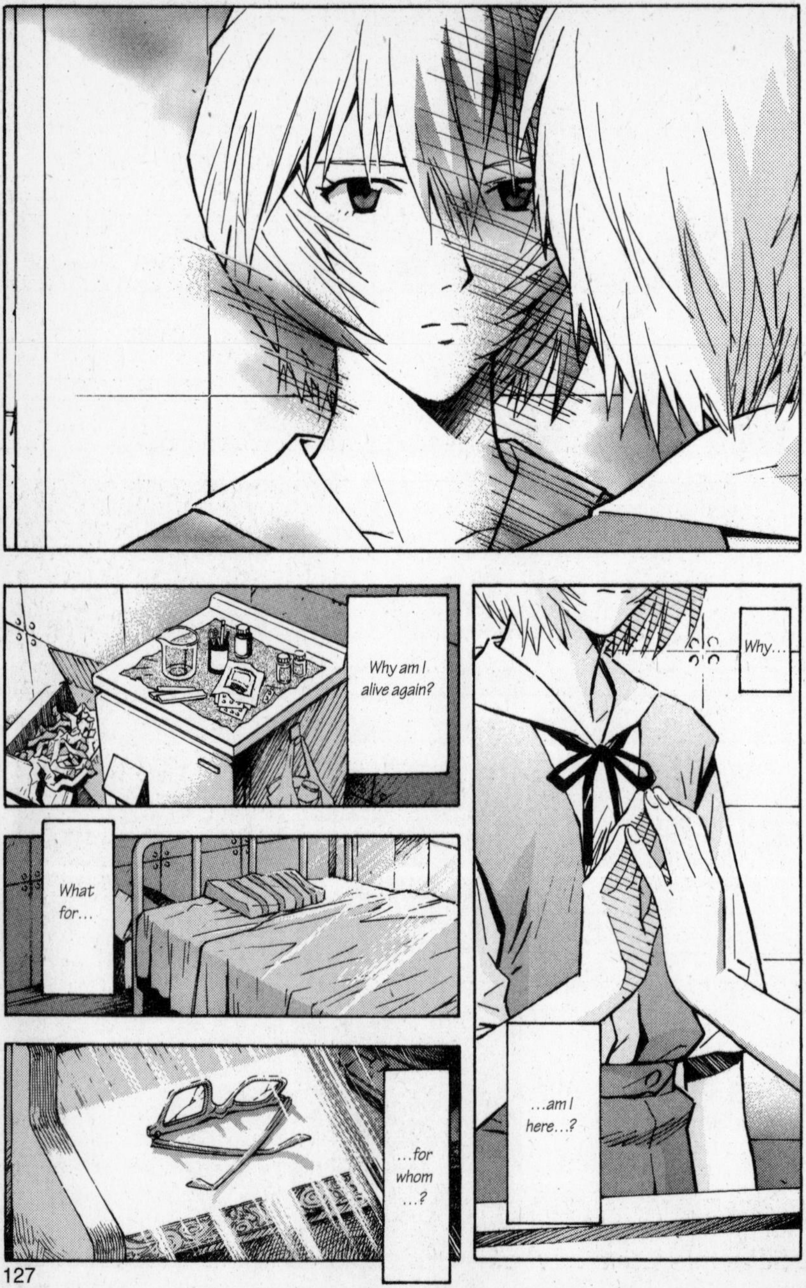
Why…
…am I here…?
Why am I alive again?
What for…
…for whom …?

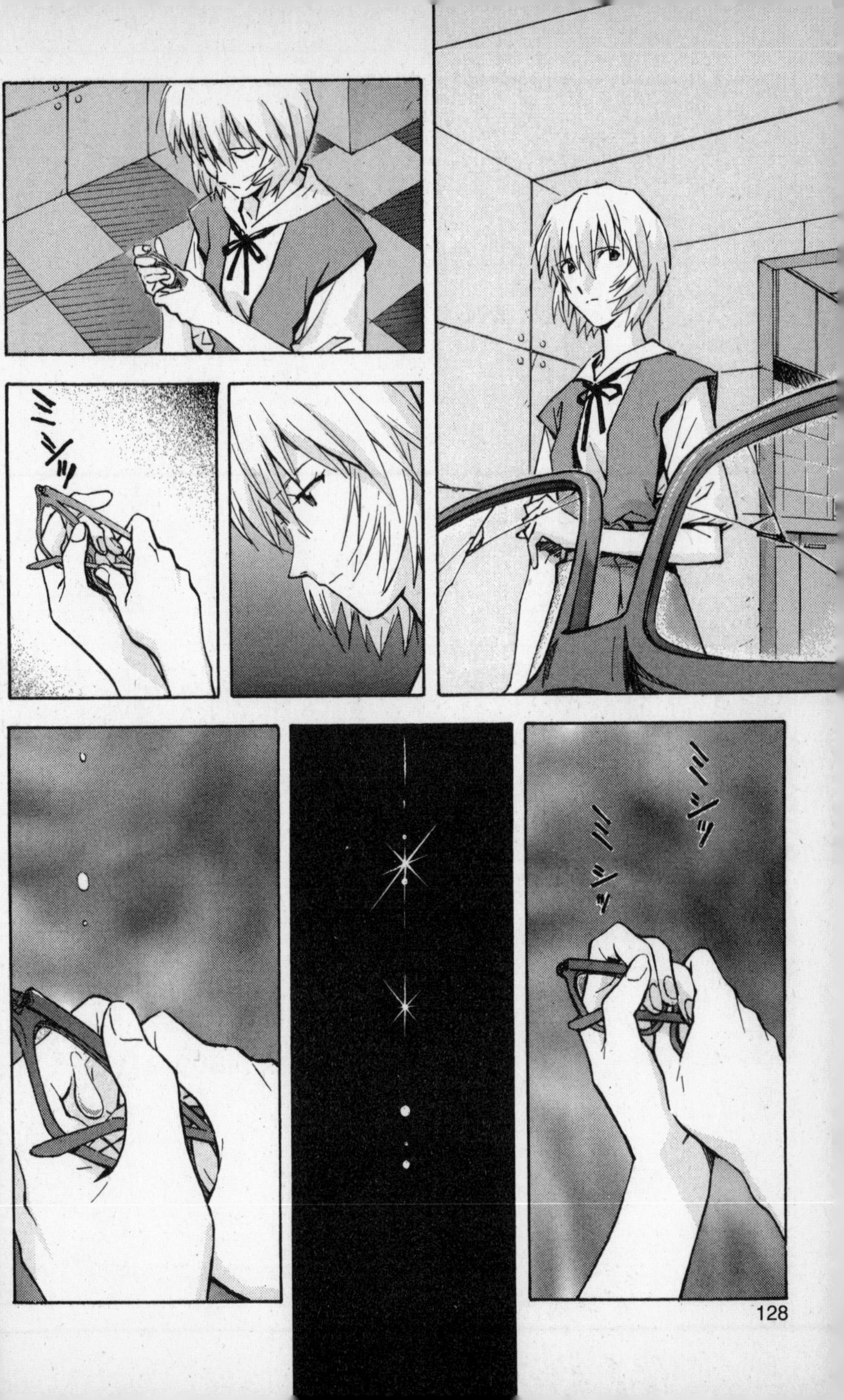
ミシッ
ミシッ
ミシッ

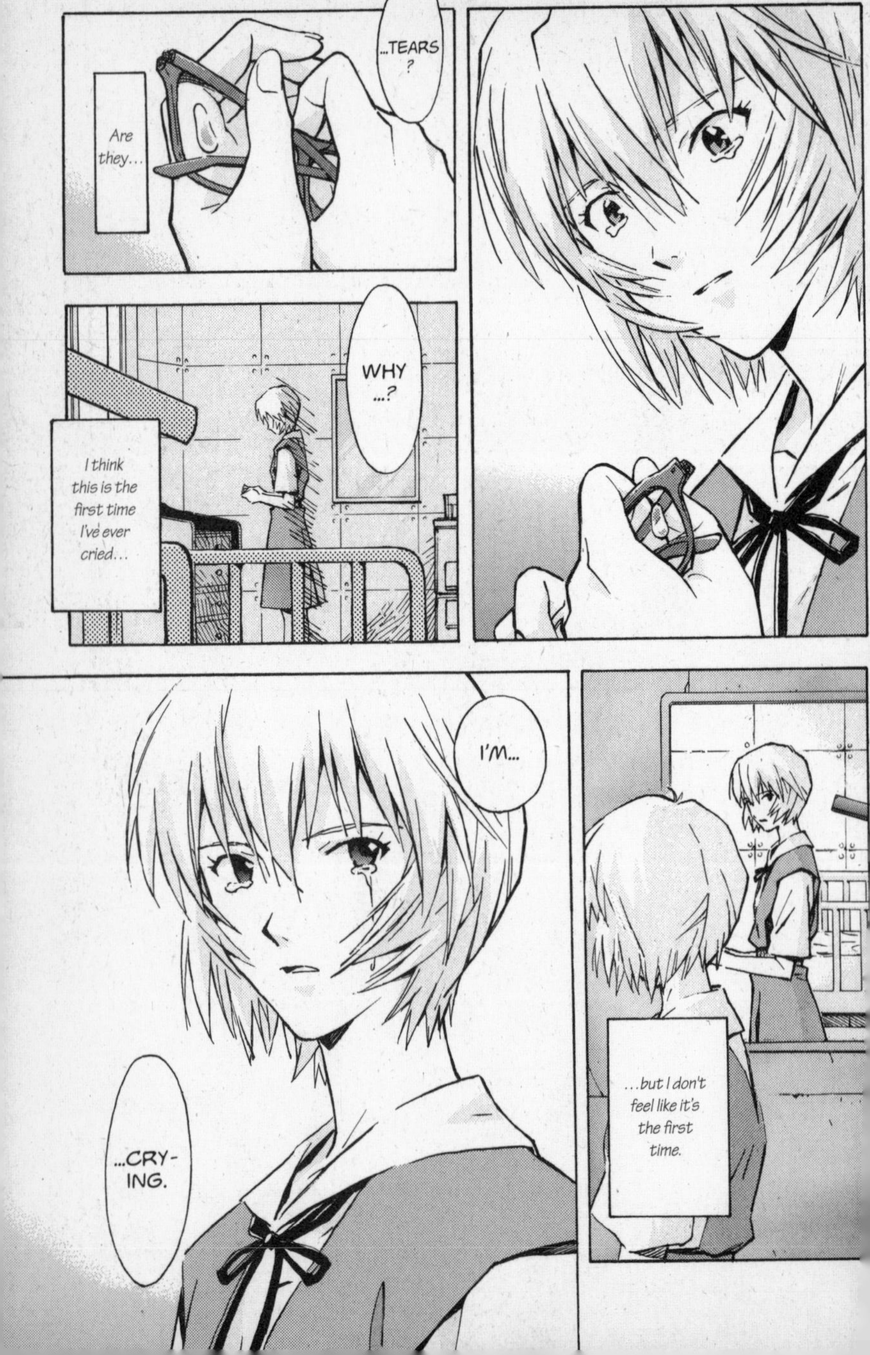

...TEARS ?
Are they...
WHY ...?
I think this is the first time I've ever cried...
...but I don't feel like it's the first time.
I'M...
...CRY-ING.

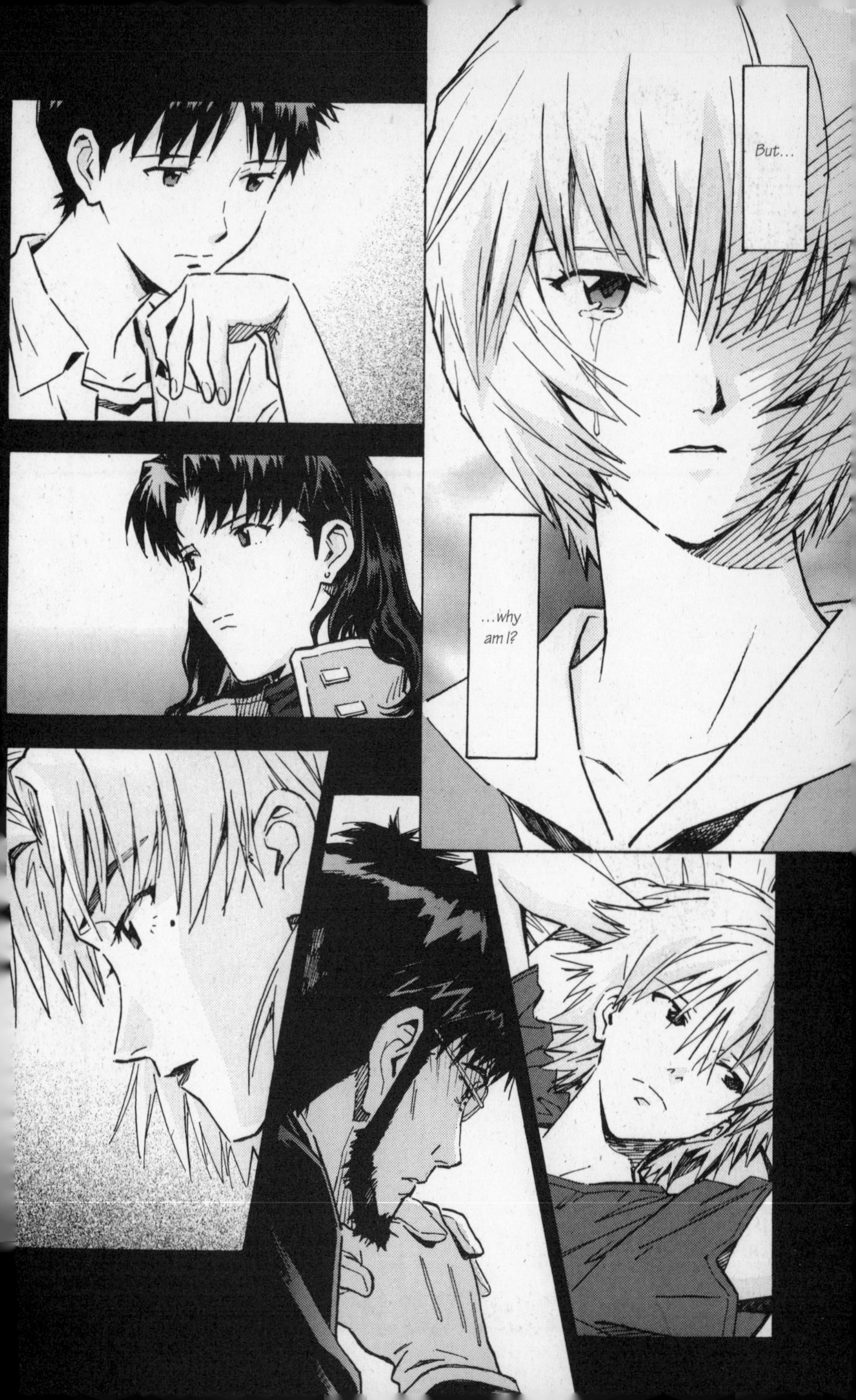
But...
...why am I?

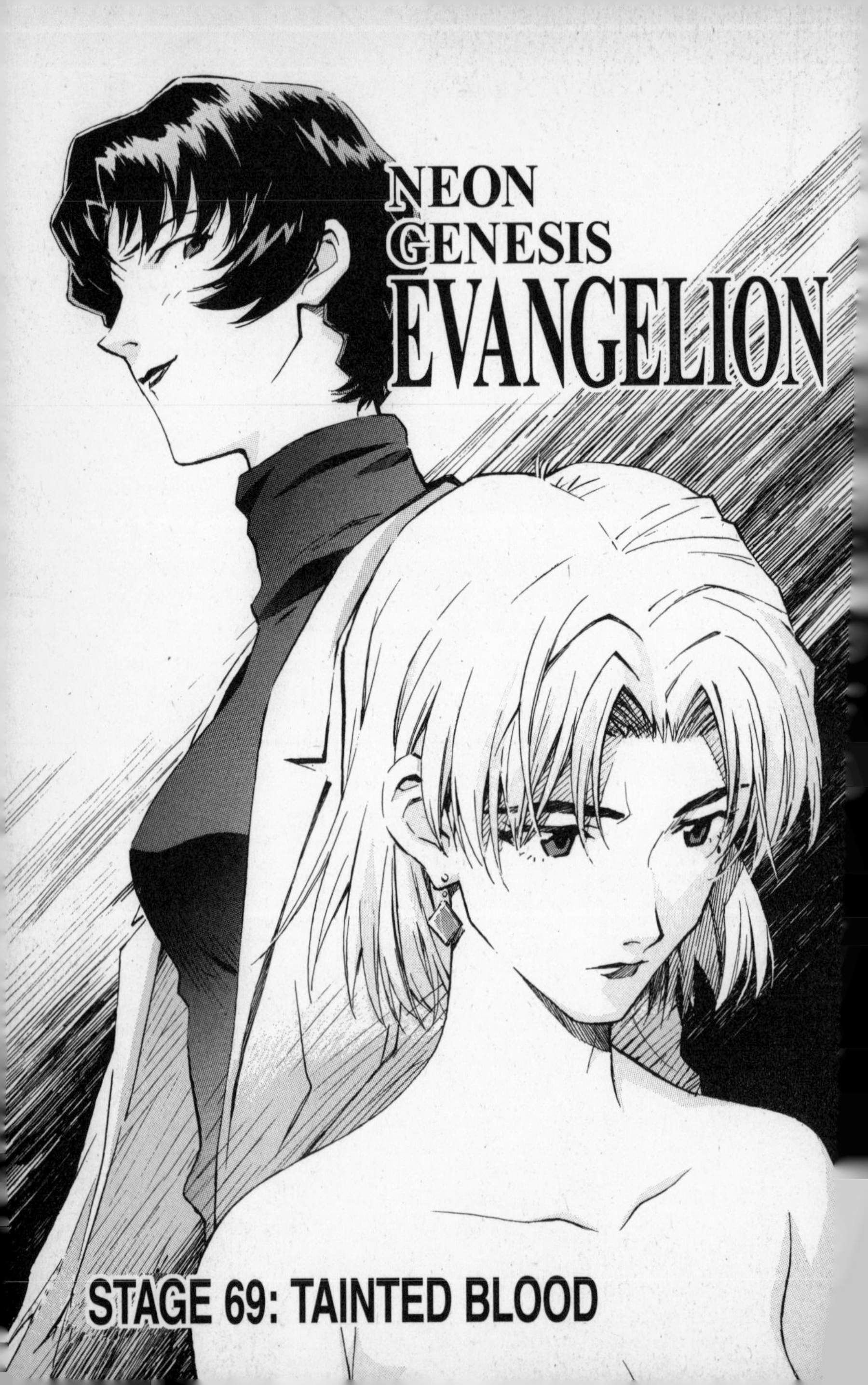
NEON GENESIS EVANGELION
STAGE 69: TAINTED BLOOD

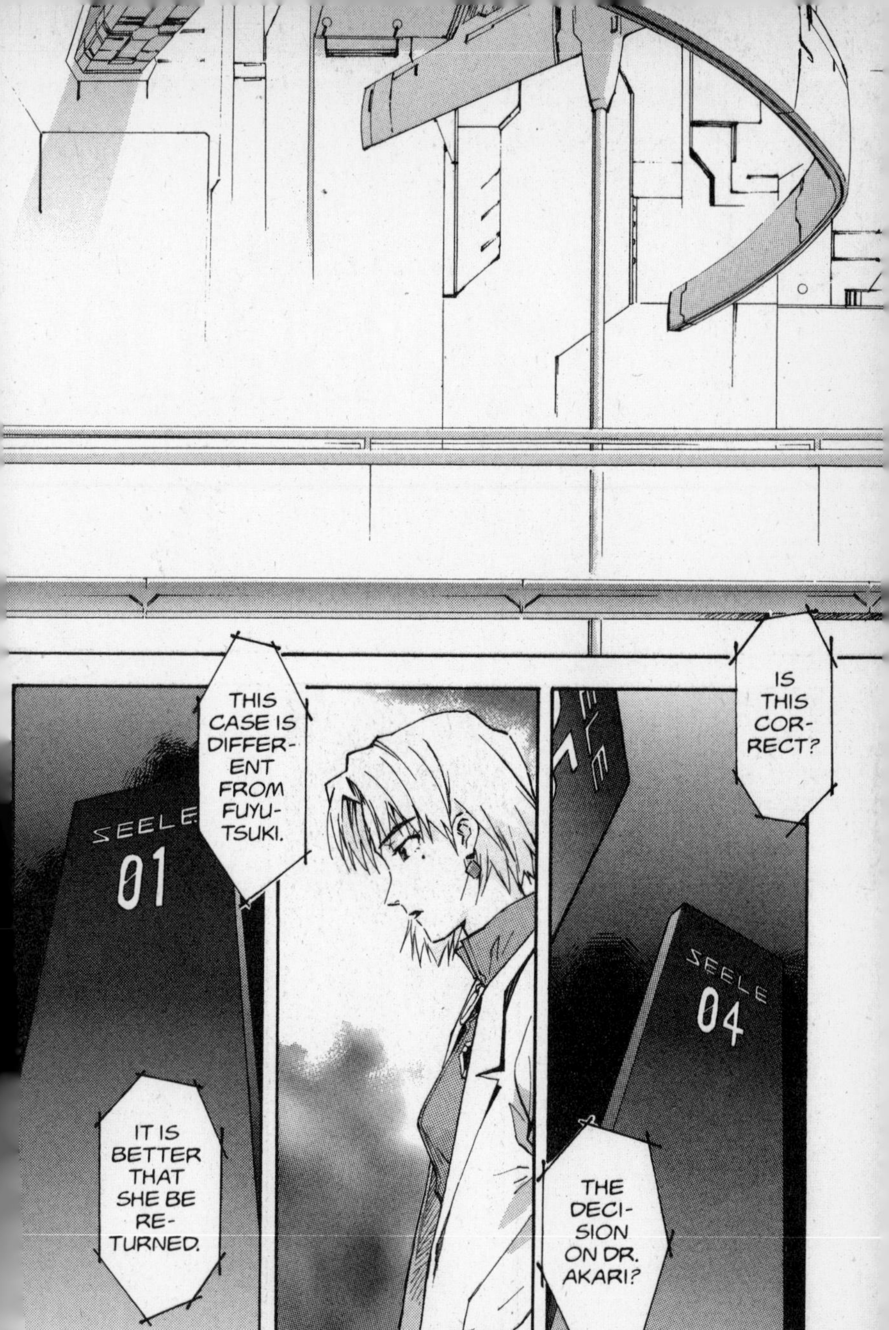
IS THIS CORRECT?
SEELE 04
THE DECISION ON DR. AKARI?
THIS CASE IS DIFFERENT FROM FUYUTSUKI.
SEELE 01
IT IS BETTER THAT SHE BE RETURNED.

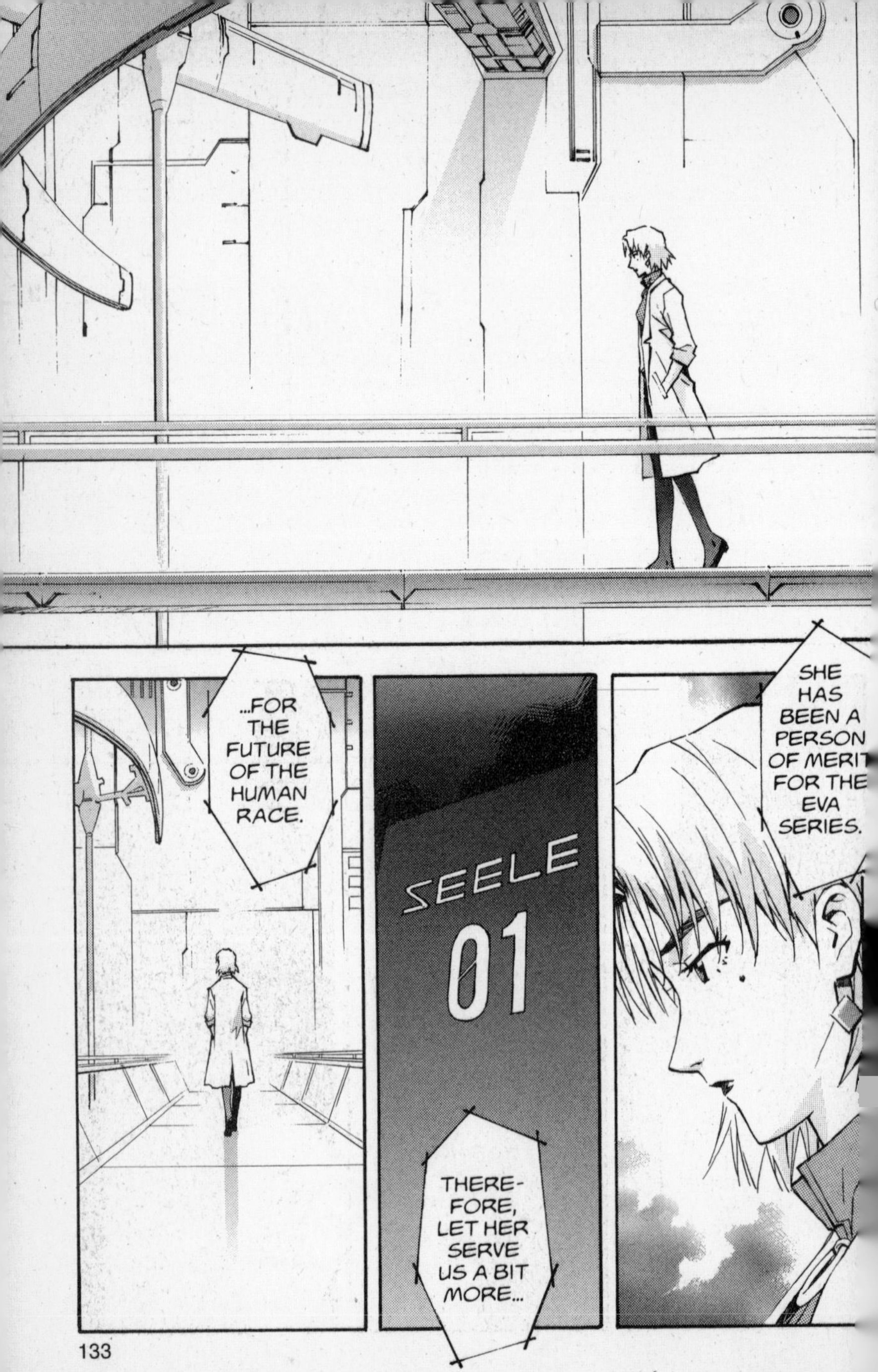
SHE HAS BEEN A PERSON OF MERIT FOR THE EVA SERIES.
SEELE 01
THEREFORE, LET HER SERVE US A BIT MORE...
...FOR THE FUTURE OF THE HUMAN RACE.

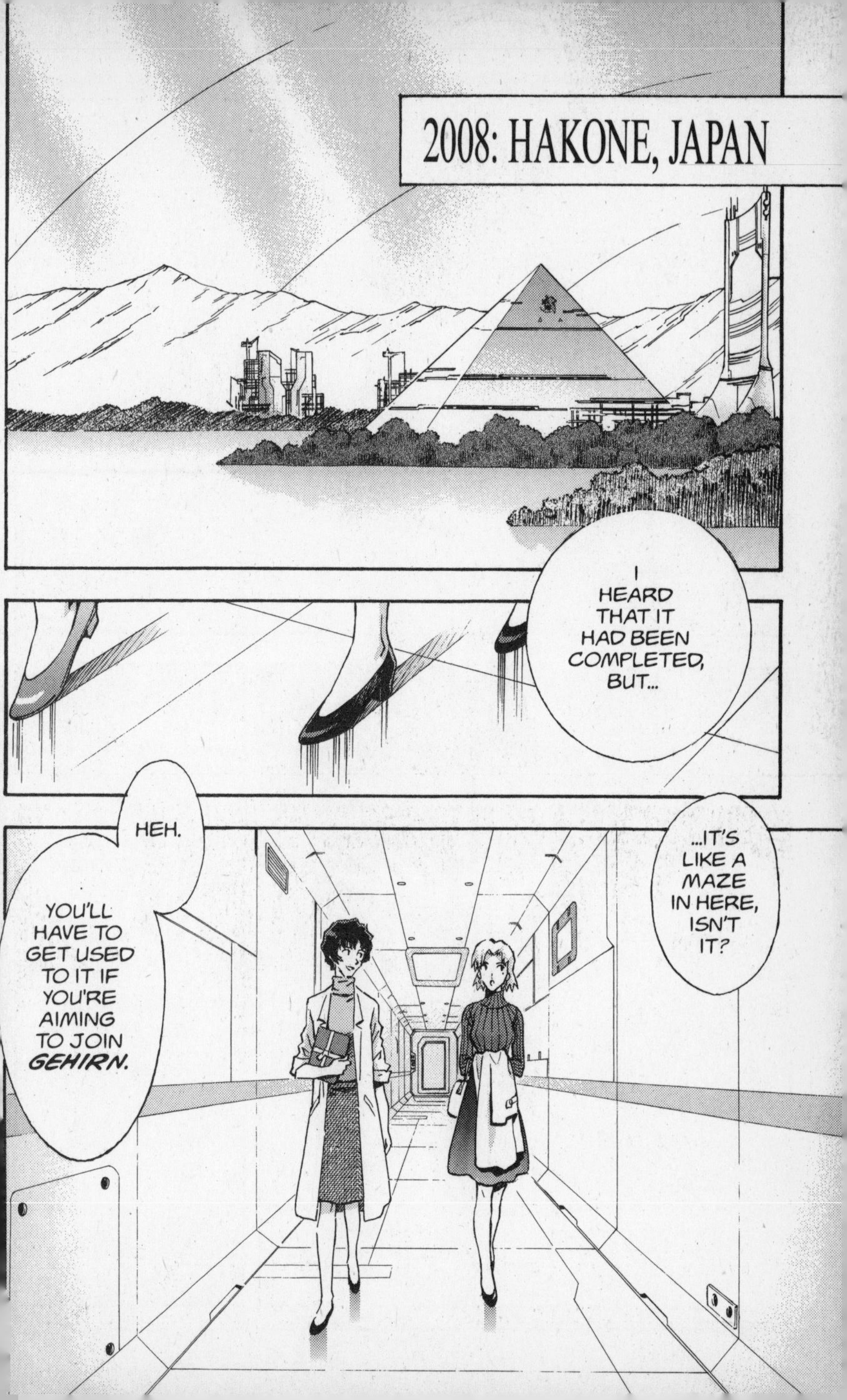
2008: HAKONE, JAPAN
I HEARD THAT IT HAD BEEN COMPLETED, BUT...
...IT'S LIKE A MAZE IN HERE, ISN'T IT?
HEH.
YOU'LL HAVE TO GET USED TO IT IF YOU'RE AIMING TO JOIN *GEHIRN*.

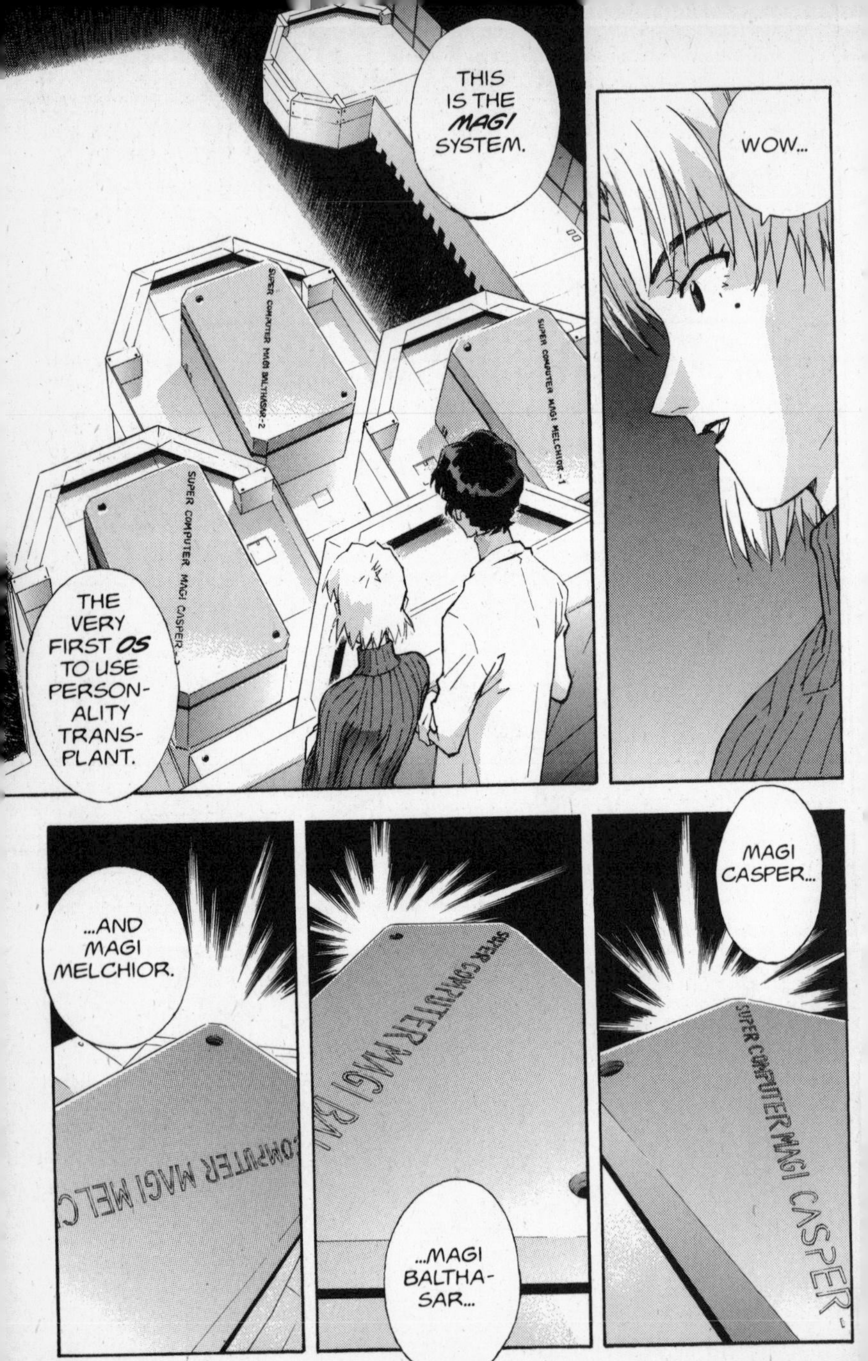
WOW...
THIS IS THE MAGI SYSTEM.
SUPER COMPUTER MAGI MELCHIOR-1
SUPER COMPUTER MAGI BALTHASAR-2
SUPER COMPUTER MAGI CASPER-3
THE VERY FIRST OS TO USE PERSONALITY TRANSPLANT.
MAGI CASPER...
SUPER COMPUTER MAGI CASPER-
...MAGI BALTHASAR...
SUPER COMPUTER MAGI BA
...AND MAGI MELCHIOR.
COMPUTER MAGI MELC

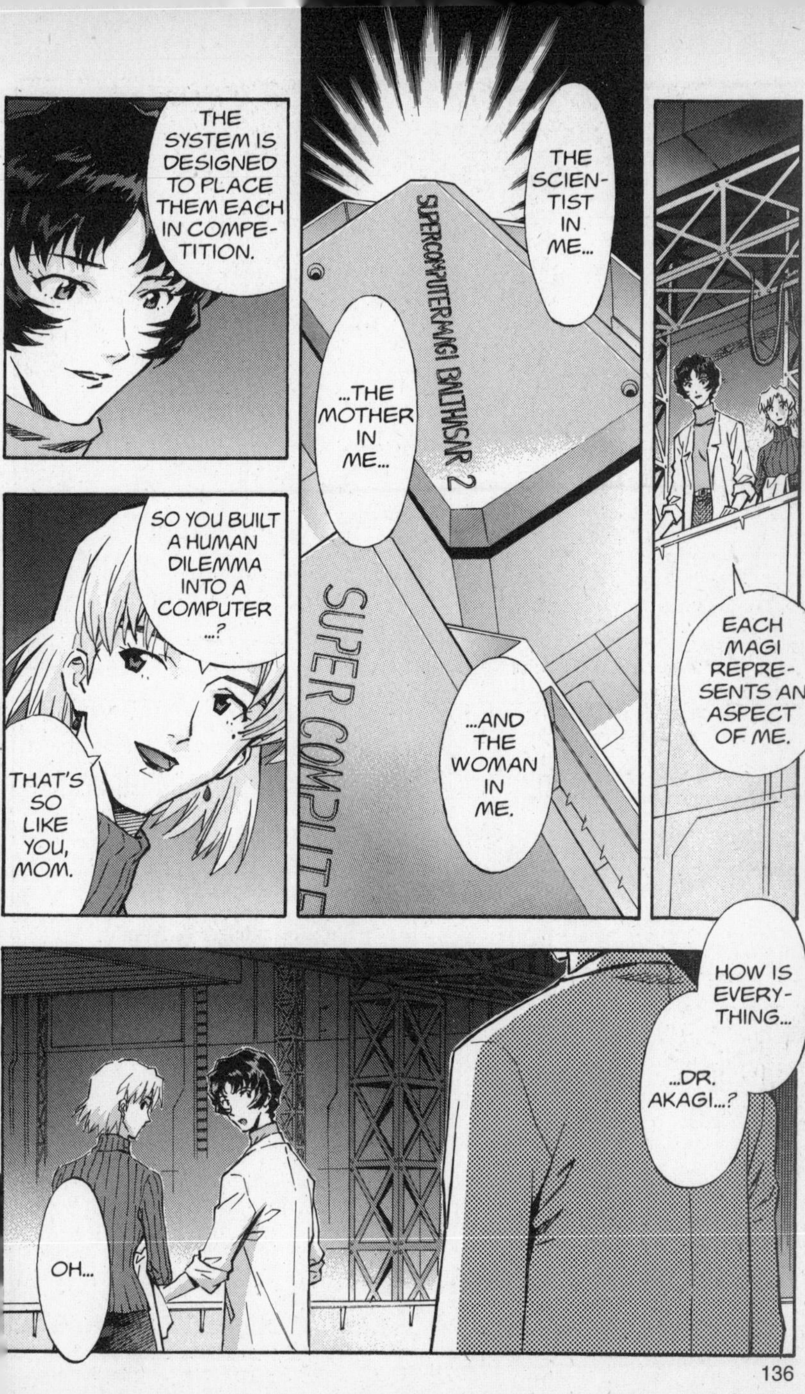
EACH MAGI REPRESENTS AN ASPECT OF ME.
THE SCIENTIST IN ME...
SUPERCOMPUTERMAGI BALTHASAR 2
...THE MOTHER IN ME...
SUPER COMPUTE
...AND THE WOMAN IN ME.
THE SYSTEM IS DESIGNED TO PLACE THEM EACH IN COMPETITION.
SO YOU BUILT A HUMAN DILEMMA INTO A COMPUTER ...?
THAT'S SO LIKE YOU, MOM.
HOW IS EVERYTHING...
...DR. AKAGI...?
OH...

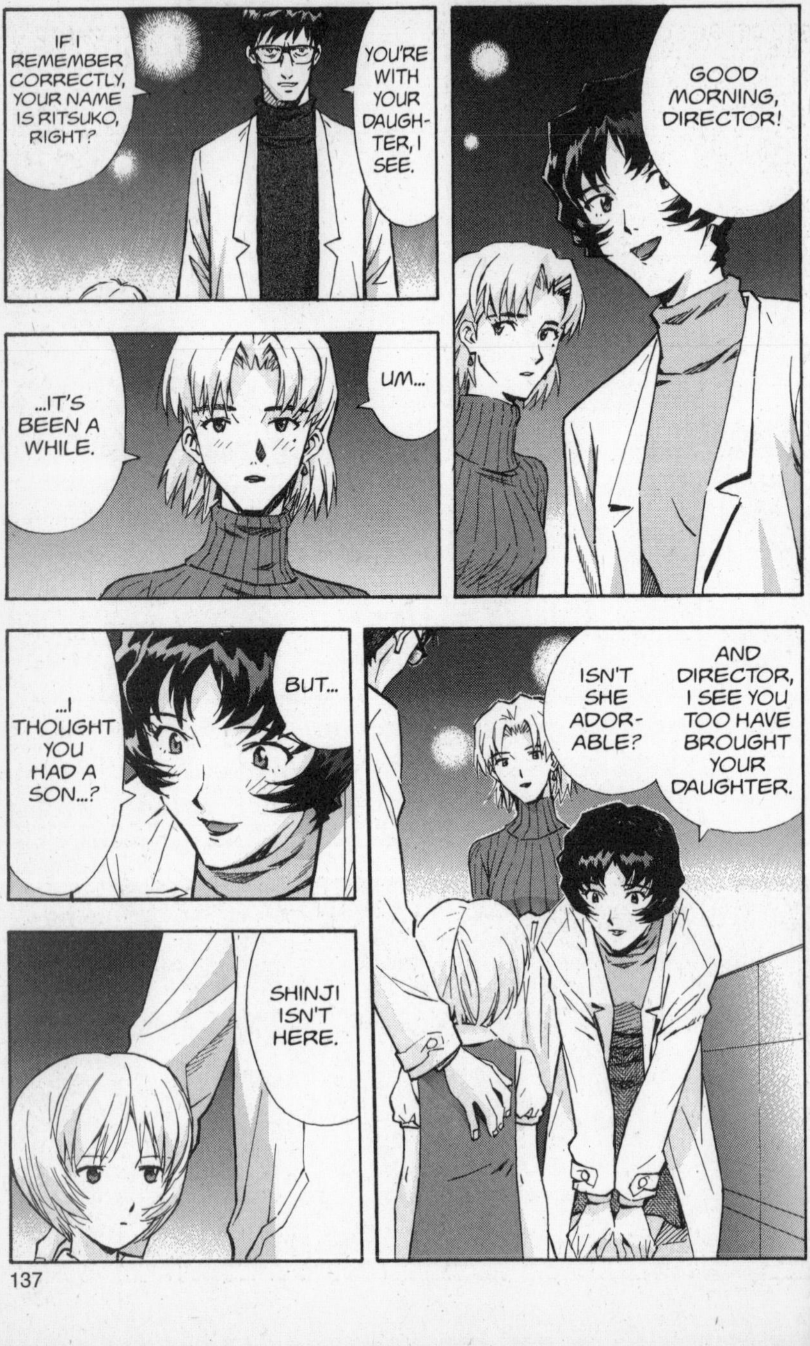
GOOD MORNING, DIRECTOR!
YOU'RE WITH YOUR DAUGHTER, I SEE.
IF I REMEMBER CORRECTLY, YOUR NAME IS RITSUKO, RIGHT?
UM...
...IT'S BEEN A WHILE.
AND DIRECTOR, I SEE YOU TOO HAVE BROUGHT YOUR DAUGHTER.
ISN'T SHE ADORABLE?
BUT...
...I THOUGHT YOU HAD A SON...?
SHINJI ISN'T HERE.

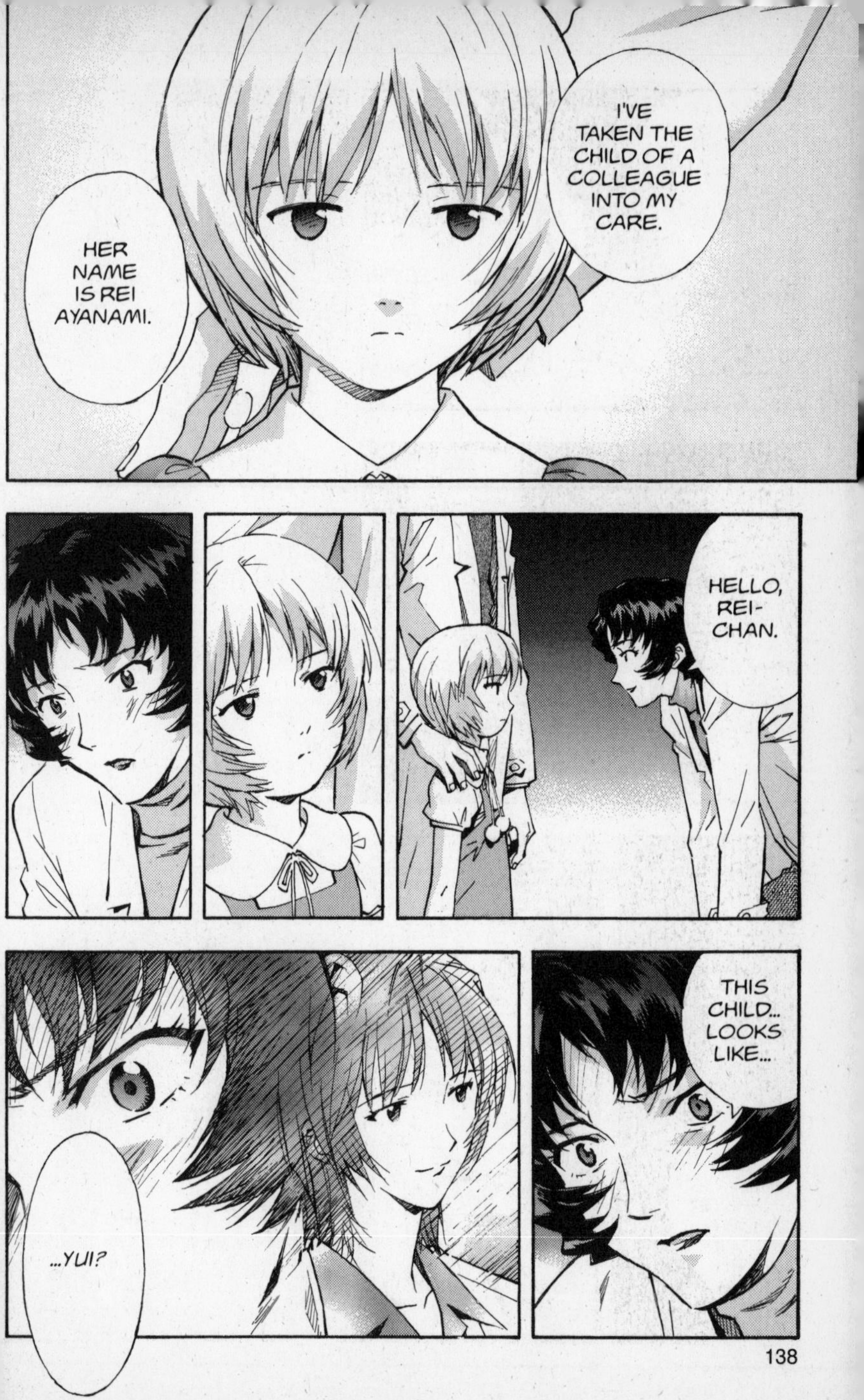
I'VE TAKEN THE CHILD OF A COLLEAGUE INTO MY CARE.
HER NAME IS REI AYANAMI.
HELLO, REI-CHAN.
THIS CHILD... LOOKS LIKE...
...YUI?

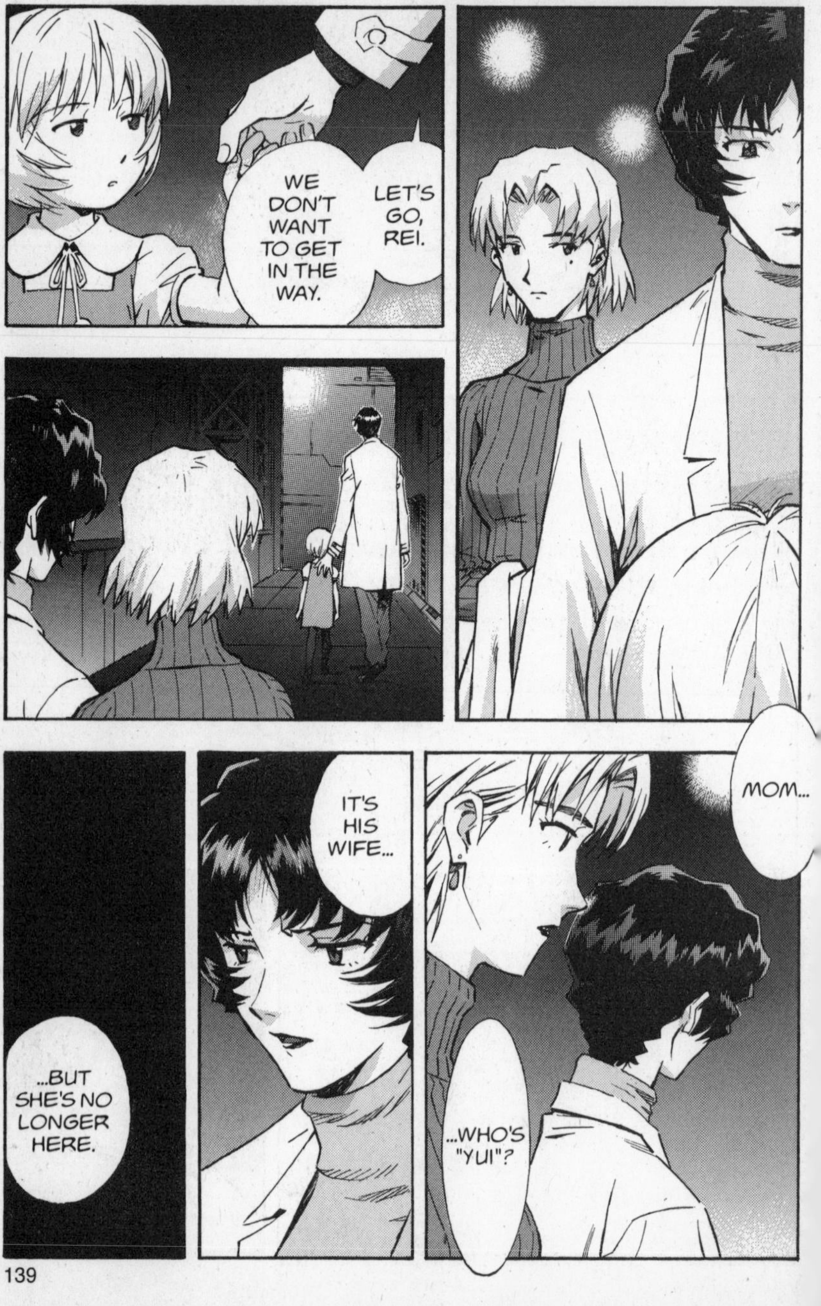
LET'S GO, REI.
WE DON'T WANT TO GET IN THE WAY.
MOM...
...WHO'S "YUI"?
IT'S HIS WIFE...
...BUT SHE'S NO LONGER HERE.

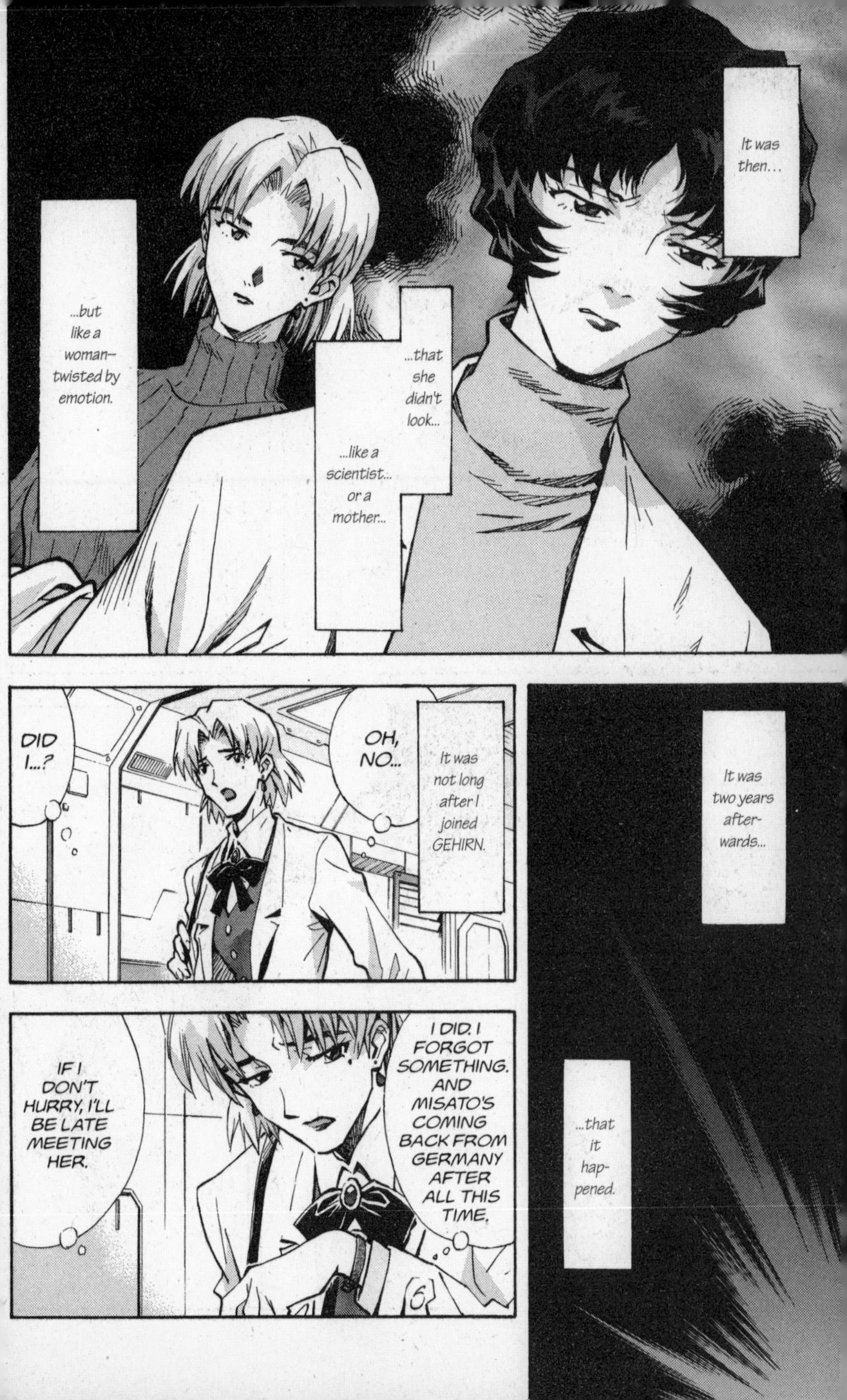
It was then...
...that she didn't look...
...like a scientist... or a mother...
...but like a woman— twisted by emotion.
It was two years afterwards...
...that it happened.
It was not long after I joined GEHIRN.
OH, NO...
DID I...?
I DID. I FORGOT SOMETHING. AND MISATO'S COMING BACK FROM GERMANY AFTER ALL THIS TIME.
IF I DON'T HURRY, I'LL BE LATE MEETING HER.

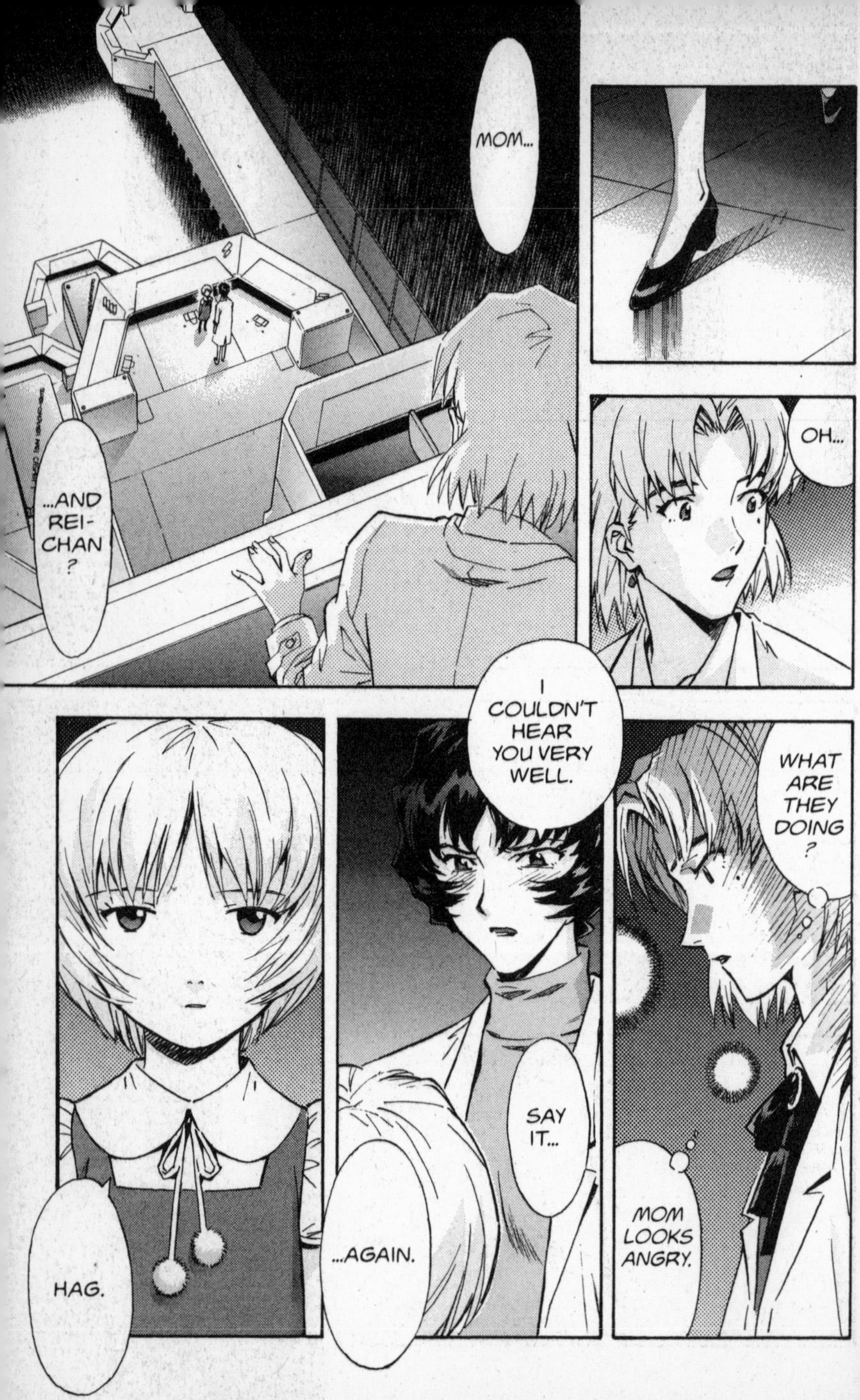
OH...
MOM...
...AND REI-CHAN?
WHAT ARE THEY DOING?
MOM LOOKS ANGRY.
I COULDN'T HEAR YOU VERY WELL.
SAY IT...
...AGAIN.
HAG.

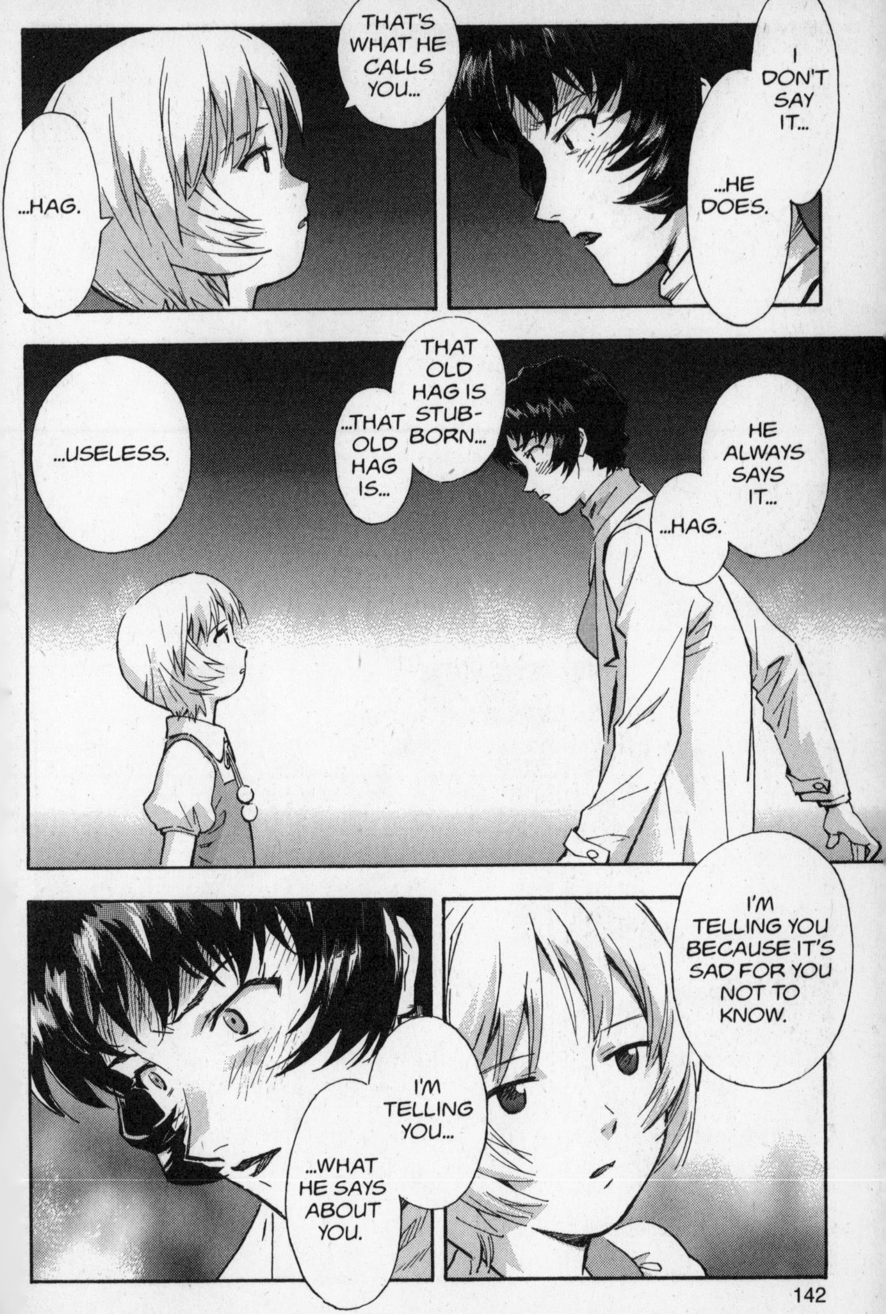
I DON'T SAY IT...
...HE DOES.
THAT'S WHAT HE CALLS YOU...
...HAG.
HE ALWAYS SAYS IT...
...HAG.
THAT OLD HAG IS STUB-BORN...
...THAT OLD HAG IS...
...USELESS.
I'M TELLING YOU BECAUSE IT'S SAD FOR YOU NOT TO KNOW.
I'M TELLING YOU...
...WHAT HE SAYS ABOUT YOU.

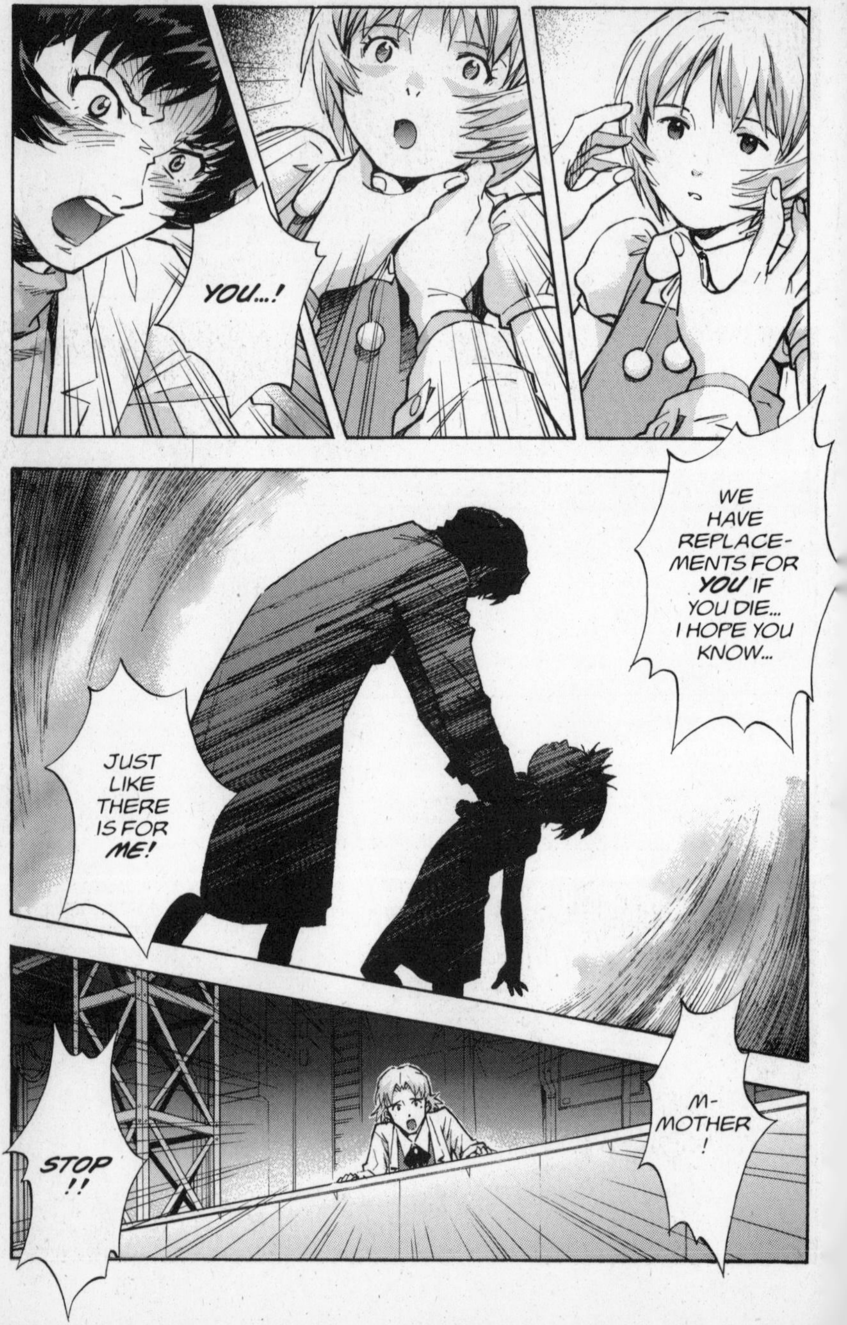
YOU...!
WE HAVE REPLACEMENTS FOR YOU IF YOU DIE... I HOPE YOU KNOW...
JUST LIKE THERE IS FOR ME!
M-MOTHER!
STOP!!

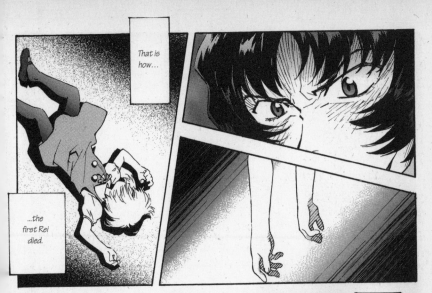

That is how...

...the first Rei died.

And my mother ran...

...and threw herself off...

...the top of MAGI Melchior.

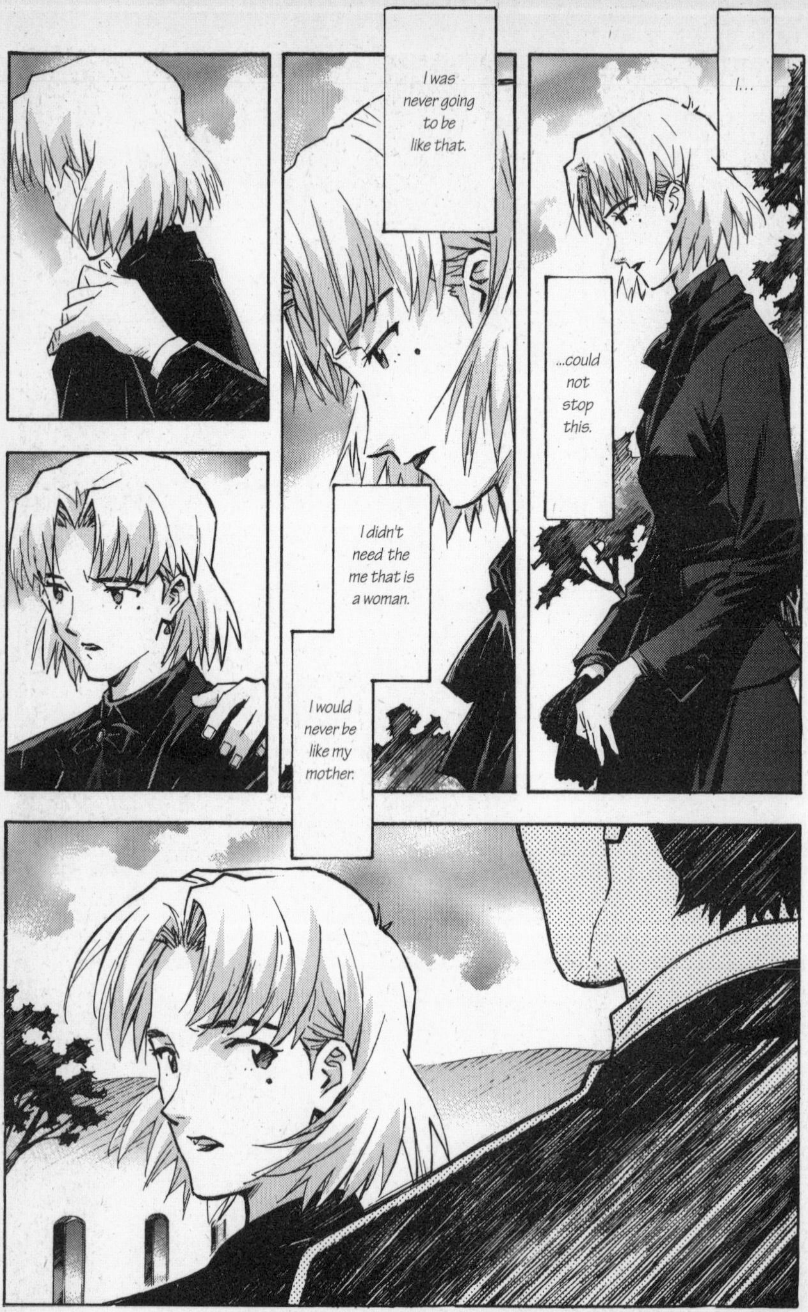
I...
...could not stop this.
I was never going to be like that.
I didn't need the me that is a woman.
I would never be like my mother.

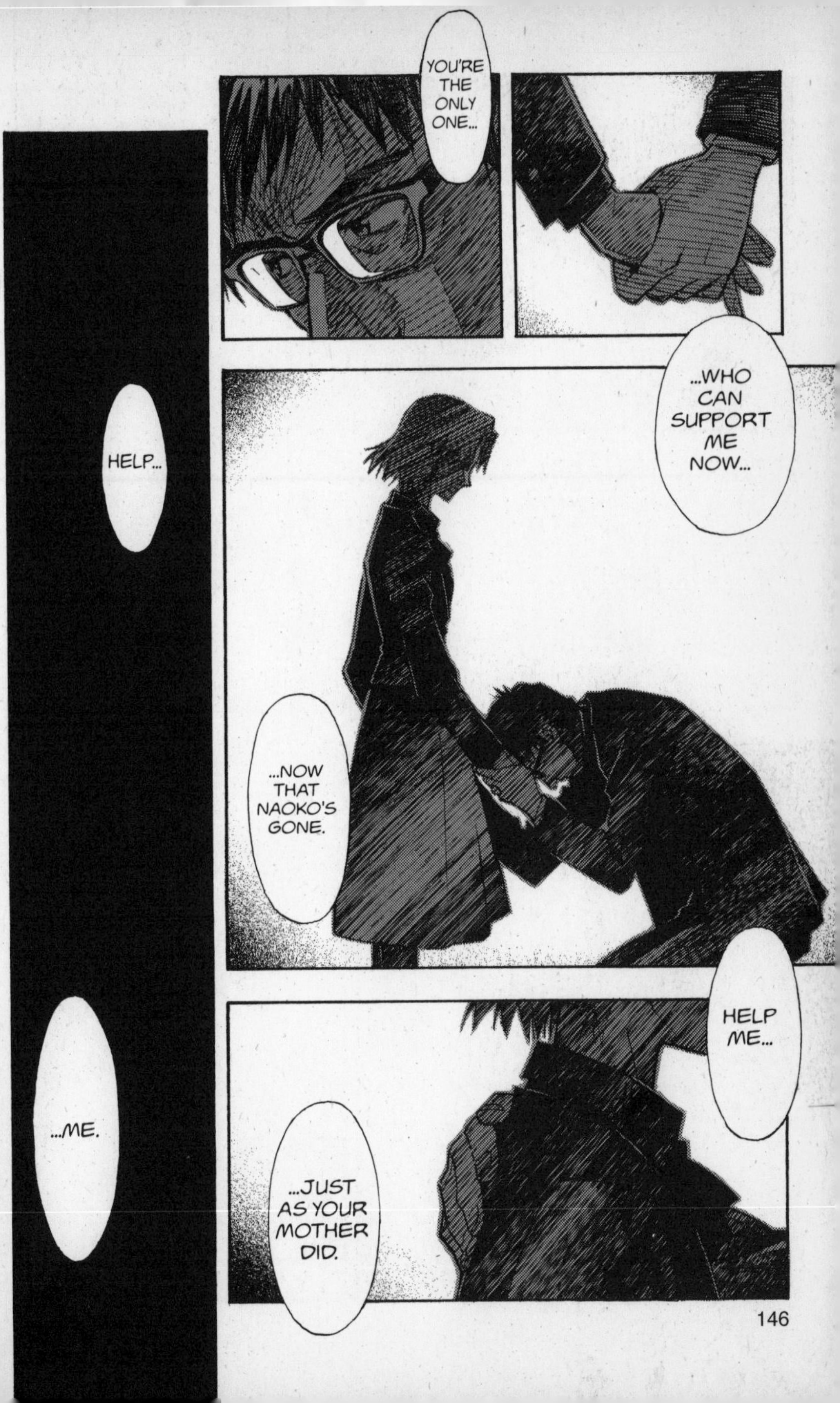
YOU'RE THE ONLY ONE...
...WHO CAN SUPPORT ME NOW...
...NOW THAT NAOKO'S GONE.
HELP ME...
...JUST AS YOUR MOTHER DID.
HELP...
...ME.

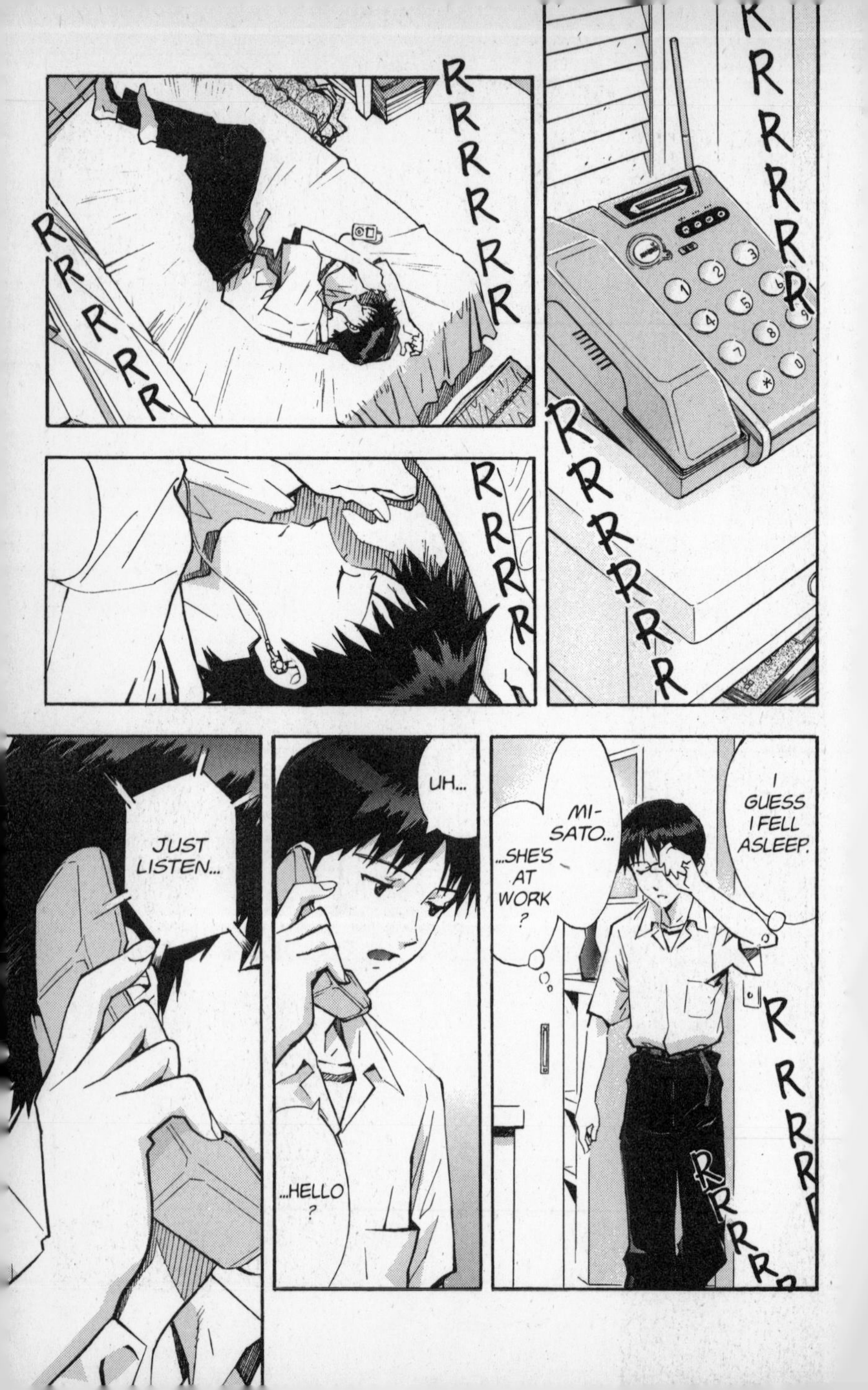

RRRRRRR
RRRRRRR
RRRRRR
RRRRRR
RRRR
I GUESS I FELL ASLEEP.
MI-SATO...
...SHE'S AT WORK?
RRRRRRRR
UH...
...HELLO?
JUST LISTEN...

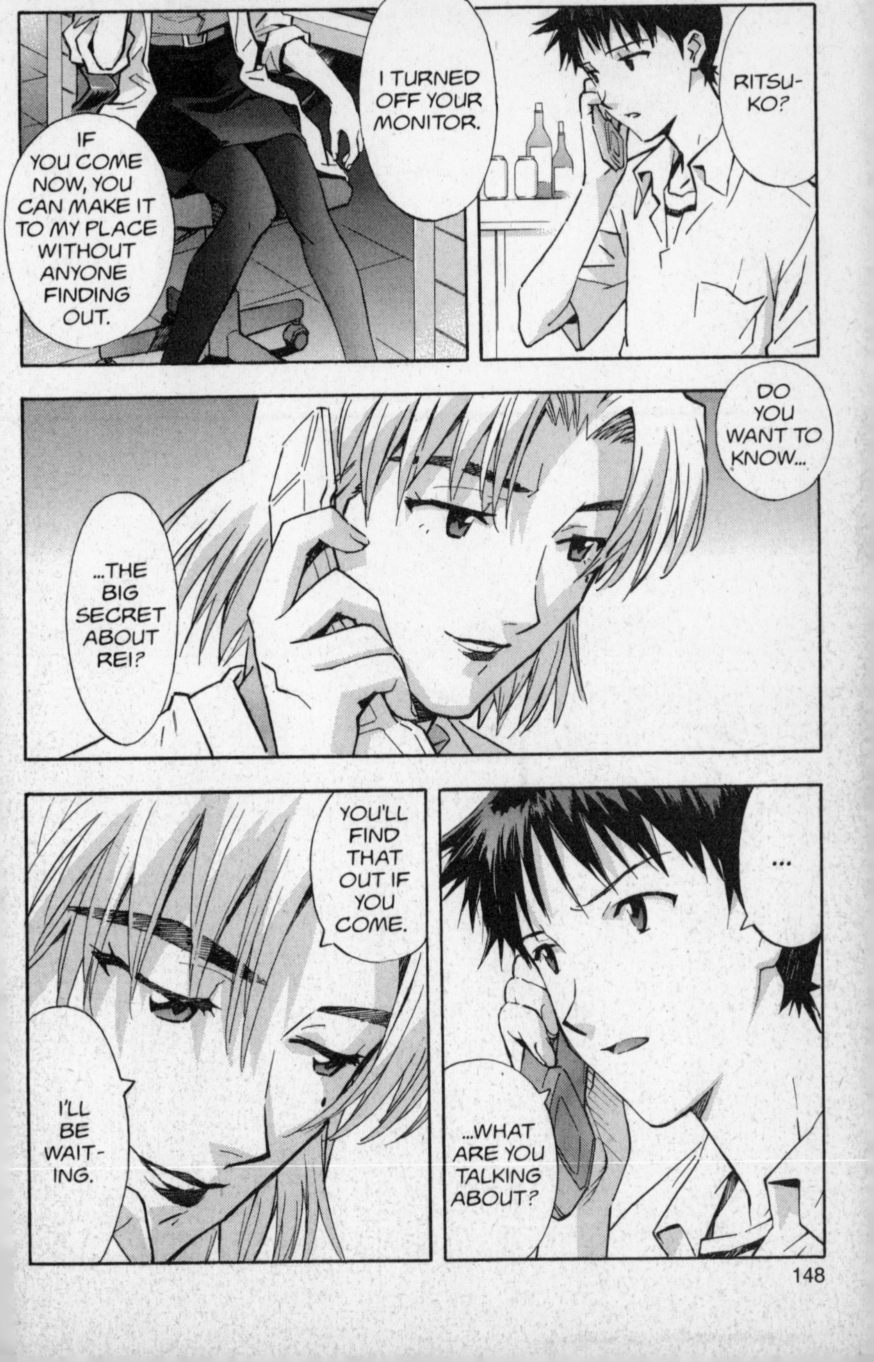
RITSU-KO?
I TURNED OFF YOUR MONITOR.
IF YOU COME NOW, YOU CAN MAKE IT TO MY PLACE WITHOUT ANYONE FINDING OUT.
DO YOU WANT TO KNOW...
...THE BIG SECRET ABOUT REI?
...
...WHAT ARE YOU TALKING ABOUT?
YOU'LL FIND THAT OUT IF YOU COME.
I'LL BE WAIT-ING.

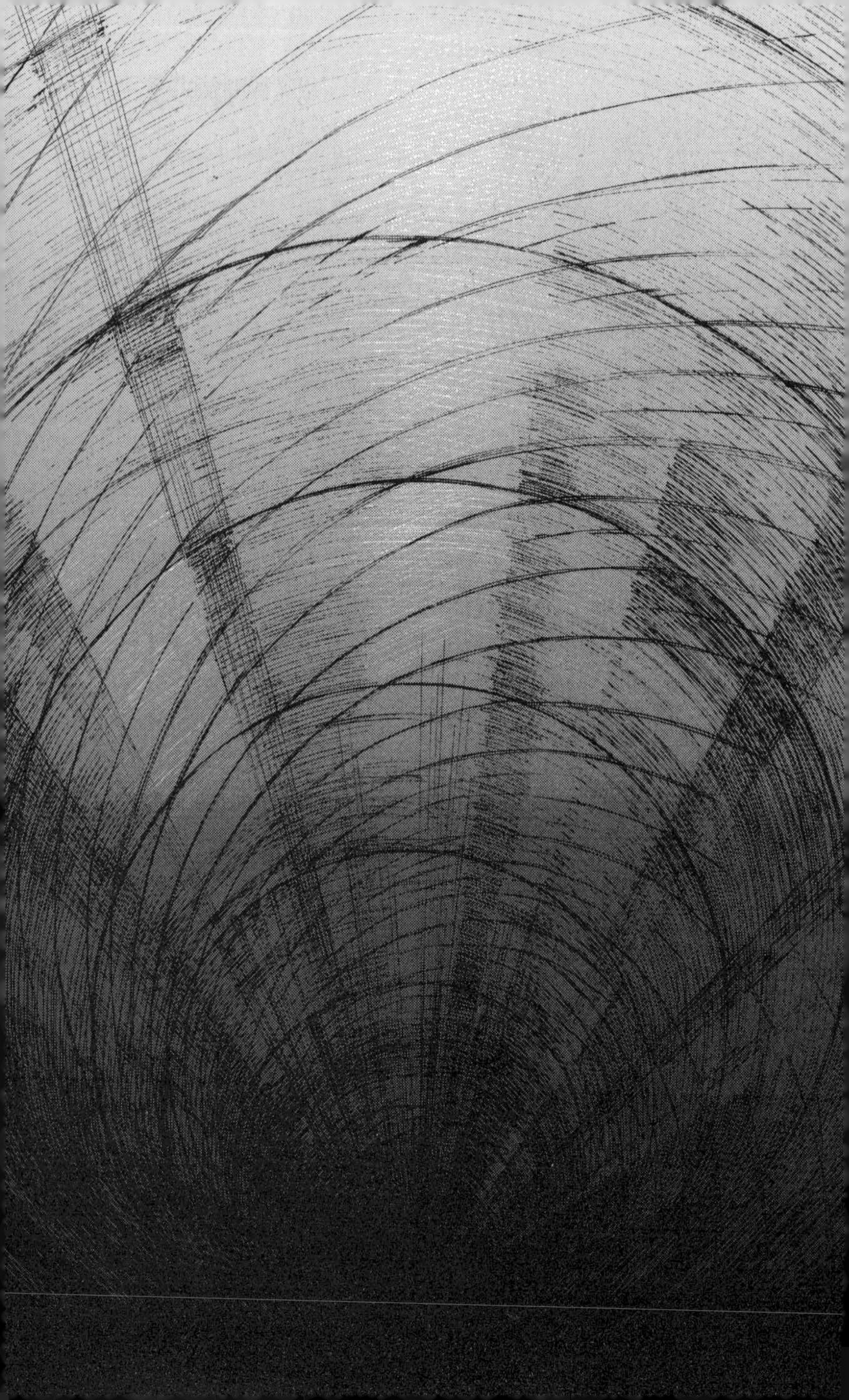

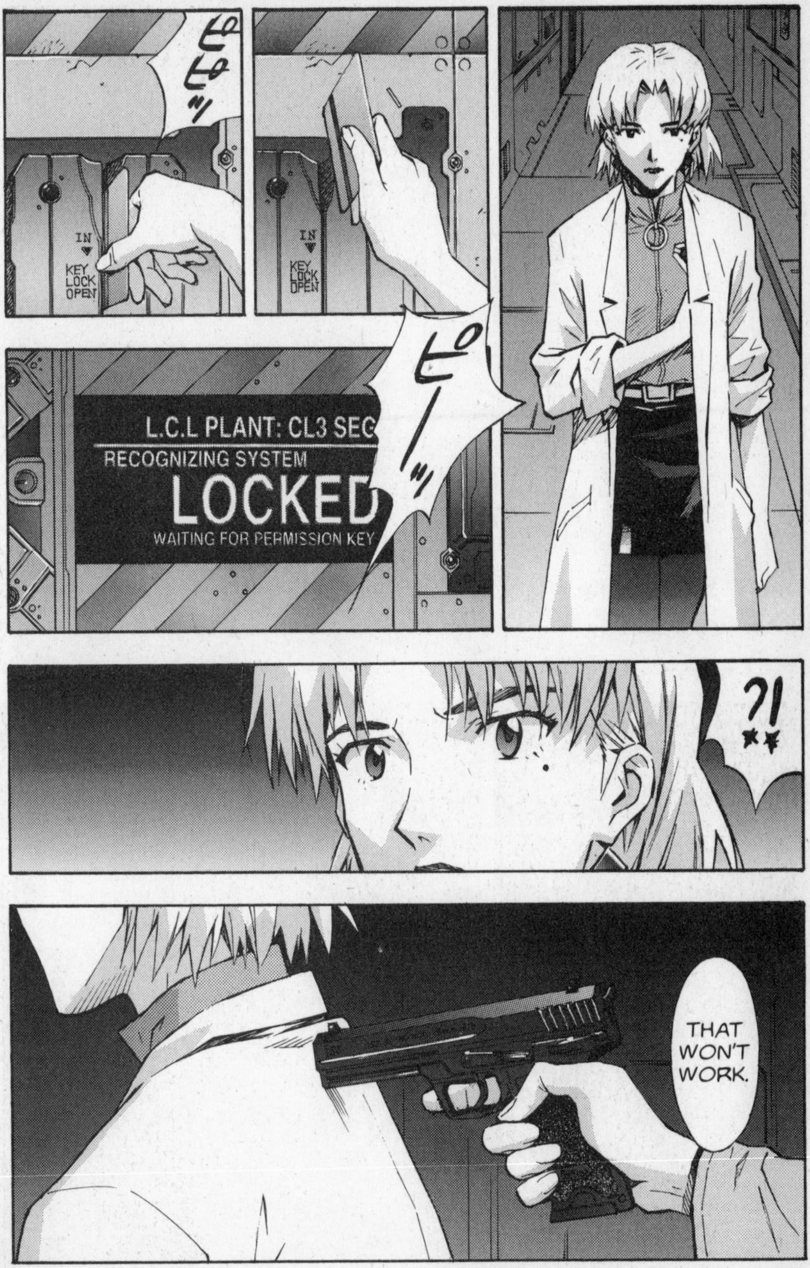
IN
KEY LOCK OPEN
ピピピッ
IN
KEY LOCK OPEN
ピーッ
L.C.L PLANT: CL3 SEG
RECOGNIZING SYSTEM
LOCKED
WAITING FOR PERMISSION KEY
?!
THAT WON'T WORK.

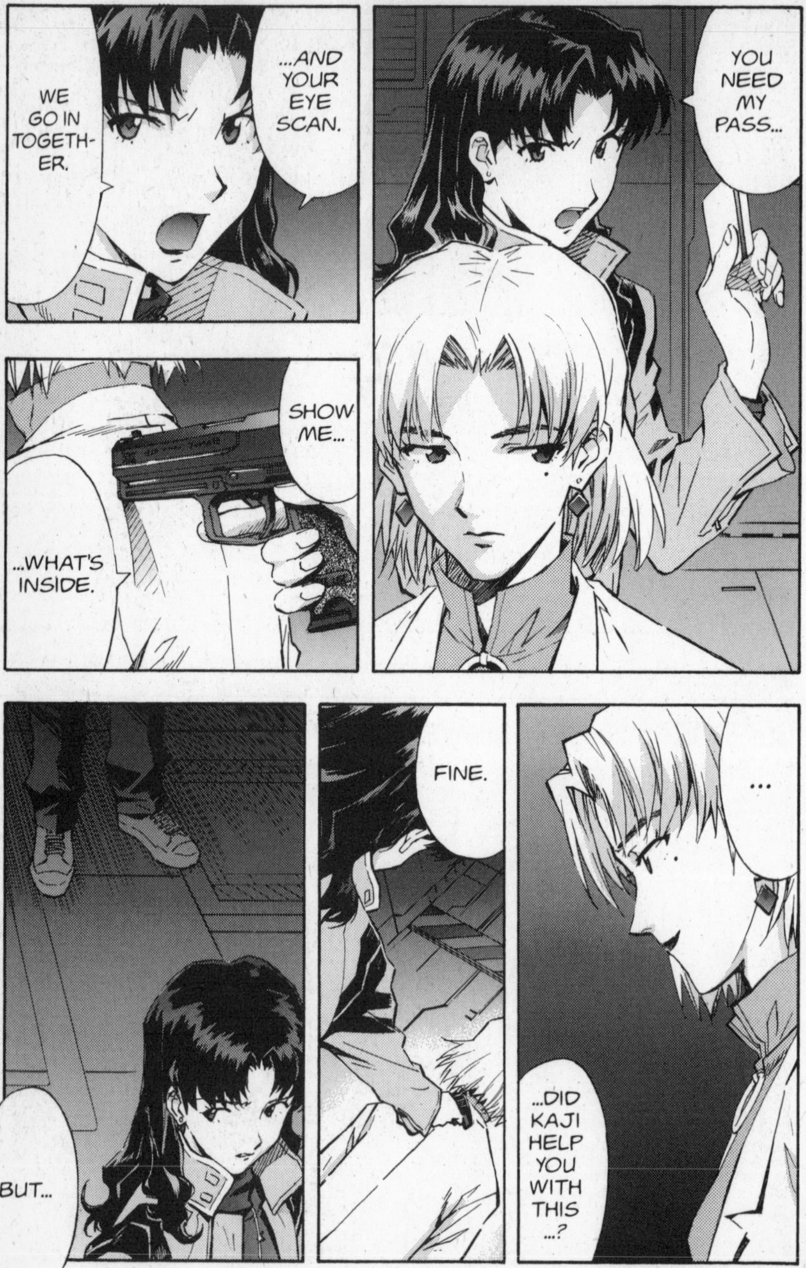
YOU NEED MY PASS...
...AND YOUR EYE SCAN.
WE GO IN TOGETH-ER.
SHOW ME...
...WHAT'S INSIDE.
...
...DID KAJI HELP YOU WITH THIS ...?
FINE.
BUT...

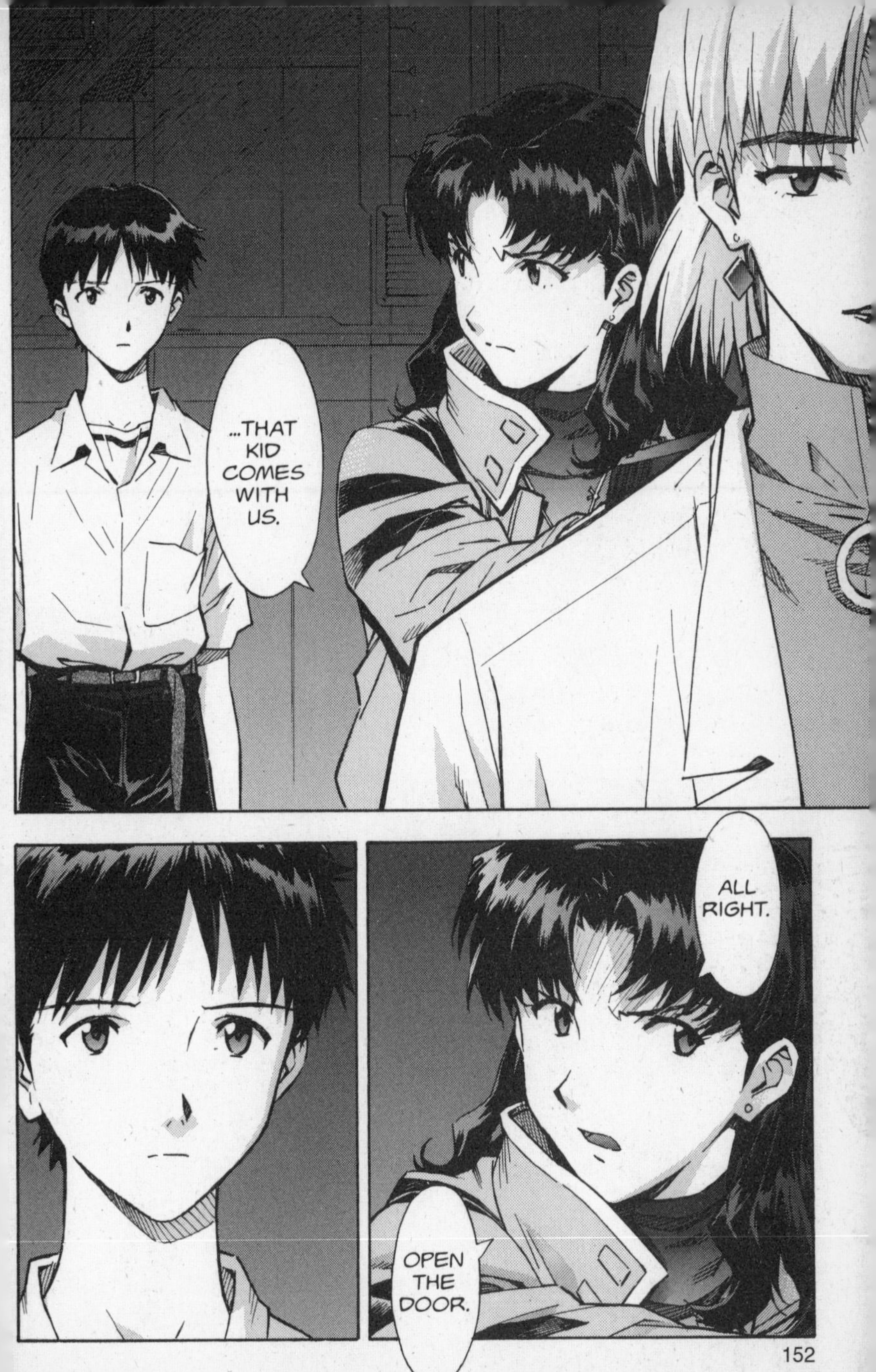
...THAT KID COMES WITH US.
ALL RIGHT.
OPEN THE DOOR.

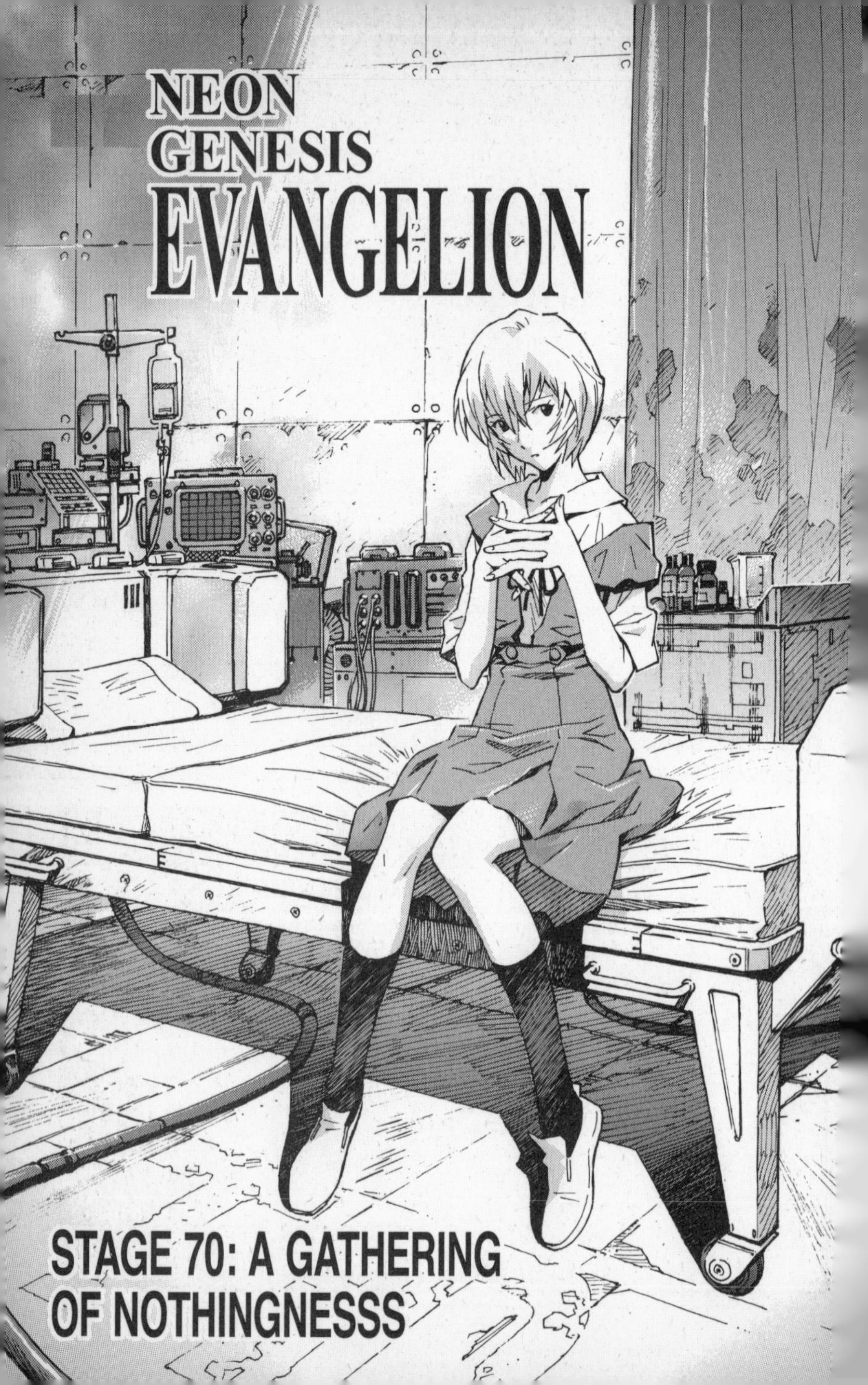
NEON
GENESIS
EVANGELION
STAGE 70: A GATHERING
OF NOTHINGNESSS

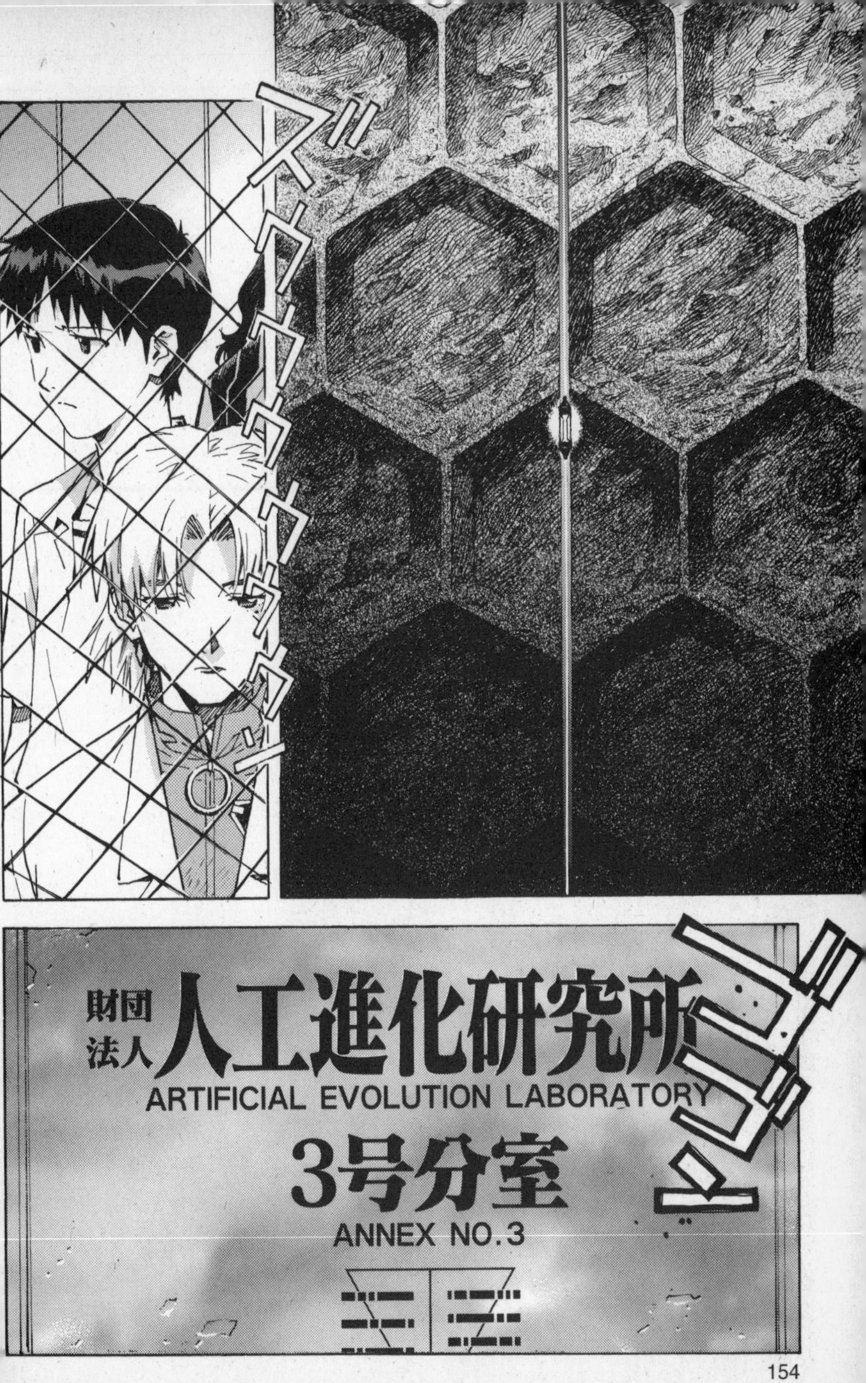
財団法人
人工進化研究所
ARTIFICIAL EVOLUTION LABORATORY
3号分室
ANNEX NO.3

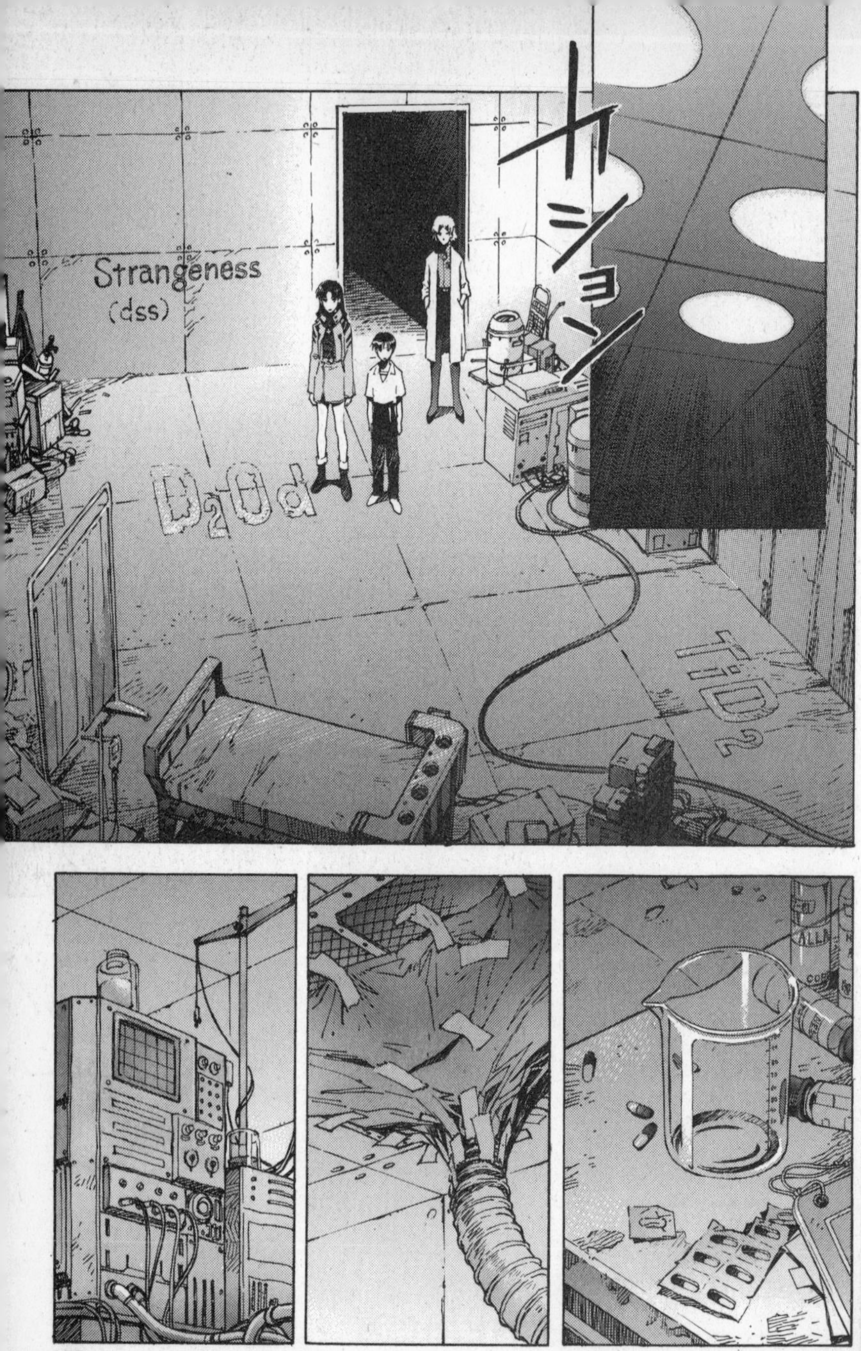
カショーン
Strangeness
(dss)
D2Od

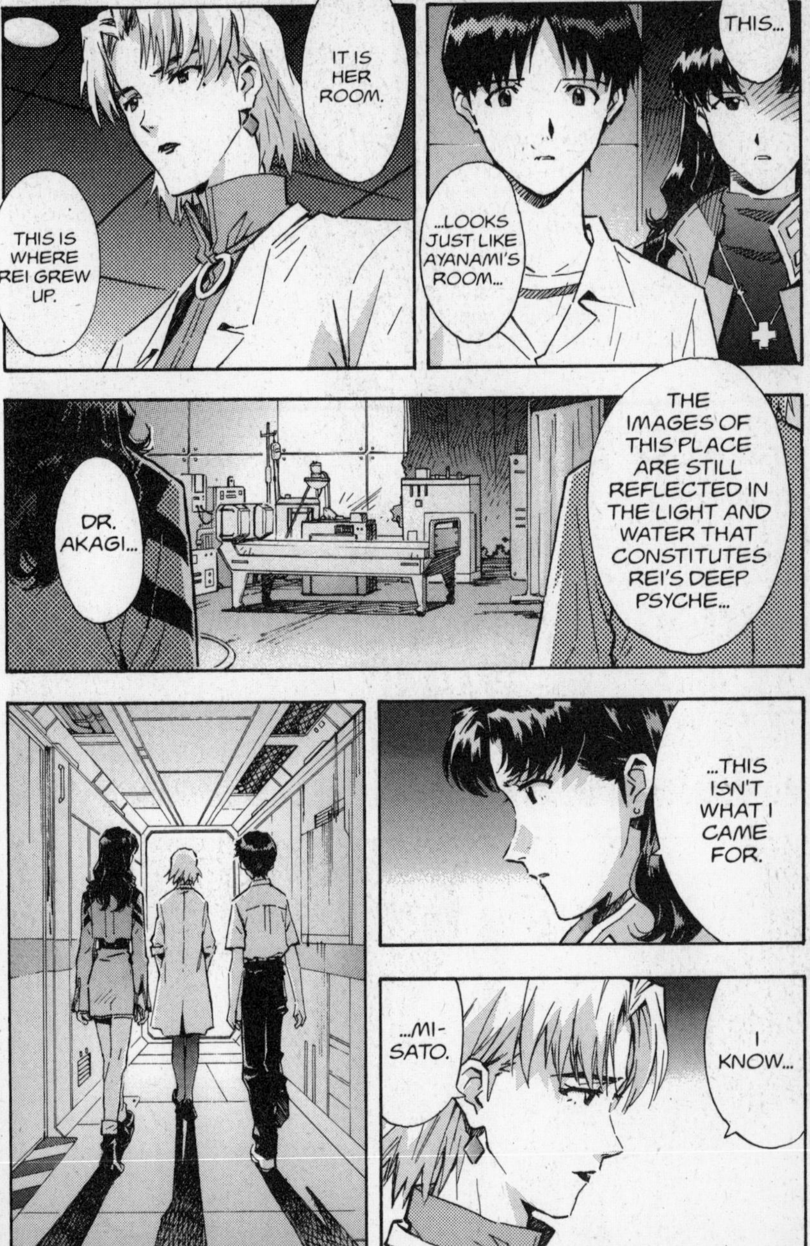
THIS...
...LOOKS JUST LIKE AYANAMI'S ROOM...
IT IS HER ROOM.
THIS IS WHERE REI GREW UP.
THE IMAGES OF THIS PLACE ARE STILL REFLECTED IN THE LIGHT AND WATER THAT CONSTITUTES REI'S DEEP PSYCHE...
DR. AKAGI...
...THIS ISN'T WHAT I CAME FOR.
I KNOW...
...MI-SATO.

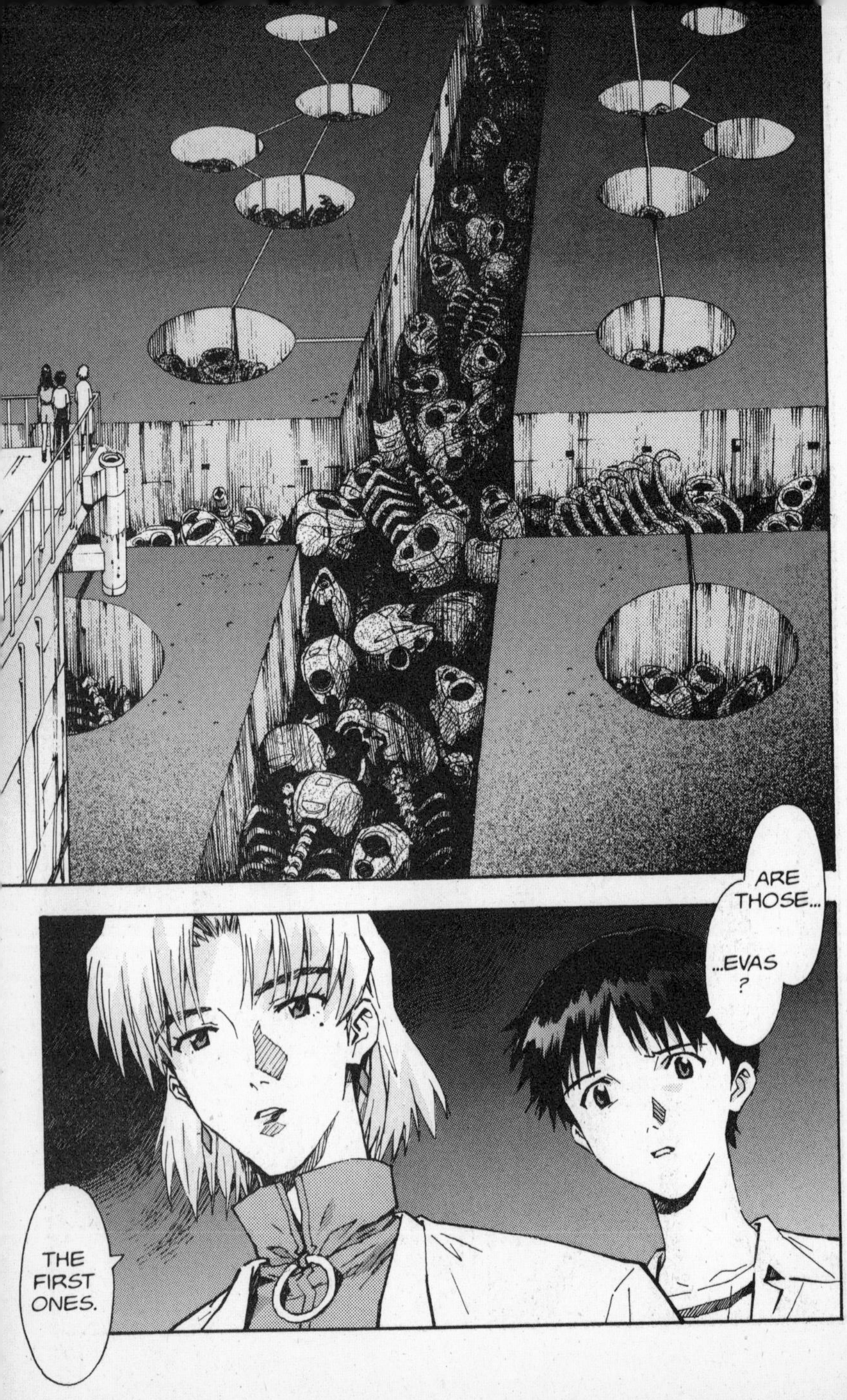
ARE THOSE...
...EVAS ?
THE FIRST ONES.

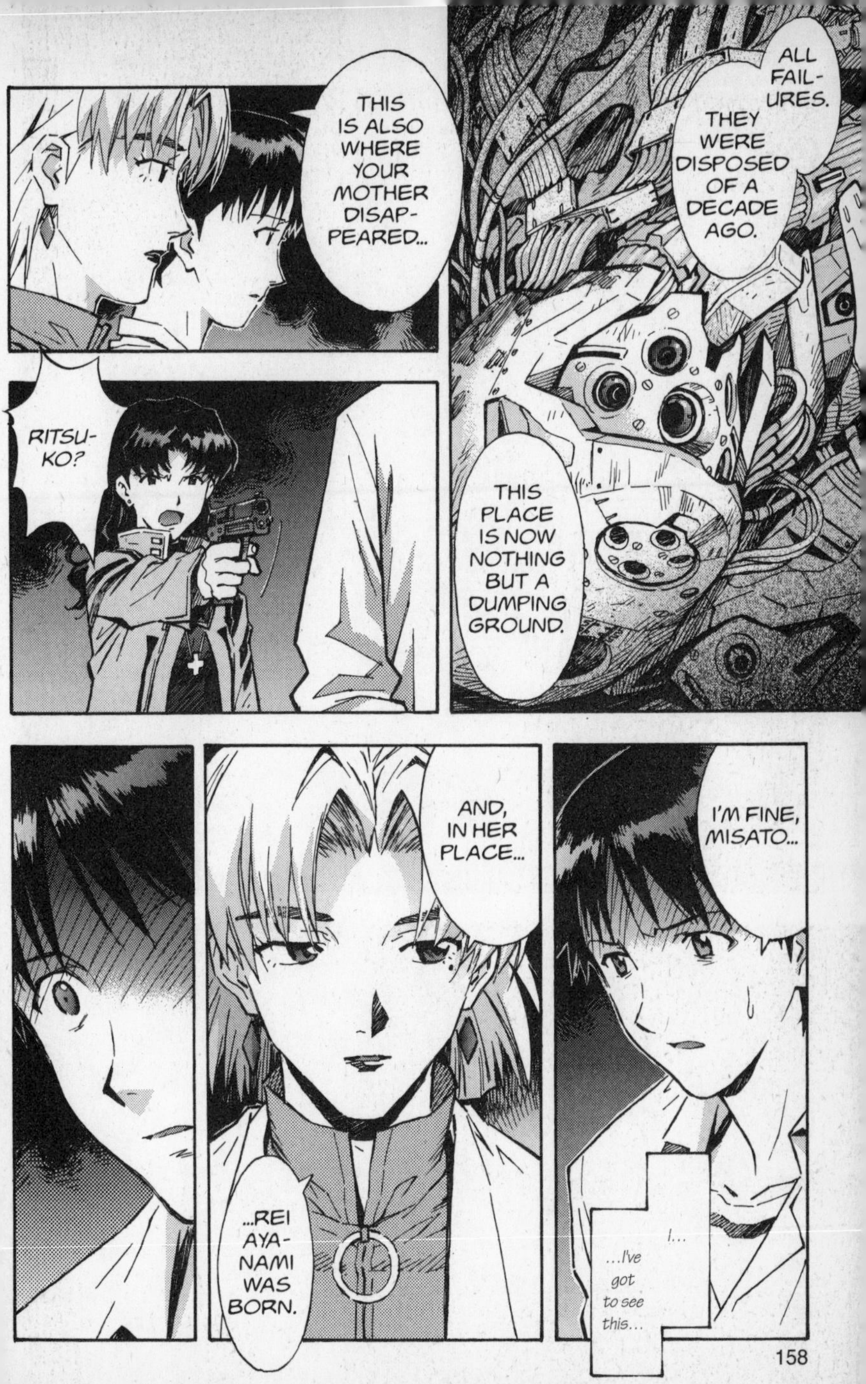
ALL FAIL-URES.
THEY WERE DISPOSED OF A DECADE AGO.
THIS PLACE IS NOW NOTHING BUT A DUMPING GROUND.
THIS IS ALSO WHERE YOUR MOTHER DISAP-PEARED...
RITSU-KO?
I'M FINE, MISATO...
I...
...I've got to see this...
AND, IN HER PLACE...
...REI AYA-NAMI WAS BORN.

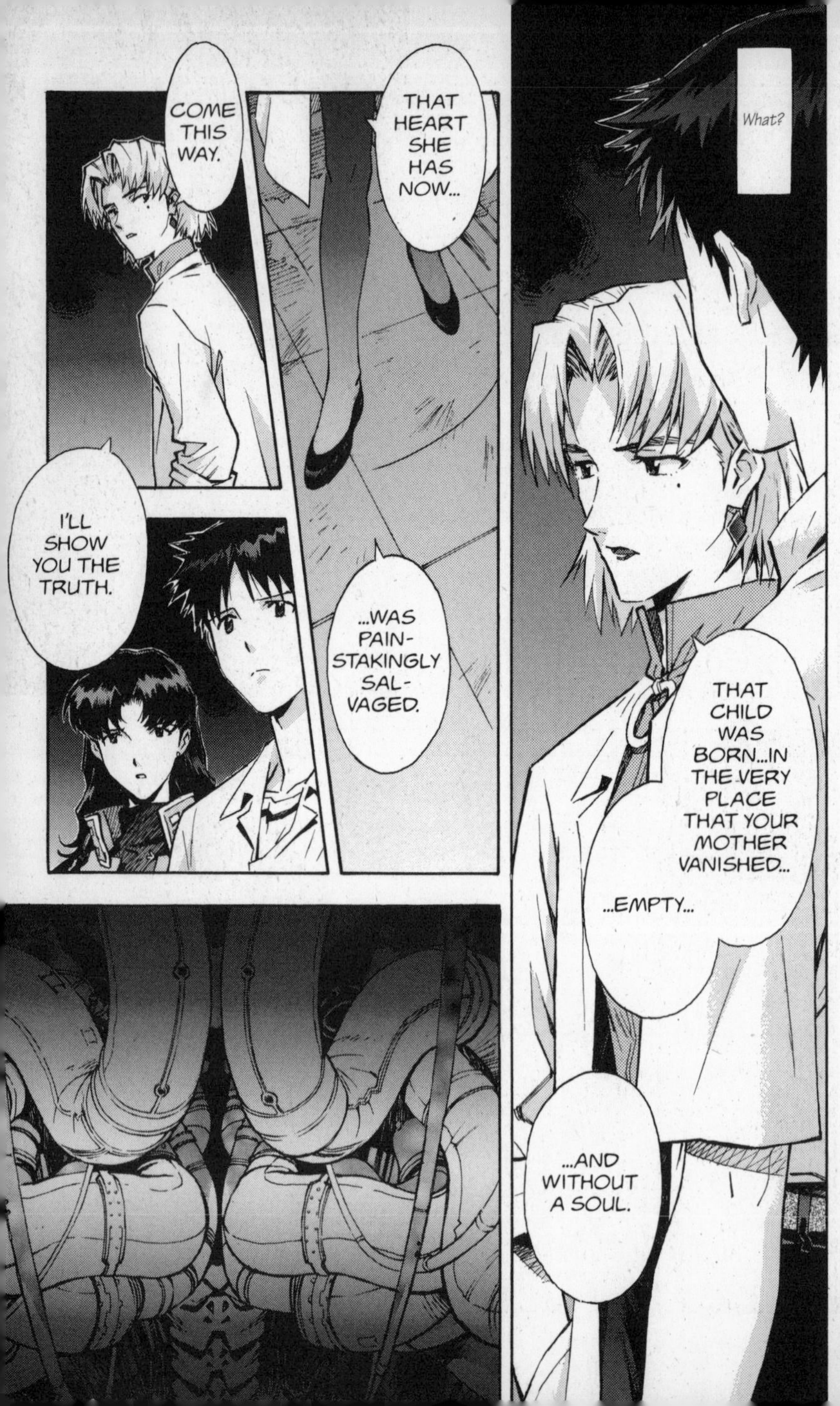
What?
THAT CHILD WAS BORN...IN THE VERY PLACE THAT YOUR MOTHER VANISHED...
...EMPTY...
...AND WITHOUT A SOUL.
THAT HEART SHE HAS NOW...
...WAS PAIN-STAKINGLY SAL-VAGED.
COME THIS WAY.
I'LL SHOW YOU THE TRUTH.

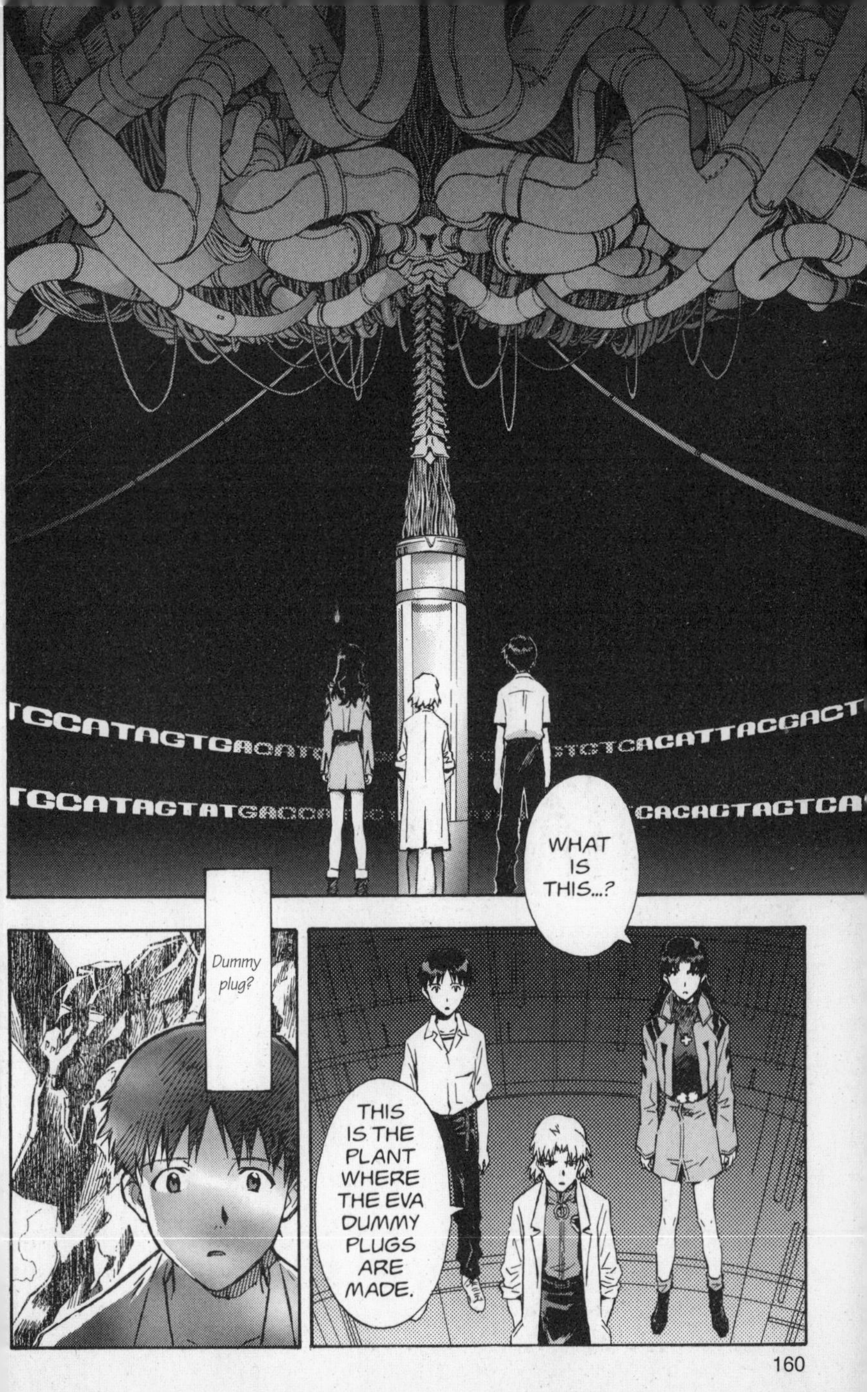
WHAT IS THIS...?
THIS IS THE PLANT WHERE THE EVA DUMMY PLUGS ARE MADE.
Dummy plug?

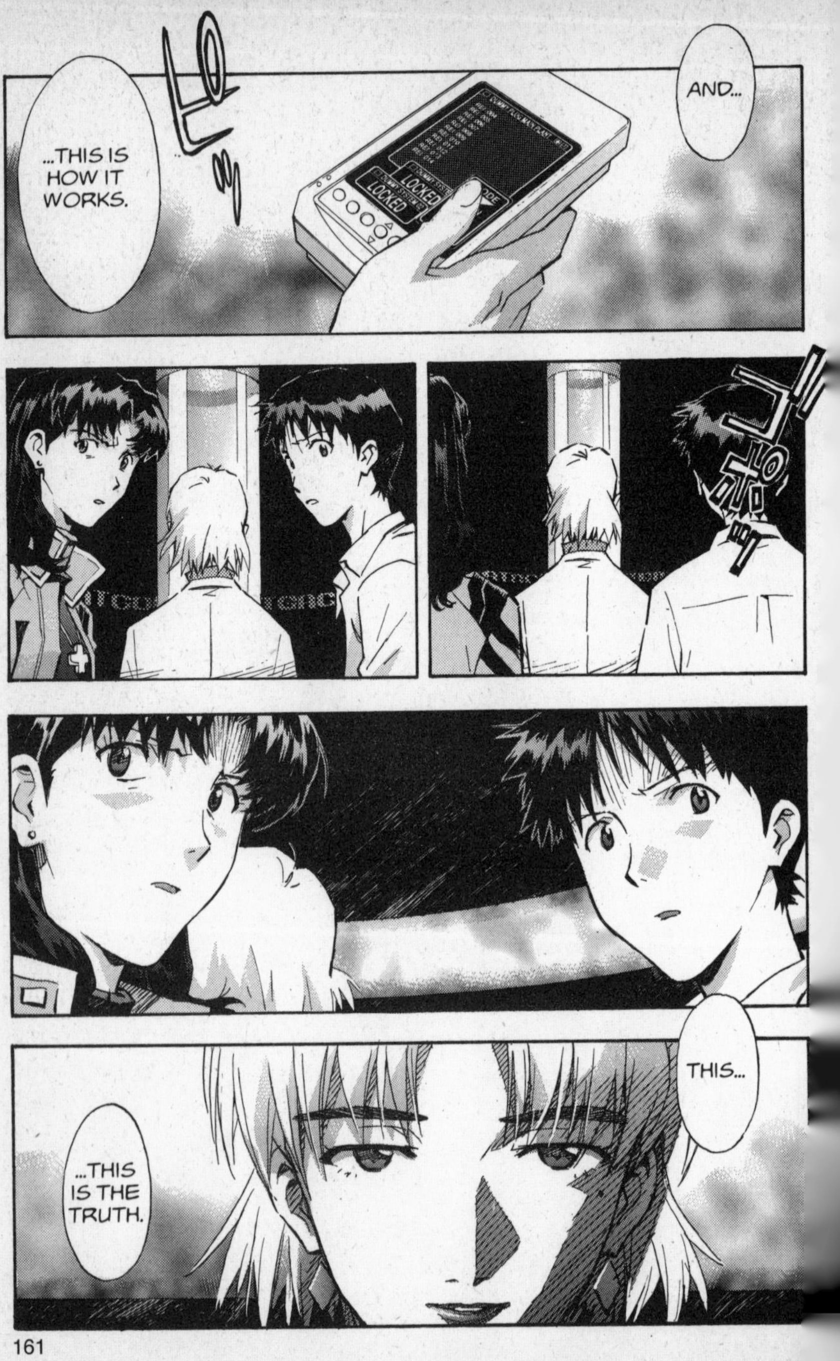
AND...
...THIS IS HOW IT WORKS.
THIS...
...THIS IS THE TRUTH.

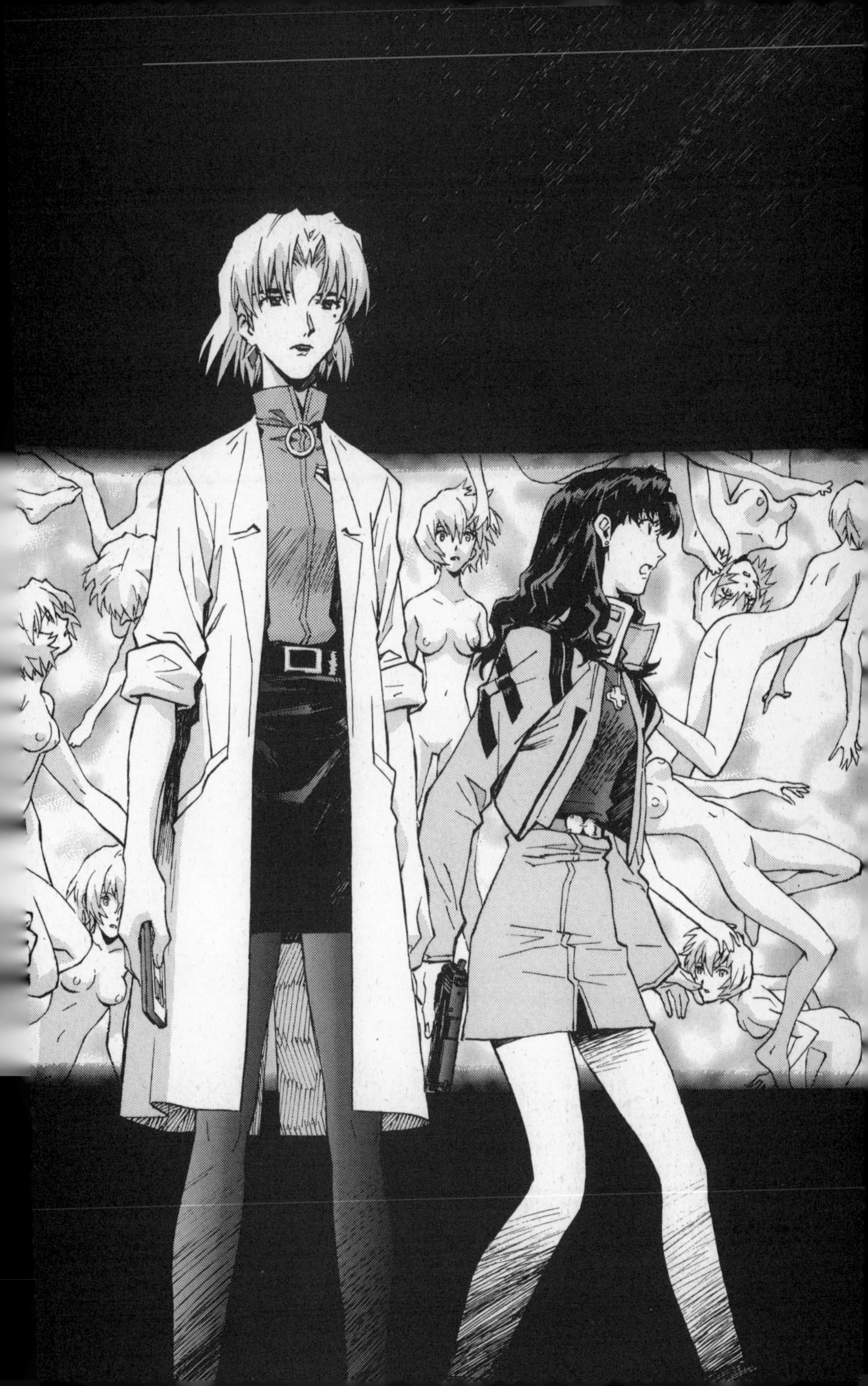

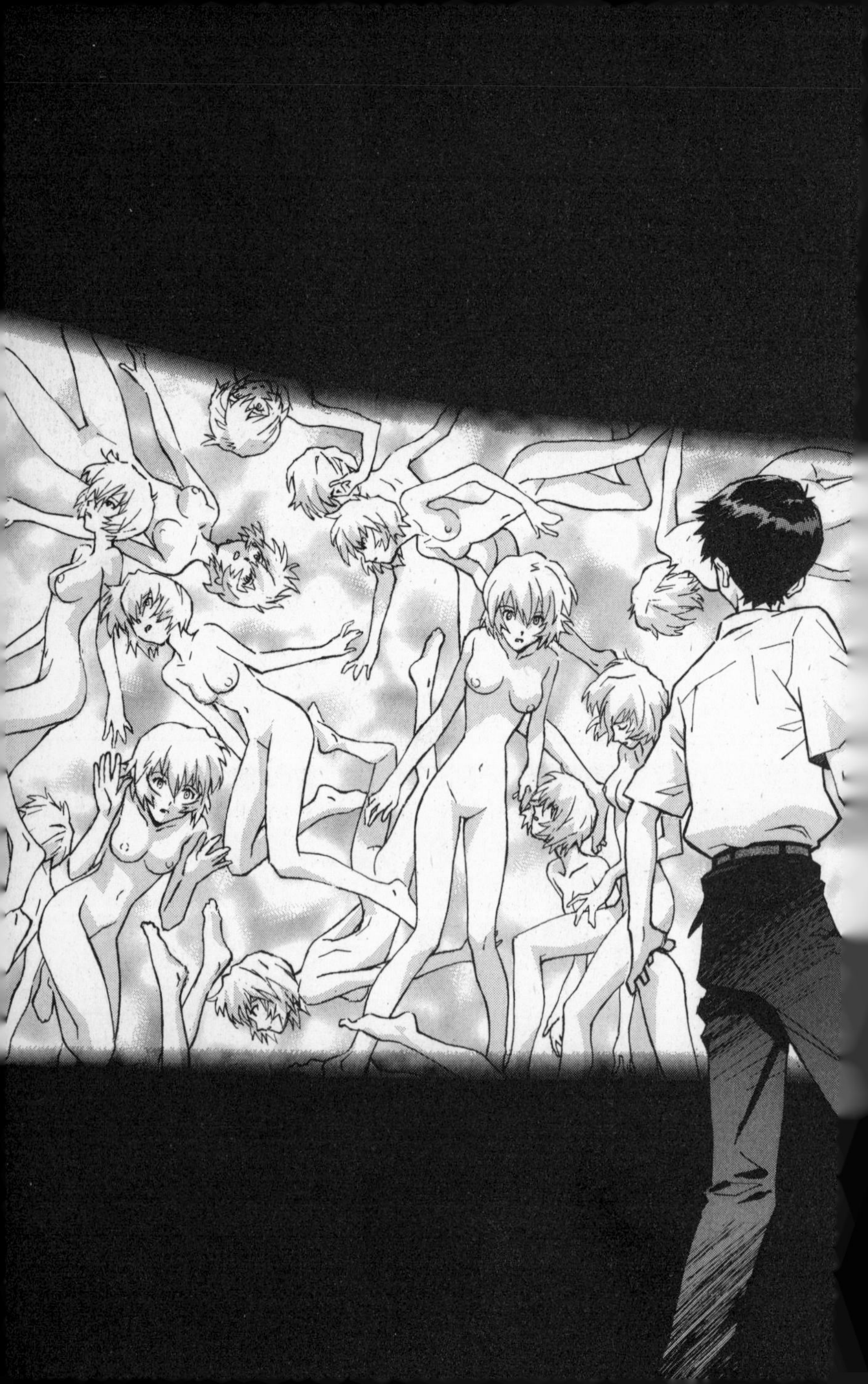

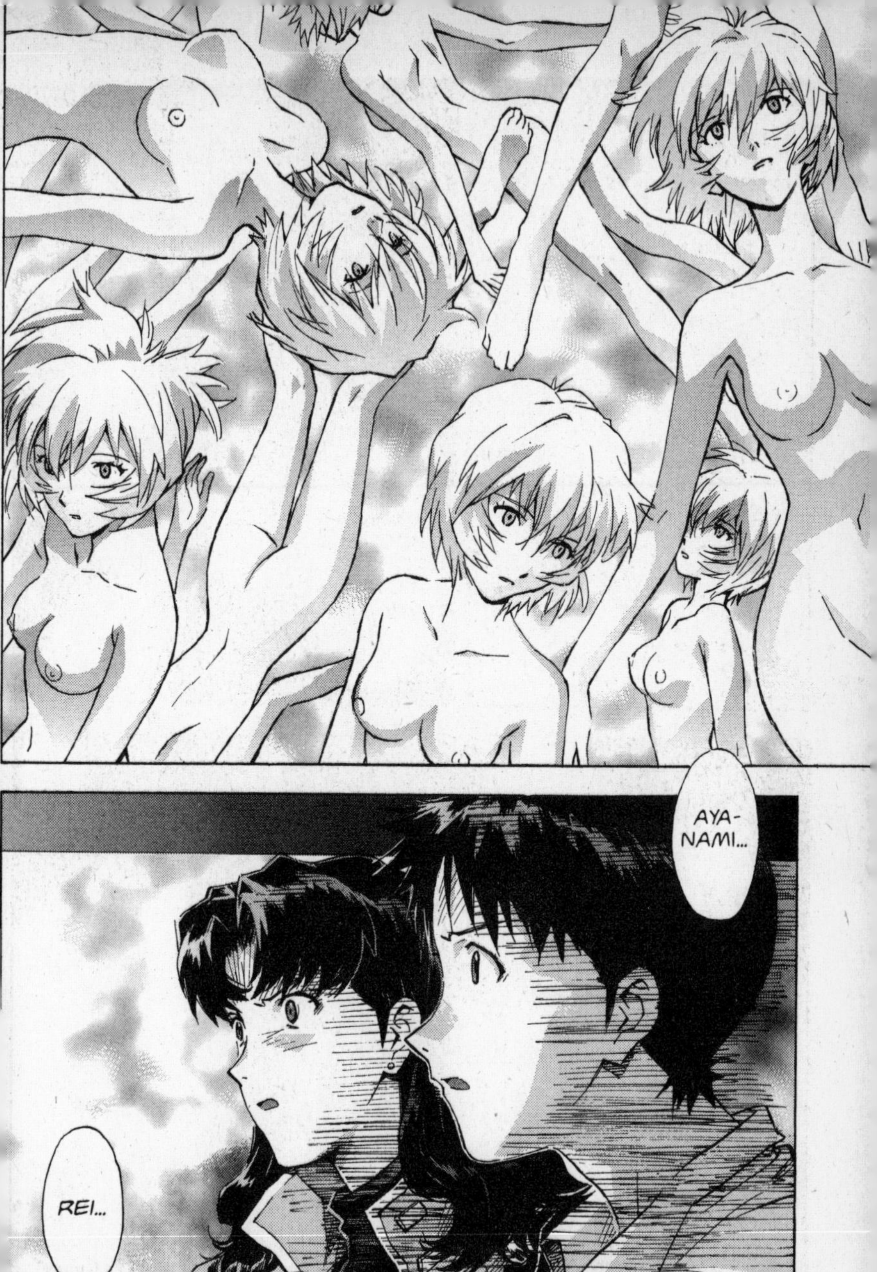
AYA-NAMI...
REI...

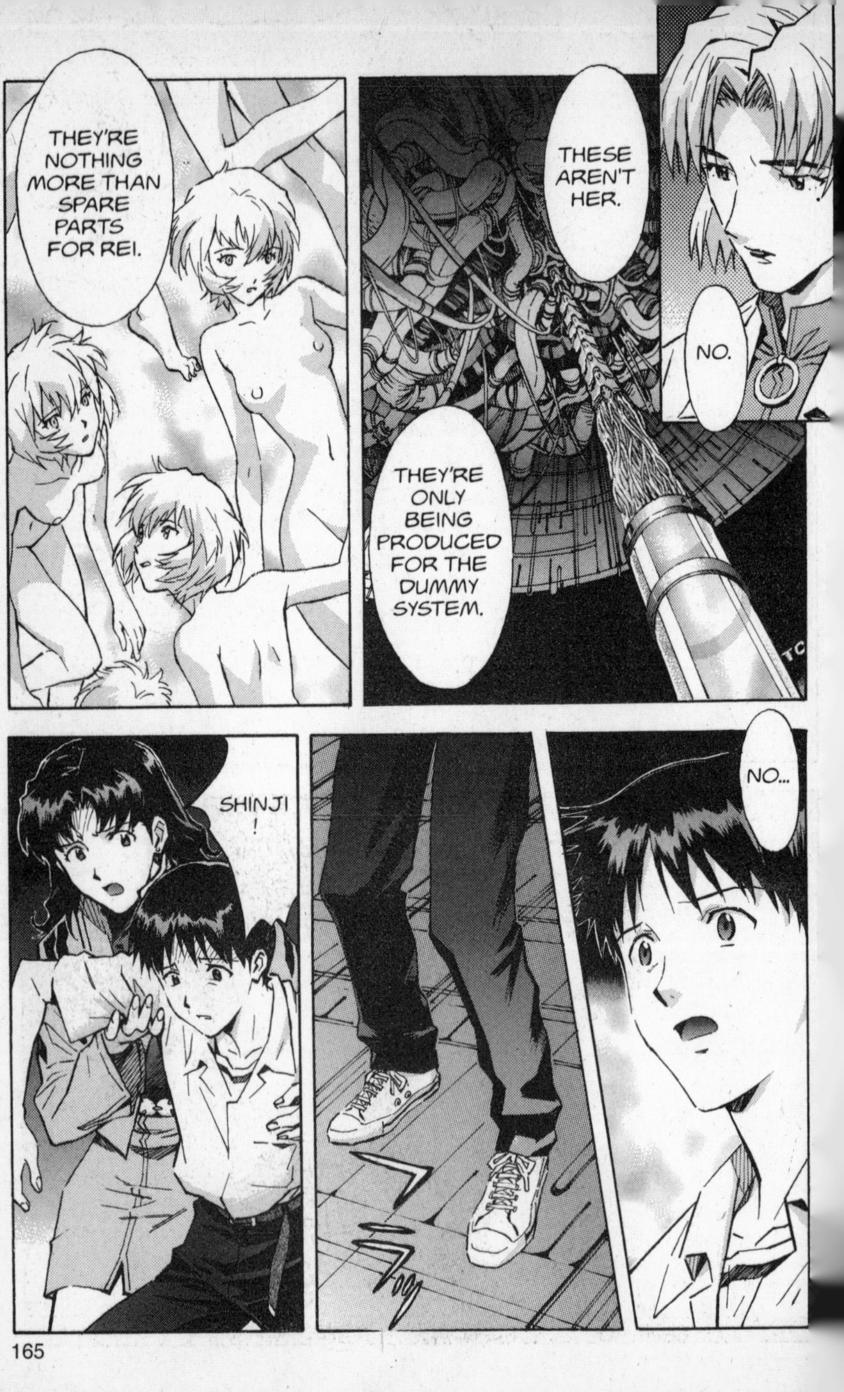
NO.
THESE AREN'T HER.
THEY'RE ONLY BEING PRODUCED FOR THE DUMMY SYSTEM.
THEY'RE NOTHING MORE THAN SPARE PARTS FOR REI.
NO...
SHINJI!

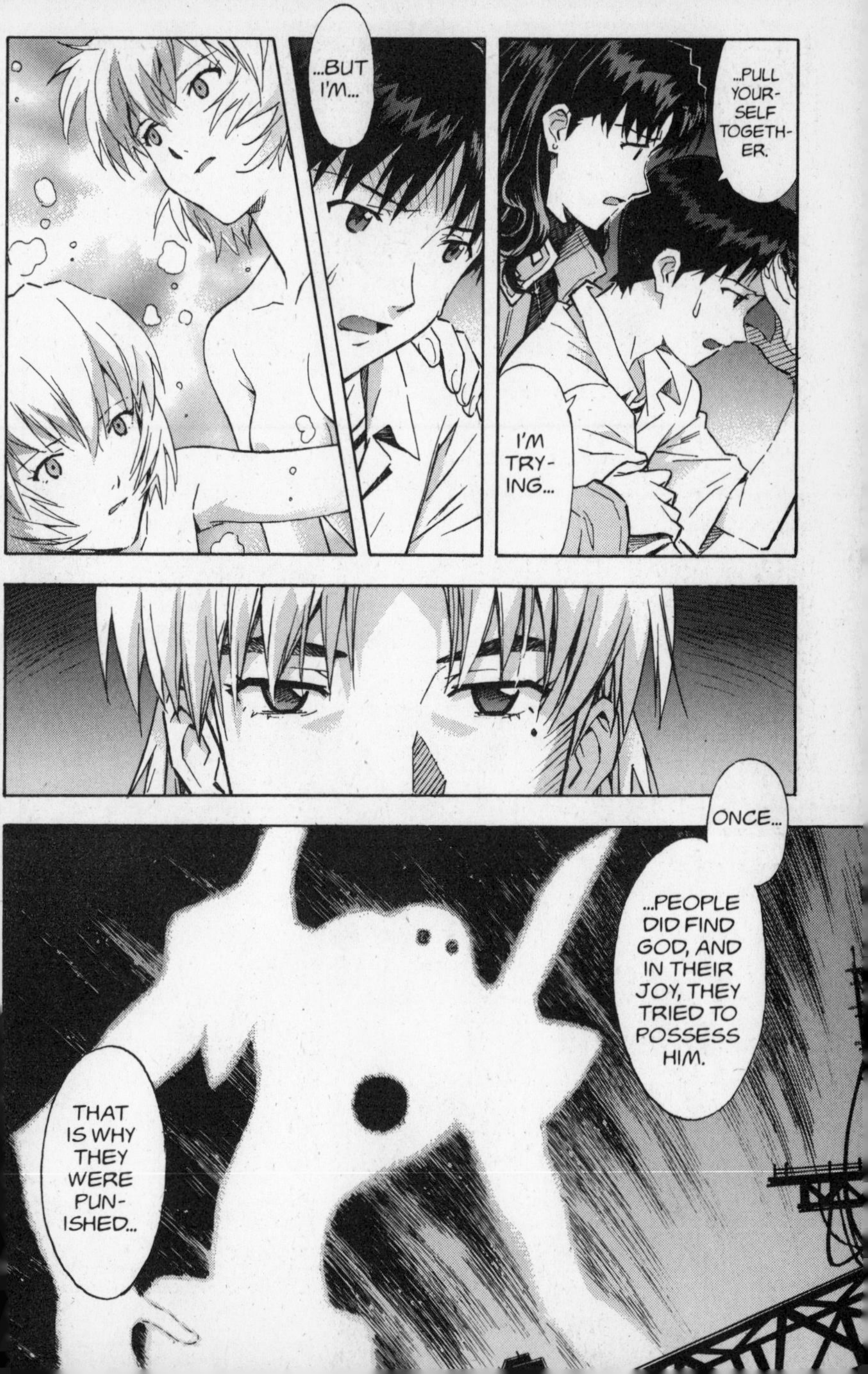
...PULL YOURSELF TOGETHER.
I'M TRYING...
...BUT I'M...
ONCE...
...PEOPLE DID FIND GOD, AND IN THEIR JOY, THEY TRIED TO POSSESS HIM.
THAT IS WHY THEY WERE PUNISHED...

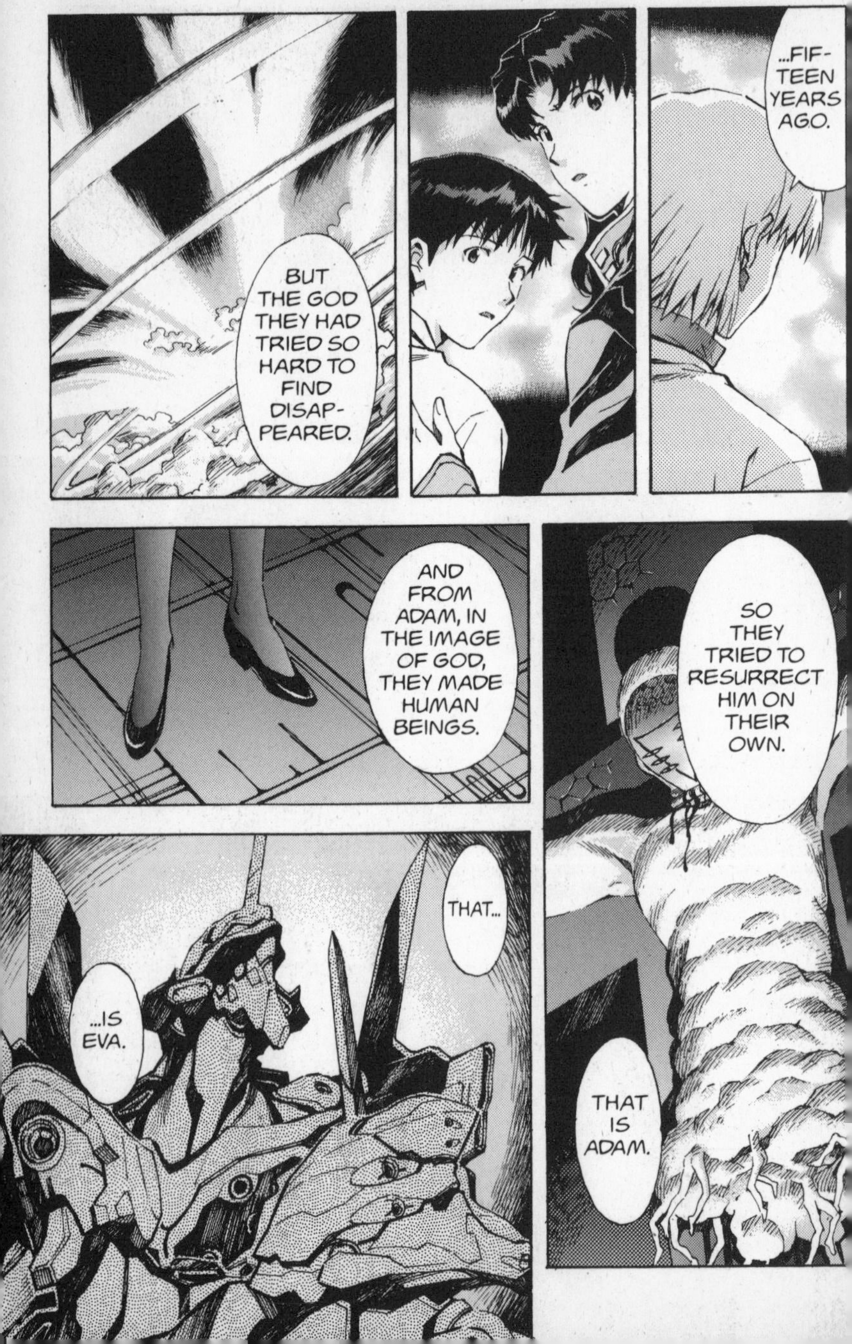
...FIF-
TEEN
YEARS
AGO.
BUT THE GOD THEY HAD TRIED SO HARD TO FIND DISAP-PEARED.
SO THEY TRIED TO RESURRECT HIM ON THEIR OWN.
THAT IS ADAM.
AND FROM ADAM, IN THE IMAGE OF GOD, THEY MADE HUMAN BEINGS.
THAT...
...IS EVA.

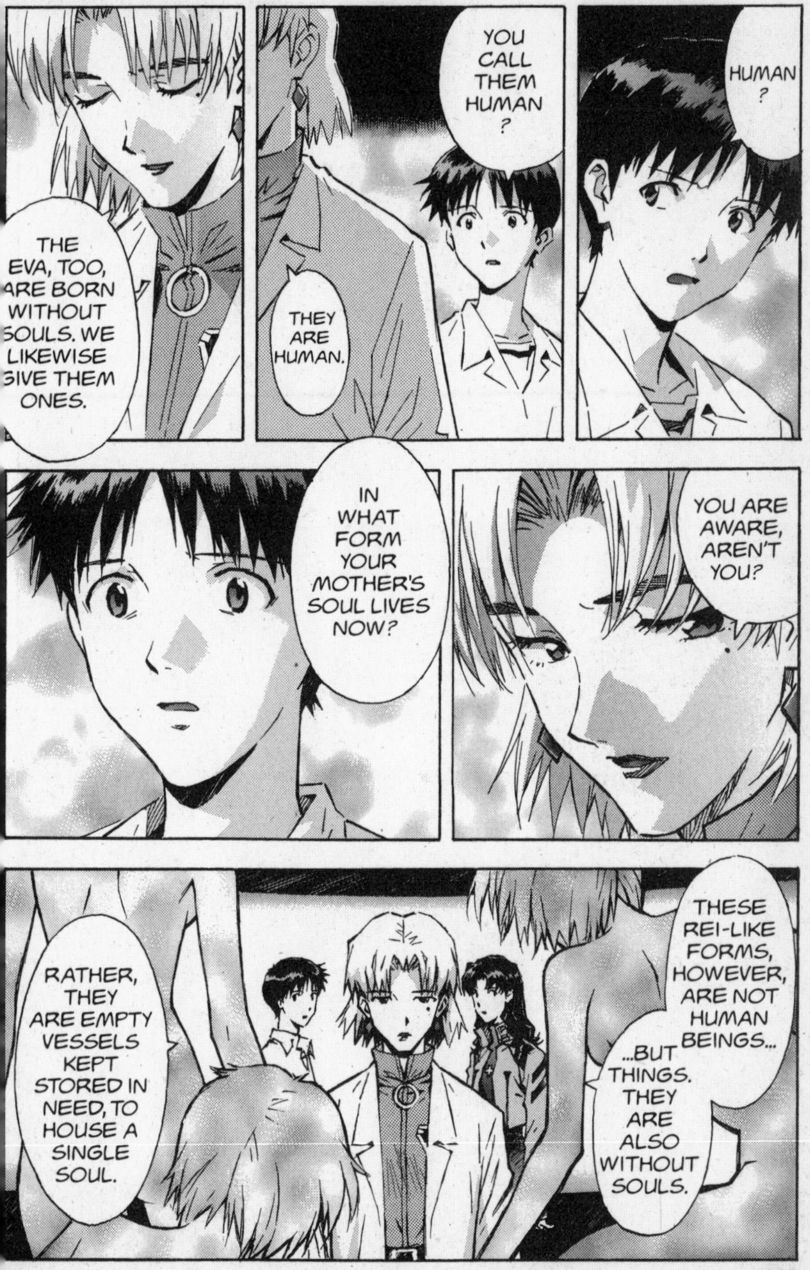
HUMAN?
YOU CALL THEM HUMAN?
THEY ARE HUMAN.
THE EVA, TOO, ARE BORN WITHOUT SOULS. WE LIKEWISE GIVE THEM ONES.
YOU ARE AWARE, AREN'T YOU?
IN WHAT FORM YOUR MOTHER'S SOUL LIVES NOW?
THESE REI-LIKE FORMS, HOWEVER, ARE NOT HUMAN BEINGS...
...BUT THINGS. THEY ARE ALSO WITHOUT SOULS.
RATHER, THEY ARE EMPTY VESSELS KEPT STORED IN NEED, TO HOUSE A SINGLE SOUL.

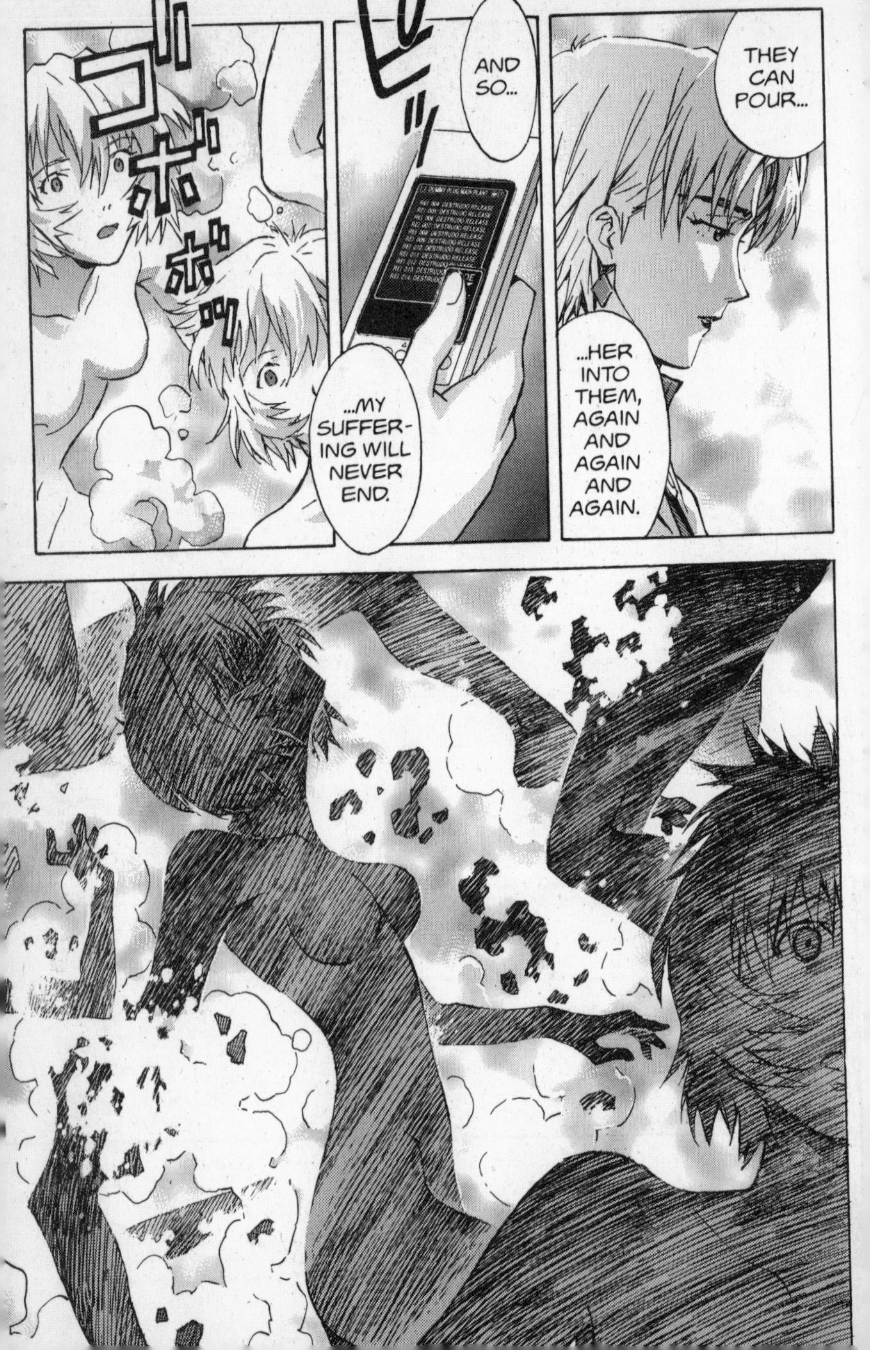
THEY CAN POUR...
...HER INTO THEM, AGAIN AND AGAIN AND AGAIN.
AND SO...
...MY SUFFERING WILL NEVER END.

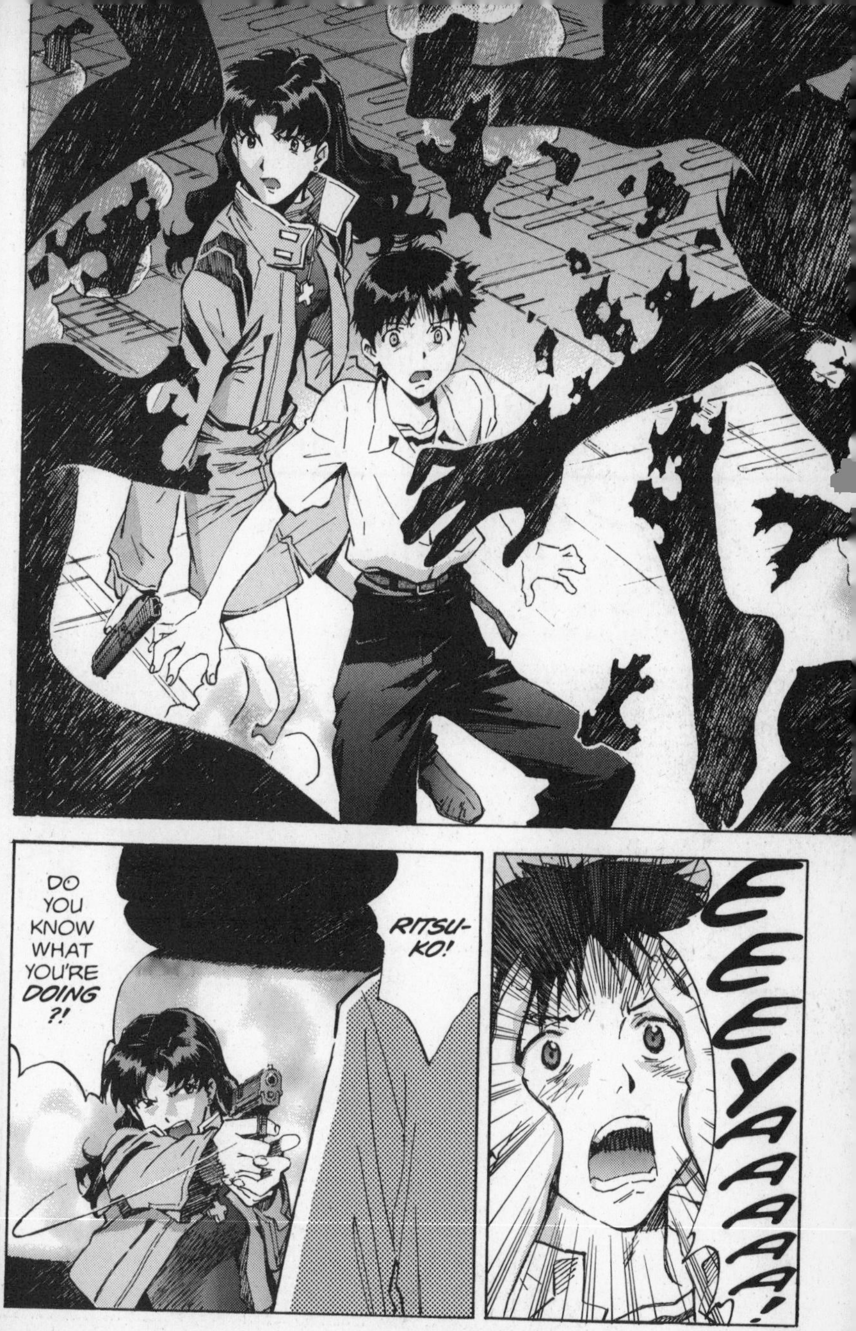
EEEYAAAAA!
RITSU-KO!
DO YOU KNOW WHAT YOU'RE DOING?!

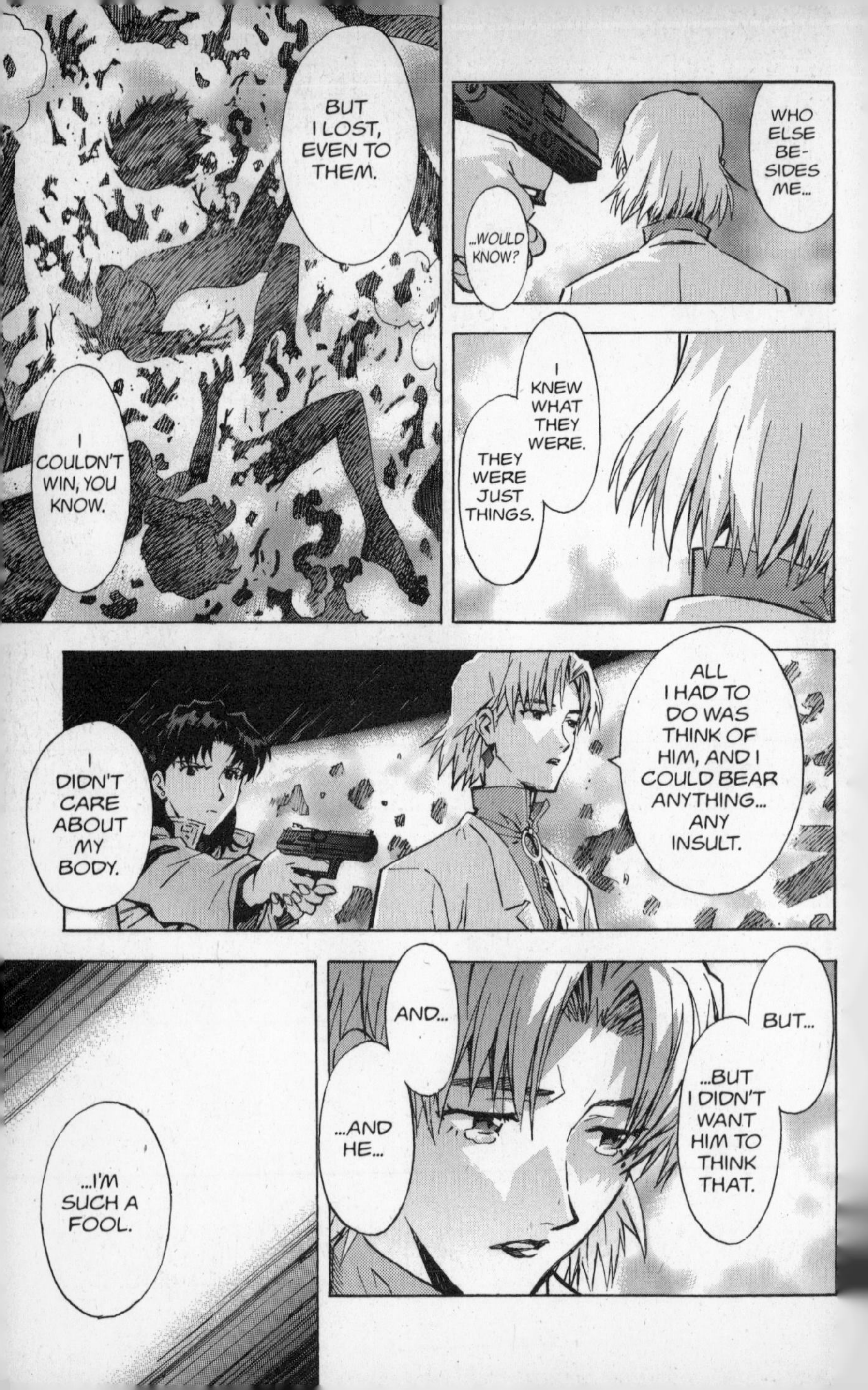
WHO ELSE BE-SIDES ME...
...WOULD KNOW?
I KNEW WHAT THEY WERE.
THEY WERE JUST THINGS.
BUT I LOST, EVEN TO THEM.
I COULDN'T WIN, YOU KNOW.
ALL I HAD TO DO WAS THINK OF HIM, AND I COULD BEAR ANYTHING... ANY INSULT.
I DIDN'T CARE ABOUT MY BODY.
BUT...
...BUT I DIDN'T WANT HIM TO THINK THAT.
AND...
...AND HE...
...I'M SUCH A FOOL.

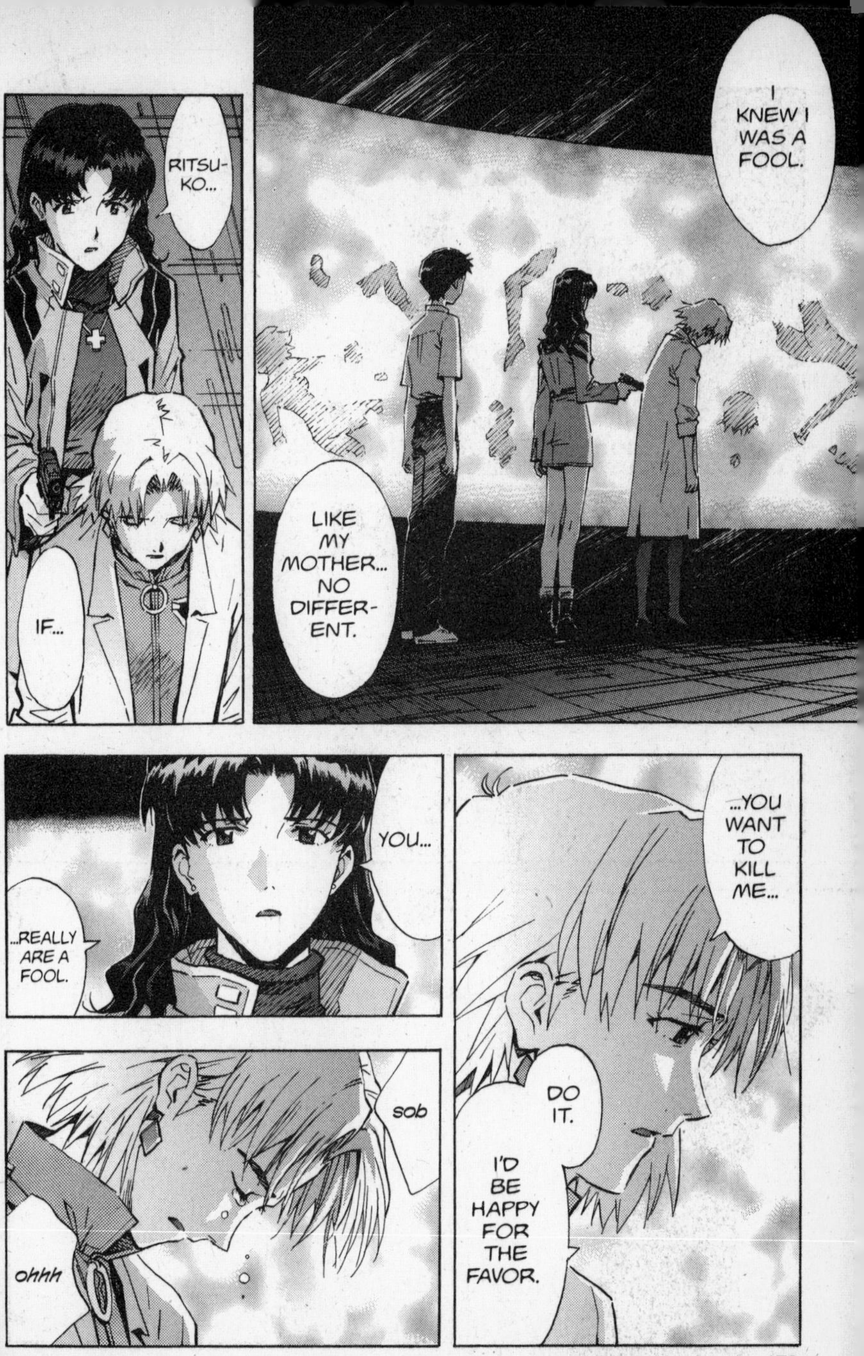
I KNEW I WAS A FOOL.
LIKE MY MOTHER... NO DIFFERENT.
RITSU-KO...
IF...
...YOU WANT TO KILL ME...
DO IT.
I'D BE HAPPY FOR THE FAVOR.
YOU...
...REALLY ARE A FOOL.
sob
ohhh

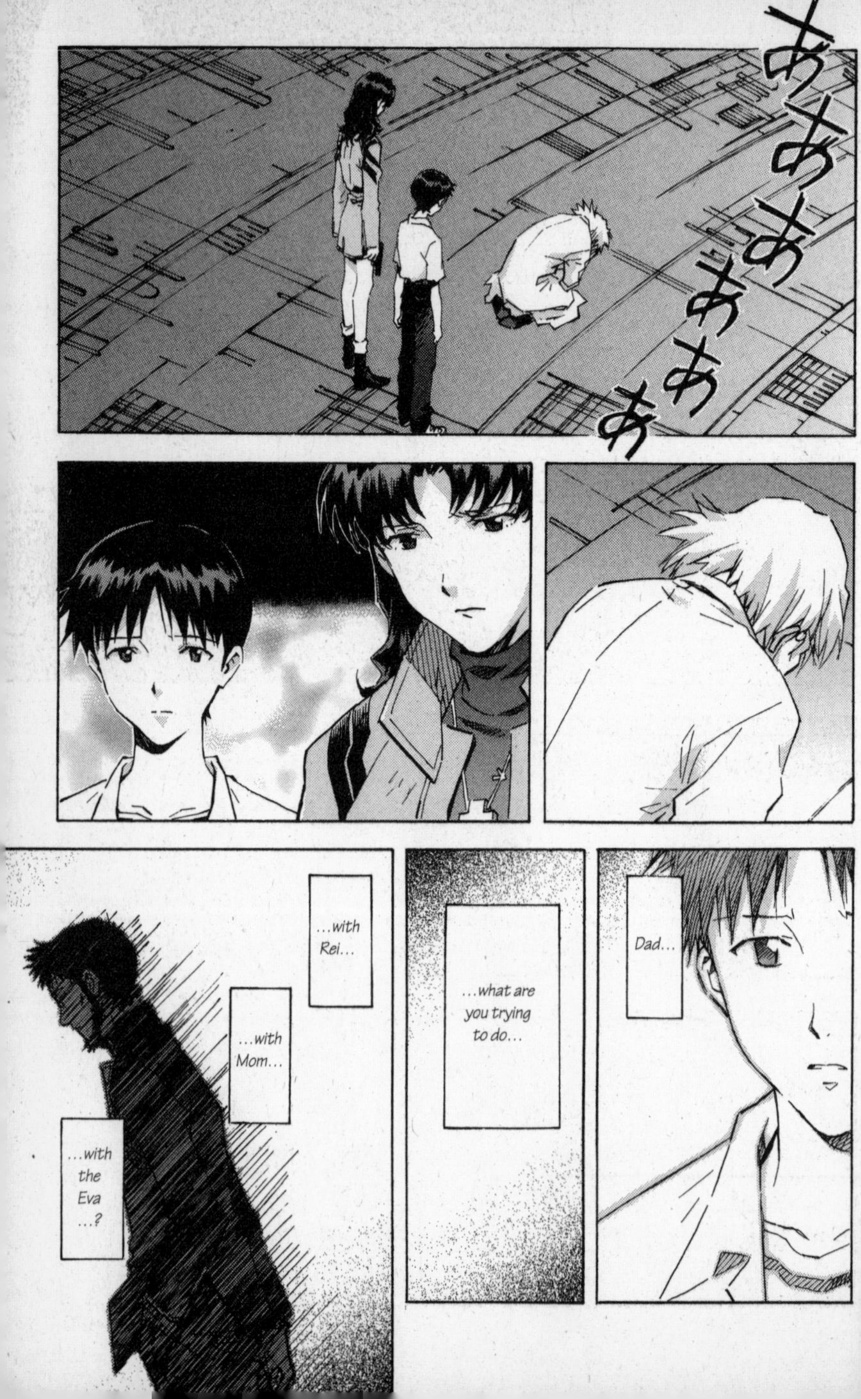
あああああ
Dad…
…what are you trying to do…
…with Rei…
…with Mom…
…with the Eva …?

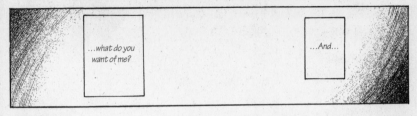

...what do you want of me?

...And...

Mom...

Rei...

what...

...do I do now ...?

TO BE CONTINUED IN EVANGELION VOLUME ELEVEN

NEON GENESIS EVANGELION

WRITER AND ARTIST

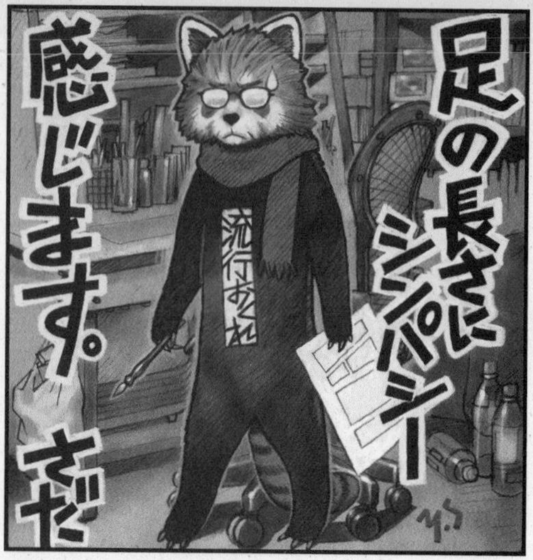
足の長さにシンパシー
感じます。
さだ
流行おくれ
M.S

YOSHIYUKI SADAMOTO

The author in his studio is labeled out of fashion, while a message from a mysterious "Sada" expresses sympathy over the length of his legs.

I've thought at great length about how nice it is to be young, especially when it comes to love. As long as you have feelings of love towards one another, you can overcome obstacles—but the obstacles become more difficult the older you get. Work, income, domestic life, health, the future—especially the future, which, even as you contemplate it, sees your pure unadulterated love go stale.

Although the world that Shinji, Rei, and Asuka are experiencing is of course a two-dimensional, imaginary one, I believe there is a place like this somewhere out there. I am writing this and reliving my youth, even if only in my emotions—while eating gelatin with coenzyme Q10.

SOUND EFFECTS GLOSSARY

Welcome to the sound effects glossary for Volume Ten of ***Neon Genesis Evangelion***! Japanese is written with a combination of *kanji*—Chinese ideograms, borrowed and modified—and *kana*, phonetic characters. There are two kinds of *kana*: *katakana* and *hiragana*. *Hiragana*, written in a cursive style, is very important in indicating grammar in Japanese.

However, when it comes to manga sound FX, we're mostly concerned with *katakana*. These are written in a more angular style, and their uses include spelling out foreign words, and giving emphasis in ads and signs (sort of like writing in block letters). It's in this role of emphasis that *katakana* are used as sound FX, and almost all of *Evangelion*'s FX (and manga in general) use it. Sometimes, however, *hiragana* is used instead—in cases where, for some reason, it would seem more "natural" to a Japanese speaker to write out that particular FX in *hiragana*. 101-5, *gui*, is an example. Note that the use of *hiragana* in manga FX is often associated with sounds that are personal or intimate.

Here's how this glossary works, taking the first example: 8-1 simply means the sound FX that's on page 8 in panel 1. The order all FX are listed, of course, is the Japanese reading order, right-to-left: so 8-1 is the upper right (not upper left) panel of page 8. In cases where two sound FX exist in the same panel, an additional number is added to distinguish them, as in 11-1-1 and 11-1-2. The reading order for such multiple kanji within a panel is right to left, or, in cases where right and left is less clear, clockwise. After each line's number and FX, you get the literal *kana* reading followed by the description of what the FX stands for in brackets.

By the way, students of Japanese might note some unusual usages in the FX of *tenten*, the two short parallel marks used to modify the sound of *kana*. Many Japanese textbooks will not show them being used on vowels by themselves, but you will see them so employed here in 8.1, where the "u" is changed to a "v" sound (not normally present in Japanese orthography). The same modification to "u" is used later on in the story to represent cell phones on vibrating mode.

A last note: Japanese vowels (whose order is taught as "AIUEO" rather than "AEIOU"), unlike English, always have the same pronunciation. "A" is said *ah*, "I" is *eee*, "U" is *ooh*, "E" is *eh*, and "O" is *oh*.

8-1——FX: vzuvzuvzuvzuvzuvzu [cracking]

8-3——FX: bikibikibiki [creaking]

9-1——FX: gakun [sudden jerking]

9-2——FX: zudododon [rumbling]

11-1-1—FX: zuvvvvvv [vibrating]

11-1-2—FX: bikibikibikibikibiki [creaking]

11-3——FX: ba [sudden movement]

11-4——FX: dodon [loud thud]

11-5——FX: guku [creaking]

12-1-1—FX: shu [sliding]

12-1-2—FX: bababa [hitting]

12-3——FX: bashu [cutting]

13-2——FX: bushuuu [cutting]

13-3——FX: zudodon [rumbling]

14-2——FX: dororo [thick substance dripping sound, like gloop]

14-4——FX: gugu [fast turning]

14-6——FX: byu [flying through air]

15-1——FX: do [hitting]

15-3——FX: zuvvvv [vibrating]

16-3-1—FX: gugugugu [straining]

16-3-2—FX: biki biki biki [creaking]

17-1——FX: pipipipi [beeping]

17-3——FX: gachagacha [rattling]

20-1——FX: gugu... [straining]

20-3——FX: biki biki [creaking]

20-4——FX: gu... [feel lump in throat]

20-5——FX: biki... [creaking]

22-3-1—FX: biki biki biki [creaking]

22-3-2—FX: zuzuzuzu [rumbling]

22-4-1—FX: zuzuzu... [rumbling]

22-4-2—FX: biki biki [creaking]

22-5-1—FX: biki biki biki [creaking]

22-5-2—FX: zuzuzu [rumbling]

27-2——FX: pata pata [pitter pattering]

28-3——FX: gigigigi [creaking]

28-4——FX: zuhyu... [flying through air]

29-1——FX: doshuuuuu [penetrating]

34-1——FX: bachi [catch snapping open]

34-2——FX: bashuuuuu [exhaust]

34-3——FX: gogogogogogo [door cranking open]

34-4——FX: zuo [rising sound, like whooomf]

35-1——FX: gan [hitting]

35-4——FX: gu [clenched fist]

36-1——FX: gugugugu [straining]

37-1——FX: gan gan gan [thudding footsteps]

37-2——FX: zuhyuru [flying object]

37-3——FX: doshurururu [flying object]

39-2——FX: pau pau [shooting]

42-3——FX: zuzu [rumbling]

42-5——FX: zuzuzu [rumbling]

42-6——FX: boko boko [clicking]

46-3——FX: gashan [crashing]

47-4——FX: doshuuuu [penetrating]

48-3——FX: ga [gasping]

48-4——FX: gugugugu [straining]

48-5——FX: biki biki [creaking]

49-4——FX: gu [groaning]

105-5-1 –FX: vvvvvvvvv [phone on vibrate]

105-5-2 –FX: vvvvvvvvv [phone on vibrate]

105-6—FX: ba [quick grabbing]

116-2—FX: shu [door closing]

116-3—FX: ka ka [sound of footsteps]

116-4—FX: dosa [falling into chair]

119-4—FX: pushun [door closing shut]

120-2—FX: basa [pages fanning out as it hits the floor]

121-1-1 –FX: ka [pecking]

121-1-2 –FX: ka [pecking]

126-3—FX: shururu [twirling]

126-4—FX: basa [falling to ground]

128-4—FX: mishu [crushing]

128-5—FX: mishu mishu [crushing]

150-3—FX: pipi [beeping]

150-4—FX: pii [beeping]

154-1—FX: zuuuuuuun [door sliding closed]

154-2—FX: gogon [door closing]

155-1—FX: kashon [turning on lights]

161-1—FX: pi [beeping]

165-5—FX: fura [staggering]

169-2—FX: pi [beeping]

169-3—FX: gobobo [crumbling]

173-1—FX: aaaaaa [screaming]

49-5 ——FX: gugugugugu [straining]

51-2 ——FX: byu byu [flying through the air]

52-2 ——FX: pikyon [releasing lever]

52-3 ——FX: ga shu... [pulling lever up]

52-4 ——FX: fiiiiiiii [spinning]

53-6 ——FX: boko bokon [hitting]

54-1 ——FX: bokon boko boko [hitting]

65-1 ——FX: gooooooo [blasting]

71-1 ——FX: gan [hitting]

73-1 ——FX: dosa [falling]

73-4 ——FX: hyuu [exhaling]

74-1 ——FX: babababababababa [propeller]

77-2 ——FX: pushu [door opening]

79-1 ——FX: gako [hitting]

95-5-1 —FX: vvvvvvvvv [phone on vibrate]

95-5-2 —FX: vvvvvvvvv [phone on vibrate]

96-1-1 —FX: vvvvvvvvv [phone on vibrate]

96-1-2 —FX: vvvvvvvvv [phone on vibrate]

96-2 ——FX: vvvvvvvvv [phone on vibrate]

98-2 ——FX: suuhaa [deep breathing]

101-5 —FX: gui [grabbing]

105-4-1 –FX: vvvvvvvvv [phone on vibrate]

105-4-2 –FX: vvvvvvvvv [phone on vibrate]

Postscript

VIZ goes back a long way with *Neon Genesis Evangelion*; in fact, VIZ goes back the longest. The first anime magazine anywhere in the world to carry a story on the *Evangelion* anime wasn't the Japanese *Newtype* or *Animage*—it was VIZ's *Animerica*, in its February 1995 issue.

Animerica wasn't as slick as today's publications—rougher paper and limited color—but founding editor Trish Ledoux had vowed in 1992 to make it the first regular monthly anime and manga newsmagazine in English, and she, and later editor Juile Davis, kept the promise. It was all the more remarkable as *Animerica* was a creation from scratch—it was neither a licensed edition of a famous Japanese magazine, as is the case with *Newtype USA*, or of a famous American one, as with Wizard Entertainment's *Anime Insider*.

The *Evangelion* story came in so quickly, there was no time to even blurb it on the cover, which was on the anime *Kishin Heidan* (based on a novel by the same Masaki Yamada of VIZ's *Ghost in the Shell 2: Innocence—After the Long Goodbye*), and, as only the cover story in the front (and the fan art in the back!) got the use of the limited sixteen pages of color, the two-column scoop led off the "Dateline Japan" section in the black-and-white newsprint.

The story, "Gainax Returns to Anime with *Shinseiki Evangelion*," reflects what was known about the new series when the story was written (in the first two weeks of January, 1995), and it's interesting to see both the limitations of that knowledge, and the difference between Gainax's conception of the series at the time, and how the series actually played out.

We can begin with the Japanese name of the series, which *Animerica* spelled out entirely in *kana*, the *kanji* that would be used to spell *Shinseiki* not yet being known at the time. The article gave the translation as "New Genesis Evangelion," which is interesting in that it implies it was known already that Gainax would prefer that *seiki* be translated "Genesis" (which is not the meaning of the kanji actually used, which

mean "century") but not yet that *Shin* (which **does** mean "new") would have the preferred translation "Neon" (which, of course, is a romanization of the *Greek* word for "new"...)

The first change made from the original plan can be gleaned by the article's statement that the *Evangelion* TV series was slated to appear in "Spring 1995"—in actuality, the series did not begin until October of that year. As the story's title "Gainax Returns..." suggests, *Evangelion*, which to many fans today is the beginning of Gainax as they know it, was actually perceived as the studio's *comeback*, following their four-year hiatus from anime since their first period of professional works, 1987's *Royal Space Force*, 1988-89's *Gunbuster*, 1990-91's *Nadia*, and 1991's *Otaku no Video*. The article described *Evangelion's* concept this way:

Beginning with what might be regarded as an update on the classic science fiction premise of aliens warning the human race not to continue their pursuit of nuclear weapons, Shinseiki Evangelion *is a near-future drama in the mode of Arthur C. Clarke's* 2001 *series. In this future age, biotechnology, rather than atomics, is the final scientific frontier as man attempts to artificially induce his own evolution through genetic engineering. Without warning, alien beings appear and demand the human race stop this direction of research...or else!*

In a bizarre twist, the aliens refer to themselves as the "Disciples," claiming to be the messengers of the divine. These so-called Disciples grant humanity a grace period of several years before they return once more, and the panicked governments of Earth embark on a crash program of building fortress-like cities and giant robot weaponry, in preparation for the Disciples' return...

Anno says that the new offering from Gainax will consider some of the ultimate questions posed by science fiction, and, indeed, philosophy, such as: What is the nature of evolution? What is humanity's relationship to his or her god? Does god, in fact, exist? What does it mean for the human race if that question can be answered definitively?

Evangelion fans, of course, will recognize the above description as ultimately not quite what got into the anime, yet it remains strangely

familiar. The biggest difference would appear to be in the role of what were here called the "Disciples," evidently an alternate rendering of *shito*, "apostle," the Japanese word used in the actual *Eva* series, which has an official English translation of "Angel."

While the Angels in *Evangelion* are arguably in a sense ultimately of extraterrestrial origin, the actual anime presents them as strongly associated with the history of Earth and the nature of mankind, so that the idea of them as alien invaders in the *Independence Day* sense (or even in the sense of the Overlords from Arthur C. Clarke's *Childhood's End*, which *Eva* can be said to also reference) seems strange—although certainly, the Angels are presented to the public as *de facto* alien invaders throughout much of the *Evangelion* story.

Stranger still, in light of the actual *Evangelion* series, is the idea of these "Disciples" communicating a warning to the human race to stop their efforts towards artificial evolution. The Angels of the *Evangelion* anime, of course, are known for their *lack* of communication with humanity—indeed, throughout most of the series, they are named and defined entirely by their human "enemy." Contrary to the image of apostles, or indeed of angels, they come bearing no word and no message, leaving the final part of the series' name—the only one which is the same in both the official Japanese and English titles—*Evangelion*, from the Greek word for "gospel," highly open to interpretation, much as the rest of the series.

The "grace period" involving the initial manifestation of the Disciples with their return seems to correspond to the gap in time between the appearance of the Angel Adam at the Second Impact in 2000 and the series' beginning in 2015. Again, however, the motive force behind events in the actual *Evangelion*, and the questioning of humanity's place, is done almost entirely by different factions and individuals within humanity itself.

Note that the unusual use of the pronoun "his or her" (rather than *its* or *their*) in reference to "humanity," and the non-standard style of referring to "god" in lower-case were the practices of *Animerica*'s original editors (it is unlikely to have simply been a mistake, as they were most scrupulous), yet it seems oddly appropriate in retrospect considering the ultimate gender "identity" of human origins in *Evangelion*, and the fact that although *Eva* presents such elements as angels, prophecy,

and apocalypse as real, it indeed lacks a presence corresponding to traditional notions of God.

Twelve years later, word comes that a new *Neon Genesis Evangelion* anime is to be made—and this time, not through a magazine scoop, but via that modern font of awareness, the Web (in the irony that seems to make the Earth turn, Gainax itself was the first anime studio to have an English-language website, beginning in the summer of 1995—yet now that *Evangelion* has made them world-famous, they no longer do).

In 2007 through 2008, Gainax plans to release to theaters four "new" *Neon Genesis Evangelion* movies, in a project being called *Evangelion: Rebuild*. "New" is put in quotes here to signify that *Rebuild* is understood to largely consist of an expansion of the original anime story. The first three films, designated 01-03, will retell that story, but with extensive use of new graphics, effects, scenes, and characters, whereas the final film, *Rebuild 04*, is to be an original story.

It's tempting here to mention the rumors and speculation surrounding *Evangelion: Rebuild*, except by the time this essay sees print in early 2007, much more definite things about it are likely to be known, and any such details said now might prove no more accurate in the end than when VIZ's *Animerica* introduced *Neon Genesis Evangelion* to the world those many years ago. There is a big difference between then and now, and this difference—not the details of *Rebuild*—is, I believe, what is worth thinking about.

It is this: the first time, no one knew how Gainax's *Evangelion* would surprise us, how it would shock and challenge its audience and its industry, a challenge that has rarely been answered. All through the first few years of the English edition, this very manga carried on the back of its graphic novels the phrase "Gainax, Japan's most progressive anime studio." And indeed, the second half of the 1990s constantly saw new approaches from them: beginning in 1995-96 with the *Evangelion* TV series itself, followed in 1997 with the incredibly bold *The End of Evangelion*—the only non-Miyazaki anime film ever to win a Japan Academy Award.

Director Hideaki Anno surprised again in 1998 by leaving his action-mecha tradition behind to do stories directed towards women, having Gainax adapt their first-ever shojo manga series, *KareKano* (released here as *His and Her Circumstances*). 1999 continued Anno's ventures into the feminine subjects with both his first live-action film, *Love and Pop* (available from Kino Video), which looked at modern *ko-gals* with surrealistic empathy, and the outrageous and as-yet-none-dare-to-release *Ebichu Minds the House*, adapted from Risa Ito's comedy manga for women office workers!

Then in 2000, Gainax seemed poised for a whole new era, as Anno's protégé Kazuya Tsurumaki emerged from assisting on *Evangelion* to direct his first solo project, *FLCL*. As Adult Swim succinctly put it, "This show will change your life." A tornado of fresh air on the scene, *FLCL*, like *Evangelion*, had people watching anime again who hadn't been excited about it in years—yet it was nothing like *Eva* and was able to look back on what anime, and Gainax, had both done and failed to do with irony *and* sincerity *and* cynicism *and* passion.

It's questionable whether the last six years from Gainax have shown the innovation which marked the late 1990s, or that of their early years. In 2001, Hiroyuki Yamaga, who had begun Gainax with perhaps their—and anime's—greatest film, 1987's *Royal Space Force*, returned to directing after fourteen years with *Mahoromatic*. Although in touch with otaku trends as much as Gainax ever was (five years later, the maid scene in Akihabara is entering the mainstream), it was nevertheless startling—as if Stanley Kubrick had come back from the dead to make *Friends*.

Instead of *FLCL* marking a new era, it seemed regarded as practice for Tsurumaki to direct a "serious" project—whereas Gainax was founded to make *Royal Space Force*, and their 10th anniversary saw them gearing up for *Evangelion*, their 20th anniversary work was their first sequel, *Gunbuster 2*. Although an intriguing and in many ways worthy tribute to the 1988 original, it arguably marked a retreat, investing their creative energy in a previously proven name instead of marking two decades with a new, original concept.

In 1995, no one could see *Neon Genesis Evangelion* coming. In 2007, we can see *Evangelion: Rebuild* coming from a mile away. My selfish wish as a fan—and not as someone who makes a living off these films—is for Hideaki Anno, and Gainax, to surprise us like they used to, to keep us watching the leisurely progress of the new *Eva* as it approaches, to go into those theaters with our eyes straight on the screen—and then, as *The End of Evangelion* did, do the trick again, and smack us right in the back of the head.

Two more things before we go. While you're waiting for the new *Evangelion* anime—not to mention the next volume of the *Evangelion* manga, which Mr. Sadamoto, on average, finishes at the rate of six chapters per year—I want to strongly recommend you check out the forums at **evamonkey.com**. With over 800 registered users, it's the largest English-language discussion board for *Neon Genesis Evangelion*, and attracts posters from Europe, the Middle East, and Latin America as well as the United States and Canada. Moreover, as moderated by its founder, Aaron Clark (whose *Evangelion* panels you might have seen at East Coast anime conventions), it's a thoughtful and informed place to talk about *Eva*, whether the topic is "who's hotter, Asuka or Rei?" (the correct answer is "Ritsuko") or "Gender of Non-Lilim Persons" (an actual topic).

Second, to quiz Gainax in person, don't forget to get yourself down to FanimeCon in San Jose, California, this coming May 25-28, 2007. *Evangelion*'s co-producer, Hiroyuki Yamaga, first came to FanimeCon ten years ago, bearing an advance copy of *Death and Rebirth*, and ever since Gainax has practically adopted the con—sometimes unashamed to get a dealer's table and hawk their ever-affordable wares in the best *Otaku no Video* manner—bringing over such studio personalities as Kazuya Tsurumaki (of *Evangelion*, *FLCL*, and *Gunbuster 2*), Yasuhiro Takeda (author of the Gainax tell-all *The Notenki Memoirs*, available from ADV Manga), Takami Akai (creator of *Princess Maker*) and the artist of this book you're holding, Yoshiyuki Sadamoto himself. Will Hideaki Anno himself finally grace FanimeCon in 2007?

—Carl Gustav Horn

P.S. Two bits of errata, both from Volume Eight: On p. 98, the caption that says "ABOVE MT. ALBERT MARKHAM," should just say, "ABOVE MT. MARKHAM." Mt. Markham in Antarctica is given in a document glimpsed in episode 7 of the *Evangelion* TV series as the site of the Second Impact, and when I came across a reference to a "Mount Albert Markham" really existing in Antarctica's Churchill Mountain range, I thought, "A-ha, this must be the mountain's full name."

Actually, there are *two* mountains in that area named "Markham," the second, being named just plain "Mount Markham," and therefore presumably the one Gainax meant, being 160km to the south of Mt. Albert Marhkam (Mt. Markham is named for his cousin, Sir Clements Markham—both were active in the Royal Geographical Society's support of Robert Scott's tragic failed attempt to be the first explorer to reach the South Pole).

Note, by the way, that both mountains are on the coast—Mt. Markham is a good 800km from the South Pole. It is not known at present why Gainax chose Mt. Markham in particular as a site, but it is worth noting that *Evangelion* co-producer Hiroyuki Yamaga has a personal interest in early Antarctic exploration, and that the Japanese themselves are world leaders in Antarctic science; Japan was the pioneer in South Polar meteorite research, discovering the first specimens in 1969. It's not difficult to imagine a real-life "Katsuragi Expedition" with a hidden agenda...

The second error was on page 129.1, referring to the 2004 experiment in which Yui Ikari vanished as having taken place using Unit-00. This is incorrect; it was, of course, Unit-01. The last thing we need is more speculation as to whose soul's in what, so I can only cringe at the mistake and pray that it didn't spawn too many online threads.

—CGH

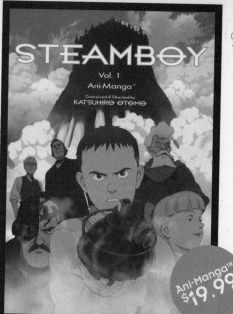
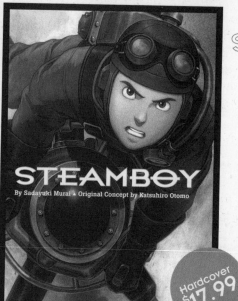

The Evolution of Science...
The Downfall of Man?

Based on the hit movie from Katsuhiro Otomo

STEAMBOY

Meet Ray Steam, a resourceful young inventor whose father and grandfather have harnessed the ultimate energy source that will transform the world for better or worse!

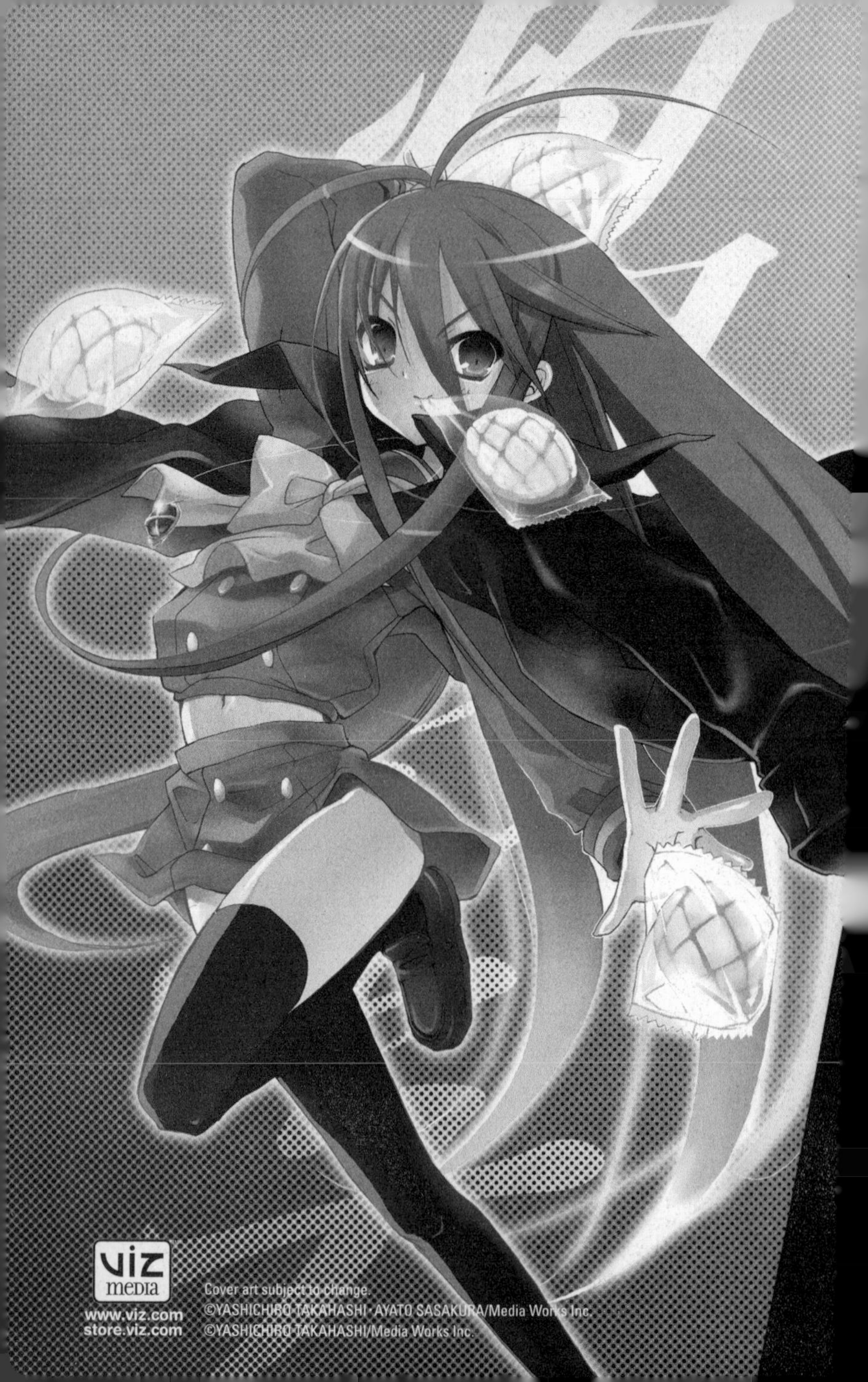
viz media
www.viz.com
store.viz.com
Cover art subject to change.
©YASHICHIRO TAKAHASHI · AYATO SASAKURA/Media Works Inc.
©YASHICHIRO TAKAHASHI/Media Works Inc.

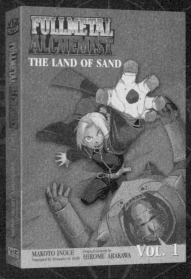

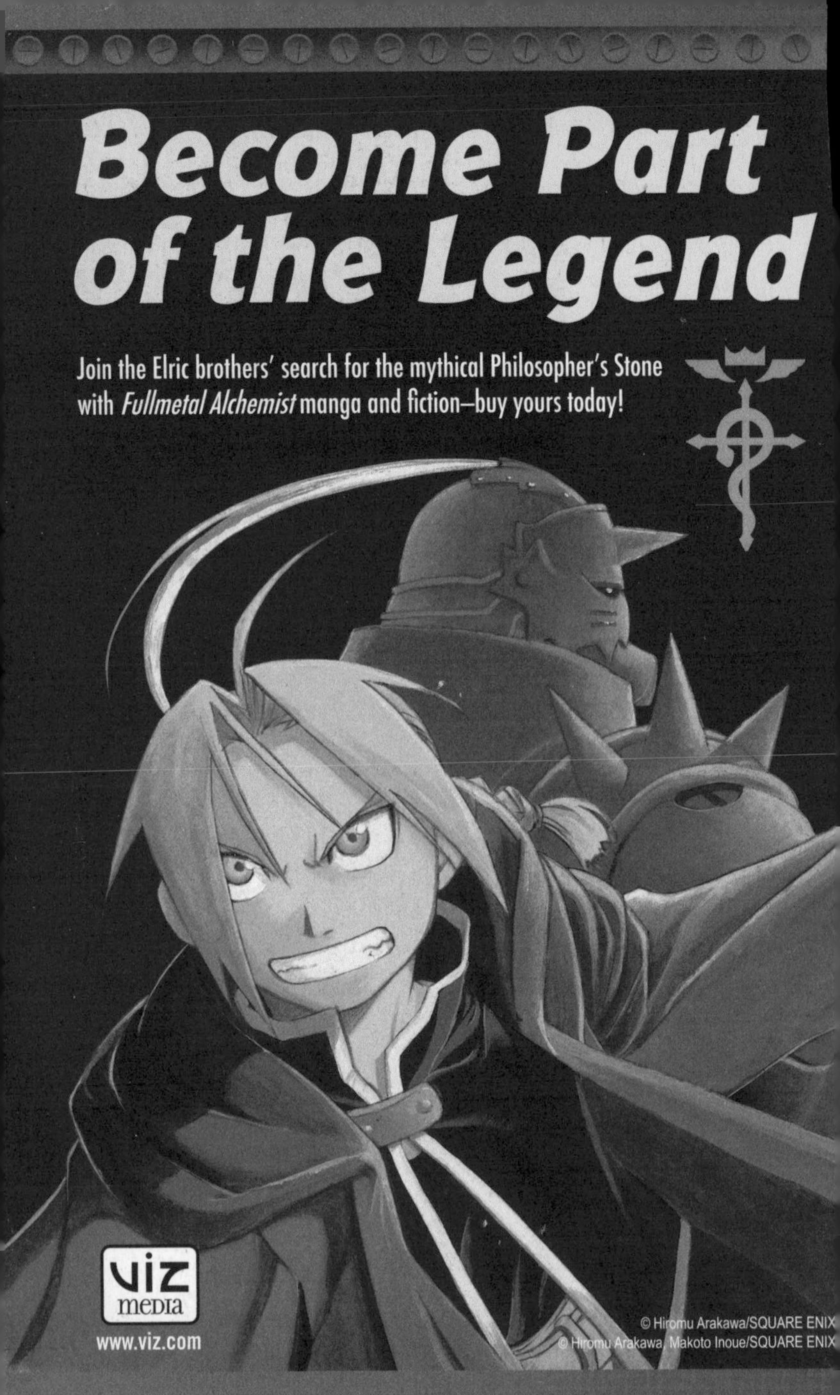
Become Part of the Legend
Join the Elric brothers' search for the mythical Philosopher's Stone with Fullmetal Alchemist manga and fiction—buy yours today!
viz media
www.viz.com
© Hiromu Arakawa/SQUARE ENIX
© Hiromu Arakawa, Makoto Inoue/SQUARE ENIX

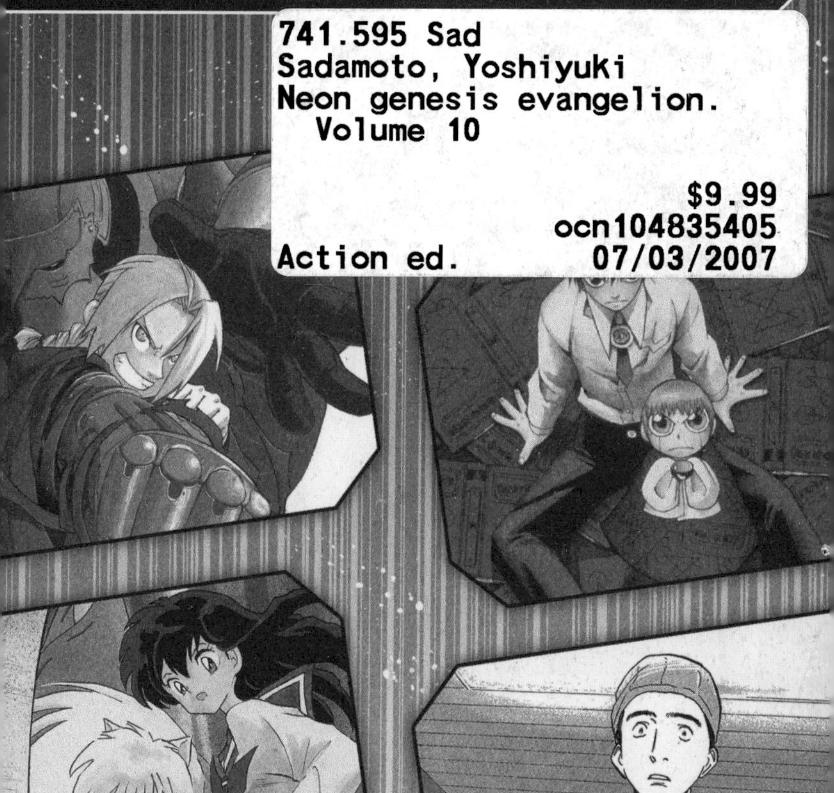

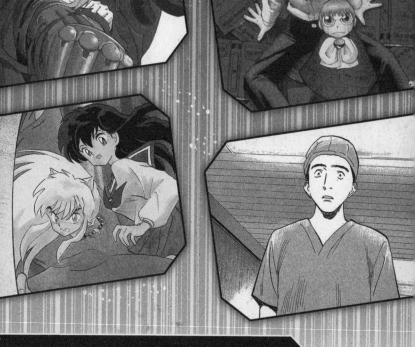